D0789752

The Prophet's Pulpit

COMPARATIVE STUDIES ON MUSLIM SOCIETIES

GENERAL EDITOR, BARBARA D. METCALF

The Prophet's Pulpit

Islamic Preaching in Contemporary Egypt

PATRICK D. GAFFNEY

University of California Press

BERKELEY   LOS ANGELES   LONDON

University of California Press
Berkeley and Los Angeles, California

University of California Press, Ltd.
London, England

© 1994 by
The Regents of the University of California

Library of Congress Cataloging-in-Publication Data

Gaffney, Patrick D., 1947–
    The Prophet's pulpit : Islamic preaching in contemporary Egypt /
    Patrick D. Gaffney.
        p. cm. — (Comparative studies on Muslim societies; 20)
        Includes bibliographical references (p.) and index.
        ISBN 0-520-08471-3 (alk.). — ISBN 0-520-08472-1 (alk. : pbk.)
        1. Preaching, Islamic. 2. Islam — Egypt. I. Title. II. Series.
    BP184.25.G34 1994
    297'.6 — dc20   93-34827

Printed in the United States of America
1 2 3 4 5 6 7 8 9

FOR P. A. W.

. . . pues si por enamorados echan a galeras,
días ha que pudiera yo estar bogando en ellas.

Cervantes, *Don Quixote de la Mancha*

Contents

Introduction

In recent years anthropologists have begun lifting their voices to dispel the impression of a conspiracy of silence as to how they obtain the data they transform into scholarship. Perhaps in reaction against the old-fashioned Indiana Jones image so suspiciously predisposed to adventure, treasure, intrigue, romance, and not incidentally the Middle East, once the field researcher returned to the somber groves of academe, the inclination was to draw a curtain over the often jumbled and unseemly raw materials of the craft. So, in reporting his or her findings an air of impersonal objectivity was adopted that feigned harmony with the muses heard by their colleagues confined to libraries and laboratories. Only at a safe distance from the lecturer's rostrum and certainly off the record of the Human Interest Area Files could one hear about the peculiar, sometimes very peculiar contextual factors that inevitably accompany the collection of such information and frequently color its interpretation.

Bronislaw Malinowski's posthumous field journal, entitled *A Diary in the Strict Sense of the Term,* is usually recognized as the great milestone that has since inspired others to attend seriously to what William Butler Yeats called the "blood and bone shop" of their ethnographies. But instead of leaving such commentaries to the discretion of literary executors, it seems preferable to incorporate at least the barest rudiments of this backstage reality within the published work itself. Otherwise questions of credibility, perhaps even of ethics, may linger and distract unnecessarily. Indeed, the unbuttoned revelations confided to his personal diary by this founding father of functionalism were at times so greatly at variance with the impressions offered in his formal expositions as to suggest grounds for reassessing the latter in this new light. Since its appearance almost thirty years ago a minor genre has emerged, first at a trickle, now approaching a rising tide, that has sought to unveil the idiosyncratic dimensions of field research. Indeed, as it continues to advance, it has gone well beyond the initial resolve to compensate for past blind spots to inaugurate a stimulating new conception of anthropology itself. Sometimes referring to it as interpretive anthropology, its advocates emphasize the acceptance of "various sorts of hybridization" as they recognize a definition of culture inspired by contemporary theories of hermeneutics which cut at odd angles across older disciplinary boundaries.[1] Such efforts are directed not only to determining the role that personalities play in the process but also, and more importantly, to exploring the theoretical and applied implications of everything that used to pass without elaboration as "participant observation."

But it was not only a realization of the great impact of individuality and serendipity upon field research that has encouraged this turn toward methodological transparency. It also derives from a fertile spillover from recent advances in philosophy, theology, psychology, and literary criticism that call into question the foundations of claims to objectivity in all the social sciences. Ernst Cassirer, a pioneer in this movement and almost an exact contemporary of Malinowski, stated the problem succinctly in terms of a logical premise: "If I put out the light of my own personal experience I cannot see and cannot judge of the experience of others."[2] Some, inspired by recent developments in economic and political thought, have set out to define the subtle linkages between institutions, interests, and ideologies as subterranean influences on anthropological writing. In both cases, however, the first necessary step toward overcoming the distortions that these arguments warn against is to provide a sort of travel brochure about the journey before it begins. At a minimum it should identify the point of departure, the itinerary, the destination, and any important facts about the traveler that may be relevant to understanding the angle of vision. Some such information is contained in later chapters, but the protocol requires that a few preliminaries be given here.

My interest in the ethnography of Islamic preaching was first stimulated by Richard T. Antoun, a foremost specialist in Middle East anthropology who was a visiting professor at the University of Chicago in the spring of 1977. With the help of several other teachers, notably Victor Turner and Stanley Tambiah, I was already immersed in the study of ritual systems and social structures. With the encouragement of Fazlur Rahman, I was then attempting to fit these insights together with issues of religious authority in the Islamic tradition and particularly the Arab world.

But my ideas about how I might trace these patterns out on the ground were still embarrassingly vague. It was Antoun who guided me patiently, wisely, in the framing of the original project. In the process he also fanned an ember of curiosity about the often mentioned but virtually never examined role of the village mosque preacher into a beacon that would eventually illuminate aspects of this potentially pivotal figure at multiple levels of involvement.

All of this occurred, of course, before the Ayatollah Khomeini exploded into the world's headlines, before Islamic fundamentalism became a byword among policymakers and journalists, and shortly before Egypt sprang over a vast diplomatic abyss in a single bound by inaugurating the process that led to the separate peace with Israel. When I began preparing the project I quickly discovered that most specialists treated my concern for local Islamic preachers as a quaint, slightly irrelevant, slightly colorful choice. When I returned from the field in the fall of 1979, however, I found almost instantly that a marvelous reversal had taken place. Now all of a sudden Islamic preachers were a topic of wide interest and great vogue, counting among the matters to be reckoned with at the highest councils of responsible concern. I, of course, while I appreciated the vindication of my early inclination, only regretted the need to disclaim any part in effecting this overdue revision of priorities.

Nevertheless, having come to this issue in advance of the great rush to understand Islam as a global force, I had already come to realize how altogether overlooked these figures were in the existing literature. It both bewildered and befuddled me at the time to encounter appalling gaps and even more the gross disparity of chronological emphasis that marked the standard literature of Middle East/Islamic studies. It was far easier to find information on preachers in eighth-century Damascus or eleventh-century Baghdad, for instance, than on their successors in the pulpits of any Arab nation in the last fifty years. I was learning by default the prevailing biases of the academic world, soon to be denounced as "orientalism," with regard to this tradition which Antoun and many other pioneers were then beginning to change. It was evident that research interests tended to cluster around the two extremes of the exotic and the powerful. But my concern was to discover the structure and the character of local practice, the familiar, the current, and the representative behavior within a given society.

Later, Frederick Denny would reflect on these same liabilities and seek an explanation for this blind spot from the perspective of religious studies. He concluded, interestingly, with a recognition of the value of techniques already forged by anthropologists:

> The study of Islamic ritual is not a mysterious business, although the paucity of published materials on the subject in relation to its obvious central importance may seem paradoxical . . . That a now generally acknowledged oversight has been allowed to persist is a testimony to the failures of scholarship and not to any opaqueness or intractability of the subject matter. But herein lies a problem. One needs to examine both texts and contexts, and the divergences between the two.[3]

One component of the issue that was especially indecipherable to me as I read widely on the question of preachers before setting off for Egypt was a profound ambiguity about the category itself. Often enough I found writers insisting that Islam had no clergy or anything like it. Versions of the celebrated axiom *lā rahbānīyata fī Islām* ("no monks in Islam") were frequently paraded forth to clinch the point that, as Snouck Hurgronje once put it, Islam is the "lay religion par excellence." And yet this blanket refutation was plainly contradicted by the existence of all manner of figures associated with mosques who unmistakably wielded variously specified types of clerical authority. It was not hard to see that around this particular issue a great and recurring controversy raged.

Perhaps no small part of my interest in this dimension of Islam stemmed from my own personal involvement in the Catholic faith. Only shortly before I took up graduate studies in anthropology I had finished a professional course in theology and was ordained a priest. Hence I was quite aware of the ambivalence surrounding the identification of a given individual with institutional religion in the Western Christian tradition and I was intrigued to explore the shape of this parallel development among Muslims. And in the course of studying preachers, I was able to do this quite effectively.

However, as I was advised by veterans and was later to comprehend more fully once I was engaged in the project, the pursuit of this or any other aspect of field research from an explicitly ecumenical viewpoint would most probably not be fruitful. In fact, in retrospect, given the situation in Upper Egypt as I experienced it, I am now convinced it would not have been possible. For historical reasons rooted in the function that religion played and largely continues to play as the basis of social identity and civil entitlement in Middle Eastern societies, it became clear to me very early that I would be unable to carry out fieldwork in Egypt if I presented myself at the start as a cleric in my own tradition. The cross-cultural static born of infelicitous, even rash presuppositions that would almost certainly arise for many Muslims would have introduced confusion of a sort that would have very probably worked to the detriment, most likely to the undermining of the whole endeavor.

Indeed, it was often difficult enough to explain to ordinary people the purpose of my unaccustomed presence in their midst. What could it mean that I had come halfway around the world to their remote neighborhood to ask so many questions and hang around mosques by virtue of being an "anthropologist"? This term has no recognizable cognate in colloquial Egyptian Arabic. I should go to the Azhar, the center of Muslim learning in Cairo, they would say, if I wanted to learn about Islam. To mark myself ostentatiously as a priest inevitably, in most cases, would have so crowded out any further considerations as to throw a conversation, perhaps a whole relationship into limbo if not to invite unwelcome apologetics. Thus with only a few carefully pondered exceptions I decided at the start to divulge such autobiographical detail only in response to a direct question. But in fact, the question never arose while I was in the field. Typically, in clarifying my purpose to those with some background in academic lore I would begin by locating my enterprise within the realm of *ʿulūm ijtimaʿīya,* that is, "social sciences." After that I could specify the actual nature of my research and offer further distinctions if needed. In less learned settings I found that the most easily understood preliminary description of my purpose was usually to explain that I was interested in studying *al-ʿadāt wa al-taqālīd,* that is, "customs and traditions."

This study is the accumulated product of several periods of field research, the longest of which was the first, an eighteen-month residence in a provincial town in Upper Egypt. This was followed by several return trips, some long, some short. The initial fieldwork was conducted between November 1977 and August 1979. I was back in Egypt again briefly in 1982. I spent another year engaged in research during 1984–1985. Once more in the summer of 1986, I was back in Egypt as a faculty fellow at the Center for Arabic Studies Abroad at the American University in Cairo. Supported by the Centre d'Etudes de Documentation, Economiques et Juridiques et Sociales, I had an opportunity to return again in December 1989. I was back once more in the summer of 1991 in conjunction with a program of the National Council of U.S.-Arab Relations.

However, in order to appreciate properly what follows, it is important to stress that these periodic revisits included ruptures as well as continuities. As will be spelled out in detail in a later chapter, the late 1970s marked the beginning of a time of exceptional socioreligious ferment in Egypt, a fact I had not anticipated. During my stay, several cities, including Minya where I was living, underwent cycles of turmoil spurred largely by religious militancy. While I was frankly oblivious to this embryonic process while making my preparation to depart for Egypt, I was quite aware of the popular unrest that was resulting from Sadat's jolting moves toward liberalizing the economy and, less certainly, political life. In January 1977 riots had erupted in many places in reaction to the withdrawal of long-standing government subsidies on staple foodstuffs. Street violence spread to the point that soon the army was called out to intervene. These events had been front-page news in the international press. Sadat then rescinded the order, calling it premature and blaming it on pressure from the International Monetary Fund. But only an uneasy calm was restored. Then, eleven months later, the signal event occurred that was to overshadow all else for some years to come. Sadat's sudden announcement of his peace initiative in November 1977 seized the attention of everyone. Egyptians too watched in amazement as he flew to Jerusalem and delivered his stunning speech before the Knesset.

By coincidence, having booked my ticket long in advance, I arrived in Egypt on the evening of the very day that Sadat himself had returned from Israel. I had scarcely unpacked my bags before I was carried off by a friend to hear the president speak of his journey before an excited crowd of several hundred thousand gathered in the square beneath the balcony of the Abdin Palace. It was an unforgettable display marking the birth of a new configuration of political and religious forces in Egypt that still remain in contention.

Upon my arrival I was told by those with experience of the local situation that social research and especially ethnographic fieldwork would not be easy to perform. I should be prepared for long waits, disappointments, and diversions. I should also hold a few alternative strategies in reserve in case the wall of obstacles around my first goal showed no breach. Among other difficulties were official restrictions that prohibited foreigners from doing research of this kind anywhere except in the capital. However, these confinements belonged to an era of tighter controls over all aspects of Egyptian society and now things were changing, although it was not clear how far and how fast. I was determined to get out of Cairo to do my research if at all possible, and several knowledgeable scholars also there at the time, most notably the late Richard Mitchaell, encouraged me to push my luck.

My first major effort to find a route into the countryside took me to Alexandria. There I met with Dr. Ahmed Abou-Zeid, a former student of E. E. Evans-Pritchard at Oxford, who was now the Dean of the College of Arts at Alexandria University. He was most courteous and immediately receptive to my research project, in fact enthusiastic. More important, he offered to set the wheels of the bureaucracy in motion in an effort to win permission for me to commence work in Egypt's second-largest population center and its major port on the Mediterranean. I was buoyed by this instant affirmative response and briefly entertained by the prospect of investigating Islamic preachers in the city haunted by the ghosts of Lawrence Durrell's famous quartet. But it was still too large and too cosmopolitan a setting to qualify for fulfillment of my lingering desire for a setting of manageable proportions, off the beaten trail.

I first visited Minya in December 1977, traveling together from Cairo with a student who had invited me to visit his home in a nearby village. In this much more modest city, so obviously embedded in its agricultural surroundings, I quickly discerned a possible site much closer to what I had in mind. Someone had given me the name of Dr. ʿAbd al-Minʿam Shawqi, the newly appointed Dean of the College of Arts at Minya University, which was itself only founded the year before, so I immediately set off to see him. He too welcomed me and expressed great interest in my project. He not only agreed to begin at once the procedures that would, I hoped, end in the permission I was seeking but also asked me at once to provide him with a number of documents to prepare the dossier that would be submitted to the appropriate powers. To make a long story short, over the next four months, I came to Minya more and more frequently, and stayed for longer periods. The train trips back and forth often seemed like rides on a roller coaster matching the invisible progress of my application. From Dr. Shawqi's always tentative but never despairing updates, I imagined it to be making its way on a slow journey resembling the phantasmagoric path of the pharaoh's soul traversing the ordeals of the netherworld, so graphically depicted on the walls of the tombs in the Valley of the Kings. Finally the day came, in April 1978, when Dr. Shawqi informed me that the waiting was over, my patience was rewarded, and I could move to Minya immediately and begin in earnest. The only provision, apart from all prudence and professionalism, was that I was to work together with one of the graduate students in the university's sociology department who was to accompany me especially on any visits outside the city of Minya itself.

I gratefully accepted this condition and began with the College of Arts as my base while I sought out information about local mosques and looked for introductions to local preachers. Initially, my designated assistant was of great help, as he brought me around to various mosques and explained what I was about in terms I could only approximate. But it soon became evident that it was quite unrealistic for him to spend the amount of time I myself was giving to the project, as it became a matter of him following me and not the opposite. Furthermore, he had a habit of absenting himself from Minya for days or weeks on end, and, as Dr. Shawqi readily acknowledged, it was not expected that I too would have to stop to wait upon his return. Eventually this student was replaced by another one who had a room in the university's student housing block who proved to be a helpful informant on obscure matters relating to Islamist movement on the campus. But by this time I had come to function more or less autonomously as I was able to establish good working relationships with numerous preachers. After meeting dozens of preachers and visiting a score of mosques, each of which has its own story, I came to concentrate my attention increasingly on four particular mosques, on the activities of the local *jamāʿa Islamīya* or Islamic Society, and on the functioning of the office that administered mosques supervised by the government under the Ministry of Religious Endowments.

From the start I had intended to attempt to tape-record sermons and as I become better acquainted with various preachers I broached the topic. Some were receptive and some were not and I always respected their wishes in this regard. But even when a given preacher consented, a formidable array of electronic, mechanical, acoustic, and human particulars still had to be properly arranged. I never imagined that the practicalities of obtaining these recordings would prove so difficult. At one point, I had five different tape recorders in various states of repair. When I was in full swing, every Friday I would leave one machine at home tuned to a radio station that would be broadcasting the sermon that day. Others I would have brought around earlier and left with helpers who had agreed to record sermons at certain mosques. Then I myself might go off elsewhere to hear yet another preacher, lest I miss something important. By these methods I heard hundreds of sermons over these months and got several dozen recordings that were clear and usable. Later I had a number of these sermons transcribed to facilitate my work with the Arabic text.

As with all such projects, there was a category of problems that had to do with being a stranger and, not surprisingly, some of these were tainted by the ideological coloring of the day. Overall I was shown enormous hospitality and countless acts of personal kindness. But as it became clear on the campus and around the town that I was not a transient visitor, that I spoke Arabic and had a very persistent interest in Islam and its local institutions, my presence also provoked a few unsettling and more tangled reactions. Not infrequently, despite initial efforts to explain myself straightforwardly, I encountered various blends of confusion and presumption about who I was and what I was doing or should be doing. Sometimes exaggerated courtesy would precede as the cover for what would later surface as implacable hostility or wholesale manipulation. Furthermore, I am sure my failure to grasp the full implications of certain delicate situations or ultimately my inability to resolve them while remaining committed to my own task only added to the debt I owe so many in Minya for their patience.

Two specific issues in this realm merit brief mention. First, the fact of being an American in Egypt at this time occasionally invited direct associations between myself and the official foreign policy maneuvers that were then in high profile. It reminded me of a remark made by that great early Victorian ethnographer of Cairo, Edward Lane, that the Egyptians of his day characteristically assumed that he must be an emissary of his monarch. Second, the fact that I as a Christian was engaged on quite friendly terms with Islamic preachers often presented what seemed indigenously an uncomfortable if not an unthinkable confounding of categories. Here, indeed, being an outsider gave me a distinct advantage. But it took constant circumspection to maintain this edge and stay aloof from an always latent and increasingly overt hornet's nest of sectarian tension.

The deterioration of civil order in Upper Egypt by the time I left in August 1979 could only nurture apprehension about its stability in the foreseeable future. However, when I returned to Minya in November 1982, the general situation at the university especially seemed to have calmed down greatly. Matters were also visibly under tighter reins. Moreover, the colleges had moved to their new campus about five kilometers north of the city center, a relocation that brought relative isolation and deterred the most disruptive forms of demonstration.

But when I came back to Egypt in 1984–1985, hoping once again to reside in Minya to follow up and elaborate on my earlier research, I found the mood had changed considerably. Within a few hours of my arrival I was summoned to "drink some tea" at the office of the Secret Police. There I was told politely but firmly to leave town first thing in the morning. When I asked for the reason, the officer advised me that it was for my own safety. I objected, arguing that Minya was like a hometown to me and after considerable discussion, plus what I suspect was a phone call to Cairo in a back room, I was told that I could reside in Minya only if I obtained permission from both the Ministry of Religious Endowments and the Azhar. So I returned immediately to Cairo and began pursuing some patron's blessing from within the Azhar and the Ministry, at both of which I had built up contacts. After jumping through bureaucratic hoops over the course of several weeks I finally discovered the cause of the delay. It turned out that the same Secret Police who had pointed my way out of Minya also had their officers overseeing the security clearance at these religious institutions. In a word, my unwillingness to accept a direct "no" in Minya was now being translated into an endless stall in Cairo with the same effect. Hence, I shifted the focus of my research that year to mosques and preaching on the national and transnational level.

From this experience and others since that time, I have come to appreciate how exceptionally fortunate I was to have been able to accomplish what I did in Minya several years before. For several reasons, at the head of them the objections by the security forces, but also in view of a more general closure in the realm of religion, it would be impossible to do today what I managed to do then. In recognition of this remarkable opportunity I have not hesitated to give copious direct excerpts and in the appendix three complete sermons taken directly from the pulpits of Minya. I know of no source that offers for scrutiny similarly extended ethnographically derived examples of contemporary Islamic preaching.

It is also necessary at this point that I acknowledge how much the realization of this book owes to a number of scholars and institutions which have played various parts in its completion. For funding two years of field research I am indebted to the American Research Center in Egypt. Many associated with this exceptional body deserve my thanks but I single out Paul Walker for his initial inestimable assistance. While in the field I relied on many for help of all sorts, but Muhammad ʿAbd al-Majid, Hamdi al-Halawani, Zakariya Sayyid al-ʿAbayd, and the above mentioned ʿAbd al-Minʿam Shawqi stand at the head of the list of the indispensables. Many colleagues have also contributed to this manuscript in their various ways; among the most significant were Richard Adams, Georges Anawati, O.P., Charles Butterworth, Juan Campo, Nazih Daher, Carol Delaney, Michael C. Dunn, Richard Frank, Jerrold Green, Mary Louise Gude, C.S.C., Yvonne Haddad, Barbara Harlow, Valerie Hoffman-Ladd, Ira M. Lapidus, Fred Lawson, Jane D. McAuliffe, Barbara Metcalf, Christiaan van Nispen, S.J., Ruud Peters, Ibrahim al-Sinjalani, Jaroslav and Susanne Stetkevych, Diana de Treville, and Jean-Claude Vatin. Earning still higher esteem, Richard T. Antoun and Dale F. Eikelman read the manuscript in earlier versions and offered much appreciated suggestions, although the finished product is my own. In addition, on a related front, I am deeply grateful to Lynne Withey of the University of California Press and her editorial co-workers, Laura Driussi and Nancy Evans. Their patient support no less than their impressive technical skills have in countless ways benefited both the book and the author.

Finally with regard to transliteration and related conventions, I have attempted to steer a middle course between a pedantic obsession with consistency and a defiant abandonment to arbitrary phonetic approximations of the sort that T. E. Lawrence justifies in the barbed and witty "Preface" to *Seven Pillars of Wisdom*. In general I have adopted the system of the

International Journal of Middle Eastern Studies although several categories of qualification are admitted. For instance, dialectical expressions are sometimes retained in their non-literary pronunciation. Arabic lexemes that have come into English as loan words are not converted back into the original idiom. Proper nouns that have their own conventional spellings in English are left in their recognized anglicization. In the case of personal names I recognize the right to orthographic self-presentation, as confusing as it may appear. Here I follow the lead of Richard Mitchaell who, in his peerless study *The Society of the Muslim Brothers*, gives the surname of two brothers within the space of three lines, one as Najib, the other as Neguib. This is a difference of three characters in the transcription of a word that has only four letters in the original Arabic. By the same token, diacritics are generally omitted in the case of names, although the ʿayn may be retained since it represents an Arabic letter that has no equivalent in the Roman alphabet. Also, with regard to the names of persons, I comply with the time-honored anthropological custom of giving pseudonyms to the actual preachers who comprise the main focus of this study. Place names, however, including names of local mosques, and the names of public figures are given accurately.

1 The Social Organization of the Ritual Setting
The Mosque in Time and Space

By its very existence, the local mosque in any Islamic community embodies a paradox. On the one hand it represents a universal and permanent ideal. To believers it recalls events regarded as unique, absolute, enduring, and of normative consequence. Regardless of the structure's physical appearance, whether it is crude or grandiose, a mosque exemplifies the pristine community of the perfect religion. It recreates the founding instance of "hierophany" when the divine will revealed itself to become human law.

On the other hand, every actual mosque is contingent, incidental, and constrained by concrete facts. It reflects some particular and incomplete set of historical experiences, theological convictions, and sociocultural relations. The empirical qualities of every real mosque, including its location, size, style, embellishments, and facilities, not to mention its personnel, its congregation, and the activities customarily associated with it, all belong to the flux of human affairs that are forever partial and subject to change. Thus, in one sense all mosques are the same insofar as all convey the recollection of an eternal presence. But at the same time every mosque is different since each partakes singly in the diversity of historical forces that shape its distinctive personality, its forms of solidarity, and its aesthetic inclination. Grasping the significance of a mosque, in other words, does not allow for a neat separation between the beliefs and the experiences of those who define themselves, to whatever degree, with reference to that privileged space.

In effect the convergence of "this-worldly" and "otherworldly" reality in a mosque reproduces the more elaborate paradox of Islam itself. Each mosque represents a microcosm of the Muslim worldview insofar as it makes concrete and accessible in ordinary life the possibilities of the sacred realm. It stands as the permanent offer of the encounter between divine and human purpose. Mosques accomplish this variously, but above all by providing a community with definite and bounded space sanctioned for the carrying out of the rituals which manifest and interpret this merger of earthly aspiration and divine invitation. Hence a mosque serves as the point of intersection, a pivot between "planes of classification," the meeting place between two conceptual opposites, understood as creature and creator.[1]

Given this symbolic character, an adequate description of a mosque necessarily involves multiple and shifting frames of reference. No single instance, not even the Grand Mosque of Mecca, which houses the sacred *ka'ba*, fully models the totality of all earthly replications. Certainly this hallowed shrine has traditionally epitomized the Prophet's message more than any other site. In addition, its associations with the creation of the world, with Adam and Abraham, as well as its consecration as the object of the *hajj*, the pilgrim's goal, add immeasurably to its special significance. But this sacred quality must not be confined to the lineaments of physical geography. Rather, the centrality of the historical Mecca situated in the Hejaz has long since given way to a dispersion of countless localized "meccas." All manner of mosques have arisen at every remove from this prototypical place of worship to become, in their own way, centripetal hubs of devotion, extending Mecca's divine aura as well as its moral and political influence. At a minimum, it can be said that Mecca is reproduced in every mosque by means of the *qibla*, the niche that marks the direction one faces while performing the *salāh*, or daily prayer.

Thus, not only does a mosque consist of space circumscribed for use in this ritual, but a key feature of its architecture, specifically its alignment, makes evident the awareness (as Black Elk, the Sioux holy man, put it) that "anywhere is the center of the world."[2] This realization is observed further in the fact that, at various times, Mecca itself has been spurned by pious Muslims critical of the way these shrines have been maintained or governed. Similarly, today there are Muslims who protest against the domination of these sites by the Saudi state. But this history of reproaches leveled at the conditions of the actual site have in their own way also contributed to the dissipation of this original spatial focus. By inspiring reforms and even revolutions, those rejecting what they found at the source have assisted in maintaining Mecca's contiguity as "the center of authority and the ritual center" wherever the patterns of Muslim civilization have spread.[3]

This double quality of a mosque, portraying the juncture of divine command and human obedience which is Islam, has, however, often encouraged the suggestion that quality and quantity are closely fused. Thus, in Egypt as elsewhere in the Islamic world, the recent dramatic building boom of mosques has frequently been cited as evidence for the strength of the so-called Islamic revival or resurgence. Figures from Egypt's Ministry of Religious Endowments, for example, indicate an increase of 100 percent between 1961 and 1979, leaping from 17,000 to 34,000 mosques. Only five years later, in 1984, the Minister of Religious Endowments, Dr. Ahmadi Abu Nur, stated in a report presented to Parliament that the nation then had a total of 50,000 mosques.[4] This points to an increase in five years roughly equivalent to the expansion of the previous two decades. Similarly, it was recently estimated that in the first two months following the breakup of the former Soviet Union, the number of mosques in the Central Asian republics doubled.[5] Setting aside the question of the motives for this explosive construction rate, as well as queries about the precision of these statistics and the political relevance of their official release, they nonetheless point to a trend that plainly confirms the importance of this ritual center as a visible embodiment of communities asserting their Islamic identity. But it also indicates the adaptive and versatile qualities of Islamic expression in response to changing needs and aspirations.

In an earlier age, when most matters related to education, law, and social welfare were conducted under explicitly Islamic auspices, the mosque commonly served a number of functions in addition to its use as a ceremonial setting. But under the modern state, as services and agencies have evolved under the direction of encompassing centralized bureaucracies, the bulk of the functions once tied to the mosque have moved out into other precincts and taken new forms. Schools, libraries, courtrooms, theaters, clinics, meeting halls, clubhouses, and all manner of administrative posts now provide specialized services, thereby leaving mosques increasingly identified with the performance of rituals, including preaching. Of course, certain remnants of these older conglomerates survive and not infrequently dedicated reformers have sought to reestablish the mosque as a multifaceted center. But generally these efforts have been token gestures, more remarkable for their inspiration than for the scale of their practical achievement.

It has often been suggested that Islam, as a category of analysis, resists any one simple definition that satisfies for all those occasions where the term is used for purposes of description and explanation. Practically speaking, the noun is too diffuse to allow for its application with consistency, precision, and comprehensiveness without the inclusion of contextual information. Attempts to isolate a single, exemplary definition usually fall short because, in Marshall Hodgson's phrase, Islam has "tended to call forth a total social pattern in the name of religion."[6] Or in the traditional formulation which currently echoes in the slogan familiar among Islamists throughout the Middle East, Islam is *"dīn, dawla, wa dunyā,"* that is, "religion, state, and [secular] world."[7] Hence, to presume the bifurcation of religion and politics into two discrete categories as they are commonly understood in the West when referring to the separate domains that correspond historically to church and state, each based on distinctive forms of legitimacy, often proves to be quite misleading in the case of Islam.[8] This certainly does not imply that the Muslim tradition lacks an understanding of the separation of functions that largely parallel what emerged in medieval Christendom as the realms of God and Caesar. A de facto division of "administrative and executive interests" as contrasted to "religious belief" emerged relatively early both along theoretical and institutional lines.[9] But the Islamic concept of the *umma* as a moral as well as a political community retains the insistence that a fundamental unity necessarily incorporates all human endeavor under one set of divinely prescribed principles.

Hence, to objectify Islam as equivalent to some particular set of persons, beliefs, or interests or to assume a unitary relationship with such a key element of the tradition as a mosque, carries all the risks of reductionism. By doing so one easily rules out or overlooks an indeterminate range of malleable discourse and action that occurs with variable significance in what is regarded as "informal" or "unofficial" sectors. Furthermore, limiting use of the term Islam to a discrete set of historical institutions or traditionally prescribed behaviors may greatly distort the way the term is understood among Muslims themselves. The resulting bias introduced by such presuppositions can be illustrated in a well-known study of contemporary "popular religion" in Egypt. The author of this study concludes with an explanatory hypothesis that pairs Islam with the "Near East" in a way that assumes their logical opposition and some measure of perennial rivalry: "If, as I have argued, it is characteristic of Islam that it should produce many voluntary societies for social and religious ends, it may be characteristic of the *Near East* that government should aim persistently to control such associations and that they should soon succumb to political power."[10]

This approach not only ignores the fusion of social and cultural elements that constitutes the geopolitical abstraction "Near East," rendering its distinction from "Islam" highly artificial at best and arguably mean-ingless, but at the same time it disregards the long and continuing history of a vast civilization in which religion has played and continues to play a decisive role in the legitimating of government authority.[11] Moreover, this uncritical combination of a materialist theory of politics with an ide-alist theory of religion also fails to reckon with the continuities and per-mutations of sacred and secular representations that can easily shift their meanings across the boundaries of different settings. In brief, such an approach imports an implied theory of secularization that envisions the relationship of the state to religion as a zero-sum game. Such a perspective leaves little room to appreciate the strength and persistence of Islamic appeals that have been recognized even in an avowedly secularist regime, such as that of ʿAbd al-Nasir.[12] Likewise, it fails to assess the manner by which raw political motives, as Machiavelli understood them, may also be asserted by "voluntary societies" or for that matter by governments, dis-guised as the "social and religious ends" of Islam.[13]

For this reason, neither Islam nor the mosque can be defined uniformly in terms of any one set of definite interests pitted against another. Instead, the contesting of what does and does not represent Islam, or does so best, involves the assignment and reassignment of values embedded in the dynamic interaction of empirical and ideological factors. Therefore, what one observes in the Islamist confrontations of contemporary Egypt is nei-ther simply a power struggle between socioeconomic classes, parties, regions, genders, lifestyles, generations, nor different alignments of elites and masses, all variously masked by a veneer of ritual display and reli-gious rhetoric. Rather, the current contending of forces within and about mosques reflects complex transformations of demography, social identity, ethical consciousness, international pressure, political process, and eco-nomic structure, through all of which religiously minded people are straining to discover and to articulate a satisfying expression of the sym-bolic links between transcendent values and the pragmatic issues of daily life. By concentrating therefore upon the authoritative ritual setting, where Islam is regularly and publicly proclaimed and interpreted, I hope that the meanings surrounding this term may be better recognized than elsewhere.

To treat Islam as a "symbol and signification system" takes squarely into account the possibility for confusion that may result when one term serves to affirm or condemn a broad and seemingly contradictory range of phenomena.[14] Such a system acknowledges the function of Islam as a source of inspiration and validation for the Muslim conscience as well as its pertinence to worldly affairs. Appeal to this notion may be flexible, but a pattern can be discerned that confirms its importance as a focus of intellectual and moral legitimation. Ali Merad has emphasized the remarkable versatility that may accompany such a system:

> This aura of ambiguity which surrounds the meaning of Islam is not deplored by everybody. In social debates, and often in political debates, each one tends to give credence to his own religious views, philosophy of history, views of his party on socio-economic or cultural matters by using the "label" of Islam, however distant these ideas may be from the objectives of the original sources of Islam. . . . Similarly, a number of political and ethical concepts which were popularized by modern culture are said to be derived from Islam. Here the objective is to support the political, socio-economic and cultural options of the dominant ideology.[15]

Mosques Evoking Mecca and Medina

Just as Islam reappears in many protean forms, so too do mosques exist in nearly boundless variety; yet each reflects an image of spiritual wholeness. While every mosque recalls, as has been noted, the sanctity of Mecca, other features of this ritual space also have their origin in the more practical arrangements that marked the customary use of the Prophet's original place of prayer in Medina. This first mosque, properly speaking, was not planned out, nor was it initially inaugurated as space reserved exclusively for sacred as opposed to profane activity. Rather, its construction and use evolved gradually, apparently with no explicit precedent, in the midst of a largely polytheistic Arab society where worship was known only in the form of ceremonies performed in highly marked cultic shrines.[16] Thereafter, while subsequent mosques were meant to replicate it, they also adapted and developed it, both conceptually and in a proliferation of actual edifices.

According to Muslim tradition, this first mosque originated with the courtyard of Muhammad's house in Medina. When Muhammad and Abu Bakr first reached the refuge of this oasis city after their escape and arduous emigration from Mecca, that is, the *hijra*, which marked the beginning of the Prophet's mission as leader of the community of believers, a dispute arose among his hosts who were vying for the privilege of receiving these distinguished guests. Legend has it that the Prophet himself suggested the solution. He was to let his camel wander freely until she stopped of her own accord. The plot where she first knelt would then be bought by the Prophet for his home. And so it happened.

It is further recorded that adjoining the place where Muhammad erected the first crude building as his house, there was a spacious area which he cleared of some palm trees and tombs. It was here that his followers began to come together, since it provided them with a convenient place for all manner of gatherings, including prayer. The different uses for this earliest "mosque" were not well defined in the beginning but they emerged as the Muslim community grew and its activities became more elaborate. There are numerous allusions to this mosque in the biographical materials and the collected sayings of Muhammad, most of which is difficult to date or to authenticate, but as a general observation, the area did not have the character of a restricted sacred space. On the contrary, this same terrain was used as a general meeting place for both Muslims and others while it was also designated as the place for collective prayer and the forum for the Prophet's public preaching. "Believers and unbelievers went freely about in the mosque, tents and huts were put there, disputes took place in it, often it had the outlook of the headquarters of an army. . . . It depended on the circumstances whether the aspect of the mosque as a social centre or as a place of prayer was more or less emphasized."[17]

As was mentioned, the concept of a sacred precinct requiring special enclosures and ritual purification was quite familiar to the Arabs at this time. In fact, Muhammad's native Mecca was famous throughout the Arabian peninsula for precisely such a sacred domain known as the *ḥima* or *ḥaram* within whose perimeters the shedding of blood, the bearing of arms, and the pursuit of outstanding feuds and other profane activities were strictly forbidden. This pre-Islamic sanctuary in Mecca had created a rare arena of permanent neutrality and brought together the cults of locative and tribal deities into a sort of pantheon.[18] Furthermore, its presence accounted, in large part, for the city's position as the dominant commercial and political influence in the region. Also, in conjunction with the three sacred months each year when hostilities everywhere were suspended, allowing for safe travel and for caravan transport, Mecca had mixed lucrative trade with popular pilgrimage for the benefit of all, but especially for the Quraysh, the leading tribe of the merchant aristocrats.[19]

Muhammad, of course, had initially sought to reform this polytheistic cult of Mecca by replacing the idolatry of his countrymen with the worship of the one God, Allah, alone. Only when this effort failed was he forced to flee to Medina. But he never lost sight of the centrality of Mecca and the *kaʿba*, around which the city was built. Much of his political and military strategy, moving gradually from defense to offense, was aimed at bringing the proud leadership of this city to surrender. Just three months before his death the Prophet achieved his ultimate victory. Upon the capitulation of his former persecutors, he entered Mecca in triumph and

purged the city of its idols. He declared an end to paganism with the can-
cellation of all its blood guilt, debts, obligations, and privileges.

Thus Muhammad retained the pre-Islamic practice of the *hajj* but he
endowed the custom with a new significance. From that time, pilgrimage
to the sanctuary of Mecca would become one of the pillars of the faith.
With this transformation of the *ka'ba* into the locus, par excellence, of
Muslim ritual, the paradox of the local mosque realizes its fullness. In
these last days of the Prophet's life, this second model of the mosque was
definitively consecrated. Henceforth, two separate institutions would
share the distinction of being the original. But the two were not conjoined.
Rather, the gap between the site of practical administration and spiritual
contemplation was not only symbolic, it amounted to the 270 miles lying
between Mecca and Medina. And a new idiom also enters Muslim vocabulary to express this doubleness with a single concept, namely the *hara-
mayn*, the "two sanctuaries."

Indeed, in the time of the Prophet other mosques apart from these two
were clearly in use, and several times the Qur'an makes reference to such
"houses of God" (14:36; 2:187). But they seem to have been few in number and apparently each new foundation required divine approbation
through a specific authorization by the Prophet, who seems to have legitimated their use by his praying in them. One instructive incident, illustrating a contrary case, again referred to in the Qur'an involves what was
called *al- masjid al- ḍarār*, the "opposition mosque," whose builders, the
Beni Salim, were allegedly motivated not by piety but by factionalism.
The Prophet not only refused to pray in this mosque when he was so
invited, but ordered it destroyed (9:107–10). The *Sira* of Ibn Ishaq, a standard collection of sources on the Prophet's life, in recounting the circumstances surrounding this revelation, is very careful to enumerate exactly
which are the "apostle's mosques," thus excluding others that lacked this
status.[20]

This episode clearly indicates that from the very outset the setting aside
of a place for prayer included the issue of representing authority in addition to considerations of convenience and propriety. In fact this symbolic
facet of mosques only increases with the development of a complex
Islamic civilization. Although Muslims can and do pray anywhere (later
jurists even allowed for modification of the rubrics so as to permit the
pious traveller to pray while riding a camel) more and more, architecturally distinct institutions arose designed to serve as permanent sites, set
aside primarily for common prayer and congregational preaching.

Almost immediately after the death of the Prophet, a series of these
formal structures dedicated as mosques were constructed along the road

connecting Mecca and Medina at places where it was remembered the Prophet had prayed. This project illustrates the inclination of early Muslims to proceed by imitating what Muhammad himself had done. In the following decades, as Arab conquests spread quickly into Syria, Egypt, and Persia, Muslim generals who were establishing new settlements or occupying older cities also founded new mosques, often within their camps, as one of their first acts. These usually consisted of simple places of assembly modeled after that of Medina—in most cases, an open space adjoining the house or tent of the commander. Here Muslims continued to combine worship with aspects of military drill, public administration, and general community activities, although the mix became progressively more difficult to coordinate. The rapid expansion of Islam had brought great opportunity but in unequal measure. Differences of opinion arose bringing great strain upon the new bases of loyalty. Disparity of ability and the vagaries of fortune in the field also caused old dissentions to surface that had been submerged as long as the unimpeachable arbiter, the Prophet, had been among them. What many pious followers perceived as unacceptable compromises at the expense of divine law also brought division. Practices rooted in the common Arab tradition also met with resistance as other communities, some with rich cultural heritages of their own, were being incorporated into *dār al-Islām*. Rival factions and competing centers of power began to spring up which diluted allegiance to the caliph, the successor to the Prophet who reigned in Medina.

Moreover, conversions to Islam from among non-Arabs introduced further complications. For instance, there was the practical matter of dealing with churches, synagogues, and temples which were sometimes converted into mosques and otherwise contributed indigenous thematic elements to the new mosques built for these new Muslims. Still more crucial was the need to translate, interpret, adapt, and enforce a legal, moral, and ritual code to peoples who lacked the sociopolitical heritage and shared cultural outlook of the Arabs. Meeting this challenge meant the grafting of Persian, Hellenistic, Christian, and Jewish elements into an Islamic synthesis. But it also brought forth the great efforts that were required to define and codify the sources of belief and practice into the *Sunna* which was set down in canonical texts placed alongside the Qur'an.[21] Some of these labors followed a legalist or a rationalist inclination while others were directed toward spiritual and mystical pursuits.

Within thirty years of the Prophet's death the remarkable unity that had mobilized virtually all of Arabia through acceptance of the new monotheism began to fragment, largely along the lines of older tribal and regional loyalties. The consolidated military alliance did not survive in its original form as the exercise of power grew increasingly detached from the profession of the new religion. Three of the four orthodox or "rightly guided" Caliphs, those first successors of the Prophet whose words and actions are taken to exemplify the ideal practice of Islamic government, died violently, two of them at the hands of fellow Muslims. The only one to die naturally was Abu Bakr, the first Caliph who had only held the office for two years.[22]

Out of this civil war, this betrayal of theocracy, as it were, known as the "great crisis" (*al-fitna al-kubra*), after failed efforts at reconciliation led to an open struggle for dominance, a leader emerged from among the old Meccan aristocracy. This was Mu'awiyah, founder of the Umayyad dynasty, who managed to reorganize and reunite most of the Arab ruling community but only by fixing his claim to authority at still one further remove from the vision inspired by the summons of the Prophet.

> He restored unity no longer on the basis of the prestige of Muhammad's city and the consensus of Muhammad's old associates there. . . . The caliphal state stood now as a more mundane imperial power, no longer directly based on Islam. Rather it was supported internally as well as externally by a particular complex of military and physical power which was partially supported in turn by Islamic faith.[23]

This new political and spiritual configuration was reflected spatially during the Umayyad caliphate by the establishment of its capital at Damascus as opposed to Medina. Likewise, Jerusalem was celebrated with new emphasis as a cult center, to some extent displacing the singularity of Mecca. Such gestures represent once again still further extenuations of the mosque as an ideal from its original setting and the incorporation of this symbolic space into the vicissitudes of human politics.

Redefining the Center and the Periphery

Since this early formative period Islam has continued to flourish with a long succession of caliphates, kingdoms, sheikdoms, imamates, sultanates, khanates, emirates, monarchies, revolutionary dictatorships, and constitutional republics reaching up to the present. But throughout these epochs and their shifting borders the mosque constantly reappears in various constellations as the center of prayer and a focus for the expression of authority. To review such a history here is hardly necessary but a portion of it has been discussed in order to frame the essential duality implied by the generic term of reference, the mosque. This sparse suggestion of its historical evolution is helpful to put in perspective a current debate widely engaged in throughout the Islamic world on the proper role of the mosque in society. Not surprisingly in this controversy, various partisans of renewal or reform, from both the traditionalist and the radical camp, habitually resort to claims that evoke an idealized vision of a unitary institution in the distant past.

The paradox of the mosque appears not only in a retrospective survey. It continues in the spatial order of contemporary ritual centers, as can be seen by contrasting two defining elements of any major mosque. These two elements, in turn, invite investigation from significantly different perspectives in the classical theory of the sociology of religion. The first element is the *minbar*, or pulpit, from which the preacher delivers the authoritative Friday sermon. To approach the mosque from this rhetorical point of access favors a Weberian analysis. It encourages attention to the interaction between leaders and groups in the light of the articulation of particular systems of belief that ultimately result in the setting of goals, the evaluation of motives, and the legitimation of authority. Seen from the perspective of the pulpit, a mosque represents a forum for the development and the transformation of power relationships.

The founding charisma of the Prophet or the subsequent potency of religious virtuosi project their influence largely through an oratorical medium. So too, the classical corps of literate specialists, the *'ulamā'*, come to the foreground since they are the teachers, judges, and administrators of the routinized doctrinal and legal system and the pulpit has long been held as their rightful prerogative. Furthermore, from this angle, typologies may be usefully introduced which specify the character of the relationships that obtain among dominant institutions that are closely linked to centers of power, rationalized administration, and those who are ruled, notably the wider populace for whom kinship and village bonds remain primary. In broadest terms, this distinction corresponds to the categories of preachers on the one hand and their congregations on the other. Here the formation and the transformation of various sociopolitical interests and ideological constellations can be recognized as the ritual oratory of the mosque displays gradations of public authority. From this point of view the mosque represents the affirmation of these hierarchical relationships embedded in a bureaucratic structure—a patronage system or some other organizational principle—or possibly a refutation of these bonds which are replicated symbolically at different levels of inclusion. Mosques, therefore, are local manifestations of the religiopolitical order that characterizes the communities that build, maintain and ideally staff them.[24]

The second key feature of a mosque that provides a somewhat different point of departure for examining its paradoxical nature is the *miḥrāb*, or the empty niche, often embellished and illuminated, that marks the direction of Mecca. To approach the mosque from this perspective tends to favor an analysis guided by Durkheim's insight into the social character of religion as the projection of moral authority. It recognizes the mosque as the symbolic origin of a community's corporate identity as Muslims. The building or area where the defining collective rituals regularly occur becomes itself a sacred space in that it embodies the society as a harmonious totality in opposition to the profane realm outside, the agonistic world of rival subgroups and competing individuals. That vitalistic surge of group sentiment through which, Durkheim suggests, an ideal world is objectified is formulated by the ritual prayer, the primary activity and arguably the *raison d'être* of every mosque. But this view need not be regarded as static since this unifying focus upon the *miḥrāb* may also frame transition and change in terms of new or rediscovered configurations that reshape and redirect the collective ideal in the light of converging pressures and emerging aspirations:

> The ideal society is not outside the real society; it is part of it. Far from being divided between them as between two poles which mutually repel each other, we cannot hold to one without holding to the other. For a society is not made up merely of the mass of individuals who compose it, the ground which they occupy, the things which they use and the movements which they perform, but above all it is the idea which it forms of itself.[25]

Thus mosques inevitably express differently conceived ideal forms of society as a result of the particular character of the moral foundation that undergirds the group consciousness of any given Muslim community.

During fourteen centuries of expansion and development the Islamic tradition which initially revolved around the two mosques of Medina and Mecca has undergone a vast prismatic diffusion. The founding ideal of unity has generated a flourishing diversity. A community's conception of sacred space once so tightly concentrated has long since spread out both historically and geographically to encompass a vast multitude of social and cultural forms.[26] The center and therefore the periphery have lost their fixed coordinates, or, to put it another way, center and periphery can no longer be consistently or objectively distinguished. In this sense, Islam is recreated in every mosque, for it is through its rituals that the memory of divine revelation encounters the subjective and intersubjective attitudes to reestablish the *umma* as a specific human experience. It is the public demonstration and transmission of this possibility that mosques are set apart to facilitate. Hence the two-fold quality that Edward Shils has called the "central value system" is symbolically projected by the social organization of the rituals which a mosque embodies.

> It is central because of its intimate connection with what the society holds to be sacred; it is central because it is espoused by the ruling authorities of the society. These two kinds of centrality are vitally related. Each defines and supports the other.[27]

Because the *minbar* and *miḥrāb* represent this highest authority, every mosque reflects the sacred center. But every mosque is also peripheral, for no ruler nor capital city corresponds to the completeness of the triumphant community of believers in Mecca and Medina in the Prophet's own lifetime. Since the center is formed through the affirmation of a social structure as well as the expression of transcendent ideals the resulting consensus may have different meanings in differing contexts. But it is precisely this plurality of forms and levels of consensus, reflected in a multiplicity of mosques or perhaps more subtly in the degrees and modes of involvement within the same mosque, that produces this seeming contradiction. It is a paradox which is only diminished under special ritual settings, most dramatically, perhaps, in the performance of pilgrimages, where a "liminal" mode is most successfully evoked to overcome the normal constraints of social differentiation and alienation that obstruct the realization of the ideal.[28]

In sum, the mosque stands as both an institution and an idea. It expresses stability as well as regeneration through reform or even revolution. Over a half century ago, Hassan al-Banna, founder of the Society of Muslim Brothers, strongly reproached his fellow Muslims in Egypt for their nation's moral and political degradation. He declared forcefully that "the Mosque alone did not suffice" to fulfill the call of Islam.[29] Nonetheless he and his many followers responded to this conviction by replicating the essential features of mosques everywhere in their campaign to revive Islam and to redirect the nation. The café, the school, the shop, the office, the factory, the clubhouse, the barracks, the bus shelter, the playing field, and the street corner could all be made over as symbolic sites for the performance of prayer and for preaching. The boundaries of the mosque were eliminated, as it were. That great assortment of activities that once characterized the courtyard of the Prophet's house in Medina was to flow through modern society, making it into an "Islamic order." But the other dimension of the mosque, as a reserved ritual sanctuary, recalling the enclosure of Mecca, did not disappear in the process. For the importance of these institutions hardly diminished in the reformers' estimation; if anything the mosques became even more prominent in their encompassing activist program. Hence, in 1987, Rashid al-Ghannoushi, the leader of the Tunisian Islamic Tendency Movement, condemned to death (he was later pardoned), made a declaration at his trial before the State Security Court that came to be celebrated as the signature of his life's work: "If God wishes me to become a martyr of the mosques, then let it be so."[30] Needless to say, he was not referring here to mere buildings, but to an encompassing sacred mission extending to all aspects of society, for which the ritual space figures as the primary metaphor.

2   The Authority of Preachers

The study of Islam or any world religion as it is actually lived in a local setting, the "practical religion" as Edmund Leach called it, challenges many presumptions of classical academe which considered texts, the more canonical the better, the essence of a tradition.[1] Tensions between these philological or "orientalist" methods and operational or "ethnographic" approaches commonly arise because religious symbols are normally expressed in a universal idiom whereas the experience of them occurs in particular times and places. The original historical circumstances and the mentalities of later adherents inevitably differ, sometimes enormously, as also do their perceptions and their responses to the sacred message.

Furthermore, by its very nature, formal religious discourse, especially in ritual settings, tends toward a mode of articulation that stresses the ideal, the absolute, the encompassing, the enduring, and the abstract. But discovering the perceived significance of these expressions in any definite sociocultural context necessarily requires an empirical inquiry. A narrow preoccupation with the study of classical texts, as valuable as they may be in themselves, easily leads the unsuspecting to succumb to what Marc Bloch refutes as the "idol of origins."[2] He points out, for instance, that a name used to designate something may be retained even long after the phenomenon itself undergoes a profound transformation. Change is the way of the world but language, and especially sacred language, often claims an unearthly timelessness. Hence a formula or a title at the heart of a tradition is especially prone to be idealized. It easily remains unchanged even when the understanding of the object being referred to has, in effect, become something quite different.

27

Also, theology, that is, broadly speaking, "god-talk," as an authoritative discourse has long been largely the prerogative of a fairly exclusive literate elite who, like others, have their own peculiar views and vested interests. From their perspective, the normative elements of Islam, notably its revealed book, the traditions of the Prophet, and the law based upon them, have been seen as the substance of the faith. The actual practices of different Muslims, on the other hand, and in particular the attitudes and behaviors of those reputed to be unlearned or deviant have tended to be disregarded, noted merely for curiosity's sake, or were considered only to be condemned. One legacy of this elaborate but blinkered scholarly heritage has been what Edmund Burke has critiqued as a "privileging [of] ideology as the central analytic category" and a relative neglect of the dynamic social forces that underlie collective action and the exercise of power within and between both formal or informal institutions, especially those at the popular level.[3]

In fact, no religion can be properly understood if its description is confined purely to its orthodox doctrinal elements. This objection is perhaps even more relevant in the case of Islam which has, at least in principle, always contested the historical separation of spiritual and temporal realms as they came to be bifurcated in classical Christendom. But this caveat also applies to the study of religion and politics in the context of modern nation-states in which, by various symbolic stratagems, "civil society" and "reason" have themselves become virtually "*sacralized.*"[4] Indeed one of the defining features of religion as a social reality, or in Geertz's famous phrase "as a cultural system," is that it is charged with an "aura of factuality" rooted in corporeal everyday reality.[5] Religion must not, in other words, be mistakenly reduced to the sacred as opposed to the profane (to recall Durkheim's seminal dichotomy). Such a view fundamentally misrepresents the "religious life" which was not a matter of pursuing the sacred to the exclusion of the profane, but rather the generative fusion of both to produce the "elementary forms" of collective consciousness, a moral order, and ultimately society itself.[6]

Nor is the holy necessarily logically prior to coercive forces of a more mundane character. Rather, stimulation works in both directions. As Radcliffe-Brown, arguably Durkheim's most influential British interpreter, put it over a half century ago: "In so far as religion has the kind of social function that the theory suggests, religion must also vary in correspondence with the manner in which the society is constituted."[7]

Religion, in other words, presumes a gap between the ideal and the real because the special property of religious symbols is precisely their capacity to mediate, fuse, transcend, and integrate what are felt to be these antipodal realms. As a system of symbols, religion may represent eternal truths but such revelation was received, constituted, and canonized at some founding moment and it continues to be handed down through a changing world for the sake of mortals who inhabit its diverse parts at different times. A creed may be viewed as immutable, but the way its language is understood, organized, and acted upon in concrete circumstances inevitably varies. Exactly how believers react to this diversity, and indeed, the degree that they are aware of it, forms yet another dimension of religion as a force of both segmentation and integration.[8]

Many who have criticized the essentialist tendencies in the study of religion, pointing out their intellectual blinders, have sought to correct the consequent oversights and distortions by employing methods that draw upon contemporary phenomenology, hermeneutical theory, and interpretive sociology. For example, some have sought to depict Islam in terms of a "pendulum oscillation"[9] or in terms of contrasting levels such as a "high" and "low" version, or an "official" and a "popular" religion, or "establishment Islam" and "Islam from below."[10] This double vision often has had the benefit of greatly enlarging the scope of inquiry. But such tactics commonly present difficulties of their own unless careful attention is also paid to the various and at time independent "cultural forms of authority" which may call into question unqualified distinctions between purported definitions of what is central and what is peripheral.[11] Hence, many scholars, notably anthropologists working within the framework of an expanded functionalism and exploring the relationship of knowledge and power, have continued to refine such approaches and to apply them creatively so as to compensate for their formal limitations.

One must avoid, for example, the tendency to insulate different tiers or segments in ways that preclude the examination of their vertical or horizontal interconnections. Otherwise, the result is often a sort of "checkerboard" or "layer cake" depiction of religious groupings whose structure is simply restated in dichotomous rather than monolithic terms.[12] Even Clifford Geertz, whose numerous studies on Islamic societies have often applied this multilevel theory brilliantly, has not escaped criticism. Interestingly, Edward Said, writing in the late 1970s, singled out Geertz as a notable exception to the "orientalist" bias, which he analyzed as the typical perspective of the Middle East adopted in Western literature and social science. But a decade later Said was led to reconsider this view and he withdrew his broad approval of Geertz's work.[13] Others have faulted Geertz for disregarding historical disharmony and for missing the "social reality that any religion encompasses a number of traditions that are in some degree in conflict."[14]

One proposed corrective of a more radical sort has suggested that anthropologists replace the singular with the plural. Instead of discussing *Islam* as though a single entity corresponded to this label, they might express their topic as the investigation of "local *Islams*" in order to emphasize the multiplicity of equally valid expressions.[15] But this reaction also has major shortcomings. Among other drawbacks, it overlooks the underlying coherence manifest in the fact that Muslims, however seemingly diverse, all share elements of a common tradition. They characteristically assert their belonging to one *umma* despite the fluid meanings they may attach to the categories related to it.

Thus in order to understand Islam in "local contexts" the task must be to combine a recognition of immediate social spheres with those relationships of continuity that make for participation in a greater totality.[16] This entails the description and analysis of key facets of what members of a given local community regard as its explicitly "Islamic" elements within a larger framework of shifting social, ideological, political, and economic circumstances. The messages and ideas that are conveyed through mosque preaching cannot therefore be isolated from other local, national, and ultimately international spheres of experience and their corresponding systems of reference without sacrificing a large measure of a sermon's actual significance to those who hear it. The transmission, transformation, and reproduction of symbolic expressions, what Eickelman has termed the "political economy of meaning," constitutes an interaction whereby "belief systems . . . shape and in turn are shaped by configurations of political domination and economic relations among groups and classes in societies at different levels of complexity."[17] In this light, we turn then to an exploration of the role of the preacher in the local context in conjunction with the related ideals and recent developments which define his cultural identity and the social basis of his authority.

Frames of Reference

The most common term used by Egyptian Muslims for the one who preaches is *shaykh*. But this is a general deferential title that also applies in many other settings quite apart from that of religion. It may refer to the senior member of a kinship group, for instance, or the head of a department or a work crew. It also indicates a formal administrative position, especially important in village government.[18] In larger towns, including Minya, where this functionary known as the *shaykh al-balad* has been supplanted by other municipal officers, the geographic designation *shaykha*, roughly equivalent to "precinct," nevertheless remains in use. Furthermore, the term may be freely used as a traditional form of address or indirect reference toward any older man or woman (in the feminine form) in recognition of the dignity of their years. Thus *shaykh* conveys an elevated social standing and a relative degree of social distance. The title is used formally and informally in countless associative ways, including sometimes ironically and in jest.

In various settings or with regard to particular preachers other terms are used in addition to *shaykh*. Most prominently, the term *imām*, literally meaning "leader" or "the one who stands in front," refers specifically to the person who formally "leads" the ritual prayer. Of course, in theological or historical discussions, especially among Shiʿa Muslims, this epithet frequently refers to the prophet Muhammad and his line of successors, but this usage is not common in colloquial Egyptian Arabic. The term *imām* can likewise denote a preacher because normally the same person who leads the prayer at the Friday congregational service also preaches. Customarily this double role also indicates that this person is acknowledged as the official or unofficial "head" of the mosque. And in that case he might also be identified as an *imām* in context-free usage. Today, only in a handful of extraordinary instances is there an express separation of these functions. For example, at some of Egypt's greatest mosques, including the Azhar itself, there is a *shaykh* who is the titular head of the institution, but his duties center primarily on administration and official representation rather than on ritual leadership. Or this distinction may be introduced as a mechanism designed to mollify or to control different elements within a given institution. For instance, in 1985, after much public controversy, including violent demonstrations, when the government finally assumed the management of al-Nūr Mosque in Cairo, which had become a rallying place for dissidents, a full-time official *shaykh* was installed in addition to the similarly trained religious professional appointed to be the *imām*.[19]

Of course, the term *imām* is also employed as a context-bound reference. Since any Muslim who has the knowledge and ability to do so is technically able to lead the prayer the term *imām* may be used with regard to any person who performs this function on any particular occasion. Contemporary English terms such as "carpenter," "speaker," "cook," or "driver," function analogously. They may denote a full-time occupation, a habitual avocation, or an incidental temporary activity that someone happens to be carrying out in some setting. They may also evolve into proper family names.

The term that specifically refers to the one who preaches, that is, who delivers the sermon, is *khaṭīb* and the sermon itself is the *khuṭba*. In the abstract neither of these terms belongs exclusively to the vocabulary of religion and for that reason they might also be glossed as "orator" and "speech." Thus when the president delivers a speech to the Parliament or a minister addresses a gathering at the dedication of a new building, or a headmaster speaks at the inauguration of the school year, each is a *khaṭīb* giving a *khuṭba*. In actual usage, however, these two terms have come to be closely tied to the mosque and religious performances.

Thus, if the same *shaykh* who preached on Friday is addressing an audience elsewhere, for example at the Young Muslims Society, at some other time, and even if he is, for all practical purposes, repeating the gist of what he said or might say from the pulpit, this address would not be called a *khuṭba* but most probably would be called a *muḥāḍara*, or "lecture." Also if he is giving a "lesson" within the mosque itself, no matter how much its content resembles a sermon, this is called a *dars*. Nor would he be thought of as acting in the capacity of a *khaṭīb* when he is not in the pulpit, even though in some cases this title may stick to a given individual not just as a professional category but as a personal epithet in other unrelated settings because he regularly preaches at the mosque. In other words, while these and some other morphologically related terms once denoted a comprehensive range of settings involving rhetoric and while they still retain these implications in classical literature, codes of protocol, and within the context of a few elevated official ceremonial settings, they are more narrowly associated with religion in the vocabulary of current popular speaking.

The *wāʿiẓ*, literally, "warner" or "one who admonishes," is another relevant term whose semantics carry definite religious implications. It also refers to a preacher, although it is currently heard less frequently in connection with mosque pulpits than the other terms mentioned. This usage seems not always to have been the case, however. Edward Lane, in his encyclopedic account of Cairo in the early nineteenth century, not only includes a rare description of mosque preaching but records verbatim one actual sermon which he notes was then known as the "khutbet el-waaz."[20] He may be referring here to the preacher or to the character of the sermon.

Today in Egypt, however, the term *wāʿiẓ* refers formally to one specific type of free-lance professional preacher who is not attached to a particular mosque but who is employed under the General Administration of Islamic Culture, a subdivision of the Azhar. As an itinerant preacher his work may include, in part, delivering a weekly sermon in some mosques as a guest preacher. On a daily basis, however, he preaches in nonritual settings which may include mosques, although not from the pulpit, as well as in schools, clubs, community centers, factories, offices, army bases, or prisons. The *wāʿiẓ* wears the same uniform as other official *shaykhs* and from his outward appearance it is impossible to distinguish him from his similarly educated colleague who serves in the local mosque under the administration of the Ministry of Religious Endowments.[21]

A number of other terms rooted in both classical or folkloric usage also occasionally arise in reference to preachers of various sorts in Egypt. But here I single out only two because of their heightened ideological significance at the current time.[22] One is a term of high generalization, *rijāl al-dīn*, literally, "men of religion." It makes no specific reference to preaching or even to Islam but it has come to be used for public spokesmen of religion who validate this identity primarily through the teaching of religion, its administration, or leadership of its ritual expressions. Recently, this term has been favored by some modernists as a replacement for *'ulama'*. It connotes a marked professional class or clergy, and the same term applies to Christian priests within a basically secular society.[23]

The second term, *dā'* or its variant form *dā'iya*, literally "one who calls, who invites, a propagandist," has no explicit lexicographical association with religion, although it has come to be understood as such. It is frequently the label preferred by those who preach in the spirit of the contemporary Islamic resurgence. The widely read monthly magazine of the Muslim Brothers which was allowed to resume publication in 1976 and suspended again in 1981, evoked this same notion in its title, *al-Da'wa*, "The Call" or "The Invitation." Although historically these terms have often been associated with Shi'ite missionaries and politico-spiritual movements surrounding figures of a millenarian cast such as the Mahdi and the "hidden Imam,"[24] in contemporary Egypt the *dā'iya* tends to denote a dedicated activist, usually a young man, advocating the totalistic application of Islam. From its etymology the term primarily signals the oratorical and persuasive aspects of this dedication, although it may extend to other more practical endeavors, giving it somewhat the sense of a "missionary."[25]

As mentioned earlier, in theory Islam insists that it is a religion without a clergy. But this claim obviously does not mean that Islam lacks persons who variously claim to represent its authority. Rather, there is an abundance of such representatives and no little controversy among them over their relative prerogatives. It is not, therefore, the absence of authoritative religious specialists that is refuted by this declaration but merely a rejection of any single hierarchical definition of what entitles one to exercise this authority. As a result, the problem of "role uncertainty" familiar from studies of clergy in other contemporary societies reappears here in its own particular fashion.[26] In fact, Islamic preachers in Egypt fall into a number of significant categories rather than a single status group.

Islamic preachers in Egypt lack a set of external restrictive features that would group them, for instance, in the manner of Anglican or Roman Catholic clergy into what Erving Goffman has called an "analytic category." Moreover, under such conditions, Goffman sounds the pertinent warning that any assumption of status collectivity when "the system-like properties of the organization cannot be taken for granted . . . is surely hazardous."[27] He further stresses that systems of reference in role analysis can be subtle since frames shift and actors may stay *in role* or may *break role* through an assortment of interactive maneuvers. Similarly, Richard Antoun, in a comparative study of local Islamic preachers in Jordan and Iran, characterized the social organization of the preachers as "polycephalous, decentralized and informal"—features, he adds, that are especially pronounced in times of crises.[28] In Egypt much the same could be said, although to different degrees and in a variety of settings. It may be added, however, that such a view reveals an elite perspective, as it may underplay the solidly established basis of a preacher's authority within a local constituency. To this degree, it may be said that the role rests on a form of *ijmā'* or "consensus," one of the fundamental principles of Islamic jurisprudence, which locates authority, not as vested in the one holding the office, but within the "religious ideological fabric of the Community."[29]

The Preacher and Knowledge

To recognize what Bryan Turner has called the "essential looseness" of an Islamic specialist's role does not mean, therefore, that religious authority is itself amorphous and mimetic, merely assuming the basic shape of pre-existing social, political, and economic institutions.[30] On the contrary, there exist variously understood yet definite and distinct cultural symbols identified with Islamic authority that are not arbitrary. The mosque, for instance, represents one such independent entity, as does the position of the preacher apart from any given individual who occupies the role. But stated in still broader terms, the one notion that probably summarizes the predominant ideal associated with Islamic authority would be the concept of *'ilm,* or knowledge.

The supreme importance of this ideal is demonstrated by the emphasis laid upon it throughout the Qur'an as well as the Traditions and in later elaborations of both the scholastics and the mystics. As Fazlur Rahman puts it, *'ilm* stands as the first principle of Islam and upon it, the *sharī'a* rests as a "total way of life."[31] It easily follows then that religious authority is tied to different definitions of knowledge. Thus, how learning is achieved and verified, how it is demonstrated in the social functions of teaching, counseling, interpreting, and, of course, in preaching are all relevant, even pressing issues. For knowledge to be socially effective, it must be converted into authority and for authority to be established it must be projected as knowledge. Thus a preacher's influence in a local context depends fundamentally on the concepts of knowing that are found there and on how these qualities are understood to be portrayed.

To speak of today's Egypt in this regard means to reckon with multiple and co-existing concepts of knowledge as well as their competing modes of validation. For instance, the specialized training in traditional Islamic sciences that is obtained at the Azhar no longer commands the respect it did even a generation, not to mention a century, ago. But the reasons given for this much lowered esteem are various and contradictory. Modernists generally dismiss the Azhar's manner of education as hopelessly narrow, archaic, and stultifying. Traditionalists, meanwhile, insist that decades of misguided reforms and slackened standards, initiated by secular leaders in collusion with corrupt *shaykhs*, have thoroughly diluted the excellence of its classical curriculum and undermined the morale of students and faculty. Fundamentalists, finally, are most vocal of all in condemning it as a formation designed to produce graduates who are obsequious toadies willing to serve as the functionaries of an Islam compromised by its subservience to an irreligious state.[32]

The introduction on a massive scale of education modeled along Western lines, leading to increases in literacy and semi-literacy along with an information boom stemming from both print and electronic media have all played their part in precipitating a fragmentation of Islamic religious authority. A once fairly unified and restricted idea of knowledge has now been called into question. Modern pedagogy has brought new ways of teaching religion—refuting, for instance, the value of the rote memorization of texts, including the Qur'an. Claims of competence and superiority based on academic achievements in specialized fields of "secular" learning also make their bids for recognition. The uncertain rating due to worldly experience and the disputed criteria for evaluating personal qualities apart from pure mental acumen also complicate the issue.[33]

Virtually all assertions of authority are represented, in some fashion, as validated by forms of knowledge. In Islamist settings, therefore, where Islam also functions as a political ideology, the problem is exacerbated because of the premise that there can be no division between religious and secular spheres. Hence, the traditional religious sciences would seem to lose their privileged status. No longer does knowledge lie in knowing the Qur'an and a mastery of the *sharīʿa*, since the *ʿulamāʾ* who may qualify on this scale are judged incapable of responding to the immediate practical needs of contemporary society. It follows then that specialists in modern technical ways of knowing, new prestigious branches of science, such as medicine or engineering, or reform-minded schoolteachers presume the right to displace these allegedly bankrupt traditional scholars.

Recognizing knowledge as the cardinal quality in the legitimation of Islamic authority suggests further the usefulness of what might be framed as a simple typology, a set of domains involving three different configurations inspired by the Weberian conjuncture of charisma, domination, and rationalization.[34] The interest here is not to trace the genesis of the role of the preacher nor the stages of its transformation throughout history but to construct for heuristic purposes a triptych of different "roads to salvation" as reflected in domains of preaching of contemporary Egypt. Needless to say, such a paradigm does not pretend to accurately portray individual preachers as pure exemplars of such categories. In fact, variations, overlaps, and combinations of each representative are fully part of the process. But such a partition of types of authority does have a strong indigenous conceptual basis and a clear institutional validity.

Preacher as Saint

The first domain of preaching derives from the relationship of human to supernatural forces which Weber associates with the basis of monotheism as a "religion of everyday life." This process, which has as one of its prerequisites "the existence of specific personal carriers of otherworldly goals," is typified as the movement from sorcery to what Weber calls religion as cult.[35] In terms of practitioners, this domain embraces the continuum between magician and priest. The first claims his authority on the basis of his power to magically coerce or charm the "functionally universal" deity or lesser demons or spirits, while the relationship of the second takes the form of prayer, sacrifice, and worship. In practice, however, he notes that the differentiation of techniques between these two is fluid and vague. Weber contrasts them more by their habitual sociological relationships than by instrumental criteria: "the term priest may be applied to the functionaries of a regularly organized and permanent enterprise concerned with influencing the gods, in contrast with the individual and occasional efforts of magicians."[36]

In the context of local Islam that concerns us, this category of the priest-magician may be associated with the *walī* (feminine, *walīya*), or "saint."[37] This Islamic "holy man/woman" tends to be most prominent among relatively small-scale, closed, homogeneous, strongly corporate social systems with a generally low division of labor. It usually has its most elaborate manifestation in the village, the popular quarters of cities, and tribal settings. This location of the saint at the margins of the high civilization is not only a feature of social structure but it is often reproduced geographically as well. Cult sites linked to these figures are characteristically situated in places where they have the effect of providing a symbolic centering for a particular community and the setting of its boundaries.[38]

Furthermore, conceived as a source of special blessings and a mediator, the function of this saint tends to be highly generalized rather than specialized. Marcel Mauss noted with regard to such practitioners that they display "almost a total confusion of powers and roles" since the elements of magic as a system are diffuse. Hence even while magician-priests themselves stand apart, their effect is to unify a community for "these individuals have merely appropriated to themselves the collective forces of society."[39] They do not, in other words, serve as specialists within the framework of differentiated organizations; they instead embody a total corporation. Peter Brown, in his study of the holy man in the local milieux of the late Roman empire, contributes a further insight by noting that the rise of these figures "coincides . . . with the erosion of classical institutions," whereas their decline or leveling-off "coincides with the re-assertion of a new sense of majesty in the community."[40] He concludes that the predominance of these striking figures as the "bearers of the supernatural among men" subsides when strongly centralized, functionally segmented institutions, such as, for instance, the caliphate, begin to develop. Then the focus of a generalized divine power which was concentrated in dispersed individuals especially at the interstices of society is dramatically redirected as though pulled by a new magnetic field toward the new formal, imperial institutions. This historical portrayal concurs with developments in Egypt over the past two centuries. The contraction of traditional popular Sufism and its related saints' cults clearly coincided with the emergence of the social, economic, and political leviathan of the modern nation-state, subsumed into the international market and security systems.[41]

The character of the knowledge attributed to the *walī* is personalistic and esoteric. It is infused rather than learned for it is "knowledge which derives from illumination, or knowledge of God's concealed purposes, of the *bāṭin* which lies behind the apparent world of the *ẓāhir*."[42] These complementary terms, *ẓāhir* and *bāṭin*, refer to two dimensions of reality. The first relates to the world as an external, visible, objective realm while the second points to the hidden, secret truths that underlie appearances. Knowledge of the *bāṭin* is distinguished as *ma'rifa* (gnosis) which has its source in a vital inner power or compelling divine force known as *baraka*. Of course, the saint, as a sacred dynamo, producing and distributing this grace for his devotees, is not limited by the bounds of space and time that confine ordinary mortal knowing. Hence, genuine saints continue to bless and their sacred munificence may even abound more abundantly after their deaths. Hence the cult of the saint and therefore access to the knowledge and power they personify frequently involves veneration of their tombs or some other spot they have designated. From out of these special sites, which may grow into pilgrimage centers, where mosques, sufi lodges, and schools may also arise, the magical and intercessory powers of the saint are diffused into the material world of *ẓāhir* to provide benefits for those whom the *walī* favors.

Preacher as Scholar

The second domain of preaching corresponds to the category signaled by Weber's notion of the "ethical prophet" who concentrates on social rather than ritual action for gaining salvation. Again, this type should not be considered a fixed state but a process or "a developing systemization."[43] Weber distinguishes between two forms of such systemization and the Islamic preacher speaking as ethical prophet moves between them. The first orientation emphasizes a legalistic approach to righteousness: "the particular actions of an individual in quest of salvation whether virtuous or wicked actions can be evaluated singly and credited to or subtracted from the individual's account. . . . It is held that his religious fate depends upon his actual achievements in their relationship to one another."[44]

The second pole of this systemization stresses intentions and treats "individual actions as symptoms and expressions of an underlying ethical total personality." In this latter case, demands at the level of the total personality increase while particular accomplishments or transgressions are dealt with as secondary. In drawing this distinction Weber appeals to the concept of *Gesinnungsethik,* a term which is variously translated as "ethic of inwardness," "religious mood," "inner religious faith," or "inner religious state."[45] The dominance of this religious inwardness implies an orientation toward ultimate ends or authentic faith while its lack points to "the increasing intrusion of intellectualism" and the growth of "rationalism" in dogma and ethics. Where religious inwardness is more highly developed, attitude and intention are weighted more heavily whereas in its absence, which Weber associated with external "responsibility" (*Verantwortlichkeit*), formalism and legalism are advanced as the ethical ideal. This concept of inwardness is important because it points to an essential tension between ethical action as strict conformity to law as distinguished from piety judged as subjective motivation.

The preacher as the ethical prophet is associated in this typology with the *ʿālim* (pl. *ʿulamāʾ*), derived from the stem *ʿilm* and meaning "one with knowledge" or the "scholar." His privileged position rests upon achievements in learning and specifically his supposed mastery of the revealed canon together with related juridical and perhaps other texts. Recalling, as Weber has noted, that "the transition from the prophet to the legislator is fluid,"[46] the *'ālim* is the agent of divine law whose task is to preserve, to codify, to interpret, and to transmit the verbal charisma of the prophet. The knowledge embodied by the *'ālim* refers therefore to an objective closed literary heritage recognized as *'ilm*, identified as the traditional Islamic sciences. Furthermore, this system of knowledge and indeed the historical origins of these scholars as the class of *'ulamā'* have been closely bound up with a specialized institution of learning, namely the *madrasa*, forerunner of the European university, which spread from its beginnings in Baghdad in the eleventh century to become an indispensable element of medieval urban life. These "mosque-universities" developed into a vast network of religious, legal, and intellectual centers whose graduates and associates were entrusted with all manner of civic, social, and religious functions.[47]

Today, in Egypt as elsewhere, this older notion of the *'ulamā'* as a class is hedged with tentativeness and ambiguity. To the extent that the category retains validity, it consists of professional preachers, teachers, and government functionaries trained at the Azhar and following careers in various institutions or under Ministries such as Justice, Religious Endowments, or Education, where their religious credentials are prerequisites for their posts. But such men lack the support of formal mechanisms that would solidify them and coordinate their common interests. Egypt, for instance, has nothing parallel to the formidable League of Moroccan Ulama which exercises great influence in that country.[48] The rapport between Egypt's *'ulamā'* and the state has often been troubled in recent history but these difficulties also reaffirm the continuing importance of the religious establishment in the political legitimation of regimes. Even though the *'ulamā'* have traditionally distanced themselves from the actual exercise of power, they nonetheless remain spokesmen for "official Islam," which retains considerable influence, especially in matters of family relations. Political scientist Ali Dessouki recently stated the relationship succinctly: "You have an unwritten contract. On political issues, Al-Azhar will defer to the government. But when it comes to civil issues like marriage and women, this is Al-Azhar's domain."[49]

Perhaps this often noted reluctance to rule on the part of the *'ulamā'*, which forms the basis of a de facto separation of religion from politics in Egypt, is not only for want of an historical opportunity. It may also emerge from the character of their *'ilm*, which is embedded in the nature of this law itself. It has been suggested that the legal system they represent is not really comparable to a modern constitution with its adjunct criminal or civil codes, but has rather an essentially hortatory function as well, in the manner of a sermon:

> Since the Sharīʿa was held to be absolutely normative for all aspects of life, even if only a small part of it was in fact applied, there is reason to consider the attention given to its elaboration as an implicit but clear protest by the religious scholars against certain social realities and government policies. To the extent that reality deviated from the norms prescribed, the elaboration of these norms and the declaration of their absolute validity implied condemnation of and protest against reality as it existed in Muslim society.[50]

Recently, the old arguments of liberal reformers that the "door of *ijtihād*," that is, "independent judgment," be reopened to allow modern jurists to interpret the sharīʿa in unprecedented ways, better suited to modern needs, have been surpassed by more radical tenets. In some quarters, the view has been advanced that the *ʿulamāʾ* themselves take charge of the apparatus of government. This position has emerged as a response to the feelings of frustration, deprivation, and injustice usually blamed on the advance of secularization. It has tended to follow along the lines of two distinct but related ideological convictions, articulated in what might be called a Sunna and a Shiʿa version. In the first case, the *ʿulamāʾ* have sought to adapt religious authority to the sovereignty of the state; by exercising their power of veto from the top, they may guide the direction of the nation. In the second version, religious leaders seek to adapt their authority to the sovereignty of the believing community which is mobilized to seize control of the state and entrust it to the mullahs or scholars who themselves serve as governors.[51]

This second paradigm reflects the radical theories of the Ayatollah Ruhollah Khomeini and his thesis of the *veliyat al-fiqīh*, the "rule of the Islamic jurist." This revolutionary form has only an approximate parallel in Egypt among certain extremist groups of an almost cultlike quality under a leader usually called the *amīr*. Far more in the mainstream of Islamist views are figures like the late Shaykh Salah Abu Ismaʿil, who made a name for himself by insisting on the application of the *sharīʿa* from his seat in the Parliament.[52]

Preacher as Warrior

The third domain of preaching derives from a Weberian type that is less immediately the transmitter of grace but more its active defender, enforcer, and a conqueror in its service. This type does not constitute a stage in a presumed scale of religious evolution; it is rather a religiously legitimated agent of action found in virtually all environments. This is the "warrior" who theoretically depends upon the higher authority of a specialist for his religious direction, although he himself may at times also claim direct access to divine charisma. In Islamic history as well as current ideology, this conjunction of religiopolitical hegemony with successful military leadership is reckoned to have begun with the Prophet Muhammad himself. For instance, one of the most popular Egyptian writers of this century, 'Abbas al-'Aqqad, celebrated this conventional image in his biography, *The Genius of the Prophet*. Here, Muhammad is depicted as a singularly triumphant military strategist, an extraordinary field commander, and a heroic combatant.[53] This same theme also often recurs explicitly in sermons, especially those of preachers who are morally associated with this domain. Of course, this persona is familiar to recent memory in the dramatic victories of the Mahdi's faithful in the Sudan, in the Pasdaran or "revolutionary guards" of the Iranian Republic, and in Egypt's violent Islamist fringe who characteristically consult with a sympathetic religious legal scholar to validate their campaigns, which may include bombings, robberies, and murders.[54] Indeed, President Sadat himself was fond of combining ostentatious military and religious emblems in his personal attire, his public gestures, and his political rhetoric.[55]

This domain of preaching associated with the "holy warrior" has its idealized contemporary counterpart in the figure of the *mujāhid*, deriving from the noun *jihād*. Such a preacher views himself in the tradition of the first militant disciples of the Prophet through whom formidable opponents were defeated and an Islamic empire was created. But this call to immediate engagement and confrontation is not restricted to combat on the battlefield. It includes concerted effort to overcome social and political corruption and in that sense it has the character of a moral crusade as well as a potential for revolution. Furthermore, the *mujāhid's* primary orientation toward action emphasizes the need to mobilize the society at large and thus to excite others to join this holy cause. Hence the *jihād* in question may begin with the minds and hearts of believers but the proof of its success is judged in the eventual domination of the worldly order.

The priority of Sufis and others who viewed the "greater" *jihād* not as that of the sword but as the spiritual struggle aimed at purifying the heart and directed against the evil within one's own self falls into abeyance here, for the preacher's discourse has primarily this-worldly objectives.[56] The methods of this combat may indeed be non-violent, such as those embodied in the Islamist concept of *jihād al-da'wa* ("home mission"). Here the preacher as warrior seeks to spread Islam among unbelievers or to "Islamicize" Muslims by means of "argumentation and demonstration," although the basic struggle is outwardly directed.[57]

This warrior, purely considered in Weber's scheme, is not readily a "carrier of a rational religious ethic" but has much more at stake in his honor: "To accept religion . . . and to genuflect before any prophet or priest would appear plebeian and dishonorable to any martial hero or noble person. . . . He does not require of his religion . . . beyond protection against evil magic or such ceremonial rites as are congruent with his caste, such as priestly prayers for victory."[58]

However, in the Islamic context, including in contemporary North Africa, this *mujāhid,* while deeply committed to protecting his "honor," is also far more an exponent of religious imperatives than Weber's figure suggests. The line that theoretically divides the military commander from the religious leader has often been difficult to define or maintain especially in conflicted circumstances. In Morocco, for instance, King Hassan retains and prominently displays his title of Commander of the Faithful. He also makes prominent gestures that signal his place at the head of his military and aroused civilian forces, such as his leadership of the highly successful Green March of 1974 meant to assert his country's claim to the former Spanish Sahara.[59] The founding president of Tunisia, Habib Bourguiba, who did not hesitate to advance his own interpretations of Islam, sometimes directly in the face of the ʿ*ulamāʾ*, also was fond of depicting himself as *al-mujāhid al-kabīr,* the Great Warrior.[60] Finally, in Libya Colonel Qaddafi has often appealed explicitly to the indigenous model of the warrior-saint in asserting his legitimacy since he took power by overthrowing King Idris in 1969. Moreover, Qaddafi's eccentric interpellations in matters of faith as well as political life, including his thorough undermining of existing religious elites, both the ʿ*ulamāʾ* and the saints' system, suggests that the "appearance of such a figure, in the form of a modern statesman rather than the mahdi of popular belief" reflects a consistent permutation in the type of Islamic authority represented by this domain of preaching.[61]

Implied in the *mujāhid's* attitude and his manner of justifying it is the view that a practical knowledge that leads to victory is superior to theoretical; that is, theological knowledge must prove itself in action. His knowledge does not derive from submission to the patronage of a distant saint nor from mastery of ancient texts but from the self-validating capacity to effectively control or manipulate the natural and social world. In this sense, the *mujāhid* is primarily oriented toward visible results. Therefore science as technology is often the model and goal of his learning. In this connection it is perhaps not surprising that so many of those committed to Islamism in Egypt are or were students of the Western-style universities rather than the traditional religious colleges. Likewise, their influence in underdeveloped village settings has been quite limited. Increasingly the leadership of this movement is derived largely from among students and professionals in the applied sciences, notably medicine and engineering.[62]

Likewise much of the popular apologetic, exegetic, and even devotional literature characteristic of this tendency is written in a style that draws heavily on scientific and medical allusions.[63] This orientation toward concrete action and the association with the acknowledged achievements of modernity demonstrate what and how the *mujāhid* knows. Among extremists, even direct provocations, assaults on property, and assassinations have been justified as a kind of modern mass pedagogy which some militants designate by the term *ghaḍab li-allah* "an outrage for God" which might be seen as a variation of the attacks called "armed propaganda" by Italy's Red Brigade.[64] In present-day Egypt, this domain of preaching is reflected most familiarly within the compass of the Society of the Muslim Brothers and its off-shoots that envisage essentially worldly goals while religion motivates and directs their moral and political aspirations.

Preachers and Mosques

Closely linked to this three-part typology and connecting these domains of preaching with Weber's concept of routinization are the actual mosques where preachers and congregations converge for the ritual performance. Here, the mosque may be understood as the institutionalization of what Bryan Wilson calls "charismatic demand" or a "tradition of credibility awaiting arousal."[65] Their variety discloses the multiple social structures and differing cultural bases of religious authority. The English word *mosque* derives from the Arabic *masjid*, from the root of which also comes *sajada*, meaning "to bow down, to prostrate oneself." This alludes, of course, to the daily prayer, the second of the five pillars of Islam at which prostration is, perhaps, the most demonstrative of the several prescribed gestures.

In Egyptian Arabic, *masjid* constitutes what linguists call an unmarked term. It can refer to virtually any sort of site, satisfying the barest minimal definition. It may be an elaborate construction on a grand scale or the merest cubicle. It could be any tiny nook, a portion of a hall, or a barely demarcated open space that has been set apart, permanently or temporarily, for prayer. Of course, variously associated other activities may also occur in a mosque, or the site may be abandoned, but by definition it stands as a sacred enclosure, belonging to God and therefore to the whole community. A mosque, like the ritual prayer from which it takes its name, is essentially symbolic in that it represents the integrity and solidarity of the whole community. It is a sanctuary that embodies a divinely inspired ideal, a blessed surface where the lineaments of another reality are evoked. A mosque provides the routinized setting for the public expression of both a given established order and what has been called anti-structure, counterculture, or *contre-champ*. In it the brute facts of power, suspended as unconstrained ideals, are collectively reaffirmed and reinterpreted. But within this sacred space, preaching perhaps more than any other activity allows a mosque to point beyond its strictly conceived function to become "not merely a physical site for prayer . . . [but] an ontological critique of man's agonistic impulses."[66]

But even as any place of prayer, regardless of its size or degree of elaboration, may be called a *masjid*, Egyptian Muslims also conceptualize different kinds of mosques which they denote with specific terms and modifiers. To oversimplify slightly, local residents distinguish between three basic categories of these religious institutions. This classification system is also reflected officially in the administration of mosques by three separate government agencies charged with the regulation of various aspects of social organization and religious expression. This division has been evolving for over a century and has only recently undergone a new series of sweeping adjustments under President Mubarak.

In the early 1980s a series of measures were implemented that were designed to tighten the state's control over religious institutions, primarily to prevent the use of mosques for what the government considered to be dangerous and illegal political purposes. But these revisions merely carried through to completion earlier initiatives that have accompanied the growth of the modern centralized state as it displaced Ottoman and British practices. Basically, the three classes of mosques that operated under separate government bureaucracies during the 'Abd al-Nasir and Sadat era have now been placed under a single broad oversight procedure. Its concern, however, has not been the administration of mosques generally, but more explicitly the supervision of the pulpit.

The three types of mosques, as reflected by official definitions, are "government mosques" (sing., *masjid hukūmī*), "private mosques" (sing., *masjid ahlī*) and those mosques variously designated which operate under the auspices of the Supreme Sufi Council (*al-Majlis al-Sūfī al-Aʿlā*). Once again, these divisions may be represented as exclusive, but in reality they also exist in mixed proportions. Quite often sets of attributes identified with one system overlap with others. Nonetheless, to depict three categories of mosques roughly along these lines conforms to popularly held notions. Furthermore, this three-part division has a long pedigree in Islamic urban typologies dating at least from the work of 'Izz al-Din ibn Shaddah (d. 1284) describing the Mamluk cities of Damascus and Cairo.[67]

It is not surprising, therefore, that a very similar version of this prototypical classification scheme reappeared in the comprehensive geographic encyclopedia of Egypt, *al-Khiṭāṭ al-Tawfīqīya al-Jidīda*, compiled by Egypt's first Minister of Public Works, 'Ali Mubarak, at the end of the nineteenth century. In that magisterial work, which ran to twenty folio volumes, Mubarak set "places of worship" at the top of his list of public buildings he described in Cairo and other cities. He divided them initially into two kinds of mosques, first, the *jāmiʿ* and then the *masjid*. Third, he cataloged the assorted establishments related to Sufism and the cult of saints (for example, *ḍarīh*, a mausoleum; *qubba*, a shrine) along with the meeting places and lodges of the brotherhoods (for example, *zawīya, ribāṭ, takīya, khalwa*).[68]

The distinction between a *jāmiʿ* and a *masjid* is set down formally in the code of classical *fiqh* although its application is frequently haphazard. Popular understanding of the contrast today is also often vague and impressionistic. According to the classical theory, the *jāmiʿ* is a uniquely large mosque founded as the place of the solemn weekly assembly for an entire community. It was supposedly centrally located and adjoined or adjacent to the ruler's residence. Here the Muslims of a given locale all came together for the Friday noon prayer at which they would hear a sermon delivered originally by the Caliph himself or the governor, his deputy in the provinces. This law also specified that the erection of a *jāmiʿ* was reserved solely for important urban centers and only the greatest cities were to have more than one of them.[69]

In architectural terms the lofty status of the *jāmiʿ* was announced externally by its size, its prominent location, and its grandiose design. Internally, apart from the probable richer decor, it contained the *minbar*, or ritual pulpit, which was supposedly constructed with features that linked it iconographically to the sacred podium and imperial seat of the Prophet and his successors. It was this pulpit and the sermon it signified that most plainly designated the defining privilege of the *jāmiʿ*. This ritual prerogative denoted an explicit political relationship since traditional Islamic law also required that the *khuṭba* be delivered either by or in the name of the legitimate successor of Muhammad. Hence the restriction of this ritual oratorical event, the Friday sermon, to the *jāmiʿ* led the great French historian Gaudefroy-Demombynes to gloss the term descriptively as *mosquée à khotba*.[70]

Government and Private Mosques

The category of the "government mosque" in contemporary Egypt emerged from a tangled history of reform efforts and state appropriations of traditional Islamic trusts, known as the *waqf* (pl., *āwqāf*). The funds from such donations, usually in land or buildings, were designated, all or in part, for the support of mosques, as well as schools, hospitals, poor houses, and other charities. The properties classified as endowments of this sort became quite extensive. But the practice was based upon legal mechanisms that had "all the intricacies of an extremely complicated and archaic land system" and as such, in modern times, *waqfs* were chronically prone to the self-interested manipulation of the very wealthy.[71] Over the last two centuries, in stages, the entire practice has been curtailed until ultimately all *waqf* properties were nationalized by the revolutionary regime in the 1950s. At the same time, the responsibility for maintaining the support for the benefited institutions was nominally transferred to the state.

Within the Ministry of Religious Endowments (*wizarat al-āwqāf*), one subordinate branch, the Office of Mosques (*maktab al-masājid*) was created and charged with overseeing the administration of the thousands of mosques that had theoretically relied on the income from these foundations. In fact, for some time previous to this takeover, the management of *waqfs* had been notorious for corruption and abuse, making the entire system a byword for the economic backwardness and political reaction associated with the traditional religious elites allied with the king and the conservative landed class.[72] But when *waqf* affairs were turned over to the Ministry, the subsidies now issued directly by the state did not follow the stipulations of the original benefactors, which had sometimes been stipulated centuries ago. Instead, the criteria for the selection and the support of what came to be called a "government mosque" were based on the state's own priorities and its budget constraints. The result was the formation of an expanding national religious bureaucracy which operated, in 1961, for instance, 3,006 mosques out of the total number of 17,224 mosques then existing in Egypt, according to the Ministry's own count. Besides full responsibility for the physical maintenance of the buildings, again at least in theory, each government mosque was also staffed with a professional preacher, a graduate of the Azhar, who was appointed and salaried through the personnel office of the Ministry. In actuality, however, the staffing levels at these government mosques were also commonly deficient. For example, in this same 1961 survey, it was revealed that only 71 percent of all government mosques had preachers.[73]

At the time these statistics were released, 'Abd al-Nasir's government announced a grand plan to incorporate the remainder of the nation's mosques into this government system within ten years. However, this did not occur. It proved far too ambitious in terms of expenditures and manpower. But over the next two decades, the state did proceed steadily to increase the number of mosques it directly supervised. During this same period, however, the increase in private mosques continued to outpace by far this rate of absorption. In 1979 Shaykh 'Abd al-Min'am al-Nimr, then Minister of Religious Endowments, released figures indicating that the total number of mosques in Egypt had reached 34,000, of which only 5,600 belonged within the Ministry's official system. He also added the important fact of a related crisis of employment since less than half, 2,500 of these government mosques, were staffed with permanent *imāms*. The rest were assigned temporary auxiliaries, recruited locally, who merely performed the Friday sermon for a small stipend paid them by the Ministry.[74] As these figures indicate, amid enormous growth in absolute numbers, the ratio of government to private mosques remained almost constant at approximately 1:6 for these two decades.

In a significant sense, the government mosque suggests a structural parallel to the historical division between the *jāmi'* and the ordinary *masjid* as understood in the classical polity. The pattern that emerged was that the central mosque of sizable villages or the most distinguished mosque of a major quarter of larger towns and cities would be incorporated into the Ministry's bureaucracy and transformed into a government mosque with a staff and building support. In another sense, however, numerous other factors had entered the picture to make the modern situation quite distinct from the one presumed by the classical paradigm. First, in practice, preaching was no longer restricted only to a small number of mosques officially designated as *jāmi'*. The special congregational Friday prayer, including a *khuṭba* in some form or other, had came to be performed at virtually any local mosque where the congregation desired to carry it out and someone was present to speak. Second, the severe shortage of professional preachers just noted cannot be divorced from the wider diminishment of the traditional religious authority systems represented by both the Sufi and the Azhari *shaykh*. In their place, a diffuse movement of new lay or amateur preachers had started to flourish.[75]

Third and most decisively, since the end of the nineteenth century a new and increasingly popular form of socioreligious organization had arisen under the initial leadership of such towering nationalist figures as Muhammad 'Abdu, 'Abdullah al-Nadim, and Sa'ad Zaghlul. It began in urban areas but, adapting itself to local conditions, it spread rapidly into the countryside. From its beginnings this new kind of organization moved progressively toward an integration of religious involvement, especially the active sponsorship of mosques with other social functions, notably education. But it was also greatly instrumental in encouraging a revival of the sermon by introducing a more colloquial style of preaching.[76] This new sort of group become known as a *jam'īya*, literally, "society, association, corporation" or more amply, *jam'īya khayrīya*, frequently rendered "voluntary benevolent society."

Interestingly and reflecting a later orientation, in circles such as the World Bank and the American Agency for International Development, the *jam'īya*, in many cases, has also been seen as the local version of the familiar PVO, that is, "private voluntary organization," or NGO, "non-governmental organization." Independent, member-supported societies of this kind have been founded in Egypt for all manner of purposes, notably to provide education or medical care, to promote sports or hobbies, and to facilitate a variety of social activities, as well as to assist the needy in a range of categories. But for decades the category of service that ranks the highest by far in the number of beneficiaries for the different offerings of these societies has been religion.[77] Although this trend toward a greater religious emphasis at this popular level was evident long before the supposed triggering of Islamic resurgence in the late 1960s, it has been the recent exponential growth in the scale and the intensity of involvement of *jam'īyas* that has given the term "private mosque" the connotation it usually carries today. For many, this term has come to connote a mosque that is specifically and intentionally autonomous, that is, one that repudiates state control as exercised through the Ministry of Religious Endowments.

This is not to say that *jam'īya* mosques, or, to be more precise, their pulpits, have been totally without government supervision in the past. In fact, since 1945, every *jam'īya* has had to be registered and was obliged to comply with a stream of regulations issued and enforced by the Ministry of Social Affairs. But because of this bureaucratic displacement under a Ministry that had no direct interest in religion, the mosques of *jam'īyas* initially tended to experience little or no direct interference with regard to preaching. Apart from some egregious incident touching upon criminal incitement or national security, it would only be in an exceptional case, perhaps only when a *jam'īya* mosque was to receive a grant from the Ministry of Religious Endowments, that such a private mosque would encounter the specific government bureaucracy which had a direct interest in its religious practice or its preacher.[78]

Statistically speaking, of course, the great majority of private mosques were neither founded by a *jam'īya* nor do they function under the auspices of such a formal association. Most of the mosques defined in this category are simply neighborhood or work-site prayer facilities, some older, many more recent, including a number that have been erected spontaneously, as it were. Generally, such mosques have no staff and no dependable support. Many such private mosques are used only irregularly at the convenience of a shifting congregation. Others have a more stable usage and may even be served by a pious volunteer who functions as an *imām*. In rural villages, the pattern has been that where a significant permanent mosque exists, it is common for someone to serve as its *shaykh*, if only on a partial basis. But he may also combine leadership of mosque prayer and preaching with other traditionally associated activities such as teaching, Qur'an chanting, overseeing life-crisis rituals and perhaps some civic functions such as the certification of marriages. Such a makeshift *imām* may nonetheless receive a modest government stipend through the Ministry which he would supplement by other employment, by donations, and by remuneration for performing extra services.

Hence, the depiction of all private mosques as ideologically motivated breeding grounds for dissidents eager to preserve their independence against the censorship that would follow upon state control is a distorting generalization.[79] On the contrary, in many cases, the residents of villages or neighborhoods actively seek to have their local mosques brought under the munificent administration of the Ministry. Indeed, they lobby to obtain this favor just as they might besiege government agencies to build them a school or a clinic, to install electricity or build them a road. Nonetheless, the implication of opposition toward the government that has come to be associated with private mosques does recognize the political undercurrents that account for the enormous popularity of many prominent *jamʿīya* preachers. Hence, their reputation for harboring intrepid firebrands in the pulpit, or for doubling as recruiting stations and breeding grounds for Islamist groups, does not fit the great majority, but it does point to the independence that makes these private mosques most visible and distinctive.[80]

Official Religion and Its Opposition

Over the course of almost two centuries of sweeping social, economic and political transformation in Egypt the structure of religious institutions and the patterns of piety have also undergone considerable change. Not the least of the factors influencing this religious dimension, including the global manifestation of what is often referred to as Islamic fundamentalism, stems from the rising "popular awareness of 'standard' Islam."[81] One by-product of improved communication and rising literacy has been a movement toward conformity with the more normative practices, especially in rituals, as set down in the classical texts. Nevertheless, it remains important that the background against which this modernizing reaction is occurring does not get overlooked. Contemporary Islamic activists generally scorn, if not condemn, the demonstrative and often ecstatic spirituality of the popular Sufism. They share this criticism with many of the 'ulamā', or at least its officialdom, who also tend to denigrate the cult of saints. Nevertheless recent developments in Egypt point to the endurance and resilience of the underlying sociocultural dynamics that form the basis of these traditional forms of expression. For instance, the strong appeal of moral arguments in public life that has been discussed as a feature of the "retraditionalization of policy"[82] has followed amid pressures that another observer has described as "a growing villagization of the cities."[83] All of which reaffirms the relevance of traditional values based on kinship, patronage, and the solidarity of religion, beneath a veneer of secular progress. Thus it happens that several of the most renowned dissident preachers in the country, including Shaykh Mahmud Mahallawi and Shaykh 'Adil 'Aid, whom President Sadat singled out for rebuke and personal insult in his since famous harangue before the Parliament just a month before he was killed, were preachers in government, not private mosques.[84] Furthermore, the blind *shaykh* who is undoubtedly the most celebrated preacher in the contemporary Arab world, a pyrotechnic orator whose sermons on bootleg cassette tapes may be heard from Marrakesh to Muscat, Shaykh 'Abd al-Hamid Kishk, has also long served as the *imām* of a government mosque in Cairo. From there, with occasional interruptions due to police intervention, he won his reputation as a forceful and mocking critic of Sadat's and then Mubarak's administration, as he preached to crowds of thousands overflowing the mosque into the surrounding streets each Friday.[85] As these personalities suggest, the lines of division that are supposed to define the difference between government and private mosques may be broached in practice. But one feature of the typology offered above is its flexibility. A few such men have a very high profile both before the religious public and to some degree in political circles although they are not the norm. But neither are they wholesale anomalies, since overflow, slippage, and switching between varied social domains and their symbolic systems merely underlines the versatility of claims to authority and the possibility of multiple roles that may be played by a given preacher.

Nonetheless, the overall view prevails that the government mosque, like the classic *jāmi'*, is the proper setting for the *'ālim*. Official Islam achieves its most articulate local expression in the sermons and lessons of this professional preacher who presides over a mosque under the direction of the Ministry. The conventional uniform, epitomized by the ankle-length coat, or *kakūla*, and the red fez surmounted by a black silk tassel, surrounded by a small white muslin band to form an abbreviated turban, identifies him publicly with the tradition of classical learning. In contrast, the mosque of the *jamᶜīya*, and thus the private mosque in its most ardently engaged form, is the place best suited to the preaching of the *mujāhid*. From here, this hortatory warrior personifies direct involvement in efforts to hasten the advance of Islamic claims in an unbelieving world. In the spirit of the Society of the Muslim Brothers (*Jamᶜīya al-Ikhwān al Muslimīn*) whose slogan for national reform was "the Qurʾan is our constitution" the ideological trajectory of this holy warrior aims at a totalistic societal transformation with the mosque serving as its center and meeting place.[86]

Finally, the saint's shrine, whether it encloses his tomb or other relics dedicated to his memory, or perhaps the lodge of the Sufi *shaykh*, constitutes the appropriate location for the preacher who embodies the *walī*. Many times, little or nothing in the design of such sites associated with saints distinguishes them from ordinary mosques. The rituals carried out there may also appear for the most part to follow orthodox practice. But conspicuous external markings do not always reflect the perception of believers regarding these performances. It easily happens that elements of the saint's complex may penetrate and perhaps even encompass a *masjid* or a *jāmiᶜ*. A saint's aura may convert the empty space of any mosque into a hub of popular devotion. It is no coincidence that the terms *zawīya* and *khalwa* remain today common expressions for a small *masjid* in Upper Egypt, for these terms are closely associated with the tradition of Sufi "mosques." Because a saint is recognized as a point of access to the spiritual realm of what is secret and hidden, preaching in the name of the *walī* may occur under various guises. Both the *ᶜālim* and the *mujāhid* may also evoke this presence. For here as elsewhere the gnostic test of genuine knowledge often applies: he who knows does not speak and he who speaks does not know.

One consequence of this paradox is the tendency for a *walī*'s power to be fully realized only after his death. Perforce, the real speech of the saint is that of the heart, which is interior and intuitive and therefore not subject to ordinary standards of coherence or eloquence. Rather, as an English poet remarking on ancient Christian saints in the Middle East has observed: "They preach a stronger sermon, their voices being silent. They summon more urgently having fewer things to say."[87] When the preacher addresses a congregation under the patronage of the *walī*, therefore, his whole meaning is seldom conveyed from the mosque pulpit alone. He speaks also indirectly by means that cannot be straightforwardly verbalized nor fully apprehended by the rational mind.

Metaphors and Metonyms

The three domains of preaching described above are therefore anchored in analogous concepts of knowledge and authority. But as the review of contemporary practices has suggested, this three-part paradigm has recently undergone a sort of flattening process resulting in another layer revealing a two-part paradigm due largely to the strong centralizing forces that have polarized the older diffuse system into a dichotomy made up only of government and private mosques. As a result, the assemblies of worship as personified by their preachers have also been evolving into a pattern of two co-existing modes of discourse. First is the case of the *ʿālim*, where the underlying theory of ritual oratory that validates his role rests on principles of rational exegesis, appeal to precedent, analogy, and implicit comparison. It has metaphor as its model. Such a view is postulated on the interaction between two separate systems, revelation and the world (*dīn wa dunyā*), which have structural parallels by which the preacher is able to relate them to one another.[88]

The preaching of formal sermons in the idiom of metaphor presumes the need for an intermediary, interpretive step that intervenes between the divine law and its mundane application. This moment of transference from one field to another may incline toward either of the two tendencies that characterize Weber's ethical prophet, that is, toward legalism or a spiritual and psychological emphasis. But in both cases a gap separating the sacred law in itself from the contingent moral universe is institutionally acknowledged since the primary task of the preacher is to bridge this gulf. The *ʿālim* as preacher shows through his performance —whether he is good or bad at it is important but a different matter— the need to forge an interpretive link that is neither intrinsic nor entirely self-evident. The qualities of this metaphor presuppose the difference between the contrasting elements being symbolically conjoined, thereby comparing the features of one field with those of the other. The metaphor is reflected not only in the rhetoric of his pulpit discourse but also in the role or cultural identity he projects, as preacher and apart from the mosque ritual as well. As a social actor, this scholar-preacher belongs to an mediating category such that his authority depends on the maintaining of a position of the kind described by Richard Antoun as a "culture broker."[89] His manner of preaching presumes that the fullness of Islam requires this explicit and permanent function of mediation, that is, the services of the specialist in the interpretation of the juridical and religious texts. At the same time, he ratifies his own legitimacy through leadership of collective ritual.

The second mode of rhetorical expression stems from the predication of inherent contiguity, intuitive transfer, and conceptual identity which may be called metonymy. Under this rubric which is associated with both the *walī* and the *mujāhid*, a logic of association dominates which does not specify an intervening interpretive phase or any distinct institution standing between the divine will and the human imperative. Rather, the movement between them is regarded as necessarily direct, intrinsic, natural, and inevitable. They represent, as George Lakoff depicts metonymic models, "cases where some subcategory or individual member of a category is used to comprehend the category as a whole."[90] For this reason, the mosque of both the saint and the warrior can be said to be marked as sociolinguistics employ the term. For these two situations commonly exhibit supplementary or exemplary attributes that symbolically associate them with what might be called asymmetric features of the broad Islamic tradition. The mosque of the scholar resembles the case of zero-marking or an unmarked term. The marked versions display what Lakoff has described as a prototype effect, that is, "an asymmetry in a category, where one member or subcategory is taken to be somehow more basic than the other (or others)."[91] But the two former instances depart from the normal pattern in opposite ways. The pulpit that serves as the pedestal for the *walī* faces the secret realm of *bāṭin* while the dais or soap-box that supports the *mujāhid* looks toward the agonistic world of *ẓāhir*. As marked terms, mosques of these two types frequently exaggerate respectively, as it were, their otherworldly or this-worldly orientation as compared to the relatively nondescript space occupied by the *ʿālim*. In these two modes of discourse the divine powers that each claims to embody are not detoured through a long and tangled history of human learning but the divine message is understood as flowing uninterruptedly from the source itself.

For the *mujāhid*, the actual meaning of revelation in the Qur'an is believed to emanate immediately from the sacred text itself. It can be understood by anyone who speaks Arabic with no further need of specialized clerical training nor of explanations by bureaucrats. In the case of the *walī* as the personified word, *baraka*, or mystical power, communicates itself through direct interaction or physical contact which may be through a visit, a dream, a trance, or by its extension through an amulet or a spell.

The *mujāhid* as preacher tends to treat scripture as a collection of unambiguous statements that simply "mean what they say." Therefore such Qur'anic injunctions as the cutting off of the hands of thieves and the absolute prohibition on interest are often depicted as a blueprint for a righteous society appropriate to all times and places. By calling for the literal and total application of the *shari'a,* they are vigorously rejecting the assumption that any self-conscious hermeneutical procedure is required for the discovery of how the meaning of revelation might be suited to different historical conditions. This presupposition of inherent connectedness is displayed in remarks like the following, by Hassan al-Banna, the charismatic founder of the Muslim Brothers, whose authority seems to draw upon both these metonymic roles: "Islam is worship and leadership, religion and state, spirituality and work, prayer and holy war, submissiveness and domination, the Qur'an and the sword and no one of these may be disconnected from any other."[92]

Each in their own particular ways, but with structurally comparable results, both the *wali* and the *mujāhid* as preachers assume a semantic of continuity and incorporation that implies a virtual isomorphism between a utopian past or an age of miracles and the present time. This pairing of the then and the now is not asserted primarily on the basis of historical similarity but rather it flows from a premise of divinely ordained cosmic order. In the perspective of ritual, time and eternity intersect through the favor of the saint or the proximity of the warrior's martyrdom. The expanse of intervening centuries melts away before such immediacy. History has no ruptures since all of its periods constitute parts of a single unified whole.

Moreover, the effectiveness of this mode of discourse associated with metonym relies more on the strength of localized solidarity than does the mode of metaphor. The metonym as a cultural idiom flourishes in social contexts that tend to be corporate and bounded, in which relationships are more generalized and roles relatively unspecialized and where members of a group share roughly similar experiences. Here, individualized, self-conscious abstract categories are seldom called forth to explain or analyze the moral dilemmas for everyday life. Power tends to be understood in personalistic terms with little differentiation between primordial bonds and institutional ties. Also, in these settings ritual leadership is often more compactly or metonymically fused with total personal identity since, as Bryan Wilson has observed, the nature of *charisma* in such societies similarly ignores pronounced boundaries between roles: "There is an inextricable involvement of a man's factual attributes with the evaluation of them, and with the emotional responses that they arouse. The individual is in effect looked upon as a total indivisible being."[93]

Hence, both the *wali* and the *mujāhid* as preachers, the one by miracles and the other by struggle, demonstrate a metonymic form of coherence projected upon them that is directly "linked to the need to concentrate symbolic capital in a single person."[94] Their manner of preaching, unlike that of the formal 'ālim, does not undertake to elevate their rhetoric or to insulate their role by situating them at a safe social distance from their adherents or their activity. Their preaching is itself the chief point of engagement overshadowing the ritual accoutrements that frame the preacher. These two metonymic representatives validate their authority by manifesting through their pulpit performance the achievements they announce. For them, the ritual process is not qualitatively different from involvement in either the internal or respectively the external reality for which they speak. The ceremony merely provides the occasion for the intensification and public presentation of their leadership which calls for a congregation's participation. Symbolically, their performance reproduces the miraculous events or the worldly triumphs of the age of glory; by making these scenes present again, they celebrate the anticipation of their repetition in present experience. Thus, in the metonymic mode, the sacred and the profane are not separate domains after all. They are merely two perspectives of one and the same reality which the saint in his way and the warrior in his continually recombine.

Given this theoretical foundation we may now embark on an analysis of actual mosques, preachers, and their congregations. Of course, as was noted earlier, the three domains of preaching that are set out here are not ethnographically pure types. Multiple functions and flexible constellations are not unusual and transformations from one mode to another are themselves often components of a rhetorical strategy. In that sense, the typology might best be regarded as a set of complements rather than a paradigm of contraries. Likewise the modes of metaphor and metonym as distinct patterns for the conversion of meaning from the "sacred" to the "secular" are also capable of being manipulated at many levels. Hence, as we proceed we shall take a cue from Henri Bergson, whose masterful study of the two sources of morality and religion features the role of the "moral hero, the genius of the will" as the pivot between the "closed" and the "open" society: "Oh, I know what society says, (it has, I repeat, its reasons for saying so); but to know what it thinks and what it wants, we must not listen too much to what it says, we must look at what it does."[95]

3   The Mosque and the
       Cult of the Saint

The first mosque in Minya I chose to focus upon seemed the most obvious candidate. When I, arriving as a stranger, began inquiring about local mosques, I usually heard most about the city's grand central mosque known as *masjid al-Fūlī*. It readily claims to be the most prestigious and, architecturally speaking, the most distinguished Islamic monument in the entire governorate. Furthermore, since the few sites of recognized ancient or medieval importance in the area are all but abandoned and largely ignored, the striking physical size and excellent condition of this modern complex lent manifest validity to this assumption.[1] There is an immediate picturesque quality about this mosque as it is set on the corniche, the broad boulevard overlooking the Nile. Directly across the river is a majestic panorama of the green shore behind which are the russet cliffs rising high above the east bank.

Graced by a few tall shade trees forming a tiny oasis in the city, al-Fuli mosque is set apart from other buildings to display a neoclassical style suggesting vaguely Arab lines and curves. The complex covers an area some sixty meters long and perhaps thirty meters across at its widest point. Upon closer inspection one notes that there are actually three distinct parts to the building. At the north end stands a relatively compact, square structure, topped by a high dome. A second much greater rectangular portion occupies the center, which has a tall, elegant minaret reaching up at one side. Then a somewhat lower section extends beyond this large middle part to form what appears to be a separate room. The entire building is constructed of the same limestone blocks in one uniform style with its various parts joined together by colonnades, wide porches, and spacious verandas, all of which leaves the pleasing effect of a unified design. There are four entrances, none of which open onto the side that faces the river which is the back of the building. The main entrance, which looks out onto the city, is at the very center. It is approached by a broad set of steps that leads through a set of heavy double doors into the mosque itself. On the north side, a small, steep staircase gives direct access to the cupola shrine, which is connected on its other side to an open-air passage leading over a raised inner court into the mosque. At the far opposite end of the building is a door to the adjoining library, which is rarely used. Finally a fourth entrance, also on the front side, but just out of the line of sight from the mosque's main doors, leads to the ample washroom where ablutions are performed before prayers.

The mosque itself is a simple, spacious hall, sparely appointed with traditional decor. It offers nothing original, yet it presents all the expected features of a prominent government mosque, a *jami'*, that seeks to convey a solid though streamlined traditional image. A thick green carpet covers the floor, for everyone leaves their shoes, if they have them, outside on shelves that look like worn bookcases. Above, in the center of the high ceiling around the circumference of a shallow dome, verses from the Qur'an are written, in gold lettering on a blue field in extravagant intertwined calligraphy. High in the four corners, again in conformity to the standard iconography of such a mosque, are the names of the first four caliphs. In the front, to the right side as one enters the mosque's main door and facing the southeast, are the usual ritual fixtures, a *minbar*, whose pulpit platform stands approximately eight feet off the ground, and a *mihrāb*, decorated with inlaid stone, indicating the direction of Mecca. Other furnishings include a low wooden stand about the size of a card table upon which the Qur'an chanter sits when he performs at the Friday Prayer.

In the smallest section, at the north end of the complex, furthermost away from the library and under the cupola is the shrine where the saint or *walī*, Shaykh Ahmad al-Fuli, is buried.[2] Inside, behind a high wooden latticework screen, or *mashrabīya*, lies the tomb, arrayed in a manner familiar to the cult of saints throughout Egypt.[3] One enters this inner chamber through a door in the latticework in order to touch the cubiform cenotaph or to circumambulate it in the manner that echoes the *tawāf*, the walking around the sacred *ka'ba* during the *hajj*. This enclosed area is scarcely four yards square and the tomb occupies about a third of that floor space, a fact which can lead to considerable crowding on Fridays or whenever some event or festival brings crowds of villagers to the mosque. The cenotaph itself is covered with several layers of cloth, the outermost being a bright green and embroidered with the name *al-shaykh Ahmad al-Fūlī* along with several pious phrases, notably the *takbīr* ("God is Great") and the *shahāda* ("I profess there is no god but God and Muhammad is the prophet of God"). At each of the four corners of the tomb there is mounted a characteristic brass fixture, roughly the shape of an onion dome atop the steeple of a Russian church, about six inches in diameter at its base, then tapering into a rounded point at the top. Pious visitors stroke these globes to gain *baraka,* or blessing, or they may tie ribbons to them signifying some vow or plea. The walls of this chapel are covered with cloth hangings, plaques, and paintings depicting the sacred shrines of Mecca and Madina or containing Qur'anic verses in artful lettering. These items, I was told, are gifts from devotees. Electric lights and lamps are also hung all about. There are also two large wooden chests on either side of the entrance where cash offerings may be deposited.

This mosque takes its name from the *walī* or saint Shaykh al-Fuli, who is recognized as its founder, although the present building is recent, dating only from the 1950s. Originally situated directly on the river's edge, the greatly enlarged mosque of today was built on a new site, some one hundred fifty yards inland away from the bank. Unusually high waters that caused serious flooding in the late 1940s, prior to the construction of the Aswan High Dam, probably contributed to this decision. Now with the seasonal fluctuations of the Nile kept under control, the area between the mosque and the river includes the handsome north-south boulevard adjoining a riverside park. The nucleus of the original building nearby is said to date from the seventeenth century. It began as a sufi lodge, or *zawīya,* presided over by the since legendary al-Fuli who was buried there when he died in 1068 A.H., i.e., A.D. 1658. Not much is known about the mosque's eponymous saint, although a plaque at the shrine, rather like an epitaph, offers a few bits of information. He was said to be the son of a great scholar and ascetic who taught at al-Azhar. For unknown reasons, he came to Minya where he settled, got married, and began to teach.[4] He was given the nickname al-Fuli (from *fūl,* meaning "beans," which then and now constitute a principal staple of the Upper Egyptian diet) for apparently he took up bean selling as his livelihood. When he died he was buried by his devotees, who continued transmitting his teachings; in time a cult grew up around his *zawīya.* Miracles (*karamāt*) were attributed to his intervention and his resting place began to draw pious visitors as a radiant center for *baraka.* Eventually local benefactors also emerged who donated property to form endowments of the sort known as *waqf* which were rented out allowing the proceeds to be used for the support of this pious establishment.[5] Over approximately the last two centuries, in various waves of reform beginning with the reign of Muhammad 'Ali (1805–1848) and ending under 'Abd al-Nasir (1956–1970), all such *waqf* properties have been taken over by the Egyptian state which in theory, at least, has also assumed the responsibility for the maintenance of the institutions these trusts were intended to support. It seems that the al-Fuli mosque saw its *waqf* properties appropriated in the midst of this process, under the Khedive Ismail Pasha (1863–1879), whose lavish spending nearly bankrupted the government and led to the British intervention that followed a few years after he was abruptly deposed. This timing suggests that the original facility fell into neglect over the ensuing decades, adding a further factor in the story of its relocation and considerable expansion.

In Egypt as elsewhere in the Muslim world, prior to the modern era and continuing through tides of change well into the present in some areas, religious practice at the popular level revolved largely around the cult of saints and related elements of the sufi tradition. So widespread was this involvement with what has been called "maraboutism," a term favored in some other parts of North Africa, derived from the Arabic term *marābit* and the rough equivalent of the *walī* in Egypt, that even the Azhar itself reflected its impact. In fact, one of Algeria's greatest modern reformers, 'Abd al-Hamid Ben Badis (1890–1940), asserted that no one in his native land thought Islam to be anything but this system which Clifford Geertz has described as the "*sayyid* complex."[6] This widespread veneration of saints, which entails some practices reputed to be nonorthodox and based on magical or superstitious elements of folk religion, has been receding for several generations under constant attacks by modernists and reformers of all sorts.

Already at the end of the nineteenth century, the *salafīya* movement (loosely, "return to the ways of the ancestors") had been campaigning vigorously and with growing official support to eradicate these unapproved devotional strains and replace them with an Islam more in conformity with this elite's stricter interpretation. State authorities, both from the indigenous and the colonial administration, likewise applied pressure with increasing success aimed at undermining the substantial prestige of the leading sufi *shaykhs* whose informal power survived as a major factor in the street politics of the nation up until the end of the nineteenth century.[7] Not only did these reformers combat what they perceived as the undesirable social effects of the *walī* but many also went further, attempting to suppress even the ritual vestiges of this piety, claiming, for instance, that the Prophet had expressly forbidden Muslims to pray near a tomb.[8] The Wahhabis at the beginning of the century had carried this enthusiasm to its extreme, going so far as to smash the tomb of the Prophet himself in Medina and to turn away Egyptian pilgrims as idolaters.

Although shunning these excessive views, the influence of contemporary reform-minded Muslims can be seen in the architectural partition that separates the mosque proper from the cupola shrine by an appreciable distance. The compromise struck between doctrine and devotion, between scripturalism and personalism, took shape in stone in the form of this composite. The resulting double functions are conjoined but only partially integrated. Nor is it clear whether reverence for the *walī* was slighted by this fusion or the status of the present grand mosque has been elevated by its proximity to the shrine. This question, which touches directly on the question of the preacher's role, might be pursued further by contrasting the conditions here with those of other local saints' cults.

Discerning Saintliness

The sixteen mosques in the old quarter of Minya all predate the reconstruction of the new al-Fuli, and some are older than its first founding three centuries before. There is or was a tomb included somewhere on the premises in virtually all of these, although today the vitality of the cult found there is negligible. One observes that those who enter these mosques generally tend to ignore the shrine except for the occasional women dressed in the traditional black, or perhaps some old men who may approach the tomb, stroke it gently, and then distribute the *baraka* with an open palm to face and shoulders. Periodically, some who come to pray pause in passing before the tomb, and spread their hands in the customary gesture of supplication to recite the *fātiḥa*, the opening verses of the Qur'an. But such activity is infrequent and usually, in the city, has the appearance of a private solitary devotion. Except for al-Fuli, none of these local *walī*s is currently honored by an annual festival, a *maulid*, where collective celebration is given full expression. Also, judging from the spatial layout, one suspects that in many cases the installation of a given saint's tomb occurred after the mosque was built. For the area set aside for the *walī*'s tomb, which is normally enclosed by a grill or screen, often seems consigned to a corner or is set like an afterthought in some open spot that happened to have the room for it. Only in a few instances is there a specially built structure clearly designed to serve as a shrine. Thus the impression lingers that the motives behind the cult of saints and the construction of mosques often diverge, deriving, apparently, from two different and unequal interest groups. It seems that the addition of a *walī*'s tomb to an existing mosque may suggest a concession to popular piety, while the expansion of a saint's cult into a regular mosque demonstrates a recognition that those with these spiritual gifts may also benefit more strictly observant worshippers.

Twelve mosques in this old quarter of Minya include the tomb of at least one *walī* located either within the mosque or in a separate shrine, usually domed, directly adjacent to it. The other four do not have this feature at this time, although three of them contain an interesting variation which will be discussed later when we turn our attention to a mosque called *al-Qushairī*. In these cases there is also a tomb present, but it contains the remains of the patron who endowed the mosque rather than a *walī*.

Leaving aside this variation of a founder's mausoleum, it is important to note that by its very presence a *walī*'s tomb conveys a symbolic statement regarding the overall authority expressed within a mosque. The great British historian D. S. Margoliouth pointed out this relationship at the beginning of this century in commenting on varieties of ritual specialists: "The preacher, then, in the sense of a religious and moral guide, is not the orator of the Friday service at the mosque, but the *Sufi* . . . [whose] function was not to preach (*khataba*) but . . . [whose] sanctity becomes an asset to the community; living or dead their presence is a protection to it; averting disaster; those whom they bless prosper, those whom they curse are doomed."[9] Likewise, Mark Twain, touring Rome in the 1860s, reached a similar conclusion while reflecting on the significance of the tomb of a medieval bishop. There, he noted, we still "receive an impressive sermon from lips that have been silent and hands that have been gestureless for three hundred years."[10] But even if the *walī* does possess the greatest share of what Pierre Bourdieu has called the "symbolic capital" and if, in addition, he tends to "monopolize symbolic production" under advantageous conditions, nevertheless the causes and consequences of this potency are not necessarily due to achievements celebrated in his actual biography.[11] Sainthood, it seems, is not simply, maybe not even primarily, a matter of the wonders accomplished by a holy person during a lifetime. Rather, as the case of al-Fuli suggests, the preeminence of the *shaykh* as a living symbol over the *shaykh* as a historical figure also demonstrates how a *walī*'s past obscurity can work, ironically, to his future advantage. In fact, the question of where a saint is buried or where his body is later moved may turn out to be no less critical in the fortunes of one's "symbolic capital" in the "religious market" than a score of witnesses to a thaumaturge's miraculous performances.[12]

In visits to various mosques in and around Minya I regularly inquired about the saints whose tombs were honored in many of these places of worship. Rarely, however, could I find out more than the name, some vague date, and perhaps a story or two that might link this local *walī* with some great figure of ancient or medieval Islam. If I persisted in my questions, my polite hosts often tried to accommodate my curiosity by offering a highly generalized catalogue of virtues or accomplishments, relating, for example, that the saint was close to God, generous, beloved, and compassionate. Frequently, any more definite trait or the person's origin would be an elaboration of the name itself. One mosque, for instance, honored the tomb of a sainted woman called *al-Sitt al-Namayla*, about whom the preacher at the mosque knew little except that she was said to be very tiny, like an ant (from *namla*, or "ant"). Another mosque is called *al-Maghribī* after the saint by that name whose tomb it contains. The one definite fact which those I asked here could say about him was that he came from Morocco (*al-Maghrib*). This same sort of limited information was given about the saint in another mosque called *Shaykh Muhammad al-Turkī*, namely, that he was originally from Turkey. The saint in still another mosque was said to be the brother of one of Egypt's most famous *walīs* whose mosque is the central *jamiʿ* in Alexandria, called Sidi Abbas. But when I asked how or when he came to Minya, the government *shaykh* with whom I was speaking simply shrugged his shoulders and moaned indifferently "*yaʿni bigūlū kidā*" ("anyhow, that's what people say").

If I were to address my questions to a devotee of a given saint, I would typically receive a much more enthused response, reaffirming the saint's powers, but seldom would it be accompanied by additional historical details. When there was little else to be told of a *walī*, however, a votary might at least quote the phrase from the Qurʾan which is often cited as the approbation, indeed the injunction to honor holy persons: "Verily, for God's friends (*awiliyā*, pl. of *walī*) no fear shall be upon them, nor shall they grieve" (10:62). In the case of some of these mosques, the preacher appointed by the Ministry of Religious Endowments may show an attitude which shows clear hostility to the cult of the local saint. In one instance, a young *imām* at a very old mosque actually shut off the room that contained the *walī*'s tomb, leaving it locked and unlit more or less permanently.

As noted earlier, the cult of saints has been declining steadily for over a century and a half throughout Egypt, due to multiple transformations that first affected the metropolis. As always, provincial Upper Egypt lagged well behind. However, by the time of World War I the fabled image of the "ignorance and inscrutability of the Egyptian peasant" had clearly begun to falter here too, as changing social structures brought about by cash cropping, land transfers, and massive commercial agriculture spurred explosive urbanization and stirred up mounting political unrest as well as cultural ferment.[13]

Social History and Saints' Cults

Between 1907 and 1927 the population of Egypt increased by roughly a fourth, from 11.1 million to 14.2 million. But at the same time the ratio of urban to rural residents soared, almost doubling from 14.3 percent to 26.8 percent. Thereafter the trend continued, but at an even more accelerated pace. By 1976, the nation's population was registered at 46.7 million, of which 43.9 percent lived in cities.[14] Generally, Upper Egypt's urbanization progressed at a far slower pace than the Delta. In fact, the statistical gap in 1976 showed a variance of three to one, with 75.8 percent in Lower Egypt living in cities as compared to merely 24.2 percent for the Sa'id. In its own growth rate, the city of Minya itself tends to mirror the national rather than the regional pattern. In thirty years, between 1907 and 1947, its population increased from 27,000 to 70,000. Then it doubled again over the next three decades to reach a total of 146,366 by the official census figures of 1976.[15] These have been times of periodic ferment for Egypt as the great waves of popular determination that erupted spontaneously in the 1919 Revolution seem to regain their momentum under the different banners of 'Abd al-Nasir's Arab socialism, Sadat's liberalist nationalism, and the current stirrings of an Islamist orientation.

Minya has moved steadily into the mainstream of the nation's history. In a modest way it participated in the uprising at the end of World War I. Its streets witnessed a series of demonstrations which led to a bloodless confrontation with the local British authorities who had several prominent citizens arrested, including two leading religious personalities.[16] But more important, for local pride, at least, Minya was also represented on the national level, since one of the members of the ad hoc delegation of three Egyptians that presented the demand for an end to the Protectorate to the British Agent and Consul-General, Sir Reginald Wingate, was originally from Minya, where he still had extensive land holdings. This was 'Ali Pasha Sha'arawi; and their famous meeting, which failed utterly in its objective, nevertheless evolved into the foundation of the Wafd Party. From the same family came the renowned Huda Hanum Sha'arawi, pioneer of Egypt's feminist movement, which had close ties to the liberal and nationalist Wafd. Today, interestingly, following the draconian land reforms and sequestrations of the 'Abd al-Nasir era, this once dominant family has all but disappeared from Minya, but a handsome mosque which they founded there at the turn of the century continues to bear their name.

Still another present-day echo from this era recalls an incident that occurred in March 1919 at Dier al-Mawas, a village on the main highway some fifty kilometers south of Minya. Here a group of excited peasants opened fire with their hunting rifles on a train carrying English troops who had been dispatched from Luxor to quell disturbances in other cities further north. This token assault led to quick reprisals from the occupying power and the affair has since passed unnoticed in the standard British histories. But today the date of this spontaneous outburst is celebrated annually as an official patriotic holiday honored throughout the Governorate of Minya.[17] In a sense, it seems the advancement of this sort of localized secular observance has sought to fill at least part of the vacuum left by the decline of the occasions for popular gatherings provided by saints' festivals. The historian Marshall Hodgson points to just such a conversion as the spread of a nationalist political consciousness in Egypt merged with an overlapping movement championing Islamic reform.

> As earlier in the cities so now even in the villages all the less
> strictly Shar'i side of village cultural life tended to be toned down,
> for instance extravagant mourning at funerals. In effect, this meant
> toning down all of the more emotional and much of the more col-
> lective side of religion; and as emotions were withdrawn from the
> cult, they were invested in politics.[18]

Given such tendencies, it might be thought that the official promotion of the cult of a local *walī* as evidenced by the new al-Fuli mosque represents something of an exception or an anachronism. Were there not other mosques in Minya where the *walī* might have been bypassed that could have been chosen for enlargement? Why didn't the Ministry of Religious Endowments strike out on new ground and build a mosque from scratch dedicated to a reformist theme such as the "oneness of God," *al-tawḥīd*? To explore these questions at the local level will hopefully serve to further illuminate the contours of institutionalized Islamic authority as a composite of malleable religious symbols and changing social dynamics.

The supposed appeal of the cult of al-Fuli is ordinarily assumed to be rooted historically in the city of Minya. But it takes only cursory observation to realize that while the cult today remains quite vigorous, the saint's devotees have apparently changed. They are principally *fellahin*, peasants visiting from the countryside, rather than actual urban residents. This suggests an interesting displacement recalling the climax of an engaging short story by the contemporary Egyptian writer Abdul Rahman Fahmy. It begins when the narrator encounters a pious indigent sufi of the old school who has taken up residence in a thoroughly dilapidated and abandoned shrine on the outskirts of town, dedicated to a certain Sidi Utaiti. The sufi places himself in the saint's service and he begins to bestow prayers and blessings upon the townspeople. This pious activity stirs up fervor and it is soon decided that a new shrine and a mosque should be built on the spot. The sufi likewise joins enthusiastically in the project. But no sooner has the construction been completed than the manager who has been brought in to oversee its operation catches sight of this shabby, unkept sufi and he instructs the doorman to bar the ragamuffin from entering it. "Get rid of him," he orders. "Tomorrow I'll go to Cairo and bring you another Sheikh who's a bit cleaner looking." Eventually resigning himself to his expulsion, the sufi departs, saying: "I'll go off and look around for a Sheikh of my own size, someone whose circumstances are as wretched as mine, seeing as how Sidi Utaiti has become too exalted for us."[19]

However, this matter of achieving a comfortable fit between religious expression and societal status is not just an issue for a sufi *shaykh*. It is also a key factor in the gathering and defining of any congregation. Thus, in order to understand better this transposition of a saint's appeal from its native town to the rural penumbra, it is helpful to review what little can be learned about the cult of al-Fuli from various clues scattered over the last century. For these shifts in the saint's following seem to dimly parallel an ambivalent drift affecting the overall direction of mosque authority as it frames the tensions between the familiar but constraining loyalties of the traditional community and the inviting but uncertain promises of a liberalized wider world.

While documentation on the development of the cult of al-Fuli, past or present, is scant, reviewing some of it in the light of other saints' cults in the vicinity is illuminating. Not surprisingly, perhaps, given what one historian of Egypt's religious elites has termed "the comparative state of institutional paucity so evident for Upper Egypt," Minya usually appears in pre-modern histories more as a geographical landmark than as a coherent community with its own identifiable features.[20] However, one pertinent source dating from the first half of this century is a well-researched study devoted exclusively to the sometimes fantastic popular festivals that marked the high point of a saint's cults, both Muslim and

Coptic. The author, John W. McPherson, a British colonial officer who arrived in 1901 and stayed there until his death in 1946, has lately himself been celebrated in a British Broadcasting Corporation series as "The Man Who Loved Egypt."[21] He worked in numerous posts in various Ministries, including a stint as head of Cairo's Secret Police. His one book, *The Moulids of Egypt: Egyptian Saints-Days*, is the product of extensive travel, observation, and inquiry clearly motivated by a personal fascination with these folkloric *fêtes votives* which the author realized were threatened by the changing times. Not only does he bemoan their demise, but he objects to the opposition against them coming from modernist, reformist, and most official circles. He argues instead that these seasonal religious fairs are harmless, charming, and socially beneficial gatherings that should be allowed to continue.

Furthermore, McPherson's book (which incidently contains a brief but glowing foreword by the young E. E. Evans-Pritchard, then teaching at Cairo University, later to reign at Oxford as the doyen of British structural-functionalism) provides more than the descriptions of dozens of specific *moulids* and a vindication of their social value. It also includes an extensive catalogue listing hundreds of saints and their shrines together with notes on the character of their cults throughout the country. In this sweep, he also includes, however briefly, the patron of Minya whom he calls Sidi Fuli, about whom he has only this to say:

> I have no information about this moulid except that it is of local importance in the Minia district of Upper Egypt.
>
> Sheikh Fuli is generally credited with being the Wali who protects us from crocodiles, by preventing their passing north of Minia: but this is contested by the votaries of certain other Walis by the side of the Nile further South.[22]

Aside from this expert observer's lack of details, which itself serves as a commentary on the marginality of Minya as well the obscurity of its major saint, it cannot be overlooked that this single credit, relating to crocodiles, was a highly generalized attribute assigned at the time to any number of *walis*. Also, unlike many great saints whose cults have spread due to miraculous appearances or the translation of relics, al-Fuli's *baraka* has remained localized.[23]

A second, quite different view is given in the standard reference for practically every kind of detail on history, geography, economics, biography, and administration in nineteenth-century Egypt, the twenty-volume encyclopedic compilation known as *Al-Khiṭāṭ al-Tawfīqīya al-Jidīda* by 'Ali Pasha Mubarak.[24] In it, the entry for Minya gives various kinds of information, mostly dealing with past military events that happened nearby and hardly involving the native population, but al-Fuli is also mentioned: "In [Minya] there are also many tombs set under cupolas (*adraḥa kathīra dakhil qabāb*) and among the most famous of those buried here from among the righteous (*min al-salihin*) is Shaykh al-Fuli whose resting place lies by the well-known river [the Nile] where groups of people visit it along the shore."[25]

Note from the Arabic text that 'Ali Mubarak does not refer to this as a mosque (*masjid*) but as a tomb (*ḍarīḥ*) inside a cupola chapel (*qubba*). Later, however, he also describes the two largest mosques in the city. One may conclude that at the time of this survey (published in 1886–1889) no mosque proper existed on the site of al-Fuli's cult, but merely a domed shrine adjoined probably to an unmentioned sufi meeting place.

Another intriguing issue touching indirectly on the saint's status which appears in *Al-Khitāt* is the name of the city of Minya itself. Not only does 'Ali Mubarak spell it with a final *hā* instead of the final *yā* as it is always done today, but he refers to it by its classical epithet as *Minyat ibn Khasīb*, named after a legendary ruler who was appointed governor of the region during the time of the Abbasid Caliphs. Today, for virtually all Egyptians and in any official document, the mention of the name *al-Minya* without further modifiers is understood to refer to the city along with the governorate here under discussion. However, sometimes in popular usage and occasionally in formal settings to avoid ambiguity it may also be called by the fuller name of *al-Minya al-Fuli*. The reason for appending this marker, as everyone says, is to distinguish this Minya in Upper Egypt from another much smaller identically named Minya which is located near the Suez Canal, which is customarily called *Minya al-Qamḥ* when it is necessary to avoid confusion.[26]

The addition of a supplementary term in order to distinguish one place from another is perfectly understandable. But curiously enough, it is not just that there are two *Minya*s that could be mistaken. Rather, a consultation of 'Ali Mubarak's index reveals that it is a very common place name. There are no fewer than 156 different village sites in Egypt that begin with the word *Minya* (apparently related to the Arabic *minā'*, meaning port or harbor). The interesting point here is that in the case of the largest Minya the sobriquet added to the generic name has undergone a change. Apparently, sometime over the last century, *Minyat ibn Khasīb* has become *Minyā al-Fūlī*. In other words, in the relatively recent past al-Fuli has advanced to become literally the "named" patron of the city. Exactly when this practice began remains unclear; the common assumption among ordinary residents seems to be that their city has been Minya al-Fuli as far back as memory can reach.[27]

Adding to this impression, in April 1979 there appeared an exceptionally forthright indication of the present stature of al-Fuli as a symbol of the city and the governorate. At that time, one of Egypt's mass-circulation illustrated weeklies issued a special sixteen-page color magazine featuring Minya. On its cover, occupying almost three-quarters of the page, was a panorama photo of al-Fuli mosque, over which was written "Minya: Jewel of the Sa'id." Two much smaller photos completed the collage. One depicted a polychrome bust of the fabled Pharaonic beauty, Queen Nefertiti, wife of Akhenaten, whose capital was at Amarna, just south of modern Minya. The other featured the pillared late Victorian facade of the governorate's stately administration building.[28]

Saints and Urban Development

Still another clue to the historical background of al-Fuli's cult are divulged by the help of a map. The only detailed city plan of Minya I was able to find was made by the British and based on the Survey of 1931. On it, all local mosques as well as many other public institutions are indicated and shown in scale. (See map.) It shows that there are two great mosques in the old quarter of Minya, both of which happen to have been established in the middle ages and are still functioning today, that are close to triple the size of the old al-Fuli. Besides these two, there are several others that either equal it or surpass it merely in terms of floor space. But clearly size alone does not suffice to establish pre-eminence. At least two other factors, namely, access to water and the criteria favored by urban planners also seem to have notable influence.

First, the setting of a mosque directly aside a continuous water source conforms to a familiar pattern throughout the Islamic world. Such a juxtaposition has the obvious practical advantage of supplying water for the ablutions, as well as for the carrying off of routine sewage, since the sanitary facilities of a mosque may also function freely as a public washroom.[29] In traveling along the main road or by train on the parallel railway line that connects the length of Egypt, one frequently sees mosques of various sizes and shapes constructed beside the large canals such as the Ibrihimiya and the Ismailiya which the highways and railroad tracks often follow. Much less common, however, and surely in large part due to the hazards of flooding, are mosques situated directly on the river bank. In Minya, therefore, the location of the old al-Fuli was unusual and the original shrine may have emerged and stayed unchallenged on this spot to

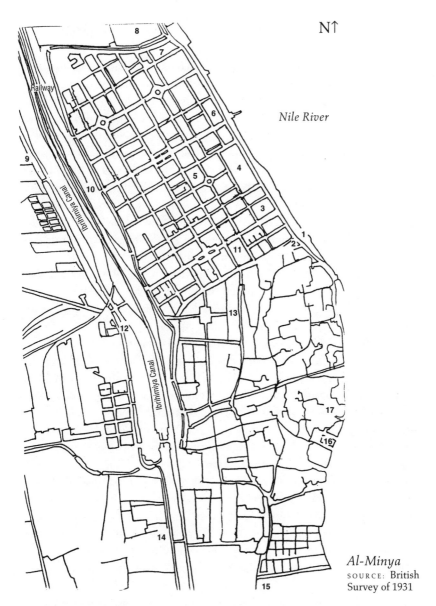

N↑

Nile River

Al-Minya
SOURCE: British
Survey of 1931

1. *Al-Fuli Mosque (original site)*
2. *Al-Fuli Mosque (present site)*
3. *Girls School*
4. *Mudariya*
5. *Coptic School*
6. *National Bank of Egypt*
7. *British Consulate*
8. *Minya University*
9. *Sha'arawi Mosque*
10. *Railway Station*
11. *Provincial Council*
12. *Al-ʿIlm wa-l-Iman Mosque*
13. *Al-Qushairi Mosque*
14. *Al-Qurtubi Mosque*
15. *Sunniya Mosque*
16. *Police Headquarters and Prison*
17. *Al-Wadaʿ Mosque*

some degree because this space was not otherwise useful and thus did not attract the interest of ordinary builders.

But the reasons behind al-Fuli's special favor as affirmed architecturally by the Ministry of Religious Endowments may also owe something to a governmental policy that treats Islam as a dimension of its centralization of authority. The building of the great mosque in Aswan, *jāmiʿ al-ṭabāʿa*, a decade and a half after al-Fuli illustrates how this logic of official sanctity works. Until it became the site of various modern hydraulic projects, Aswan, now a city of almost exactly the same size as Minya, was a modest border outpost, near the first cataract, where the Nile's easy navigability ends. Its population was largely Nubian, an ethnolinguistically distinct people who extend further upstream into what is today the northern Sudan. During the colonial era, Aswan's rich archaeological remains drew a regular stream of foreign visitors and its moderate climate in winter months had also made it a favorite seasonal resort. But the real boom came in the 1950s with the commencement of the High Dam, an expensive, ambitious project that preoccupied the energies and resources of ʿAbd al-Nasir's Egypt for years.

It was just at this time of rapid change and growth brought on by the dam project that a new mosque was built by the Ministry of Religious Endowments right at the center of what was becoming the new expanded Aswan. It is a monumental building set majestically with a high dome and a tall minaret, built upon a raised mound surrounded by sloping lawns. Its general design, in fact, looks fairly similar to that of al-Fuli. Looking down from the top of one of Aswan's high-rise tourist hotels, an observer might easily conclude that this imposing cathedral mosque simply by virtue of its centrality and size must qualify as the great and enduring cult center for the entire region. However, visiting the mosque itself fails to confirm this initial impression. Also upon inquiry, one learns that this mosque is altogether new and that the residents of Aswan generally have no interest in it commensurate with its dominating location and scale. It is also pointed out that in order to build it, the government had to appropriate a densely populated lower-class neighborhood and send its occupants to featureless concrete housing blocks far on the distant outskirts of the city. Prior to this massive project of religiopolitical urban renewal, there had been a small mosque which included the tomb of a *walī* in the vicinity, but apparently its cult was quite limited.

By contrast, a cemetery exists just outside of Aswan, dotted with cupola shrines, some of which enjoy considerable regional or even wider acclaim. Most renowned among them is a large ancient site whose tomb chapel honors the "seventy-seven saints" (*sabʿa wa sabʿīn awliyāʾ*), a succession of holy men stretching from Noah to ʿAli. This latter monument apparently dates from the early Fatimid era (tenth century) and despite its great distance from the capital, Cairo, it is regularly singled out for discussion as one of the great saints' shrines of Egypt.[30] Nothing in the entire region of Minya evenly faintly compares to it.

But this great shrine, regardless of its historical claims, was not the choice of city planners who apparently considered location above popularity and authenticity in choosing their site. Here, religious claims seemed to weigh little as a criterion for the investment by the Ministry of Religious Endowments in the construction of such a mosque. Yet this new, disruptive, centrally situated, ostentatious mosque was built at exactly that time when a substantial Russian engineering corps was residing in Aswan to oversee the construction of the High Dam and its electric generation plant. But with the presence of so many "communist" military and technical personnel, most visibly in Aswan, provoking discomforting questions about Egypt's moral orientation, it is easy to understand that the regime would reply to suspicions of contagion by such "atheists" with a vivid, if hollow, architectural assertion of the nation's Islamic identity.

Admittedly this comparison between Minya and Aswan is somewhat loose, but on the question of the official motives for "creating" a central mosque there is a close similarity. A study of the statistical profile of spending on mosque construction by the Ministry of Religious Endowments from 1942 to 1964 clearly demonstrates a tendency to invest great sums in very few grandiose mosques rather than to distribute smaller allotments more widely.[31]

But these priorities regarding mosque construction at the highest reaches of the national bureaucracy are not to be mistaken for the patterns that prevail locally. As the above examples illustrate, a political will and economic resources exterior to the community were largely responsible for these decisions. It follows, not surprisingly, that the character of the construction also derives from the outside. Some further points of interest are shed on the trend in an article written by the Director General of the Engineering Department of the Ministry of Religious Endowments in Egypt. There he confirms that the uniform religious architecture observed in Minya, Aswan, and elsewhere is a matter of central planning:

> As for the establishment of large principal mosques (*masājid
> raʾīsīya kabīra*) in the capital cities a suitable design should be chosen with an appropriate exterior and a comprehensive, beautiful

decor, while maintaining a traditional Islamic style [suited to] the modern age. Thus, [we] return to the idea that assumes one site [as the point] where guidance is concentrated and from which [the city's] political and religious activities emanate.[32]

Several times in the course of the article, the author repeats this theme of building mosques in an "Arab classical style" (*al-tarāz al-ʿarabī al-klasīkī*). He is articulating a concern that is quite evident in the consistent design and the replication of stylistic features that has become the trademark, as it were, of mosques built all over Egypt by Ministry of Religious Endowments in recent decades.

Beyond this architectural assertiveness, the motives of a centralizing authority in the rise of al-Fuli to such prominence are discernible from yet another spatial perspective. Returning to the map, it can be seen that this mosque is situated right at the juncture where the old "traditional" quarter of Minya, characterized by irregular dense construction, winding streets and cul-de-sacs meets the "modern" new quarter laid out in straight measured blocks, with central squares and broad streets intersecting at right angles. Looking from the vantage of the modern city, al-Fuli lies just beyond the southeast leg of a large triangle formed by the railroad station, the British Consulate, and the Minya Provincial Council Building. Looking from the direction of Cairo it stands last in a line of adjacent buildings on the corniche including the National Bank of Egypt, the *Mudarīya*, or municipal government center, and the city's major school for girls. Looking from al-Fuli southward, it is the first in a more angular set of mosques and villas that is bounded at its far end by the police headquarters and the prison. In sum, the re-making of al-Fuli as the city's principal mosque suggests that it was to serve as a sort of socioreligious hinge fusing two communities by identifying with variant expressions of Islam.

The Saint on the Border

This conjuncture of the modern and the traditional in the combined shrine and the mosque of al-Fuli illustrates what Victor Turner has described as the extraordinary force that often concentrates at points of transition or liminality. Here again, it is not the definiteness of al-Fuli's past but its malleable obscurity that generates his *baraka*. Those who visit his tomb and reverence him do not recall historical achievements. They acknowledge, rather, a figure who must be holy because he has successfully bridged the gap between two separate but adjacent societies and so has proven his capacity as a mediator. By occupying a position of such prestige in both and in neither realm simultaneously, he embodies the paradox of *communitas* where one meets "the structurally inferior as the morally and ritually superior, and secular weakness as sacred power."[33] His status as a *walī* is inseparable from the incongruity of his surroundings.

The deeds al-Fuli accomplished long ago in his lifetime matter little because by the self-evident importance of this monument he displays such "anti-structural" potency in the present. Having once been transformed from a mortal into a *walī* he has since undergone a second remarkable metamorphosis. At one time he was identified as a symbol of the strongly personalistic, affective, ritually profuse piety of closed, introspective village life. As a local patron saint and therefore the emblem of the group's solidarity, his shrine was typically "more popular than the mosque because [here] there are no distinctions as to age or sex."[34] In addition, those most commonly frequenting the shrine shared a place at the bottom of a locally defined world order whose great ones spared little care for their needs and aspirations. But now, relocated to the center of the capital city, this saint has acquired another persona. He has come to represent the pinnacle of moral authority as it is ratified by the state and tended by the *'ulamā'* in this lavish and well-subsidized house of prayer. From here he invites his humble devotees to join together with the rest of the *umma*, the universal community of all Muslims, sharing equal rights and obligations before God and his holy law. Here too, with his support, the distinction between peasants and pashas, at least within the ritual process, loses its foundation, for the last and greatest gift of the patron is to deliver his faithful into that blessed condition where there is no longer a need for mediators and no cause to fear the scourges of poverty or injustice.

Appeal to the intercession of a saint implies, of course, an underlying system of pronounced status differences. The resort to this intermediary is based, first of all, on the assumption that the *walī* occupies a higher rank on the mystic scale than does the petitioner and that this elevated station translates as privileged access to divine favor. But secondly, it presupposes a special relationship, some firm bond of loyalty or mutual interest between the mediator and the petitioner who seeks his or less commonly her intercessory services. Given the logic of such a system, it is desirable, naturally, to enlist the most powerful intercessor available. But to obtain a hearing from the saint requires that some symbolic link be forged that establishes a claim upon these mystic services. Hence the vows, the visits, the votive offerings, fasts, sacrifices, and prayers of entreaty are like investments in an advocate.

Needless to say, a pious petition may always be addressed directly to God. But since the unmeasurable distance between the creator and his creatures has been bridged by countless holy men and women, especially the Prophet and his family, it seems to follow that resort to their aid will charge a prayer with special urgency and efficacy. Hence the power associated with relics and sacred places. If one venerates a lock of the Prophet's hair or a thread from the cloak of one of his Companions, or if one makes a pilgrimage to a site favored by a *wali* who may have appeared there or instructed a disciple to build a shrine on the spot in his memory, one's prayers are almost certainly heard with greater attentiveness. Thus, the greatest shrines of Egypt, in Cairo, house the relics of such lofty saints as Hussein, the Prophet's grandson, or Sayda Zaynib, one of the Prophet's daughters; at the heart of the Delta, in Tanta, lie the remains of Shaykh Ahmad al-Badawi. Meanwhile at countless intermediate levels further up the river and further down the elaborate sufi hierarchy of spiritual patron-client exchanges, other *walis* oversee the "operations of grace" and "guard the gates of blessing" for the purpose of guiding, protecting, and even empowering those believers who trust in God and recognize His "hidden" friends.[35]

After recognizing this social parallel to popular religious conviction, it is hardly surprising to observe that the cult of a given *wali* waxes and wanes with shifts of political and economic domination. There can be no doubt, moreover, that for the vast majority in rural Upper Egypt, family and village loyalty still constitute the core of their social identity. Furthermore, it might be noted that the rural to urban ratio in the governorate of Minya stands just over four to one, which is one of the lowest urbanization figures in the whole country.[36] Likewise the overall economic state and the living conditions of central Egypt reflect this same pattern of comparative underdevelopment. Infant mortality rates, for instance, often seen as a general indicator of social welfare, are the nation's highest in Minya and its neighboring governorates, well over three times greater than the rates for Cairo despite its overcrowding and slums.[37]

The penetration of state agencies and the informal pressures of modernity affecting virtually all areas of life including agriculture, industry, commerce, education, health, housing, utilities, communication, dress, entertainment, politics and religion continue, albeit most unevenly, to impinge upon this primordial sense of collective self-sufficiency. A new realization of national and international interdependency is steadily coloring attitudes and behaviors. But official perspectives on these changing realities, which freely reduce their complexity to bureaucratic categories emphasizing "progress," are notoriously blind to the traditional mechanisms that frame the actual social fabric and material circumstances, especially among the poorest.

In the governorate of Minya, where it is estimated that nearly two-thirds of the male agricultural work force is landless or near-landless, the solidarity of the family and the persistence of patron-client relationships largely define the moral universe. The pace of Egypt's economic development in this century, largely offset by demographic strains, has not been matched by corresponding qualitative changes in social and cultural structures. As a result, the vast network of monopolistic state agricultural cooperatives, begun in the late 1950s to fill the vacuum left by the revolutionary regime's eradication of the great landlords, have largely been judged a failure. As a recent study of local politics in village Egypt notes, this lag in integration has in effect left the "wealthy peasants [to] act as rural gatekeepers, restricting or inhibiting state efforts to develop the countryside."[38] Thus, for many, the role assigned to any saint echoes a wholly familiar pattern in the conduct of their practical affairs. But the next step, the selecting of which particular *wali* offers the best hopes of gaining divine assistance is, as the following incident suggests, sometimes no less a matter of availability as it is of proven *baraka*.

Choosing a Patron Saint

Given what has been recounted, it might still be argued that Shaykh al-Fuli, though obscure in origin and only fairly recently accorded the apotheosis of his shrine overshadowing the city's central mosque, was nonetheless chosen for this dignity because all other *walis* in the area were, one might say, even less qualified. But interestingly this speculation has in the case of Minya a circuitous refutation. It so happens that unlike most Upper Egyptian settlements that bury their dead in the desert (that is, in the red earth at the edge of the black earth, which is the Nile Valley's cultivated land), Minya follows a custom reminiscent of Pharaonic Thebes. For this city sends its dead by boat across the river to a vast ancient cemetery on the other side. In this sprawling ageless "city of the dead" there lies the tomb of one of the most famous of all medieval Qur'an commentators and litterateurs, namely Muhammad ibn Ahmad al-Qurtubi.[39] Originally from Spain, he traveled widely, and toward the end of his productive life he settled in Minya (that is, *Minyat ibn Khasib*, according to the chronicles). He apparently lived there for some time and he also died there in A.D. 1272. Author of numerous works, he is perhaps best known for his monumental Qur'an commentary in twenty volumes, still considered by specialists to be a work "of great richness and utility," entitled *Summary of the Perfection of the Qur'an and the Exposition of What It Contains from the Sunna and Other Evidence.* Furthermore, his biographers point out that "in addition to being a conscientious scholar, he was remembered as a pious man, inclined toward asceticism and towards meditation on the life after death."[40] Given these stellar credentials as both a scholar and a sufi plus the fact that he had lived, died, and was buried at Minya it is hard to imagine a more suitable candidate for a local *wali* than this heavenly windfall of an adopted native son.

Accordingly, sometime in the 1960s an official effort was mounted to build a mosque that would appropriately honor this "local" great scholar. Construction was completed in the mid-1970s consisting of a mosque and shrine similar to the complex of al-Fuli but on a considerably more modest scale. It is located in a recently developed area south of the city and west of the canal. Physically separated from the mosque proper, but linked by a paved courtyard, stands the cupola shrine built to enclose the tomb of al-Qurtubi, for his remains were to be moved from their original resting place across the river. This planned installation of al-Qurtubi as a *wali* was, however, never brought to completion. The mosque itself was brought into regular use, under the government's auspices, but the body of the *wali* was never moved, nor has any other saint taken his place as the patron of this mosque.

I asked repeatedly about this most curious suspension of grace but I could never get an answer until I put the question to an Azhari *shaykh* who had grown up in a village near Minya and who now occupies the second highest post in the governorate's Directorate of the Ministry of Religious Endowments. He told me that the tomb of al-Qurtubi had not been moved because the members of that small community that lived beside the cemetery and served as its guardians would not cooperate. He said they had hidden the body to keep Ministry officials from taking it by force.[41] Furthermore, the *shaykh* noted, the body was miraculously whole and uncorrupted, further attesting to the saint's divine favor. Finally, he assured me that the matter was by no means closed. Thus, though several years had passed since the *masjid al-Qurṭubī* was built, staffed, and fully in service, the adjoining cupola dome was said to be only "temporarily" empty. Meanwhile, as I learned by glancing inside, the mosque's custodian had already appropriated the space intended to house the tomb and accommodate devotees as a storage area and turned it into a sort of garden shed.

This capsule summary of how al-Qurtubi was at once honored and manipulated presents a quaint variation on the same triangular dynamics involving religious officials, a *walī*, and a local Muslim community which were played out over a longer period and with a higher profile in the case of al-Fuli. Clearly, the inspiration for al-Qurtubi's new mosque-shrine grew out of a convergence of general ideals which in reality contained numerous contradictions. The site itself was very well considered. It lies at the corner near what was rapidly becoming a major crossroads where the highway connecting Cairo to Aswan intersected with a road leading to a bridge over the canal entering into the city proper. One could easily imagine that unless construction proceeded with some dispatch this prime real estate would surely attract the interest of a competing government agency or an enterprising developer who would know which palms to grease to obtain the plot. The residents themselves, having only recently moved into the quarter, were undoubtedly divided on the question. Those of a pious conservative temper might have been pleased that their neighborhood would acquire such a stately moral anchor, notably at no expense to themselves. Yet others, for example, secularists, Christians, or even Islamists would almost certainly have preferred different uses for this opportune space. Also, the local Islamic bureaucracy's initial proposal for the funds needed from the Ministry's limited budget had argued their case in the name of al-Qurtubi's memory, a factor that definitely assisted in winning the approval for this costly endeavor. But just how determined were these religious functionaries to realize their nobly stated intentions remains an open question. Hearing the various accounts of the supposed arrangements made and the promises broken in the course of negotiating what was nominally the key element in the entire project, that is, the transferring of the saint's body, plainly suggests that quite different and ultimately incompatible interests were at stake from the outset.

In brief, the complete realization of this lofty al-Qurtubi mosque-shrine raised dilemmas that were apparently best resolved by this strategic and purportedly provisional non-conclusion. In this way, all parties to the scheme could in some way boast of their sincerity and their efforts while none lost face. The resulting compromise seems to venerate an absent *walī* while it also satisfies the modern reformists' disapproval of saints' cults. It has also produced a new government mosque in a growing neighborhood in compliance with national priorities on the support and management of religion. Precisely by its incompleteness this mosque-shrine has found a format suited to this particular social setting. But to admit this hardly qualifies as a commendation for any of the parties involved, since it has become a rather bland institution offering little more than perfunctory spiritual services.

The mosque of al-Fuli, on the other hand, is a singularly successful merger of genuinely popular and thoroughly official Islam. Every Friday morning, well before the time of the noon prayer, the open areas around the mosque and shrine start filling up with great crowds of spirited and raucous peasants who often spill over into nearby streets. They turn the entire space into a sort of impromptu carnival grounds. Fortune-tellers, folk-preachers, vendors of sweets and fantasies as well as peddlers of practical items, musicians, dancers, and young men duelling with staves all converge on the spot as old and young, men, women, and children, all clearly country folk, create a sort of truncated version of a *maulid* celebration. Many from this throng press into the shrine to reverence the tomb of al-Fuli, often mobbing the steps and jamming the doorway, prompting the guardians to shout for order and slap their cane rods menacingly in a fashion that only adds to the festive cacophony.

But as the hour for the noon prayer approaches, eventually signaled by the first calls of the muezzin, the peak of the crowd's excitement declines rapidly. At the same time, an altogether different clientele begins arriving, not to visit the shrine, but to mount the main steps to enter the mosque. The tone for these worshippers seems to be set by the many stout middle-aged male burghers among them, wearing their starched Sunday best, as it were. When the muezzin's call sounds again to indicate the imminent start of the formal prayer ceremony, the preacher, dressed in the traditional garb of the ʿālim, as though in a vestment, emerges from a preparation room at the side of the pulpit and a great calm settles upon those gathered both inside and outside the mosque. The men within are all seated on the floor, having arranged themselves in rows that include some of those who have just passed an exuberant hour or more honoring the saint. But most of this recollected multitude who are about to hear the sermon have only just arrived, having come from their homes around the center of the city in order to partake in this prescribed weekly ritual.

The performance of the Friday prayer in this setting is accompanied by more ceremonious elaboration than anywhere else in Minya. It incorporates several stylistic adornments that are identified with the great mosques of Cairo, as seen, for instance, on television broadcasts. The sermon here too conforms closely to the high linguistic and rhetorical standards that are the mark of an urbane classical pulpit. Thus the contrast between the stateliness of the assembly presided over by the professional *imām* and the merriment evoked by the spirit of the *walī* could hardly be more striking. Yet the broad umbrella of local Islamic practice embraces both modes and it manages to blend them with a modicum of functional coherence. The dichotomy comes rather in the puritanical tenets of Islamism which refute the charms of the saint as magic and the learning of the scholar as complacent blind imitation. The character of this countercultural movement, to which we now turn our attention, likewise bears its share of internal incongruities that in their own way strain the social fabric up to the breaking point and even beyond it.

4   Islamization
The Tarboosh and the Beard

Ever since the arrival of Napoleon at Alexandria in 1798, the event that marked the beginning of the modern era in Middle Eastern history, Egypt has been depicted as a land in search of its place in today's world. At first Egypt's new rulers sought to establish an independent province, indeed to create an empire, under token Ottoman suzerainty. Failing that, the Khedive Isma'il by the end of the nineteenth century was fond of declaring that his country was part of Europe. Later, reactions against colonial rule gave rise to opposition that fused under the banner of nationalism. Then, in the middle of this century 'Abd al-Nasir emphasized Egypt's role in the leadership of transnational communities, notably the Arabs, Africa, the third world, and the non-aligned movement. Sadat, in turn, liberalized the policies of his predecessor, calling this redirection of policy toward the West *thawra al-taṣḥīḥ*, the "corrective revolution." Meanwhile, alongside these secular currents a variety of religiously motivated claims upon the character of the nation have also arisen that cross a wide spectrum from reactionary to progressive.[1] During the 1970s, Egypt, like other countries in the region, felt the impact of a dramatic wave of Islamic activism that spread quickly, very soon becoming what many regard as the central factor in its political stability.

Prior to the climactic assassination of Sadat and the brief insurrection in Asyut that accompanied it, the most significant episode in the mounting conflict between the regime and its Islamist opponents occurred in the summer of 1977. On July 3, a few months before I arrived in Egypt to begin my research, the members of an obscure, clandestine cell committed an act of violence that instantly vaulted them into the nation's headlines.

This organization, which became known as *Jamāʿat al-Takfīr wa al-Hijra* (Society of Repudiation and Holy Flight) was a relatively small extremist group that carried out one of the most daring assaults perpetrated in the name of religion since the Muslim Brothers' attempt on ʿAbd al-Nasir's life in 1954.

The youthful members of this secret society who called themselves *Jamāʿat al-Muslimīn* (Society of Muslims) kidnapped and subsequently killed Dr. Hussain al-Dhahabi after the government refused to yield to their demand that some of their number who had recently been arrested be released from custody. Their victim was a distinguished public figure and a leading member of the *ʿulamāʾ*. Among other prominent posts, he had served as head of the Institute of Islamic Research, which is closely affiliated with the Azhar, and as Minister of Religious Endowments in Sadat's cabinet. This crime was treated in the media and official pronouncements as an outrage, touching on sacrilege as well as treason. Immediately police responded with a nation-wide dragnet that prompted several shootouts and resulted in scores of dead and wounded.[2] Within a few days after the discovery of the body of the murdered *shaykh*, approximately 135 alleged members of the group had been arrested. This was followed by further roundups until in the end a total of some 600 persons were detained. A special military tribunal was convoked of the sort that presides over matters of highest state security. Then a public trial was held, lasting from late August through the end of November, which was covered extensively in the press.

During the course of the prosecution and again even more vigorously in the defense, the radical ideology of the group was thoroughly aired. The defendants insisted on justifying their act in the name of Islam, claiming its legitimacy on the basis of tenets expounded in the later writings of Sayyid Qutb, the Muslim Brothers' ideologue, whom ʿAbd al-Nasir had executed for conspiracy in 1965.[3] Their efforts to refute the moral integrity and the doctrinal soundness of their accusers brought about a most unusual spectacle. Eventually leading scholars from among the *ʿulamāʾ* and professors from the Azhar were called in to offer expert testimony. The courtroom at times took on the appearance of an inquisition chamber as juridical form gave way to heated and not infrequently obscure theological debates. In the end, five leaders of the group were condemned to death and executed in March 1978. Of the 204 others who stood trial with them, only 36 were found guilty and given various terms of imprisonment.

The importance of these unanticipated events for the project I was about to begin concerns first of all the wide public exposure they afforded to these Islamists' convictions. Likewise the attempts to refute them by the official representatives of Islam had also been heard. Second, it demonstrated the intensity of their indictment against both the religious establishment and state authority. The frustrations and disappointments popularly associated with what was trumpeted as the nation's failures due largely to reliance on borrowed ideologies, such as nationalism, Arabism, liberalism, socialism, and finally Sadat's new capitalism, received an interested hearing among many younger Muslims with some higher education. Though perhaps disapproving of the extremism that had led to such violence, many felt inclined nonetheless to sympathize with the arguments of the militants. In short, their case against the privileged, corrupt, and complacent elite had by no means been defeated by the *shaykhs* serving as apologists for the government. To some, therefore, the righteous warriors of *Jamāʿat al-Muslimīn* took on an aura of martyrs.

Third, there is a geographic factor. Unlike the Muslim Brothers of their fathers' and grandfathers' generation and unlike most other militant groups of the time such as *al-Jihād* centered in Alexandria and *Jund Allah* based in Cairo, the so-called *Jamāʿat al-Takfīr wa al-Hijra* drew its membership almost entirely from Upper Egypt. Its autocratic and charismatic leader, Shukri Mustafa, was from near Asyut, the next large city south of Minya. Moreover, one important feature of this radical group was a scheme to break thoroughly from the present-day sinful society in order to establish a new *umma* at the edge of the desert. And one of the sites which was already being occupied for this purpose was in Minya Governorate.[4] Patterns of recruitment in this cultlike group relied heavily on kinship, friendship, and village ties, while its authoritarian leadership and rigid discipline also figure as recognized characteristics of the general Upper Egyptian ethos. Thus while I have no definite proof of the influence of this shadowy group upon the largely student membership in *al-Jamāʿa al-Islāmīya* (that is, the activists of the Islamic Society of Minya University which was already quite prominent when I arrived in the city in December 1977), the probability of familiarity if not direct contact between them is considerable. Likewise, the blind Shaykh ʿUmar ʿAbd al-Rahman had also been working in Minya in the mid-1970s before moving to a post in Asyut and later to self-chosen exile in New Jersey. Not long after my departure from Minya in August 1979 this outspoken advocate of the Islamist cause, already well known locally, would rise to national prominence when he was identified as the *mufti* for the group called *Tanzīm al-Jihād*. In this capacity, among other things, he authorized them to commit armed robberies of Coptic businesses and to kill Sadat on the grounds that he had

abandoned Islam. A decade later this same *shaykh* would acquire international recognition for his suspected part in the car bomb planted
beneath the World Trade Center in New York.[5] Thus the ideological
resemblances and, to an indeterminate degree, the interpersonal links
between the now stigmatized *Jamā'at al-Muslimīn* and the Islamic
activism of Minya in the late 1970s point to an unmistakable overlap.
This sequence of calculated aggression by Islamists and the similarly
violent response of the state would have its effect both on *'ulamā'* in
government mosques and on independent *jam'īya* preachers.

Finally, anxieties roused by this confrontation starting in Upper Egypt
were shortly to flare up again due to the crisis of Iran in 1978 and the
emergence of the Ayatollah Khomeini. The image of this fully turbaned
and bearded mullah at the head of a revolutionary Islamic government
provided a rallying point for a sudden wave of mobilization, especially
among the youthful enthusiasts at Egypt's provincial universities. Awareness of their dim prospects for the future, given the lack of opportunities
offered by their country's troubled political and economic systems, now
combined with religious zeal in efforts to resolve what Saad Eddin Ibrahim
has called their "collective status incongruity."[6] In retrospect, therefore,
the assault on Shaykh al-Dhahabi, who personified the official Islamic
establishment upholding the state, clearly alerted others associated with
these institutions that they were regarded as standing in the way of an
advancing political order with the Qur'an as its basis.

Islamization in Practice

The term Islamization has been used to describe both the official and the
revolutionary aspects of the processes involved in the conflict represented
in the Shaykh al-Dhahabi incident. For example, Richard T. Antoun
speaks of Islamization as the proliferation of formal state-sponsored institutions explicitly identified with official religious authority. These include
not only mosques and shrines, but also courts, schools, festivals, and pilgrimage tours, all of which employ personnel incorporated into a religious
bureaucracy.[7] Others have used the term differently, in referring to the
enhancement of popular compliance with Islamic norms including perhaps
measures of enforcement. Thus the historian Rafiuddin Ahmed in discussing nineteenth-century Bengal speaks of Islamization as a movement
intended to increase the religious and social participation especially of
rural areas in affairs of a wider, urban centered Islamic community. Such
initiatives, he notes, occasionally involved conflicts between an assortment of personalities and their rival parties. But on the whole he points to
its positive outcome, suggesting that activities associated with Islamiza-

tion "indirectly worked as mobilizing and integrating forces generating a sense of *communitas* across social divisions."[8] Finally, Islamization is now often used as the term of art favored by many activists and militants themselves to indicate what they envision as the total transformation of society in conformity with the *sharī'a*.[9] This view inevitably presupposes the political control of the state by qualified Muslims fully dedicated to this cause.

The term Islamization therefore embraces a number of perspectives. But all of them share the notion of a qualitative and/or quantitative increase in ideas and institutions identified with Islam over against other interests that are presumably alien, hostile, or indifferent. It is this agonistic element that allows Islamization to be used as a term suited to describe both its official and its oppositional components. The fact, however, that the process has recently emerged as a central issue in the public life of a nation derives from causes not directly related to arguments over the potential benefits of theocracy. Rather, the conflict surrounding Islamization arises from a crucible of particular ideological and historical factors that have combined to produce new forms of consciousness and solidarity. From these has followed the resolve to apply certain principles in order to change the fundamental character of social reality.

The point of origin for the religious resurgence that so greatly heightened the tensions implied by Islamization is conventionally given as 1967. This year marks the dark hour of ignominious defeat when the Arab allies lost not only militarily but territorially to Israel's surprise attack that began and ended in less than a week. Virtually all commentators concur on the significance of this sudden reversal of fortune. I also frequently heard this same view echoed by ordinary Egyptians, both Muslims and Copts alike, for a decisive turn toward religion affected the society at large. The traumatic effect of this disaster on the battlefield was instant and enduring. It thoroughly deflated the nation's confidence not only in its leaders but in the overall vision of its moral character. In its wake a groundswell of religiosity arose on all levels. At the top, a chastened 'Abd al-Nasir resorted to expressions heavily colored by Islamic images. This was widely recognized as an appeal for increasing the role religion played in society and as such it met with an overwhelming positive response among the wider population.[10] Within the government this newly aroused interest in religion led to sizable increases in spending for mosques, religiously sponsored schools (especially the Azhari secondary schools) and the facilities to train the professional staffs to serve and operate these institutions. Also more Islamic programming was added to the state-controlled radio and television. At the same time, this new mood prompted a flourishing of private religious incentives on a local and a national scale. Many surviving voluntary religious organizations, including sufi fraternities, began expanding again and intensifying their activities. New groups were founded adopting in various configurations the ideals of a society regenerated by a return to Islam.

After Sadat's ascent to power in 1970, there followed still further openings toward the long suppressed Muslim Brothers. Sadat, who had been the Free Officers' liaison with this organization while they were preparing for the 1952 revolution, now released those imprisoned for membership in this society. He also relaxed the enforcement of the strict laws controlling religious groups, tacitly permitting them to recommence many of their activities including meeting, preaching, and publishing. These reconciliatory gestures he combined with frequent public demonstrations of piety, being proclaimed in official declarations as the "believer president" (*al-ra'īs al-mū'min*). Moreover, in the early years of his presidency Sadat employed this appeal to Islam as a political strategy to assist in overcoming certain opponents of his regime including student groups and party cadres who remained loyal to the Arab socialist orientation of 'Abd al-Nasir's heyday. Then in 1973, Egypt's redirection toward Islam received what many perceived as a form of divine approbation. The October War of that year, in Egypt also known as the Ramadan War (and in Israel the Yom Kippur War), which ended with an internationally brokered cease-fire, was quickly proclaimed by Egypt as a national victory. Moreover, this triumphant "crossing" (*'ubūr*), referring to the military advance across the Suez Canal but also to a symbolic rebirth of the nation, was widely credited to a return to religion. It was pointed out, for instance, that instead of the battle cry of 'Abd al-Nasir's troops "Land! Sea! Air!" Sadat's soldiers had shouted "Allah Akbar" as they overran the Bar-Lev line. It was even broadcast on the national radio that angels had been seen fighting on the side of Egypt.[11]

Sadat gained further approval from those representing an enhanced role for religion when he expelled the thousands of Soviet advisors and technicians. He also encouraged Egyptian labor exportation to the oil-rich Gulf states where vast new wealth went paired with conservative Islamic observance. Similarly, the peace initiative of 1977, which began with the highly symbolic flight to Jerusalem on the feast commemorating Abraham's sacrifice (*'īd al-aḍḥā*), the greatest of Islamic holy days, was also thoroughly couched in religious terms. Accompanying these enlargements of religious expression on the national and international plane, a remarkable boom of mosque and church construction occurred throughout the country. Along with this surge of devotion the fanning of smouldering embers of Muslim-Christian sectarian antagonism also caused a dramatic rise of incidents to flare up.[12] In Minya, the militant student membership of the group that called itself *al-Jamā'a al-Islāmīya,* (the Islamic Society) likewise included a pronounced anti-Coptic element. Its preachers often referred to the Copts, at times baiting them, with terms like "unbelievers" or "Crusaders" (*salībiyūn*). Because local Copts, as Christians, were associated with the Western world and its capitalist culture which was now fully accepted by the agents of official Islamization, radical Islamists displayed both political and confessional motives in attacking them. Moreover, they could strike at Christians with relative impunity as surrogates for the state, which had shown it would not tolerate such challenges to its own authority.

Tarboosh

The form of Islamization depicted by the symbol of the tarboosh is concentrated within the context of official government institutions. The tarboosh is the rounded maroon cap made of felt which usually has a dark silk tassel attached by a short cord at the top. In Egypt it is surrounded at the base by a simple white cotton band wrapped tightly around the bottom portion. The tarboosh worn in this fashion represents to Egyptians the office of the traditional Islamic authority. Although this garb may be worn by others such as sufis who adopt it all or in part by imitation, for *shaykhs* who have studied at the Azhar and who hold positions in the nation's religious establishment it is an official uniform. It is associated with classical religious learning, authoritarian politics, and conservative social views. The tarboosh represents the established principle of Sunni Islam that even a tyrant should be tolerated for the sake of preserving the order and unity of the community.[13] In the Cairo of the 1830s, observed by Edward Lane, the tarboosh was the appropriate headdress for "men of the middle and higher classes" while a variation of another larger and fuller sort of headdress, known according to Lane as the *mukleh,* was worn by specifically religious specialists. A later reform promoted by the Ottoman Sultan did away with this plethora of differently colored and shaped turbans denoting religious sect, rank, and purported prerogatives. But curiously, the symbolic value of this higher and fuller turban did not disappear when this sacred headgear itself became obsolete. Instead its religious aura was taken up by the preservation of the once secular tarboosh.[14]

As noted, the tarboosh today constitutes the crowning feature of the obligatory garb of a man trained in the traditional Islamic sciences who works either under the Ministry of Religious Endowments or as a teacher of Arabic or religion under the Ministry of Education or in the Azhar's own system of religious schools. In addition, it is frequently also worn by lower-echelon mosque employees such as muezzins, Qur'an chanters, the deputy *imām* known as the *muqīm al-shā'ā'ir*, and even by general attendants who may have little or no formal schooling.

The overall pattern of the staff organization in government mosques is quite simple. Often it consists solely of the preacher and one or two service personnel who look after maintenance and may occasionally assist at rituals. A fuller complement would include such figures as just mentioned plus perhaps, in a few of the very large mosques, an administrator.[15] However, certain additional factors touching on the leadership of government mosques should be noted to illustrate the context of this approach to Islamization. For instance, preachers trained at the Azhar and employed in mosques under the Ministry of Religious Endowments are widely regarded today as functionaries, that is, as *muwazafūn*. This places them in the same category as hundreds of thousands of their countrymen, also college graduates, who earn minimal wages as employees in one or another of Egypt's hopelessly bloated and notoriously dreary government bureaucracies.[16] A few exceptional salary supplements such as a monthly clothing allowance and travel allotment and holiday bonus may boost their earning slightly but generally *shaykhs,* despite their supposed elevated dignity, suffer the same unsettling income privation as do the rest of the nation's chronically impoverished civil servants. Furthermore, *shaykhs* work under very similar bureaucratic conditions as do their counterparts in other ministries. They are answerable to intrusive inspectors, directors, and paper-pushing clerks who supervise compliance with time-consuming duties that may have little bearing on the actual performance of a preacher.

Also, in recent decades there has emerged a clear and easily discerned generation gap among preachers usually working to the disadvantage of the younger men. It has its roots in a tendency to denigrate the education and therefore the competence of anyone who was trained at the Azhar after the purge and restructuring of this ancient mosque-university in the 1960s by 'Abd al-Nasir. Most senior *'ulamā'* and many laymen share the view that since that reform, imposed by the government, the overall quality of this once-revered education has steadily declined. By consequence, the caliber of the entire profession has also slipped, leading to lowered esteem and an erosion of interest on the part of bright young men in traditional religious studies. Then, seeing that these mediocre graduates are now occupying pulpits it can hardly be wondered that the appeal of a career as a preacher falls off. To meet the growing need, the critical view continues, the Azhar has lowered its standards still further. For instance, the fact that most younger *shaykhs* have not memorized the entire Qur'an, which was until fairly recently a prerequisite for admission to the Azhar, is commonly cited by elders and conservatives as sufficient evidence of their laxity.[17] Derogatory views such as these pointing to uncomplimentary conclusions are also prevalent of course among young Islamic activists.

In reaction to these and other factors sapping the prestige of the tarboosh and leaving a shortage of preachers for government mosques, the Ministry of Religious Endowments has moved outside its internal ranks in order to fill empty pulpits. One practice has been to hire respected local personnel, who lack the formal credentials of an *ʿālim* but who are tested to assure a mastery of the basics, who are then assigned to carry out the routine tasks of ritual leadership. A second approach has been to recruit Azhar graduates living in the region who are employed as teachers to preach on Fridays in otherwise unstaffed mosques. They perform this service, often dressed in their usual lay garb, for a special free-lance remuneration *(b-il-mukāfa'a)*. Even so, the staffing of government mosque pulpits remains problematic and, more important, the popular response to the substitute preachers has generally not been warm.

Nevertheless, there are certain benefits to having a local mosque under the supervision of the government which make this status desirable for many communities. Most notable are the financial subsidies that relieve local Muslims of the task of supporting such an institution. Hence villages and neighborhoods constantly petition to obtain this sponsorship. Many times while visiting at the regional office of the Ministry of Religious Endowments *(mudariyat al-āwqāf)* I witnessed such requests being presented. But almost invariably they would be met by regretful rejections, for the government's interest in actually controlling mosques far outreached its resources. On the other hand, there were others who plainly objected to government appropriation of mosque facilities and any attempt to regulate the pulpit. These are represented by a contrary socioreligious current in Minya, which may be depicted as Islamization of the beard.

The Beard

The beard, as presented here, stands as the key symbol of that diffuse movement which has been variously called the Islamic Revival, Islamic Resurgence, Islamic Impulse, Neo-Traditionalism, Fundamentalism, or Islamism. Of course, a host of more colorful and often prejudicial epithets are also occasionally heard which has prompted an understandable sensitivity in some circles over the choice of the proper name for this phenomenon. Although the theoretical implications of such labelling cannot be ignored, in fact the varied manifestations of this movement do not allow for a strict and harmonious definition. I accept therefore the use of the most commonly used term, "fundamentalism," despite its initial historical ties to Protestantism. However, I do not restrict myself to it alone. Rather I embrace as sufficiently descriptive several labels that have similarly widespread application.[18] Notably, the adjective Islamist, for all its generality, seems to translate most adequately the self-presentation of contemporary Egyptian groups whose members customarily identify themselves simply as "Muslims" and their cause as "Islam."

Like many scholars, R. Stephen Humphreys has settled on fundamentalism as his chief term of reference. He defines it broadly "as the reaffirmation, in a radically changed environment, of traditional modes of understanding behavior" thereby catching the scope if not the force of the movement.[19] Such generality has the benefit of avoiding the implication that all those covered by such terms are inherently prone to extremism or violence. Nevertheless, for the context of the contemporary Middle East one could be a bit more specific regarding the nature of this "radically changed environment." For the widely perceived cause of this conflict is the intrusion of a Western secular worldview into all areas of today's Muslim life. Hence Bruce Lawrence's emphasis on the ambivalent "instrumental" dimensions of this orientation is also important to register. "In sum, fundamentalism is above all a kind of ideological formation, affirming the modern world not only by opposing it but also by using its means against its purposes."[20]

But regardless of the vocabulary one chooses, ethnographically speaking there was an unmistakable concreteness about the movement itself and a wide consensus on the image that most prominently represented it. Among those taking part in this movement as well as those who opposed it or merely observed it, the beard came to serve as the determining mark of identification or sympathy with fundamentalism. Hence in Minya during the late 1970s, especially among the youth, men who sought to display their agreement with Islamist views and especially those who were active at its functions took to growing beards. So pronounced was this tendency that some men who might have already worn beards came to discover quickly that strangers were quite likely to mistake their "secular" whiskers for a badge of affiliation with these religiopolitical views. In short, a beard, especially in the case of a young man, became the mark of membership in the movement which locally meant some degree of participating in the Islamic Society, composed largely of university students. This is not to say, of course, that every man who shared in these activities complied with this tonsorial norm, for some did not. But nevertheless the beard became the symbol of the group and their ideas to such an extent that the gesture of pointing to one's chin rapidly evolved as a mute short-hand to signal that someone or something under discussion was linked to the Islamist cause. Moreover, in the regional patois one common expression used by outsiders, including unsympathetic *shaykhs*, to refer to the group was *birubū dign*, which can be glossed as the "bearded ones" or more colloquially as "beardo's." Eventually, as confrontation between Islamists with government authorities intensified, some concluded that the beard could also be a liability insofar as it drew the attention of police. To adopt a clean-shaven look would very probably save one from being subjected to such suspicions, but it would also count as a coward's compromise. Finally, it must not be overlooked that the beard is an entirely masculine issue. Among women, the wearing of distinct sorts of veils played a similar part in the assertion of an Islamist identity.[21] But in Minya, both in mosques and in the student-based Islamic Society, virtually all leadership roles and certainly public preaching were exclusively in the hands of men.

The place of the beard as a token of authority and piety is well established in traditional Islamic literature.[22] It also belongs as a mark of dignity in the folkways of Egyptians. But for these fundamentalists its only justification was said to be the imitation of the Prophet. It stood in contrast not only to smooth cheeks, but to the more familiar male accoutrement of the area which was the moustache in the style of ʿAbd al-Nasir. Views on the particular cut of a beard were also much discussed, as there was some dispute over the exact form recommended by the *Sunna*. There was also a lively debate, decried by many as an unfortunate diversion away from more important matters, over whether the beard was a normative prerequisite for authentic Islam.[23] Among members of the local Islamic Society, however, it seemed clear that in case of doubt it was best to follow the strictest, most literal interpretation. Therefore they would hold at arm's length those who said, as did a modernist *shaykh* at a *jamʿīya* mosque, who incidentally wore a full moustache, that his beard was in his heart.

The Islamic Society of Minya University was one of many such organizations which were founded on Egypt's campuses during the Sadat era. In purely organizational terms, all these groups acted fairly autonomously at the time although, as in all things, it was the *Jamāʿa Islāmīya* at Cairo University that tended to serve as the model and to receive the most attention. In fact, some of the pamphlets and flyers that were distributed by the Islamic Society in Minya were originally published by the chapter at Cairo University.[24] All these societies were technically illegal in that they lacked official sanction, although in the late 1970s they functioned openly within the confines of the universities which enjoyed a somewhat privileged status in regard to political expression. But increasingly these activists were using the student world as bases from which they advanced a steadily more assertive agenda.

Given the formally independent character of these organizations, which nevertheless shared a body of general ideals, it is not surprising that each one showed the effects of localized interests and attitudes. Thus the provincial character of Minya as contrasted with Cairo or Alexandria plays a prominent part in the development of its Islamic Society and its appeal. It should be noted initially that Minya University was at the time a newly established institution. It had brought together thousands of largely village youth into a city that lacked adequate facilities even for such basic needs as their housing and recreation. When Sadat became president, there had been four universities in the country and only one in Upper Egypt, opened in the 1950s at Asyut. By 1976 he had established nine more, including Minya, where an existing teachers' college, an advanced agriculture school, and a polytechnic had been combined, expanded, and upgraded overnight to become Minya University. Until 1981, when the large new campus several kilometers north of the city center was completed, its several academic units were also widely divided spatially, making for aggravated transportation problems. Moreover, everything was greatly overcrowded. The lecturers and administrators consisted almost entirely of commuters who came to spend at most three or four days a week in Minya and then returned to their homes in Cairo or Alexandria. This arrangement made access to the faculty extremely difficult and it left them with very little impact on the intellectual or social life of the student body.

Furthermore, everyone recognized that the overall quality of the education itself was quite poor as compared, for example, to Cairo's academic institutions. Nevertheless the value of the university credential was itself an incentive, for at that time the government still guaranteed a position in the civil service to every graduate. Even those who did achieve high marks were well aware that there was little hope of advancement in Minya and uncertainty colored prospects elsewhere. Dr. ʿAbd al-Minʿam Kamil, then president of Minya University, was quoted as saying, "I think we are giving diplomas to help people emigrate to Cairo," a realistic observation which raises the issues of cultural identity and social mobility that were so much a part of the strong current carrying the Islamic Society as well its opponents.[25] The dream for most at the time, faculty and students alike, was somehow to find a job in Saudi Arabia or some other oil-rich Arab El

Dorado in order to leapfrog the inevitable ordeals of financial insecurity which were dawning as a major consequence of the country's faltering steps toward economic liberalization. For most students at Minya University, therefore, restlessness, boredom, and frustration, added to a sense of exclusion from the distant centers of meaningful opportunity served to create an environment where the reassertion of traditional values found fertile ground.

Another of the differences between the young Minya University and those of metropolitan centers that is clearly reflected in the careers of their respective Islamic Societies deals with the former's narrowed range of ideological options and reduced scale of political dynamics. Whereas in Cairo one finds numerous centers of intellectual stimulation to choose from and exposure to an elite directly involved in national and international issues, Minya's student world had very limited horizons and offered little encouragement for intellectual curiosity. Also, Minya's student body was relatively small and more important still too underdeveloped to accommodate a tolerant community of discourse. Rather, a small, highly authoritarian core of militants who led the Islamic Society could function without the need to face comparably dedicated and organized rivals. The Islamic Society in Minya was essentially run by a clique of young men of whom one dominating personality whom we shall call Sayf was the undisputed leader. Interestingly, he was not the nominal head of the Society, for another student fronted as the "president." But Sayf combined an imposing physical stature (he was slightly over six feet tall) with a compelling self-confidence, indeed an extraordinarily shrewd audacity, that gave the inspiration if not the direction to the rest of the group.

The Local Islamic Society

This strong leadership and the clannish character of the Islamic Society at Minya University gave it a cohesiveness that was frequently reaffirmed by public demonstrations. Here the beards were important as the indelible markers of a collectivity that extended beyond the activities of ritual display. This solidarity enabled the group's loose membership to appropriate a number of public areas for their exclusive control in the name of "Islam." They usually began this process by subjecting common space to a sort of physical occupation. They started by taking over bulletin boards and wall space reserved for posters. Then they moved into portions of the cafeteria, onto the shady spots on open lawns where students were accustomed to gather during breaks. Eventually they sought to dictate the use of playing fields, auditoriums, classrooms, and even the rooms shared by students in the university's housing facilities. In the process, ordinary social controls seldom held up against them. Otherwise acceptable norms for conduct were overridden, sometimes publicly and flagrantly. But as they proceeded it became evident that university officials were not inclined to intervene and there were no other groups among the students that could effectively counter this burgeoning bid to monopolize moral judgment and enforce allegedly proper decorum accordingly.

A second factor peculiar to the evolution of the Islamic Society at Minya University derives from the relatively small range of perceived political-religious alternatives noted above. In Cairo, it would be likely that a dissenter could define his opposition on a fairly wide spectrum of recognized opinions and probably expect support from a number of representative groups. In Minya, the categories available for justifying a minority view or nonconformity are few. They are also vague and are prone to a lumping effect that pushes all particulars to the outer edges of a scale that records little more than good or bad. This occurs, for instance, when fundamentalists freely lump Copts together with Zionists, Imperialists, and Christian missionaries, all of whom are seen at only a slight remove from the Egyptian government and the Azhar. But it also happens in the opposite direction as one may hear from those who oppose fundamentalism that those who wore the beard are really communists or supporters of Qaddafi's scheme to unite Egypt and Libya under his leadership or in the pay of other pernicious foreign agents. Hence, especially within the student subculture, not only did the beard signify positive approval and even advocacy of the line forwarded by the vocal leadership of the Islamic Society, but the absence of a beard could be construed not as indifference but as active opposition unless a person made his views quite clear by some other form of outward expression.

All manner of intrigue and conspiracy often follow to explain the compatibility of ill-fitting pieces of this lumping process. There was frequent talk among the opponents of the Islamic Society (who were also its most frequent targets) such as officials at the university, the Azhari *shaykhs,* not to mention the Copts and the civil authorities, that despite appearances the beard did not represent religious conviction or even a sound knowledge of Islam at all. The beard was simply a cover for troublemakers, poor students in search of an excuse for their lack of achievement, and similarly maladjusted, unstable, or thoroughly opportunistic elements. I was told that those now in the forefront of Islamist demonstrations were the very ones who shortly before had marched at the head of the Arab Socialist cadres. I was also told that students and others were paid to grow beards by money smuggled in from Saudi Arabia or Libya. Although I heard this rumor in many such circles, and many actual figures were quoted to me (such as three Egyptian pounds a month, or five, or seven) I at first tended to discount it. Eventually, however, a young village schoolteacher I spoke with confirmed the story, telling me that he had been offered a respectable sum if he would grow a beard. He turned it down though, he said, since he was unwilling to be associated with a group he felt to have confused the line between pious zeal and crime. Nevertheless there may have been others who found the offer too attractive to turn down.

A third factor that distinguishes the Islamic Society at Minya University in any comparison with its counterpart in Cairo derives from the contrasting sociocultural traditions of Upper and Lower Egypt.[26] Upper Egypt, known as al-Saʿid, and especially the heart of it where Minya is located, represents an ethos of proud, rugged, religious, conservative, country folk who cling to the traditional code of honor and shame. They look after themselves, and do not seek outside officials to settle their disputes. Rather they convoke a council of reconciliation (*majlis al-sulḥ*) or, if the occasion merits, they engage in the vendetta, or *thāʾir*, whose social obligations underlie all intergroup loyalties. Among Saʿidis, popular admiration persists for legendary figures who resisted outside oppressors and vindicated their victims in a Robin Hood fashion. Likewise, they uphold the traditional place of women as virtuous in their modesty while it is for men to defend the honor of the family.[27] Carlo Levi's insight of fifty years ago into traditional brigandage of rural southern Italy reflects a moral climate quite similar to what continues to prevail in large parts of present-day Upper Egypt. "[T]hrough the brigands the peasants defended themselves against a hostile civilization that never understands but everlastingly enslaves them; instinctively they looked on the brigands as heroes."[28]

Thus from all appearances, the pattern of recruitment into the Islamic Society at Minya did not consist mainly in the application of detached religious convictions to an analysis of contemporary socioeconomic conditions in the light of classical Islamic learning. Rather, while not disparaging the piety and sincerity of its adherents, the evidence also points to a strong basis for its appeal in the dynamics of peer pressure and an urgent summons to defend group honor against perceived threats to the values and the ideals cherished as the substance of Islam.

The Islamic Society's Strategy

The 1978–1979 academic year marked the high point of success for Minya University's Islamic Society, but it also spelled out its collision course with the authorities which soon afterward led to its fragmentation. The group embarked on a series of aggressive displays of its determination to bring student life into compliance with its vision of an Islamic order. Through a series of incidents, members of the Islamic Society baited not only their student opposition but faculty and other university officials both on and off the campus. Each new imposition upon existing practices and each flaunting of formal regulations that went unchallenged seemed to increase their temerity. The process also increased the polarization between the Islamic Society and its opponents, most conspicuously the Coptic students who comprised about a quarter of the student body. These Christians felt especially vulnerable since they were not in a position to counter the assaults against them without leaving themselves open to charges that they were engaging in sectarian conflict. And any confrontation that was reduced simply to Muslim versus Christian risked inflaming passions of another sort altogether that might be very difficult to contain within the context of the precipitating incident. Increasingly a "reign of terror" came to displace the relatively open casual interaction that had earlier characterized the student world.[29]

Almost from the start this emerging state of affairs on the campus had caused the anxieties aroused there to spill over into the city. The activities of the bearded ones became a topic of constant discussion and wide concern. While some Muslims tended to admire the vigor and dedication of these young activists, others expressed disapproval of their tactics or had doubts about their doctrines. Among Copts, on the other hand, rumors of menacing incidents were accumulating in all quarters.

Soon news of this burst of Islamic activism in Minya began to spread outward across the entire country. This flush of national attention was reflected for instance in laudatory articles in *al-Da'wa* and other Islamist publications. Meanwhile, among Coptic leaders, alarms were being sounded and deliberately unspecific allusions to "religious intolerance" were cropping up more and more frequently. Moreover, by the middle of this year, it became clear that what Islamic militants were accomplishing in Minya had also won them the admiration of other similar societies, most of which were still consolidating their forces on their various campuses. This prominence not only encouraged emulation but it allowed Minya to contribute disproportionately to nascent efforts to bring the scattered Islamic Societies of the country under one umbrella. One landmark step in this direction, signaling both the rapid rise of Minya's Islamists on the national scene and the development of an interest in coordinating all the elements of the movement, occurred just when the domination of the campus by Minya's Islamic Society was at its height.

In early March 1979, a meeting was held in the auditorium at the College of Arts at Minya University which brought together leading representatives from the Islamic Societies of other universities throughout

Egypt. It proclaimed itself to be the First General Congress of Islamic Societies. Speaking out on what were then pressing topics of public concern, the delegates of the congress passed such resolutions as a rejection of the Camp David Accords (which were scheduled to be signed later that month) and an affirmation of the inseparability of religion and politics (thus refuting Sadat's much repeated slogan, "no politics in religion and no religion in politics"). But in addition they issued pronouncements on several local matters which were thus being recast as issues concerning the entire national movement. Most important, they registered their strong objections to the pending proceedings of an extraordinary disciplinary council that was called upon to investigate and adjudicate an incident involving members of the Islamic Society at Minya who had severely beaten up a dozen students a couple of months previously. At the end of their meeting these and other resolutions were posted on the bulletin board of the College of Arts. It could only be seen as a straightforward gesture of defiance by a group that had already demonstrated its willingness and its capacity to use force. In the event, however, this congress's support for the local militants proved to be one of their last unanswered provocations at Minya University. Just a few weeks later, this disciplinary board ended its deliberations and announced its findings. It pronounced those who had assisted in the attack to be guilty of aggravated assault. Their sentences were also significant. Most of them were temporarily suspended from the university while the ringleaders were dismissed permanently. From this point on, the tide turned against the Islamic Society as far as the university community in Minya was concerned. Although they continued to be active and intermittently disruptive they had lost their firm grip on the campus. Soon the torch of leadership of Upper Egypt's Islamic movement would pass to the much larger setting at Asyut University, where its confrontations with academic and civil authorities would escalate precipitously.

One further factor that set apart the Islamic Society of Minya at its height from many others was its involvement in the mechanisms of student government. In 1977, the Islamic Society of Minya had gained control of the Student Union (*ittihād al-ṭulāb*) through the ballot box. Its ascent to office did not imply a mere change of administration but amounted to a takeover that effectively placed the Student Union's authority, its funds, and its facilities directly in the hands of the Islamic Society's leaders. About this time, similar efforts to converge the formal structures of student representation with the Islamist agenda were occurring at other Egyptian universities. But Minya was a pioneer in the process since its Islamic Society's slate had taken the election after a campaign that combined a burst of religiopolitical rallies with an undertow of bullying tactics aimed at discouraging any rivals and their supporters. The militants presented themselves as the embodiment of the proven path to total societal regeneration while their opponents were rebuked as representing the doomed and discredited ideologies that had brought the nation to its present crisis. Needless to say, this campaign also provided them with opportunities to propagate their cause before audiences that were otherwise normally not inclined to attend indoctrination sessions.

Given the character of sectarian relationships in Upper Egypt at the time, it was not possible for a Christian to win in these student elections, and it was thought dangerous to try. Likewise, given the climate of ideological purity aroused by those declaring themselves the spokesmen for the reestablishment of an Islamic Order, it was also difficult for a moderate Muslim candidate to stand without pledging allegiance to the leadership of the Islamic Society. In the end, therefore, it was Sayf rather than the elected president and other officers of the Student Union who, in effect, made the key appointments and dictated policy. Under this direction the activities and responsibilities of the Student Union came to be more and more closely identified with the interests of the Islamic Society. Announcements of forthcoming events on the campus and fliers promoting Islamist views handed out on various occasions were appearing signed jointly by the Student Union and the Islamic Society. Opposition to either was freely interpreted by the bearded ones as the disapproval of both.

The following year, in the fall of 1978 as student elections approached, the campaign deteriorated progressively into an open confrontation between candidates of the Islamic Society and an ill-defined coterie of Muslim moderates who were beginning a tentative alliance to counter the militants. Posters and speeches, often framed as arguments about what is and is not the teaching of Islam, grew increasingly acrimonious as the Islamic Society resorted to personal intimidation and eventually beatings. Finally, the governor of the governorate intervened and ordered the postponing of the elections indefinitely. Until further notice the Student Union would be managed by an appointed committee of students, faculty, and administrators. This was an extraordinary measure which not surprisingly caught the attention of the nation. But locally it accomplished little since practically speaking the Student Union functions were paralyzed. Moreover, much of the leverage the Islamic Society lost by its lack of direct access to the Student Union facilities it recouped by drawing the support of those objecting to the government's intrusion into the purportedly sacred democratic processes at the university. In addition, the fundamentalists were not slow to exploit this decision as further demonstration of their case against an unjust secular state.

They continued therefore to assert themselves prominently and often aggressively in the routine of daily life at the colleges. For example, on the grounds shared by the College of Arts and the College of Education, a relatively small enclosure where the largest number of students were concentrated, the Islamic Society made the daily noon prayer into a long and ostentatious display. They chose as their place of prayer a large area located partially on the lawn and partially on a sidewalk connecting the two main buildings of the colleges. This centrally situated spot had been a popular gathering point where students were accustomed to chat and mill about during breaks from class. It was now appropriated as a sort of open-air mosque, making it off-bounds for such informal worldly socializing. The Islamists accomplished this by spreading out mats on the ground, at first temporarily during prayers, but eventually permanently, thereby defining and restricting the space. They then brought in portable sound amplification equipment which they used to broadcast a thunderous call to prayer and to preach and teach at other times. Often when the mats were not occupied in the performance of ritual worship one saw bearded individuals or small groups studying the Qur'an there or instructing a neophyte. Relatively few apart from those active in or sympathetic with the Islamic Society ventured onto these mats even to join in the prayer. Interestingly, there already existed a mosque on this campus, which was scarcely thirty meters from the spot now taken over by the fundamentalists. It was a solid attractive building in good repair. But given that it was relatively small, completely enclosed and slightly off-to-the-side of the major thoroughfare, it was considered unsuited for the purposes of the Islamic Society. This original mosque, they decided, was to be used solely by women students who were to pray separately from men.

These activists did not limit themselves merely to the extracurricular sphere. They were also eager to extend their influence into the strictly academic activities of the university, although this was not as easily accomplished. They would, for instance, approach professors whom they would pressure into surrendering lecture time so that they themselves might instruct students on Islamic topics. Or if a teacher was late in arriving or absent it was not uncommon for one of their number to take the rostrum and use the occasion for a similar purpose. Classroom behavior was also subject to oversight. Doors were guarded, for example, during these impromptu lectures by Islamic Society leaders to prevent students from exiting.

Fundamentalists insisted too on the separation of men and women students in the classroom and they sought to bring compliance not only by appeals to religion but by pushing and shoving when necessary. In acting in this rough fashion, they were often seen as overstepping the bounds of traditional civility. But they typically replied that they were confronting behavior incompatible with Islam. Accepting this premise as the grounds of a dispute would then most likely divert the discussion away from the matter at hand and into the sensitive areas of moral integrity or theological comprehension where it was difficult to proceed without implying slights on one's character. Thus both Christians and Muslims who did not share the outlook of fundamentalists often felt constrained in rebutting these activists lest the defending of a contrary view be construed as an insult.

Escalating Tensions

The character of the movement portrayed here as Islamization of the tarboosh and the beard extends into countless particulars that might be furnished to deepen and broaden the discussion. But since this study concentrates on preaching and it is based primarily on ethnographic research it might be more helpful to offer a schematic chronicle of a dozen selected incidents that occurred during the course of my fieldwork in Minya. An awareness of what was happening on the campus and in the surrounding streets during this period will greatly assist in understanding the context in which local sermons were delivered. The events highlighted by this summary catalogue will also illustrate the escalating pace at which the Islamic Society of Minya University made its emergence from provincial obscurity. Ostensibly it rose in a matter of mere months from the cause of campus ferment to an incipient insurrectionary nucleus whose ever more overt and more violent challenge to the government and its official religious establishment would soon draw the Egyptian armed forces into action against them.

Church vandalized. From the time of my first visit to Minya University in December 1977, it was clear that the Islamist movement there was on the ascent. Minor demonstrations inside and outside the campus gates by its advocates and conspicuous displays of its slogans and iconography were already common. However, in April 1978 an incident occurred that brought local tensions to a new threshold of brinksmanship. One night, a band of students belonging to the Islamic Society, under the leadership of Sayf, broke into a Coptic Church that was under construction in a residential area near the block of multistory flats designed as student housing, called University City. The Student Union office is also in this same complex. They vandalized the building, breaking windows, inflicting other damage, and leaving the site a shambles. No less significantly, they chose the vigil of Easter, the greatest Christian holy day, as the date for their assault. Privately, the local Coptic community was extremely agitated by this action. But no public response was delivered by the Church. Neither did the police or other civil authorities take any visible measures to apprehend the culprits, who boasted of their feat.

Play closed down.   On the evening of November 11, 1978, as the new semester was getting underway, a large group belonging to the Islamic Society forced its way into the university auditorium. They came in order to disrupt the dress rehearsal of a student theater production that was scheduled to be begin its performances the following day. The play was a popular musical comedy which was then enjoying a long and successful stage run in Cairo, entitled in the colloquial *Minayn Agīb Nās*, or "From Where do I Get People?" It was sponsored by the drama club of the College of Arts and was directed by a professor in the Department of Arabic. The bearded militants entered forcibly and took over the stage, expelling the actors. They declared that the production was not in keeping with Islam and they demanded that it be cancelled completely. In its place, they announced that they would conduct an Islam program which they called *al-iʿtikāf*. Traditionally this refers to a sort of monastic retreat, featuring prayer, meditation, and study normally undertaken in solitude. But they wished to introduce a transformed version of it in a collective form featuring Qur'an chanting, preaching, and speeches that conformed to their approach to religion and its demands. Furthermore, they threatened to return the next night at the opening performance in still greater numbers to prevent the show from going on if their ultimatum was not respected. In a word, the performance was summarily halted and it was never revived. Shortly afterward, an evening of religious programming staged by the Islamic Society was conducted with much fanfare in the same auditorium. A great deal of anger, disappointment, and anxiety followed upon this incident, especially among the students who had worked on the play. But from all outward appearances, no official reaction was forthcoming from the university authorities and the Islamic Society was not subjected to any public criticism.

Sunset prayer demonstration.   On November 28, 1978, the word went out that Shaykh ʿAbdul-Hamid Kishk was going to come to Minya and would preach a *dars*, a religious lesson, after the *Maghrib* ("sunset") prayer in the university auditorium. Kishk is a blind Azhari *imam* who began his career as a promoter of the Muslim Brothers in the 1950s and 1960s. He was jailed more than once under ʿAbd al-Nasir, but after being released he continued his preaching in the same vein. Today, he is officially tolerated and he has now become by far the best-known preacher in Egypt despite the fact that he is banned from all state-controlled broadcast media. Cassette recordings of Kishk's sermons and lessons can be found throughout cities and villages of Egypt and his distinctive and easily recognized oratorical style is appreciated as much for his verbal finesse as for his fundamentalist views. Virtually everyone who appreciated listening to these recordings regarded Shaykh Kishk as an Islamic celebrity of the first order.

The news that he was coming to Minya only broke on the actual day he was supposed to arrive. But word spread quickly in all directions. As a result, by mid-afternoon students and others had begun to gather at the university and by the time of the sunset prayer, thousands, mainly students, had come together outside the locked auditorium doors to await his arrival. But the time of the sunset prayer came and went with no Shaykh Kishk in sight. As they waited this swelling crowd clearly grew restless. The initial air of excited anticipation was being diluted by bewilderment and disappointment. But then suddenly a message started moving quickly through the crowd. A sign had just been posted on the college's bulletin board announcing in bold script that the government, suppressor of Islam, had forbidden Shaykh Kishk's coming to Minya. Thereupon the president of the Student Union, who was also the nominal head of the Islamic Society (this was not Sayf, for he claimed no official position), climbed the steps of the auditorium and called for calm to address the crowd. He reaffirmed the notice just issued and then launched into a stinging denunciation of the Sadat regime at the end of which he invited the assembled students to join him for the prayer on the mats of the quasi-mosque set up by the Islamic Society a few meters away. The call to prayer was then sounded and those who wished to do so formed rows behind this *imām*. In fact, no more than a couple hundred persons, principally the students with beards, joined in the ritual which was carried out with much solemnity. The greatest majority of those who stayed stood about watching, as if wondering what would happen next. When the prayer was completed, another of the bearded activists of the Society arose and delivered a fiery polemic once again in defense of Islam against those who would muzzle its preachers. Then he inaugurated a chant and, as though on cue, he led those at prayer in a march out of the campus gates. Their chant was this:

> There is no God but Allah,
> And we serve none but Him,
> We rise up in the way of God [*fī sabīl allah*]
> We strive to raise the banner,

For Islam is power [*quwa*] and youth [*shabāb*] and noble
  manliness [*futūwa*],
And honor for [our] fathers [*li-l-abūwa*].[30]

Those affiliated with the Islamic Society responded en masse in following this preacher's lead while a few hundred of the other bystanders also
joined the throng. As they marched toward the city center they turned to
other slogans, including denunciations of imperialism and "Crusades."
Riot police several ranks deep were waiting for the demonstration as they
approached the main square, about a kilometer away from the campus.
These police made a baton charge that quickly broke up the demonstration
and somehow a violent confrontation in the street was avoided. I was later
told by a senior official in the local Ministry of Education that Shaykh
Kishk has for many years been forbidden to leave Cairo, and restricted
from speaking publicly outside his mosque. Hence it was quite unlikely
from the start that he would be appearing in Minya or anywhere else in
Egypt to give an evening lesson. This man also said that he believed that
the rumored announcement that Shaykh Kishk was coming was probably
no more than a pretext for drawing the crowd and staging the illegal
demonstration. One could not help but notice that from this time onward,
it became common to see a few policemen in the vicinity of the campus
and sometimes trucks filled with the anti-riot squad of the Central Security Forces stationed quietly at the major intersection between the university compound and the city center on occasions when the Islamic Society
was holding gatherings on the campus. Although no efforts were made to
constrain activities within the perimeter of the colleges, plainly a decision
had been taken to discourage a repetition of this eruption of Islamist
protest onto the city streets.

Proposed café canceled.   Another confrontation took place on December 27, 1978, on the campus of the College of Arts, this time bringing university administrators and not just students into direct conflict with the
Islamic Society. It happened when the Islamic Society was conducting a
Sūq khayrī, that is, a sort of "charity bazaar," on the campus grounds at
which they sold fundamentalist publications, tapes, and various parapher-
nalia associated with the movement in addition to certain household
items. The affair was staged both to raise funds (an admission was charged
for entry in exchange for a ticket labeled *tabarruʿ,* i.e., "contribution")
and, as became quite apparent, as another occasion for fundamentalists to
demonstrate their prowess. As had been the practice before, it was cospon-
sored by the Islamic Society and the Student Union.

The clash occurred when the Islamists who had arranged the bazaar refused to vacate the premises after the several days allotted for it had passed. Instead, they insisted on holding on to the area because, they said, it had just been leased to a local merchant who was going to set up a café on that site. It should be noted that at this time there were no such facilities on the campus, not even so much as a coffee and tea stall for student use. The Islamists objected because they felt that a café would only encourage idleness and mixing of the sexes which they regarded as forbidden by Islam. Negotiations then followed, at the end of which the university officials agreed to cancel plans to allow a café to be established on the campus. Interestingly, I later discovered that the particular merchant who had obtained the franchise for the café was a relatively young businessman who already operated a large shop selling sweets in the city. He was a person who had a beard and always wore a white cap on his head. In his shop one commonly hears Qur'an chanting and sermons playing on his tape recorder, and he frequently steers the conversation around to Islamic topics. He was, in other words, from all appearances very well disposed toward, if not a partisan of, the fundamentalist movement. The fact that he would be the agent of this purported corruption rather than a Copt or worse, a local Greek entrepreneur, is yet another of the ironies reminding the observer that the slippage between ideology and practice may be as great in Upper Egypt as elsewhere.

Copts attacked. The outcome of the wrangle over the café precipitated by the occupation of the site by the prolonged charity bazaar upset a number of students. Once again it spurred the greatest concern among Copts, whose complaints were necessarily muffled lest their objections be recast to their detriment in a sectarian light. Already the local rumor mill was buzzing with accounts of incidents of Islamist provocations in the city and extending into the countryside. Insults, beatings, and acts of vandalism directed against Copts, it seemed, were becoming common. One of the most violent incidents carried by the grapevine had occurred in a village some twenty kilometers from Minya, called Tawfiqiya, at the end of Ramadan, late August, 1978. The onset of the clash is tangled and variously rendered, but the key event was the killing of an elderly Coptic priest in his home by local Islamic fundamentalists. No reports of such incidents, including this murder, were carried in the Egyptian press at this time. The unstated policy of suppressing indications of confessional tensions in the official media was then self-evident. However, one could find coverage of these happenings in the foreign press at the time. For instance, *Le Monde*, on September 4, 1978, carried an ample account of the above-mentioned crime written by their regular correspondent in Egypt, J.-P. Peroncel-Hugoz, with the headline: "Le Meurtre d'un Prêtre Copte par des Intégristes Musulmans Suscite une Vive Emotion dans la Communauté Chrétienne."

Angered over the way that university authorities had instantly caved in to the demands of the fundamentalists and in the absence of any meaningful process of appeal a group of a couple dozen student moderates who opposed this decision took an unusual initiative. On the evening of January 3, 1979, they gathered together in a college classroom and announced their intention of remaining there, staging an occupation of their own, until they were granted a hearing with the governor of the Governorate to discuss their grievances. A few hours later, however, that same night, as news of their protest quickly spread, a large group of bearded members of the Islamic Society marched to the campus from their stronghold in the University City. They broke into the room, which had been barricaded shut, and with fists, sticks, and odd pieces of broken furniture, they attacked their detractors, severely injuring a number of them. The police finally came and broke up the mêlée, arresting no one although assisting several of the victims who required hospitalization.

This open clash involving serious injury and requiring the intervention of police on the campus roused an entirely new level of concern among students and others. Apart from the outrage felt especially by those in sympathy with the protesters, the introduction of blatant thuggery in the name of religion brought forth the real prospect of a cycle of retaliation playing upon factional and sectarian divisions. Very shortly after this, in response to an outpouring of student demand and very likely in consultation with local government, university officials announced the convening of an extraordinary disciplinary board (*majlis al-ta'dīb*) to handle the matter. Four days after this, the Copts celebrated Christmas, and it was widely feared that this feast would provide the Islamists with an occasion for further displays of defiance. Police patrols and army vehicles moved through the streets of Minya in force during the next several days. All churches were provided with armed guards at their entrances as the war of nerves continued to escalate.

City government offices occupied. During the night of February 10, 1979, a handful of Islamic Society members broke into Minya's municipal government building and claimed to be occupying it as a step toward the declaration of Egypt as an Islamic Republic. Only a week before, the Ayatollah Khomeini had returned in triumph to Teheran, an event that had been celebrated with unbounded enthusiasm by the local militants. When this group was discovered in the morning, the police were summoned and quickly routed them out, leaving a heavy guard posted outside the building for some time afterward. Once again, no arrests were made. While some shrugged off this gesture as a youthful prank by confused Islamist millenarians, others in the community were not at all amused. Among the latter were many who remarked more and more openly on an apparent paralysis on the part of local law enforcement officials. It was widely held that they were under orders directly from Cairo to act with extreme gentleness toward the fundamentalists, probably so as not to allow local incidents to build into a national crisis.

Reaction to Camp David Accords. Aggravating incidents occurred steadily over the next several weeks, but the proximity of an event of major international significance finally brought tensions to a new climax. It also brought to the surface an overt political challenge on the part of Minya's Islamists. On the morning of March 27, 1979, members of the Islamic Society set up barriers and formed a picket line before the gates of the campus. They then declared that they were closing down the university that day. Students would not be permitted to enter. They were acting in protest against Sadat's signing of the Camp David Accords which had just taken place in Washington, D.C., a scene that had been broadcast repeatedly with great fanfare on Egyptian television. By accepting this treaty, they said, Sadat had betrayed Islam and the Palestinians. But on this occasion, their message took a particularly sharp turn. They had displayed, as usual, a number of posters which echoed and elaborated their slogans. Among them was a quite unusually inflammatory "poem" directing their objections toward Sadat personally in a manner designed to convey insults. Its first line reveals the substance of its fairly predictable contents: "*Ya bayyāʿ al-dīn wa-al-waṭan*," that is, "Oh you who have sold out religion and homeland." This kind of public abuse was not to be taken lightly in Sadat's Egypt. Neither the police nor the university officials reacted immediately to this maneuver which succeeded in preventing classes that day. But the gravity of this action could not allow it to pass unchecked. A new bold disregard for authority was stirring in the Islamic Society. The fear that they might act again, that they could close the university down whenever they chose, began to be expressed among faculty and administration.

Hostages taken. Shortly after this closing, there came an official response to this increasing assertiveness. It occurred as the Islamic Society seemed to be tentatively extending their domination of the campus into a few parts of the city itself, starting with certain mosques. On Friday, March 30, just after the university had been shut down the police came out in force in the early morning and surrounded a large mosque in one of the city's poorer districts. It was a *jam'īya* mosque closely associated with fundamentalist ideology and presided over by a popular bombastic orator, Shaykh Umar, whom his congregation fondly compared to Khomeini and whose preaching will be examined in detail in later chapters. As I was told later, the Islamic Society had planned a massive protest to follow after the Friday noon prayer at this mosque. The police had decided to move pre-emptively, stopping not just the march but the prayer and sermon too.

The fundamentalists were furious at this intervention by the government and they immediately sought to exploit it as a clear and intolerable assault on Islam. Later, on the university campus where they were the masters, they called a rally to denounce this closing of a mosque in tones of righteous defiance and indignation. That evening, a large number of them staged a demonstration of a sort familiar from other occasions, but this time conducted with a new measure of calculated provocation. They marched into the city center and proceeded to pray the evening prayer in the middle of the street on an important bridge, thereby blocking vehicle traffic in both directions and causing enormous congestion. Patience was not always in evidence among those who were being held up by this display and the air was thick with the portents of a confrontation. The police arrived and quickly surrounded them and it ended without incident. But a couple of days later, the news flashed through the student community and outward in all directions that four leading members of Minya's Islamic Society had been arrested and had already been sent to be detained in Cairo.

The remainder of the Islamic Society, led by Sayf, responded immediately by seizing control of the student residence block, University City, in a sort of paramilitary fashion. They expelled other occupants and sealed the entrances, but not before they had taken approximately thirty Coptic students whom they declared their hostages. They issued a statement demanding the release of their arrested comrades, threatening that otherwise, they would kill the Christians they held. Local government officials tried to negotiate an end to the occupation but without success. The help of several religious leaders, including the aforementioned Shaykh Umar, was also enlisted but no breakthrough was reached. Finally, after two days of stalemate, about a thousand troops arrived by train in Minya and were trucked to the housing compound where they formed an armed cordon around the site. Food and water were cut off as the face-off continued. Volleys of stones, bottles, and rubbish from the bearded students were met by intermittent wafts of tear gas and calls from the bullhorn outside for surrender. Various auxiliaries also took to the streets, mostly in support of the embattled Islamic youth, including a march by veiled women students from their hostel about a kilometer away. On the fourth day, a settlement was finally reached. The exact terms were variously reported but it appears that it apparently included some pledge of amnesty. The captive Copts were released unharmed. However, from then on, police were posted permanently at the University City and they were also appearing far more frequently on the outskirts of the campus precincts. Then, within a week, the other shoe fell. Word went out that some twenty-five fundamentalists were now being detained by the Minya police.

Sadat's response. This unprecedented sweep, small as it was, stunned Minya's militants. But before they could mount a response an event on an altogether different scale occurred which had a seismic effect on the entire situation. On April 14, 1979, on very short notice, President Sadat called for the faculty and administration of the universities of Minya and Asyut to attend a special meeting to be held at Asyut University. These cumulative local events were suddenly cast into official and national significance by a striking speech and public discussion of universities and Islamic organizations which was held by President Sadat in Asyut, the largest city in Upper Egypt, some eighty miles south of Minya. At this gathering, which was broadcast on radio and television and then rebroadcast several times over the next few days, Sadat delivered a speech that was followed by an open question-and-answer session which dealt entirely with the problem of Islamic activists and their disruption of academic life. At times appealing, at times menacing, his remarks went directly to the heart of the issue of the conflicts that had become the overwhelming preoccupation of everyone at Minya University. In brief, Sadat announced that the government would no longer tolerate the disruption of education by these undisciplined elements and that the abuse of religion as a cover for illegal political organizations would also be met with strict rebuke.

At this time Sadat was seeking to identify himself very closely with Carter and the Carter image, a process that had climaxed with Carter's almost apocalyptic reception in Egypt when he had visited it in early 1979 as part of the Camp David process. Sadat's small gestures imitating Carter were manifold in these months, and one of them was the idea of a "town meeting" which Carter had launched in America. This speech and its discussion setting was apparently modeled on this supposed Americanism. A more formal speech in terms of policy, dealing with the same matters of

Islamic Societies and order in the universities and in the nation was delivered three days later in Cairo at 'Ain Shams University. This text was printed in its entirety in the semi-official newspaper, *al-Ahrām,* and the broadcast was repeated more than once on radio and television. The Asyut speech and discussion session were also printed verbatim in their entirety in *al-Ahrām* on April 15, 1979.

As a local event, this speech was quite remarkable for two reasons. First, it exposed publicly, as had never been done before, the situation in Minya as both grave and as under full government surveillance. Reversing in one blow the earlier total blackout in the press, Sadat himself was now at last presenting before the entire nation the indictment against the Islamic Society's behavior. Furthermore, he was doing so in great detail, describing specific incidents, naming names and dates, reading directly from a police dossier which he had before him. He spared no words reprimanding not just the fundamentalists but the faculty and other university officials whom he called on to instruct the youth in the development of responsibility, order, respect, and patriotism. In addition, the speech had the effect of reestablishing in the popular mind the image of a president who was indeed in control of the society's complex parts. Despite the apparent neglect of Minya and the mounting problems it was enduring at the hands of Islamic militants, the truth was now on full display, namely that Sadat had known all along and was only waiting for the right moment to set things right. A substantial undercurrent in his speech was the reiteration of a major theme of the last year and a half since his peace initiative had been launched. It promised a new era of prosperity in Egypt just over the horizon provided its citizens recover the traditional virtues of cooperation, hard work, faith in God, and confidence in their leader who liked to call himself the "father of the Egyptian family."

The total effect of this speech went well beyond the considerable public-relations impact it had on the beleaguered citizens of Minya and elsewhere who were caught up in anxieties over the Islamist wave. In the days following the speech, I heard from several acquaintances that a series of very senior officials from several ministries had suddenly been descending upon Minya to issue special new instructions with regard to their policies toward the Islam movement. The local directorate of Religious Endowments was one office where such a distinguished superior called, but others responsible for education, justice, and internal security also had their visitors sent to issue revised marching orders. The local directorate of Religious Endowments received instructions to step up the efforts of Azhari preachers in their campaign to combat the confusion spread by the fundamentalists. Also, mosques without assigned preachers, which in many cases the fundamentalists had virtually taken over, were to be reclaimed and brought under the control of the bureaucracy by hiring Azhar-trained schoolteachers to preach. Thus a spurt of ostentatious official concern was suddenly inaugurated, but as time would tell its momentum would soon fade.

Leaders arrested. Also, not surprisingly, shortly after Sadat's bolt from heaven from the podium at Asyut (the domestic equivalent of his famous sudden moves in foreign policy matters which he fondly called his "electric shock diplomacy") a further crackdown followed in Minya. On April 19, 1979, the leadership and the core of activists of the Islamic Society of Minya, including Sayf, were apprehended and jailed. Also the work of the extraordinary Disciplinary Board, which had not yet been heard from, was now declared to be completed and its verdicts and sentences were announced.

Summer lull. The period of final examinations began in early May at the university and proceeded without serious incidents although tension remained high. However, it was now clear that the grip of the Islamic Society on the campus had been broken; student identification cards were now often checked by security men at the gates. With the end of the academic year, the University City was also largely vacated. Thus, over the summer months the gathering spot for what remained of the student fundamentalists shifted to other locations, most prominently to a small, recently built mosque just inside the compound of a major hospital that was close to the older part of the city. For the next several weeks the bearded ones and their sympathizers kept largely to themselves, as they waited for the outcome of the legal proceedings against their leaders.

Abu Talib's address. One final significant event illustrating the restored confidence of the government and the resilience of the Islamic Society occurred at the end of the summer, a few weeks before I left the field. Without remarking any published announcement, as seems typical of such affairs in Upper Egypt, I found out on August 13, 1979, that Dr. Sufi Abu Talib, the President of the People's Assembly (the Egyptian parliament) would be in Minya that very evening to deliver a public address in the auditorium of the Young Men's Muslim Association. It turned out to be a crowded and yet quite dignified affair that brought together all manner of dignitaries including the governor of the Governorate, ranks of senior functionaries, and the elite of the regional Azhari *shaykhs*. The hall itself was adorned with colorful bunting and banners welcoming the special guest amid Islamic and patriotic slogans. Among those sharing the platform with Dr. Abu Talib was a nationally known Azhari *shaykh,* now retired, who had once been a celebrated radio personality. The evening's program opened with some Qur'anic verses recited by a professional chanter who had been invited for this purpose. Then the elder Azhari was called upon and he spoke for almost an hour touching on themes of Islam's glories and the modern world's need for religious guidance.

At last, after prolonged introductory courtesies, the floor was turned over to Dr. Abu Talib. His topic centered on the progress of a special commission of which he was the head that had been charged with restructuring the Egyptian civil and criminal codes in order to bring them into conformity with the *sharī'a.* As former dean of the School of Law at Cairo University and later as president of this preeminent Egyptian academic institution, he was abundantly qualified to direct this task. But, needless to say, the commission's work was surrounded by heated religiopolitical controversy. Earlier that year, Sadat had overstepped the normal procedures of the Parliament to introduce a new liberalized Personal Status Code which was fiercely criticized by fundamentalists.[31] Now, the prevailing opinion in these same circles was that the government was stalling, perhaps reneging, on its promises to eliminate the influence of the European laws which had been the basis of Egypt's modern judicial system since the time of its introduction in the nineteenth century. This issue of establishing the basis of law in the *sharī'a* serves perhaps as the central point in the debate over whether a nation may be considered to be truly "Islamic." As such, fundamentalists demand it while many ordinary Muslims, seeing it as a step toward reform, also tend to favor the suggestion in principle. But as Dr. Abu Talib pointed out that evening, the *sharī'a* is an archaic jurisprudential artifice, not readily translated into the cultural idiom of the contemporary world. Nevertheless, he emphasized that virtually all of Egypt's current laws, regardless of their inspiration by European civil and criminal prototypes, were wholly compatible with Islam. He was alluding, of course, to the considerable technical features of the question familiar to experts that render this convoluted form of "traditional law" all but impossible to implement as a wholesale replacement for the application of modern codes and their procedures.[32] In fact, however, Dr. Abu Talib did not go into these specialized dimensions of the question. He concentrated rather on the accomplishments of the commission which, he noted, had very nearly completed its work. He assured his listeners that he and his colleagues expected to finish it by the following November after which time the few new measures required to bring Egypt's laws into compliance with the *sharī'a* could be enacted through legislation.

But as it happened, Dr. Abu Talib's speech was upstaged at approximately its halfway point by a sudden commotion at the entrance. Pushing their way through the overflow of the crowd huddled near the auditorium's doors there arrived en masse some fifty bearded members of the Islamic Society and at their head was Sayf, who had only recently been released from jail. Immediately a nervous quiver went through the audience as the fundamentalists moved to places around the perimeter of those seated. They remained fairly calm through the remainder of the distinguished guest's address, but in the question-and-answer period that followed decorum eroded quickly. With visibly increasing impatience Sayf sought to be recognized by the chair in order to pose a question, but he was clearly being ignored. Finally as a number of his supporters turned to heckling the moderator for overlooking their spokesman, Sayf was called on for his question. A hush fell over the assembly as Sayf immediately broke the grip of the two men holding him on either side who were undoubtedly plainclothes police officers. Then, as all eyes turned toward him, he left his place in the far corner of the hall and marched to the podium and took the microphone in hand. He then launched into a forceful denunciation of the government for its purported abuse of Islam. A fair portion of this stately public was obviously agitated and some were visibly outraged by this rude behavior. Cries arose from the floor for him to sit down and show respect to their visitors. Eventually, amid overloud repetitions of "thank you" and a little muscle, an Azhari *shaykh* succeeded in wresting the microphone from Sayf whereupon he proceeded to deliver an excited counter-sermon. The scene grew raucous and ominous as many of the fundamentalists pressed forward to the front of the hall. Finally, the governor of Minya managed to get the microphone back from the *shaykh* and he quickly handed it over to the Qur'an chanter. As the din continued a very brief perfunctory recitation was intoned whereupon the master of ceremonies hurriedly thanked the guests and the audience. At that a score of police in uniform and plainclothes converged around Dr. Abu Talib and, forming a flying wedge, they hustled him through the crowd, out the exit, and into a waiting sedan that departed immediately. Those who witnessed the event could not help but conclude that an assault, if not a riot, had only narrowly been averted.

But no less interesting for those who had been present was the coverage this event received in the national media. Two days later, on August 15, 1979, a news story appeared in *al-Akhbar* that mentioned Dr. Abu Talib's visit to Minya and reported on the address. It gave as its headline that the committee studying the application of the *sharī'a* expected to finish its work in November. Nowhere in the article, however, was there the slightest hint alluding to the other "real event" which made the speech so memorable, namely the outburst that almost ended in a physical confrontation. It should be noted that a number of reporters from Cairo had accompanied Dr. Abu Talib and were seated prominently on the stage during this whole affair, bending intently over their note pads. I realized in retrospect that what I had witnessed was a small example of the way happenings of religiopolitical sensitivity in Egypt are simply filtered out of official information sources. An awareness of this sizable flaw in the credibility of the nation's public voice also provides important insights into the context of preaching to which we now turn.

5 The Sermon as Public Discourse

The era following World War I was characterized throughout the Middle East by a growing anti-colonial sentiment. A mounting popular thrust for political independence, economic development, and cultural autonomy was voiced largely through such secular ideologies as Arabism, nationalism, socialism, or liberalism, which frequently overlapped with activists' initiatives seeking variously to revive, to modernize, or to reform traditional indigenous and notably religious institutions. In Egypt, these developments had already begun to stir up a discernible mass consciousness several decades earlier. The 'Urabi uprising of the early 1880s, with its battle cry "Egypt for the Egyptians" and featuring the novelty of leaders addressing enthusiastic crowds in the colloquial dialect of Arabic provides a double historical landmark. Not only did it precipitate the military intervention that led to the long British occupation but it aroused an awareness of new and contrary possibilities that spread rapidly not only through the growing population of the cities but into the very fabric of peasant village life.[1]

These varied currents reached their climax through the virtually bloodless revolution of July 1952, led by a faction within the army known as the Free Officers. However, in the next decade, and especially after facing the disillusionment that followed the collective shock caused by the sudden and devastating military defeat at the hands of Israel in 1967, stubborn questions continued to arise regarding the applicability of these ideologies. Increasingly these doctrines of progress were perceived as alien and inherently unsuitable. Many would begin to say that imported visions of society had now been tried in the Middle East and been proven failures. Therefore inspiration from outside sources should yield to authentic, native solutions.[2] In place of these spurned promises forged elsewhere, widely depicted in the extreme terms of the Cold War slogans as the alternatives of East or West, that is, exploitative capitalism versus repressive communism, Islam was advanced as a "third way." Islam was described as offering an ideology in its own right, which was divinely sanctioned and hence far superior to those of mere human provenance.

Some regimes in the region paid little more than lip service to the interpretation of this crushing defeat as a decree of divinely ordained "destiny" or *qadr*. But others, including Egypt, reacted more sympathetically to the initial signs of this religious resurgence. Many leaders began to move, cautiously at first, toward a more openly displayed integration of Islam into the fabric of state policy both in an effort to explain the disaster and to mobilize religiously minded citizens toward furthering national objectives.[3] Already in the last few years of his life, ʿAbd al-Nasir had begun sounding this motif of religiosity, whereas his successor, Anwar Sadat, brought these themes still more conspicuously and more consistently to the forefront through various official statements as well as his personal image. In one of his first broad declarations, for instance, entitled *A Plan for Political, Intellectual and Administrative Action*, issued in August 1972, Sadat asserted that "our socialism emanates from our heritage and from our faith" adding that it was scientific because it was Arab.[4] He also encouraged the formation of religious activist groups in various politically strategic settings, notably on university campuses, as a countermarch against the cadres still loyal to an earlier Nasirist vision.

This attempt to fuse the primordial ties represented by Islam with the loyalties characteristic of a modern political community has been variously described. The resulting "integrative revolution,"[5] or "Islamization of nationalism,"[6] emerged well before the so-called fundamentalist trends evidenced by "the veto power that Islamic consciousness continues to exercise over the whole realm of political ideology and action."[7] In many instances, this process has brought the traditional symbols of Islam and the modern symbols of the nation-state into such close conjunction that they not only overlap, but also, in the eyes of many, seem to coincide. Indeed, even beyond the boundaries of the state as such, as Michael Hudson has pointed out, "the profound significance of Islam as a component of Arab identity lies in its pervasiveness in society, its integrating function beyond kinship, its adaptability and its socio-political values."[8] Perhaps nowhere in recent Egyptian history is there a more finely nuanced and politically pregnant example of this fusion than in the speech delivered by Sadat as a sort of secular sermon before the Knesset in Jerusalem as the centerpiece of his epochal visit to Israel in November 1977, when he inau-gurated his peace initiative.[9]

In an effort at formal analysis, David Apter has described recent Egyptian political culture as organized around a unitary principle that tends to be personified in a "messianic leader" whose legitimacy is founded on a "political religion" of a type he calls the "mobilization system." Such a regime, he suggests, "begins by politicizing all political life. As a result, politics as such disappears. . . . Progress is its faith. Industrialization is its vision. Harmony is its goal."[10] While this description may have been most immediately applicable during the era of 'Abd al-Nasir, that is, prior to the liberalizations that were haltingly begun under Sadat and have continued somewhat problematically with Mubarak's administration, certain broad tenets of this depiction retain their relevance. The major difference that should be added points to the manner and the extent of the use of Islamic symbols and Islamic institutions in recent years, not just by the state but also by those who oppose it.[11] In fact, a parallel between the popular enthusiasm framed in religious terms arising since the 1970s and the ear-lier appeal of secular ideology has been noted by any number of observers. Saad Eddin Ibrahim, for instance, in reviewing trends of the 1980s, has suggested that "religious populism is proving to be the functional equiv-alent of Nasser's national socialism."[12]

It is within this wider context that our essentially ethnographic investi-gation of preachers and sermons in a provincial capital finds a place. For here, quite concretely, it becomes evident that an official strategy of appro-priating traditional religious symbols in the course of what amounts to a power struggle between different social groups and rival interests can very quickly blur any boundaries that might normally obtain between zeal for piety's sake and straightforward political activism. Almost unavoidably in such a setting, the government's calculated adoption of the religious man-tle has the effect of starting or greatly escalating a sort of unruly bidding competition. The volatility of such a process results in large measure from the fact that it is conducted in more than one mode simultaneously. Not only are bids advanced, as it were, between supporters and dissenters of specific policies or of an entire regime, but by pious voices seeking primar-ily to protect what is essentially religious from profanation by mundane abuses. Meanwhile all invoke the same symbols. The result may be a sub-tle or even strident conflict of interpretations. But frequently such circum-stances lead to the appearance of new forms of expression which claim for themselves the contested authenticity. A process of rapid ideological infla-tion caused by a flooding of the opinion market through the formidable

mechanisms of officially controlled mass media may almost spontaneously produce a new, more convincing currency.

One highly visible example of this cycle, in the realm other than rhetoric,
may be witnessed in the general area of fashion and dress in Egypt. Emerging from two decades of relatively drab socialist quasi-uniforms that suited
the new post-independence generation of the nation's swelling industrial-
sector workers and the burgeoning corps of functionaries, shading off in the
direction of discrete *haute couture* for those who could afford it, the mid-
1970s saw the introduction of a distinct and, until then, largely unfamiliar
wardrobe. It featured garments that covered the body fully while evoking
vaguely ritualized overtones, notably in the addition of veils for women and
girls and an assortment of caps and turbans for men and boys. This new self-
declared religious ensemble was first noticed among women students at the
university and from there it spread steadily among both younger and older
participants to offices, shops, and factories, burgeoning into what was soon
widely described as a movement.[13] Not the least of the most dramatic indicators of the strength of this shift was the appearance of a streamlined version of this gown and veil combination among female pupils. For in some
instances, notably in Azhari institutes for girls, it began to be prescribed as
the school uniform, usually replacing the variously colored simple trouser
and jacket styles which had been the standard dress of most such public educational facilities in the past. Those who promoted the adoption of this garb
cited such factors as convenience, modesty, or cost; regardless of these supposed utilitarian advantages, the wearing of such garments was explicitly
meant to declare that one adhered to a purer or stricter code of Islamic values. Men also shared in this trend, as has been noted, principally by growing beards. However, a number of other marked items of apparel could be
employed that served to signal this commitment more elaborately, such as
favoring white over other colors, wearing a loose fitting *galabīya* of a certain
formal cut, the preference of sandals to shoes, and the choice of a skull cap
or turban. Nevertheless, the female versions of this fashion trend have been
far more prevalent and clearly more controversial, which is understandable
given the significance of the charged questions surrounding the role of especially educated and working women in a contemporary society that insists
on its Islamic character.

This women's dress exhibits a remarkable variation in its choice of fab-
rics, colors, and design. But what all styles have in common is a long-
sleeved, ankle-length gown with a high neckline that tends to be ample
although in many cases such drapery may be belted and pleated in a manner that does little to disguise the female form. Initially, it seemed apparent that many of these gowns were homemade, some more skillfully than

others. From the start there were various degrees of envelopment reflected in differing styles. Thus it was not unusual to hear criticisms voiced, especially by men, that combined both aesthetic and ideological disapproval. President Sadat himself was not above such comments as denigrating such style of dress as a "tent" (*khayma*). Remarks of this sort, not surprisingly, easily provoked Islamic activists to reply in kind with derogatory barbs about Sadat's penchant for sartorial display.[14] But soon enough, quite chic and highly embellished versions of such gowns began to appear and they came to be included in many of Cairo's most exclusive dress shops alongside of or even displacing the latest offerings from leading European designers. In fact, by the mid-1980s, widely advertised Islamic fashion shows held in the city's best hotels were not uncommon. Of course, crowning this single outer garment and giving the whole its symbolic name was the head covering or veil. Here again the diversity is considerable, as a wide assortment of turbans, scarves, hoods, cowls, and snoods can be observed. But at least initially, the most widely worn style of head covering associated with this dress was a two-piece affair that combined a sort of knit cap covering the hair, over which was drawn a separate and larger piece cut in the style of a ski mask or balaclava. It was designed in a way that left the front of the face exposed from the chin to the forehead while covering the top, back, and sides, and extending down over the shoulders. The image suggested, as so many have commented, is that of a classic nun's habit. Nor was this patently religious, and more specifically Christian (since Islam has no direct analogue to nuns) implication resisted by many who chose to wear this outfit. Once, for instance, when the wearing of such garments was still fairly novel in Minya, I asked a group of young women students who were so attired what their form of dress meant. One replied, and then the rest nodded in agreement, that "it means that we are just like nuns (*rahibāt*)." "Except," she promptly added, "that we will get married." She was referring, of course to the veiled Christian nuns, who are a common enough sight in the area, as they staff schools, clinics, and other religiously sponsored facilities. Interestingly, this costume came to be called *al-zayy al-islāmī*, meaning simply, "the Islamic fashion," implying at least to some that other dress was somehow less Islamic.

This use of clothing, and perhaps most explicitly the head covering, as a vehicle for expressing values and meanings is by no means restricted to the Middle East. Here, however, it continues to reflect the high sensitivity attached to the public assertion of cultural identity. At the beginning of this century the wearing of the fez for men was frequently vested with high symbolic connotations that could acquire direct political implication, as occurred in Turkey where Ataturk declared its use an act of sedition and a capital offense. But at present, attention seems more centered on the dress of women. What is intriguing is that this particular style, which claims to assert the "tradition," is itself clearly an innovation. These garments, increasingly popular among younger Egyptian women (especially in the workplace), do not have a direct precedent. They are certainly a bold departure from the unmistakably traditional dress still commonly worn by Egyptian peasant women, namely the black dress and matching head scarf, over which is draped the voluminous black *malaya* or cloak. Nor is this current fashion in any direct way imitative of the type of face-covering veil that was the typical public apparel of urban and upper-class women in Egypt until the feminist movement after the First World War gradually succeeded in discouraging the practice.

In fact, one curious and intriguing feature of this process is its experimental dimension. One sees, for instance, among other temporary trends, occasional extremes or idiosyncratic adaptations of this garb among some of those who adopt it, lending a theatrical effect. Such exaggerations—for example the cases where devotees envelop their faces to such an extent that they are virtually blinded and must be led by the hand along the sidewalk or street—clearly illustrate this attitude of searching for the suitable symbolic vehicle. In other words, these young women have not gone back to wearing the *yashmak* of their grandmothers because, as one frequently hears, such old symbols have lost their meaning. Rather it is precisely because they retain their meaning that they have been now rejected as symbols.

A parallel process can be seen in the articulation of novel symbols conveying new meanings, advanced in terms of a return to the past, on the part of contemporary Islamic preachers. Their traditional role has lost its self-evident character and they typically find themselves at a tenuous juncture of social transition and religious uncertainty. The old formalism has been shattered and rendered obsolete whereas a new "struggle for the real" requires them to both redefine their own identity as well as give voice to the heritage of learning that they represent.[15] The preacher has emerged in very recent times in Egypt as a pivotal figure in the redefining of symbols imparting the religious legitimation and moral affirmation of new social, political, and economic options. It has produced a glut of untried possibilities that can both terrify and exhilarate as it sets before the pious and the impious not only the freedom to choose, but, inevitably, the need to make a choice.

The Ritual Rhetoric of the Mosque

The development of the Islamic sermon, or *khuṭba*, as a regular feature of mosque ritual (more specifically known as *khuṭba al-minbariya*, that is, "sermon of the pulpit" or *khuṭba al-jumʿa,* that is, "sermon of the [day of] assembly," meaning Friday) along with the evolution of the *khaṭīb,* the one who preaches it, has not been a subject of extensive interest among modern students of Middle Eastern history. In fact, many have virtually ignored this enduring oratorical dimension of Muslim social life even while presenting vast and marvelous detail dealing with countless other aspects of religious culture.[16] But it is also true that the sermon and the functions of the preacher are not well documented for many periods and places. Frequently these topics are scarcely mentioned, if at all.[17] Notable exceptions to this archival gap, however, include the chronicles of persons and events associated with the origins of Islam. Likewise, the accounts of many renowned centers of learning where religious and literary culture flourished have noted the part played by preachers. Also, in certain court circles where preachers enjoyed the patronage of powerful leaders, some record of sermons and their influence may remain. Finally, in the case of certain great movements, like that of the Wahhabis, where religious claims have served to justify the call to moral reform or even to political revolt, instances of the preaching involved in the mobilization of followers have been preserved.

Of course, incidents of preaching during the Prophet's own lifetime represent a special case insofar as these occasions came to be included in the *Sira* or the authoritative biographical compilations. Similarly, accounts from the first few generations immediately following his death also contain abundant references to the contents of preaching. A substantial number of important pulpit texts from this period have been preserved. In fact, a few such sermons—some by ʿAli ibn Abu Talib, for instance, or the one that Hajjaj ibn Yusuf, the severe Umayyad governor of Iraq, delivered to the congregation of recalcitrant Basra in 692—are considered paragons of classical Arabic rhetoric. As such, they are familiar to educated persons because they are commonly featured in the standard literature anthologies used in the Egyptian schools. This high regard for their literary merit has not, however, prevented numerous recent scholars from questioning their historical authenticity on philological as well as other grounds.[18]

Quite early during Islam's formative era, the assembling each Friday noon for congregational prayer had emerged as an important public forum with multiple functions. This occurred first at Medina and Mecca but it spread rapidly to other urban centers and then more gradually into their hinterlands, wherever the Muslim conquerors were establishing their settlements. The close juxtaposition of the new community's political or military headquarters alongside the central mosque also became a typical feature of urban design. For the free adult males among the Muslim residents, attendance at this weekly gathering was considered obligatory, amounting to both a moral and a civic duty. By consequence, the preaching that occurred at this ceremony provided a major channel of official public communication for the ruler to address the ruled. In the beginning the preacher had been the head of the community who spoke from the pulpit in his own person, that is, the caliph, or, away from the capital, his deputy, such as the general of an army or a provincial governor. They used the *khuṭba* not only to exhort but also to explain and interpret religious and moral elements of Islam. But at the same time, the Friday sermon was also the recognized formal setting for the promulgation of major decisions. It was also common therefore for such a preacher to issue warnings, to confirm loyalties, and to seek to mobilize opinion on issues of general political, social, economic, and military relevance.[19]

At its origin, the *khuṭba* of the mosque was patterned on the discourse that was customarily presented by the Prophet Muhammad himself during the Friday noon assembly for prayer in the courtyard of his house in Medina. It is this precedent, therefore, which is credited with establishing the practice as an essential component of orthodox Muslim worship. Like other exemplary behavior of the Prophet which subsequently became normative, this one too came to be codified as *Sunna*, and as such it is described and elaborated upon in legal treatises as the prescribed form of ritual.[20] However, as history advanced, changing this primitive community into a great civilization, major modifications continually took place. For instance, increasingly the mosque sermon evolved into a task that was not performed by the ruler himself, nor his deputy. Rather, it was delegated to a spokesman, usually a scholar, gifted in oratory, who was appointed to preach in the name of the caliph or governor. Even though such Abbasid rulers as the caliphs Mansur, al-Mahdi, and Harun al-Rashid "made it a point to lead the Friday prayers . . . as heirs of the Prophet" they left the pulpit to a trusted rhetorician.[21] This *khaṭīb*, or preacher, already in the annals of the Umayyad dynasty, was mentioned as a dignitary who received a stipend from the treasury, in recognition of his direct service to the ruler.[22] This formal designation of a replacement of the ruler amounting to a professional preacher, drawn normally from the ʿulamāʾ, soon became the established practice in the great mosques of major urban centers. Later, especially during the period of creative florescence that has frequently been referred to in the Orientalist tradition as Islam's Golden Age, or as the "High Caliphal Period,"[23] coinciding with the middle centuries of the Abbasid era, sophisticated literary criteria were applied to preaching.

These efforts resulted in a delineation of the proper stylistic features belonging to the *khuṭba,* variously defined as appropriate for different types of sermons. In time, the refinements of pulpit rhetoric came to be designated as an important subdivision in the "science of eloquence," or *ʿilm al-balāgha,* which borrowed elements from Greek, Latin, Persian, and other sources while producing its own original idiom rooted in the distinctive character of Arabic and inspired by Islam. While these literary developments were largely centered in elite circles, their influence was by no means restricted to these learned urban settings. For several centuries after these prescribed patterns of sermon composition and delivery were set forth they remained in circulation—abridged, canonized, and continuously incorporated into preaching manuals meant for instruction and demonstration.[24]

During this same era the institution of the *madrasa,* often regarded as the prototype of the university, was also emerging. Starting in Baghdad, and copied elsewhere, it soon became a distinct urban entity throughout the Muslim world. It began primarily as a center for higher legal and religious learning, although other related sciences were steadily added to expand its curriculum. Here the scholars destined to serve as judges, jurisconsults, teachers, and administrators, as well as preachers were provided with formal training while they also acquired aspects of socialization that consolidated them into a distinct scholarly class.[25] It was in this environment that such preachers as the celebrated ibn Nabata wrote their ornately cadenced and highly embellished sermons in the form of prose poems, employing archaic grammar and drawing heavily on obscure and antiquated vocabulary. They were often composing works within an established genre of belles lettres as much as producing texts for actual pulpit use.

Meanwhile, the cultivation of ordinary mosque preaching, like many other forms of religious and legal expression which originated and developed within the confines of specifically urban institutions, gradually spread out into towns and even villages. The Muslim tradition of traveling scholars together with the popular practice of pilgrimage—both to local saints and further, to celebrated shrines located at such sites as Fez, Kairouan, Cairo, Jerusalem, Baghdad, and especially the Hejaz—also greatly contributed to this diffusion.[26] Of course, this traffic in ideas and customs was by no means all in one direction, from the top down, as it were. Many features of a folk religion and extraneous traditions, emphasizing asceticism and mysticism, eventually had considerable impact upon the more learned.

This complex process of expansion and interpenetration, resulting in layers of adaptation and modification, has contributed steadily to the condition described by some as a general blurring of the strict meaning of "orthodoxy" with regard to Islam in many respects.[27] Nevertheless, in formal terms, it did not diminish continuing efforts, especially on the part of the *ʿulamāʾ*, to isolate the *khuṭba* of the mosque as a privileged rhetorical event marked by its own particular constraints and structure. Even today it is consistently held to be a distinctive oratorical moment, which is contrasted stylistically with other related forms of religious discourse.

Thus, while admitting some variation, trained scholars seeking to follow the principle of *taqlīd*, that is, to avoid deviating from the *Sunna*, have generally insisted upon preserving differences marking various forms of public religious address. Even so, it must also be recognized that their local applications clearly vary. Hence the *khuṭba al-jumʿa* has been defined over against such other recognized religious forms as, for example, the *muḥardra*, or "lecture"; the *dars*, or "lesson"; the *waʿẓ*, or "admonition"; and the *dhikr*, or "commemoration."[28]

One of the formal features of the Friday sermon which came to have a disproportionate significance in certain situations was a blessing upon the caliph or ruler which the preacher pronounced toward its conclusion. It was required that this invocation mention the sovereign by name. As a result, it sometimes happened that the sermon could function as the platform for the public declaration of the *ʿulamāʾ*'s ratification of one contender among a number of rival claimants to power. By the same token, in times of crisis, such as a siege, an insurrection, an interregnum, or an invasion, a sermon might provide the occasion for a signal to muster in a mass uprising or it could serve notice of shifting loyalties, by means of the preacher's naming of some emerging aspirant to the throne instead of its current disputed occupant. This practice could also place the one in the pulpit personally in a precarious situation. Thus history records a number of cases where a preacher was required to deliver a *khuṭba* in the midst of a vicious power struggle, where he would slur or whisper the name so as to make it inaudible or he would delete the blessing altogether.[29] However, the importance of this symbolic legitimation of authority was by no means always the equivalent of real dominion. In many cases, ritual obeisance could be made to some figurehead while some strong man actually governed. In fact, at least in some circles it became a proverbial usage to say that one had the *khuṭba* and *sikka* (the ruler's right to have his name inscribed on minted coins), meaning that such a person had the superficial trappings of power but not its actual substance.[30]

The deterioration of formal mosque preaching into the ossified rhetorical setpiece which it became, for the most part, in the postclassical period, is closely related to the stylistic requirements associated with this ritual idiom. But clearly the concurrent decline of Arabic learning due to the erosion of its institutions, notably under Ottoman hegemony, also contributed to this fossilization of what had once been a key channel of authoritative instruction and exhortation. Nevertheless, the symbolic force contained in this medium was not entirely lost. Thus, shortly after the parliament of the new Turkish Republic officially abolished the caliphate in 1926, several leaders in various Islamic lands laid implicit or explicit claim to the vacant title, including the Khedive Fuʾad of Egypt. Interestingly, he asserted this aspiration by assisting at a Friday prayer service which had the character of a state function at which his own name was evoked in the traditional formula at the end of the sermon.[31] This self-aggrandizing gesture was not widely noted outside of court circles, nor did his attempt to have preachers throughout the country initiate this practice meet with success.

From this, however, it remains evident that despite the fall of sermon rhetoric into relative obsolescence in early modern times together with the progressive marginalization of preachers as opinion leaders, the potential of the mosque sermon for religious as well as political life continued to echo. While this particular ritual forum was unmistakably undergoing a serious lapse of relevance in contrast to its classical importance, the role of Islam as a vehicle of both official and popular mobilization persisted. Consequently, those who have lately sought to reform this stilted idiom and by doing so to use the pulpit as a basis for redirecting their societies in the Islamist path have found themselves before a formidable dilemma.[32]

The seeming collapse of the traditional religiously inspired worldview in the course of de facto secularization under so many recent governments by no means indicates the extinction of the force latent in these religious symbols. Nor does this decline represent their abandonment by the ʿulamāʾ, who have long perceived themselves as its authoritative guardians and interpreters. Thus, enthusiasts who might have recourse to the pulpit as an innovative instrument in the service of their particular political goals inevitably discover sooner or later that the sermon does not lend itself freely to every message or every speaker. Just as mastery of the oratorical form does not alone suffice, so too, conviction, determination, and radical analysis, pointing left, right, or center, cannot be merely translated into the language of the *khuṭba*. It is as though communication from the mosque pulpit is only successful within a virtually indefinable range that nonetheless prompts recognition as the charisma of the Prophet.

6   Security and Belief in the Rhetoric of the Sermon

Amn *and* Imān: *Background and Current Use*

Anthropologists have often remarked that in a given sociocultural context a limited number of dominant themes representing central values have special importance as multivocal symbols. Such focal concepts stand out from among the vast webbing of images for their greater condensation, broader applicability, and more primordial attraction. Frequently, one of the most difficult tasks of anthropological exposition is, in the words of Evans-Pritchard, "to determine the meanings of a few key words, upon an understanding of which the success of the whole investigation depends."[1]

The Arabic terms "security," *amn*, and "belief," *imān*, which will guide our analysis of sermon material in this chapter, qualify as terms that belong to this exclusive category of potent symbols. Likewise, the terms "peace," *salām*, and "islam," *islām*, to be treated in later chapters, have such properties. The two sets are linked conceptually in a number of ways, as will be evident shortly, but we are separating them into two pairs in order to isolate certain patterns of "dramatic" usage. These four words are chosen because, in the words of Kenneth Burke, "what we want is not terms that avoid ambiguity, but terms that clearly reveal the strategic spots at which ambiguities necessarily arise."[2]

On a simple phonetic level, these four terms when strung together, *al-amn, al-imān, al-salām, wa-al-islām*, display an unmistakable internal rhyme which is a favorite feature of titles and slogans in Arabic as in other languages. The repetition of vowels and consonants combines with a metric flow, reminiscent of a good jingle. Of course, a morphological relationship also supports this acoustic resemblance, for *amn* and *imān* both derive from one root just as *salām* and *islām* are both derived from another single root.

All four of these terms are perfectly normal nouns used widely in reference to an almost unlimited range of topics in both modern colloquial Egyptian Arabic and in the classical language. However, the semantics relevant to these two linguistic environments may not always be easily equated. In addition to this overlap, the joining of these terms into a singsong sequence tends to qualify their individual elements taken singly, adding still another dimension of significance. The usage of this composite first struck me soon after I arrived in Minya when I went to a large mosque to hear an evening lesson to be given by a distinguished *shaykh*, an Azhari, who was visiting from Cairo. In what can only be called a magnificent display by a professional orator, he built his entire talk around these four terms, often repeating them together like a refrain. Alerted by that initial exposure, I began to notice that these terms recurred in many other instances of formal oratory, which led me to understand that they have a rhetorical force as a gestalt that exceeds their meaning as single lexemes. The foursome had a cohesiveness like the trio "faith, hope, and charity" or "truth, justice, and the American way." Fundamental among the factors that provide *amn* and *imān* with their semantic compactness is their frequent and significant use throughout the Qur'an. A concordance lists hundreds of entries for this one triliteral root. *Amn* and *imān* comprise only two forms of many, while others include such verbal and nominal meanings as:

AS A VERB

amn	to be faithful, reliable, to be safe, feel safe
amman	to reassure, safeguard, entrust, insure
amn	to believe
atmana	to ask for protection or a promise of security, insurance

AS A PARTICIPLE

mu'min	believer

AS A NOUN

amān	security, safety, peace, clemency, immunity from punishment
amīn	superintendent, custodian, chief; *as an adjective,* trustworthy
amānah	faithfulness, honesty, trustworthiness, fidelity, good faith
ta'mīn	protection, reassurance, guaranty, security, insurance[3]

From this same stem derives the Arabic word for "amen," which reaches English via the Hebrew where the cognates for "security" and "belief" have a similarly fertile polysemic quality.[4] The choice of the English gloss "security" for *amn* from among other candidates connoting trust, safety, peace, etc., is partially justified by its wide use as the Arabic term in direct translation for such cases as the (United Nations) Security Council which is *majlis al-amn.* Following this same pattern, *amn* is commonly used in formal references to modern police or matters they are concerned with in much the same way that American English speaks of "security personnel" or "security questions." *Imān,* on the other hand, in contemporary usage has immediate religious or socioreligious coloring. It is often used as a broad cover term for religion in general, its opposite being *kufr,* or "disbelief." Both in the Qur'an and in colloquial speech, the centrality of what we gloss as "belief" can hardly be overstated. Toshihiko Izutsu, in his penetrating semantic study on the ethico-religious concepts in the Qur'an, makes this point squarely:

> Just as *kufr* constitutes . . . the pivotal point round which turn all qualities belonging to the sphere of reprehensible properties, so *imān* "belief" or "faith," is the very center of the sphere of positive moral properties. "Belief" is the real fountainhead of all Islamic virtues; it creates them all, and no virtue is thinkable in Islam, which is not based on sincere faith in God and His revelations.[5]

Among the numerous citations in the Qur'an that could be drawn upon to illustrate the potency of this term, the following verses provide what is essentially a definition of what true "belief" consists in:

> Those only are believers [*al-mu'minūn*] who, when God is mentioned, their hearts quake, and when his signs [i.e., verses] are recited to them, it increases them in faith [*imān*], and in their Lord they put their trust, those who perform the prayer, and expend of what we have provided them, those in truth [*haqqan*] are the believers [*al-mu'minūn*]. (8:2–4)

We might also note that there is another term in contemporary Egyptian usage which translates as "faith" or "belief," namely *'aqīda,* derived from the root with a base meaning of "join together, knot, convoke." More precisely, *'aqīda* might better be glossed as "doctrine" or "creed," for this term only evolves later and does not appear in the Qur'an as a noun. In those few cases where the verbal form appears in the sacred text it bears a more literal reference and means "binding" or "knotting." Hence, *'aqīda* is originally a theologian's term, although today it is often used almost interchangeably with *imān* and the term *dīn*, which is the abstract term for belief systems of all kinds like the English word "religion." Certain semantic undertones still cling to these separate expressions, of course, and this is especially visible in the relation of *amn* to *imān*.

The Building-up of the Nation

We begin our discussion with the examination of a sermon that was preached on the special occasion of the visit of President Sadat to Minya in December 1978. This was the chief executive's first visit to this provincial capital in many years, and it was staged like a triumphant reception to honor the "hero of peace" and the "hero of the Crossing" (*'ubūr*, that is, the "crossing" of the Suez Canal in the October War of 1973), for Sadat had only recently been awarded the Nobel Prize for Peace along with Israel's Prime Minister Menachem Begin. Elaborate preparations were made, including the arrival of several thousand soldiers who lined the route of the motorcade like a human fence, with only a few paces between each. Local officials outdid each other in this great opportunity to display their enthusiasm and loyalty. They mounted lavish bunting and colorful banners inscribed with all manner of welcomes and laudatory attestations. The visit had been announced only a few days before it was to occur and the remarkable speed with which these decorous fixtures arose was only matched, curiously, by the way they were almost instantly cleared away within hours after Sadat's ceremonious departure. For the masses of peasants who crowded the streets on that day, many of whom benefited from transportation at government expense from their villages, it was a grand holiday.

One featured event of this visit was the attendance by Sadat and his sizable entourage at the Friday noon prayer at al-Fuli mosque. Often in his tours Sadat prayed the Friday noon prayer in local mosques, an event which is always noted by the media. In fact, it was common to see a front-page picture of Sadat in Saturday's newspaper showing him entering or leaving or at prayer in whatever mosque.[6] This service at al-Fuli was also broadcast live on national radio, for it is the practice in Egypt to present the Friday noon prayer on the radio, although this was the first time within memory that it had ever been done in Minya. It was preached by the regular *imām*, Shaykh Muhammad.

His introduction includes certain stylized opening phrases which are pro forma for every sermon, although a good preacher can turn these formalisms to his advantage by exploiting them for various rhetorical effects. Note how the four key terms just noted, while frequently heard with reference to contemporary Egyptian social life, are here reframed as modifiers of the society the Prophet established at Medina:

Praise to God, Lord of the world, who gives prosperity to workers and victory to warriors [*al-mujāhidīn*]. I witness that there is no God but God, he alone, no associate with him. He made us to love faith [*imān*] and he made it the ornament of our hearts and he has caused us to despise unbelief [*kufr*] and infidelity and disobedience. I witness that our master [*sayyiduna*] is the Prophet of God who built the society of Medina upon the strong foundations of security [*amn*] and belief [*imān*], peace [*salām*] and Islam [*islām*] and he made this the motto for believers: "They prefer others above themselves even though poverty be their portion, and he who is guarded against the stinginess of his own soul, those, they are the prosperous" (59:9).[7]

The sermon goes on in florid classical language to specify three promises that God had made, by way of the Prophet, to his faithful servants for their benefit in this world and the next. These promises are made to those who take the Prophet as "their excellent model, who follow his lead [*iqtadū bihi*] and who stand in excellent rapport with all people, for they are the ones who have security [*lihum amn*], they are the rightly guided." This emphasis on security continues to overshadow all other themes as the Shaykh enumerates the three promises. The first guarantees to mankind authority over the earth and its resources for man has been charged to seek here for his provision. The Shaykh stresses that produce will only be yielded by work, by striving, and by suffering. "For this reason," he continues, "God made men to love work in agriculture that security of nutrition [*amn al-ghadhā'*] will be realized and that every living creature will obtain all that he needs." To this, he adds a long quote from the Qur'an describing the earth's bounty as a sign of God's blessing (36:33 ff.) adding then a *hadīth*, that is, a saying of the Prophet expressing something similar. What should be noted especially in this remark is the idiom rendered as "security of nutrition." This was one of the ringing catchwords of Sadat and his domestic policy which recurs often in his speeches and it is echoed in a wide variety of official and quasi-official public announcements. The phrase is an Arabic version of the familiar phrase "food security," although when Sadat is speaking in English he at least sometimes called this the "green revolution."[8] However, I preserve the literalness of the Arabic in order to point out how *amn* bridges a number of different realms. Also, references to "security of nutrition" appeared on many of the banners which greeted Sadat, as might be expected in a predominantly agricultural area.

The Shaykh then adds that authority over the earth's resources includes industry as well as agriculture, for which testimony he enlists the Qur'an, by paraphrase as well as by quotation:

And just as provision on the earth is accomplished by work in agriculture, so it is also accomplished in the area of industry. The holy Qur'an strengthens our determination and directs our attention to different kinds of industries in what is related about the activities of ancient peoples, for the Prophet David, peace upon him, made shirts of iron with which the warrior was protected from attack of the foe as God, exalted be He, says: "We taught you the fashioning of garments to protect you from your violence, are you not grateful?" (21:80)

Following this, the Shaykh also mentions God's instructions to Noah for the building of the ark. These references to the importance of industry reflect another leitmotif of Sadat's domestic policy which the preacher restates in the idiom "security of industry" (*amn ṣanā'i*), an idiomatic parallel to the "security of nutrition." Then he brings both these slogans together in what he frames as the second promise of God to his faithful:

The second promise is the consolidation [*tamkīn*, that is, strengthening, firmly establishing] of religion [*dīn*]. This is realized in the security of nutrition and the security of industry, for any nation [*umma*] independent in its materials will need no others besides themselves as they take steps to build and construct and to promote the progress of work toward welfare in the afterlife as well as their welfare in this world. No enemy can take away these [resources] from [the nation] and for that reason, they consolidate the nation in its religion [*dīn*] and in its performance of good deeds, its link to its Lord, and the nations which strive for glory [*ghaza*, that is, esteem, strength, fame] and honor [*karama*, that is, nobility, magnanimity, prestige, munificence] are provided with these [resources] by heaven as they turn their eyes to God who gives and withholds, who makes happy and renders miserable, who exalts and brings low, for in His hand are all kingdoms, and He is mighty in all things.

The third promise raises security out of the sphere of human striving where the Shaykh had initially set it, beyond the idea that security permits a community to pursue successfully what religion bestows, to a sense of security as grounded purely in faith. Then, in summary, Shaykh Muhammad returns to the agonistic world of workers and warriors which is the forum for divine as well as human activity.

The third promise: In the establishment of [the nation's] full security [*al-amn al-kāmil*] and in the possession of its religious faith [*al-'aqīda al-dīnīya*] it shall fear God alone, for how shall it fear a creature when it has with it the power of the almighty Creator who responds to dangers when He is called upon and who uncovers evil? For God, exalted be He, entrusted [*aminit 'ali*] to the Quraysh two blessings, the blessing of nourishment in hunger and the blessing of security from fear. God, exalted be He, says: "They worship the Lord of this House who has fed them in hunger and who secures [*aminahum*] them from fear" (106:4).

These three good wishes God has written for his faithful servants who translate their faith into work and behavior [*tarjimū imānahum 'amalan wasalukan*] and who are not satisfied with raising their feelings in faith [*imān*] without action and who do not live pessimistically, isolated from life, satisfied merely to raise their voices. Oh God, provide for us and make us learn that heaven does not rain down gold or silver. For God, exalted be He, says: "God has promised those of you who believe and who do good deeds that He will make them successors on the earth as He has made those before them successors and He will establish their religion for them which He has approved for them and will give them, in exchange, after their fear, security" (24:55).

The sermon goes on from this point to recount the trials of the Prophet, specifically his painful disappointments in his native Mecca, whose leaders finally drove him to emigrate to Medina. There, with nothing but his faith, he established the society that became the nucleus of a new and blessed civilization. The preacher notes that the first act of Muhammad in Medina was the building of a mosque, wherein "he educated men to be knights [*farsān*] to subdue the Persians, to conquer the Byzantines and Caesar." Then, adds the Shaykh, the Prophet "set to work spreading love and brotherhood between the sons of this one society which he fixed firmly upon the foundations of security and peace."

We note here the reduction of the four foundations of the society of Medina (by analogy, contemporary Egypt) to two, namely "security and peace," a synopsis he repeats again later. These are the result of the "translation" of faith which he spoke of earlier. There is a sense in which these two elements belong together as experienced in the social order while the other two terms, *imān* and *islām*, are contrasted as spiritual and transcendent. The shift between these two frames, the physical and the metaphysical, is concretized by the shift from Medina and the lifetime of the Prophet to Minya and the present moment. The Qur'an and the Prophet are the common bond between these diverse times and places.

Shaykh Muhammad in this sermon attempts to bridge these realms by forging a syllogism that hinges on the equation of national self-sufficiency with the establishment of religion in society. The logic is charted in the three promises and then developed in remarks on how the Prophet himself struggled to unite factions and to establish a productive coordination (here expressed in a military image) in order to insure social harmony and hence material prosperity. The progression moves on two levels, culminating in the implication that the meaning of *imān* in the language of God corresponds to *amn* in the language of man. Contrarily, *amn* in God's talk has the meaning of *imān* in man's talk.

God's talk	Man's talk
God guarantees mankind authority over creation	Man trusts God's word, and accepts God's gifts
God's religion is secured by man, the social creature	Man strives in agriculture and industry, in obedience to God
Full security is based on faith in God's promises	Full security is assured through blessed self-sufficiency

The Shaykh employs an image that moves from minimum security to maximum security. It coincides with a movement from a promise to its fulfillment. They are linked by the assumption that the intervening step is synonymous in both instances, for the mastery of nature can only be accomplished by religion. Hence material prosperity is the triumph of God's providence. Man's efforts to obtain his security, coordinated by religious duties, result virtually automatically in success, leaving all credit to *imān*.

Two extremely important preoccupations underlie Shaykh Muhammad's expression here which I found to be practically universal, to various degrees of explicitness, in almost all sermons delivered in Egypt. First is the premise that security is lacking in contemporary society, or, stated positively, it is presently under siege. Hardly any religious rhetoric such as I heard can be understood without putting it in the perspective of this powerful and pervasive background sentiment that emerges in even the most unsuspected context. Of course, some *shaykhs* have developed this theme of being under assault to such a pitch that their sermons are virtual philippics denouncing the often vaguely specified enemies of Islam. Shaykh Muhammad is not one of these, although this sermon, delivered as it were, in the setting where it aspires to address a national (instead of local) audience is markedly more sociopolitically engaged than is normal in his case. This explicitness with regard to the sense of being under assault may also reflect some sort of outside influence upon the Shaykh in the composition of this particular sermon or an effort to meet external expectations. To what extent this or any of his sermons rely on ghostwritten trots, or cues from superiors, whatever their source, I cannot determine. But the general drift of this sermon as a loyalist affirmation, along with its ornate form, is quite consistent with Shaykh Muhammad's preaching on less officious occasions.

The second premise which underlies this sermon and will recur very widely, though not always overtly, is the identification of Islam with societal order and personal well-being in the most general sense. This is not merely saying that "religion" (meaning Islam) as a concept embraces a broader semantic range of worldly obligation and otherworldly benefit than does the correlative, more spiritualized term "religion" in contemporary English. That much is obvious. It is affirming also that most Egyptian Muslims tend to speak of and largely to perceive moral laws (meaning Islam's dictates) with a givenness that the contemporary Western mind might reserve to the laws of nature, as they are called. In other words, even though controversy may surround some moral or doctrinal question, no argument is allowed or even conceived of that appeals to any criteria above or beyond Islam.[9] Blaise Pascal's famous phrase that the God of Abraham, Isaac, and Jacob is not the god of the philosophers would lose much of its force here. The sense of an absolute "lawfulness" in God's creation makes no self-conscious Kantian distinction between a moral and a natural order. Thus one methodology seems to apply with only superficial modification to both "social" and "natural" sciences.

This sermon of Shaykh Muhammad also contains a seasonal feature that should be noted. It was preached on December 8, 1978, which was in the middle of the month of *dhu hajj* in the Muslim lunar calendar. During this month, when the holy places in the Hejaz are bursting with pilgrims, preachers frequently dwell on the events surrounding the Prophet's forced migration from Mecca. They highlight the adversity and rejection suffered by the Prophet in contrast to his own patience and endurance. Shaykh Muhammad's sermon has touched on these points repeatedly, while his evocation of the new society at Medina is rooted in an implicit comparison with present experience. He concludes the first part of his sermon with a *hadīth* of the Prophet that neatly ties together all four of the foundations: "The Prophet of God, prayers and peace of God upon him, spoke truly when he said: 'You will not enter paradise until you believe [*tu'minu*] and you will not believe until you show good will [*tuhabu*]. Shall I point out something to you? Oh, that you would do it! Show good will by making peace among yourselves.' "

Then follows a characteristic appeal for believers to be penitent before God. The litany of petitions which ends every sermon, includes in this case a special blessing for President Sadat, mentioned by name, recalling the practice of naming the Caliph in sermons in classical times. I never otherwise heard this done in Minya, although it frequently occurs in sermons broadcast on the radio. In fact, if Sadat himself is present at the mosque from which the broadcast originates, as is often the case, it seems to be quite common.

To summarize, Shaykh Muhammad's dramatic movement pivots on a metaphor that connects the historical achievement of the Prophet at Medina to the hoped for achievement of Egypt's future. Although he spoke of translating belief into work and behavior, on another level and with greater emphasis he has described the reverse process of translating hard work and good will into security. The fulfillment of God's promises to mankind and the full faith of mankind in these promises, that is, obedience, are articulated in the one code, which is spelled out in religious duties. Any shortcoming in belief will keep man from entering paradise while at the same time it hinders the establishment of security. As is implicit in this sermon, but comes out clearly in other addresses by Shaykh Muhammad, it is the commitment to the classically defined rituals of religion (prayer, fasting, almsgiving, pilgrimage, and so forth) that are the basic expressions of religion, and their performance in sincerity points the way to security while also demonstrating faith. It is for humans, therefore, to freely take what God freely offers. On earth, this transaction turns the blood and sweat of workers and warriors into peace, glory, and honor.

Integrity of the Revealed Word

An altogether different image of *amn* and *imān*, one that is simpler in its presentation but considerably more complex in its exposition, emerges in the sermons of the preacher already introduced as Shaykh Umar. He is a retired schoolteacher, formerly very active in propagandizing 'Abd al-Nasir's policies, though now he is the *imām* at a large mosque built and maintained by a *jam'īya*, or benevolent association. As framed in our initial typology, this sort of organization tends to coincide with the traits of the preacher as warrior rather than saint or scholar and this impression of militancy is borne out in any encounter with Shaykh Umar. In both his ideas and his style of delivery he affects more of the popular than the classical mode although he is a most accomplished practitioner of his particular genre of preaching. Though his admirers tend to be low-brow, they are not few. With apologies for the analogy, one might say that he would be more at home in the meeting tent than in the cathedral. Furthermore, his perceptions may be unsophisticated intellectually, but they are greeted by his listeners as inspired. By any standards, Shaykh Umar has extraordinary oratorical talent undaunted even though he is a septuagenarian.

One of his favorite rhetorical devices which he resorts to endlessly and which he frequently turns with magnificent effect is to string together lists of near synonyms, usually nouns or adjectives but sometimes whole phrases which he poses in apposition or opposition. Frequently such sequences exploit metrical and rhyming patterns inherent in Arabic morphology, but credit is also due to this preacher's sheer virtuosity in word choice and dramatic elocution. Unfortunately this vocal talent largely disappears when a sermon is reduced to a written text, and it is further diluted by translation. Shaykh Umar also has a gift for creating and sustaining rousing hyperboles which he often uses contrastively.

The following passage from a sermon delivered on January 5, 1979, gives a glimpse of the way he uses religious symbols in the introductory portion. This particular sermon kept his listeners attentive, if not spellbound, for close to an hour and a half. For another characteristic of Shaykh Umar is verbosity. As in the case of Shaykh Muhammad seen earlier, there is a certain amount in this preface that is formulaic, but Shaykh Umar masterfully turns the formulas to his own thematic purpose.

> I testify that there is no God but God and I testify that Muhammad is His servant and His messenger, the prayers of God, His commendations, His peace and blessings be upon him, and on his brothers, the prophets and messengers, and on his wives, the mothers of believers, and on his own, the people of his house, and on his companions and his community and those who follow his way [*sunna*] until the day of judgment. For God, exalted be He, said to the Prophet, prayers and peace of God upon him, when first he sent down upon him [something] from His holy book: "In the name of God, the merciful and the compassionate, recite in the name of the Lord who created, created man from the blood clot. Recite and your Lord is most gracious who taught men by the pen, taught man what he did not know" (96:1–5).
>
> The one who recites in the name of God does not lie [*lā yakdhib*]; the one who recites in the name of God stands in no need; the one who recites in the name of God is not lured into his own caprice, nor is he self-important; the one who recites in the name of God loves goodness [*khayr*] and piety [*birr*] in all people in every time and place; the one who speaks in the name of God does not speak of God except by what God has inspired in him; and in what God has spoken; the one who recites in the name of God reverences life and fears God in every condition and inclination; the one who recites in the name of God cannot possibly permit himself or his tongue or any of his members to perpetrate any vile deed or dishonorable act [*munkar*] in the past, present, or future.[10]

Therefore we see that the Prophet, prayers and peace of God upon him, came in complete trustworthiness [*al-ṣidq kullu*] and complete truth [*al-ḥaqq kullu*] and he transmitted complete trustworthiness and complete truth.

And we see that he educated his community [*umma*] from the first individual among his companions, both men and women, to believe in his truth [*ḥaqq*] and to pronounce in trustworthiness [*ṣidq*] to act in goodness, to undertake piety for the performance of good deeds in the love of peace [*salām*] and security [*amn*] in the love of creatures, in striving for the face of the Creator, majestic and sublime; and this is a demonstration of the internationality and humanity of Islam.

The Muslim, wherever, whenever, and however he is, is molded by the morals of God, exalted be He, and he pursues them by the guidance of Muhammad, prayers and peace of God upon him. He knows well the rights he has over himself to ward off disgrace, defectiveness, error, and foolishness and to ward off corruption and weakness. And he knows well the rights of God upon him and he avoids any mistaken assumption about God, any mistaken belief in God, any mistaken perception and any misstatement or any misrepresentation of God in whatever God did not say. And he knows the rights of others upon him, beginning with his parents and relatives, those near him and his companions and the companions of those around him or travelers, for he does not harm, does not sow discord, nor is he disrespectful nor is he unfaithful [*lā yakfir*] nor does he quarrel or shed blood, nor does he alarm or terrorize. Rather, he is total peace [*al-salām kullu*], total security [*al-amn kullu*], total goodness [*al-khayr kullu*].

For in the Islamic state [*dawla islāmīya*] there live together individuals and groups, states [*duwal*] and governments, a peaceful way of life with co-citizens [*mawaṭanīn*] wherever they are and whatever creeds ['*aqā'idahum*] they hold and Muslims have not been hostile either to individuals or to groups nor have they surrendered their homeland [*waṭanahum*] to their enemies, for they always provide for their homeland. They defend the land and safeguard their honor and they are always thriving in this world and in the next. They are always trustworthy [*ṣidqun*] in speech, truthful [*ḥaqqun*] in deed and bestowing benefit on great and small.

There live in their midst some, be they many or few in number, who do not believe in their creed ['*aqā'idahum*] and not one of them suffers harm in either his honor or his property in any way, large or small. There live non-Muslim minorities among Muslims, secure [*amīna*] in their practice, secure [*amīna*] in their families, secure [*amīna*] in their property. This is the morality of Islam among Muslims and the morality of Muslims in their Islam: Peace [*salām*], security [*amn*], piety [*birr*], goodness [*khayr*], love [*muḥabba*], protection [*ḥimāya*], supervision [*ra'ayya*] patriotism firmly established [*waṭanīya thābita*] that knows no treachery, no deception, no baseness, no malice.

But as for the enemies of Islam and of Muslims, they do not recite in the name of God, but in the name of Satan and in the name of raving madness, godlessness [*kufrān*] and tyranny. For they do not strive after trustworthiness [*ṣidq*], nor do they strive after justice ['*adl*], nor do they strive after truth [*ḥaqq*] but they turn matters around, turning them to their own self-interest, turning them to their own advantage, turning them to their own positions.

Thus we always see them in the vileness of their character, in the depravity of their customs, in the error of their worship; we see them to be a people of betrayal, a people of snatching, a people of trickery, a people of Satan. They do not adhere to responsibility nor to any contract, neither upon themselves, nor upon their honor, nor upon their property.

So we have seen it in the father of disbelievers [*āb al-kifār*] in dealing with the father of believers [*āb al-mu'min*] when he tries to justify his falsehood to Abraham, "for surely if you do not give up, I will stone you" (19:46) so that the father of disbelievers denies the truth of the Prophets, preferring what he received from his forefathers, and he wants to stone his son (Abraham) to death for the sake of his belief [*imān*] in God and his disbelief in idols.

This last section refers to an episode in the Qur'an which is partially recited. It records that shortly after Abraham is called to be a prophet, he invites his father to abandon his polytheism, whereupon the father threatens his son. From here the preacher goes on with other Qur'anic references illustrating the same point. He notes, for instance, the hostility of Pharaoh to God in refusing to grant Moses' requests. Then, without any overt transition, the preacher begins railing against more historically demonstrative enemies of God and Islam, beginning with what Shaykh Umar considers the most perfidious of races, the Jews, and sweeping along in turn, Christians, Communists, and eventually a bevy of contemporary or near-contemporary leaders of Arab and Islamic states, including President Sadat.

There are many features in this passage that make it a good example of how Shaykh Umar uses religious symbols in his preaching. Most immediately is the impression that the moral and social universe is divided between categorical absolutes, all black and white with no intervening shades of grey. Reverence for God, respect for the Prophet, devotion to Islam and being a Muslim appear to be so compactly interwoven one might almost regard them as identical rather than related. By semantic extension of value-laden terms such as *ḥaqq*, "truth"; *ṣidq*, "trustworthiness"; *ʿadl*, "justice"; *khayr*, "goodness"—terms which can, in other contexts, stand as substantives denoting God—Shaykh Umar elevates the Prophet, Islam, and Muslims to a logical fixity that seems to withdraw them from any contaminating involvement in an uncertain human world. The eternal, unchangeable, inscrutable source of these virtues has by association detached Muhammad, Islam, and, to some degree, Muslims, from historical particulars, freeing them from the world of limited possibilities in which they perforce otherwise participate. Shaykh Umar does not explore nor even recognize the complexities of history that impinge on moral judgment, but like the warrior he is possessed by the proximity and force of a perceived enemy whose stratagems he must reconnoiter, only to defend against or to attack as the occasion requires. Of course, taken purely by themselves, and motivated as they are by pious fervor, totalistic moral declarations are not rare, neither in the devotional language of Islam nor in other religions. In Shaykh Umar's case, however, they are more than isolated exclamations; they form the broad foundation for a pyramid of rhetoric which encompasses, as we shall see, a program of social and political action.

On the level of semantic consistency, an interesting problem appears in his insistence that security is enjoyed by non-Muslim minorities in the midst of Muslims. On the one hand security is so thoroughly identified with Islam that incorporated non-Muslims are depicted as secure simply by this association. On the other hand, however, security is so exclusively Muslim that it is not clear how any exception could include non-Muslims. This apparent non sequitur in Shaykh Umar's presentation masks exactly such a tension, for whenever Shaykh Umar baits Coptic Christians, as this sermon will go on to do most fulsomely, there is always a lofty attestation to the Islamic tradition of the *dhimmī*, the so-called "people of the book" or "protected" people. Despite this ideal, as despite all ideals, there have, of course, been occasions where Christians and Jews have experienced great insecurity and even massacres at the hands of Muslims, a most unfortunate reality not just ignored but emphatically denied on the surface of such statements by Shaykh Umar. No less certainly, Christians and Jews have in the past and most sadly continue to assail Muslims in various settings. But the point for Shaykh Umar is not to review history, not even in the interests of justifying the righteousness or innocence of Muslims, for his objective is at once more abstract and more concrete than the constraints of actual historical reference allow. It is not so much that Shaykh Umar fails to distinguish between theory and practice as regards to security, it is rather that the intensity of his categorical oppositions has lifted the discourse out of any realm where personal experience or historical inquiry can validate a worldview or be accepted as evidence. He has entered a realm where personal experience and historical reflection, if they are "true" and "trustworthy," must themselves be validated by the source of what is truth itself, which is the Qur'an. For Shaykh Umar, the relationship between security and belief, therefore, is demonstrated in terms of attitudes or interpretations surrounding what he regards as the unmediated word of God.

Many of Shaykh Umar's sermons have as their primary content the concentrated analysis of words or terms in the Qur'an. Of all the *shaykhs* I heard, he resorted to this text most frequently and most urgently. He would also expound upon principles of Qur'anic interpretation (*tafsīr*) self-consciously. But this is not to say that his interpretations would be perceived by local Muslims generally, not to mention the *'ulamā'*, as correct, consistent, or convincing. Shaykh Umar deployed the Qur'anic text most ostentatiously in his preaching, but for all that volume, his understanding of its message was fairly single-minded. Shaykh Umar had memorized the Qur'an as a child and had taught it throughout his career. His intimate familiarity with this text, its vocabulary and its rhythms, its images and its contrasts enabled him to bring forth an impressive store of related verses to adorn seemingly every topic. He combined this immersion with an insistence on the text's "literalness," although he very seldom brought specific texts to bear on concrete local issues in a manner often associated with fundamentalist preachers. This is an intriguing exception because the Qur'anic texts that may be applied almost directly to such celebrated discrepancies with current familiar practices such as interest on loans, the sale of alcohol, the rights of women to inherit, the rights of men to divorce, or the implementation of penalties such as stoning or amputation of limbs were virtually never referred to by this preacher. Indeed, at this time there were in Egypt very active discussions, frequently appearing in the press, on exactly such controversies. These debates are by no means recent, but it is noteworthy that Shaykh Umar rarely touches directly on these questions. Instead, he treats the Qur'an as though its meaning was not primarily disclosed in its practical specificities but in its totalistic invocation.

The Qur'an as Source

The complex question of the role of the Qur'an in the preaching of Shaykh Umar has as its first element his select use of its vocabulary as symbols to convey his own message. Second is his use of the Qur'an as a symbol in itself. This second dimension is epitomized in another favorite rhetorical device in which he recites Qur'anic passages, often long ones, at a tempo and in a tone that renders them phonetically incomprehensible except perhaps to someone who already knows the text well. It gives the impression of someone racing through Hamlet's "To be or not to be" soliloquy in thirty seconds rather than the three or four minutes needed to enunciate and enable a listener to appreciate the meaning of the text. This analogy is apt in another sense because the language of the Qur'an, for all its celebrated poetic splendor and its doctrinally defined unsurpassability, remains in many respects a text that requires for its actual understanding an education such as one could not fairly assume in the case of masses of Egyptians, nor for a good percentage of Shaykh Umar's audience.[11] Even if it were recited with excellent diction, for the untrained listener obscurities would still abound. The frequency of ellipsis together with the differences in its grammar and vocabulary are reminiscent perhaps of the difficulty an unlettered twentieth-century English speaker might encounter in grasping what the melancholy Prince of Denmark is talking about when he meditates upon whether he "might his own quietus make" with a "bodkin" instead of bearing "fardels." Quoting Qur'anic passages in the manner of a 33 rpm record played at 78 rpm is impressive oratorically, but it is altogether different than presenting the text to be understood for its propositional content.

One sermon that illustrates his use of the text as a symbol quite apart from its contents in a "semantico-referential" sense was preached on April 13, 1979. On this occasion he announced that he would speak on *al-duʿāʾ*, that is, "prayer or supplication," not to be confused with *al-ṣalāh* which is the obligatory ritual prayer involving the characteristic prostrations. He begins with a few general remarks about *al-duʿāʾ*, noting its importance, before he sweeps it up into a reiteration of his general preoccupation, which is to defend the Qur'an as the uncreated divine word against any detraction from its truth and goodness.

The way Shaykh Umar validates *al-duʿāʾ* or supplication is by linking it to belief, *imān*, by way of *ʿilm* ("knowledge, learning, information, science") and *ʿirfān* ("perception, cognition, recognition"). Knowledge and perception, he then says, are inextricably tied (*mutaʿlaq*) to excellence in vision (*naẓr*) and thought (*tafkīr*) with regard to what God has created in the universe and set down as his law in the Qur'an. He then compacts them into a neat associative equation by restating it, this time putting what seemed to be the empirical basis, vision and thought (which he declares are inextricably tied to perception and knowledge) into the preconditions defined by belief:

Therefore whoever is not perceptive or knowledgeable as to what God has created in his world and commanded in His book, he has neither knowledge nor perception, and whoever has no knowledge or perception has no share of belief, except the smallest, and he who has no belief is not proficient at supplication [*al-duʿāʾ*] to the One Divine, for supplication is the summit of belief [*imān*] of knowledge, perception, and thought, of all that God, exalted be He, manifests in His universe and His book.

Here then is a chain of exclusions that set out tightly the relationship of belief (*imān*) to knowledge, both as sense-data (*ʿirfān*) and as intellectual concepts (*ʿilm*) while it states the Shaykh's notion of supplication in relation to thought. On the surface, it reveals a kind of dogmatism in the sense of Stephen Pepper's famous definition, where "belief exceeds the cognitive grounds for belief."[12] But even granting that a certain dogmatism is unavoidable when dealing with religion, there is an unusual fusion or confusion in the constituent elements of Pepper's components of judgment, which are: (1) *content* (what I know or believe); (2) *attitude* (minimum to maximum certainty); and (3) *grounds* (evidence or authority supporting it).

The premise of belief, according to the Shaykh, is knowledge and perception, and yet there can be no knowledge and perception except knowledge and perception of God's revelation (His world and His book). This can only mean that the *content* and the *grounds* of belief are in effect identical. And, given the alleged source of this deduction, it is infallibly certain, therefore assuring a maximally secure *attitude*. But by such a train of thought, Pepper's definition of dogmatism is stood on its head for "belief" is not based on "cognitive grounds" but rather knowledge and perception are predetermined as themselves acts of "belief." The assumption behind this argument that places knowledge and perception after "belief" rather than prior to it is to be found in the equation of revelation as God's world and God's book. The epistemology as formulated here rests on a presupposition about the character of the Qur'an, quite apart from an inquiry either into its text or the world which it supposedly describes. For as a matter of fact, Shaykh Umar often expresses a belief that all the "laws of nature" are already given in the Qur'an so that his reference to "God's world" is only another way of referring to the sacred text.

Knowledge and perception can have no independent basis in the experience of a knowing and perceiving subject, for according to Shaykh Umar such knowledge and perception are not discovered but revealed and since the Qur'an is the ultimate source of all revelation, all knowledge and perception emanate from there. Ultimately, therefore, supplication is merely another form of thinking, albeit the highest, for the only essential difference between belief and knowledge is the degree of intensity. The revealed word of God embraces what is believed and also supplies the cognitive grounds for believing it. It is not only self-evident and therefore compelling but self-explanatory and therefore reasonable. Here the cognitive grounds cannot exceed belief because what Pepper calls a "judgment" cannot be made, or, to be more precise, it has already occurred in the restrictive definition of knowledge. The charge to reason to distinguish between the "known" and the "believed" has disappeared and with it, any qualitative differentiation between an intellectual and a moral act. It is by such logic that the Shaykh turns this argument (and every argument) back to the credibility of the Qur'an.

In the sermon he goes on to insist forcefully that every word, every letter of the Qur'an unambiguously articulates its portion of ultimate truth. He then begins to demonstrate. He starts with the first Sura of the Qur'an and then leaps forward to the second, then the third, then the fourth and fifth, reciting at terrific speed whole blocks drawn from the beginning, middle, and end of each. These citations are not meant to comment on supplication in any direct way, except by chance; instead they are presented as standing for the whole Qur'an from which the Shaykh then extracts four "realities" (*ḥaqāʾiq*):

1. the absolute power and absolute mercy of God
2. the complete weakness and incapacity of man
3. the complete guarantee of provision and security God has made to his weak and needy creatures
4. there can be no forbidding what God gives and what God has forbidden cannot be given or permitted

Finally, the shaykh returns to the question of supplication by pointing out that man must supplicate God alone, for God alone provides and no one can stand between man and God. He then singles out for example Copts and Christians generally for condemnation pointing to the fact of priests and Popes. Then he lashes out at sufis, for they have their *walīs*. Finally he reproaches obedience to kings or presidents as a form of idolatry. Here is an example of how a doctrinal principle is transferred "literally" to a societal setting. Those who would "trust in" government officials are tarred with the same brush as Christians and sufis because, the argument goes, all of them place something or someone as mediator between "belief" and "security."

For Shaykh Umar, on the level of his use of symbols, there is no possibility of differing opinions, not only among reasonable men, but even between God and man, for all share one reason, one knowledge, one vision, one truth, most perfectly embodied in the Qur'an. Therefore, disagreement over what the Qur'an means is impossible among sincere men, for the presupposition is that divergent interpretations can only result from willful bad faith, or less politely, a lie. In this connection, Shaykh Umar often refers to the cardinal Muslim doctrine of *tawḥīd*, the assertion of God's oneness or unity, yielding a principle that is applied to His book and His world. If God is one therefore the Qur'an must be one and thus believers are either one or they cannot be believers. The link between the nature of God and the nature of the *umma* (community of believers) pivots on the Qur'an. God is like the Qur'an just as the community is like the Qur'an. It is the character of this "like" that unveils the social motive of Shaykh Umar's logic, for this "like" does not impute a similarity in certain properties but a differential sharing of the same properties. It is in this sense that the master expressive mode for Shaykh Umar is not metaphor but metonym, for he posits the relationship between security and belief as the part for the whole.

Another dimension of the metonymic mode is illustrated in another sermon of Shaykh Umar's, this one delivered on October 27, 1978. The topic for this occasion, he announces, is to demonstrate the perfection of the Qur'an as seen in its style and rhythm. Typically, however, it is soon clear that Shaykh Umar's real motive is not to illustrate but to defend. He opens by recalling an incident when the polytheists of Mecca approached Muhammad in the interest of discussing some of his sayings, that is, the Qur'an, as compared to some of their own sayings. In reply, the Sura *al-kafirūn* was revealed: "In the Name of God, the Merciful, the Compassionate. Say: 'O unbelievers, I serve not what you serve and you are not serving what I serve, nor am I serving what you have served, neither you are serving what I serve. To you your religion, and to me my religion [*dīn*]" (109:1–5).

This short Sura, which is frequently invoked in Muslim religious polemics, is given extra force due to the polysemy of the Arabic verb *ʿabada*, translated above as "serve," which might also be correctly rendered as "worship." From this base, Shaykh Umar proceeds to the elaboration of several familiar themes. He insists on the unity of the Qur'an, its clarity and scientific integrity, declaring that in it is set down the "straight path" which consists in "one religion, one earth, one book, one people, one community [*umma*]." This list occurs in a long flamboyant exposition which I will not attempt to summarize, but will cite the concluding section, the finale, as it were, since it offers a remarkably graphic illustration of the social implication of the Shaykh's use of these symbols. The explosive rhetorical pitch that accompanied the delivery of this passage is impossible to preserve in translation, but it was hardly lost on the congregation which was quite visibly and audibly aroused by it.

This passage which follows contributes a new feature to our understanding of Shaykh Umar because it is so explicitly an eschatological vision. As a depiction of heaven and hell on the Last Day, it is a statement of conclusive and definitive judgment, a proclamation of God's final decision about his creatures. Yet at the same time, it matches the Shaykh's depiction of the contemporary world. What this similarity suggests more transparently than we have yet seen is that the fusion of security and faith, *amn* and *imān,* into one category is further achieved by a de facto withdrawal from the here and now where distinctions between the ultimate and the immediate are often clouded. In this Day of Reckoning perspective, however, worldly effort has no bearing on security because it is only belief that matters. Here, the warrior of our typology becomes more than ever a "holy" warrior. This vacillation between the absolute certainty of eternity and the utter contingency of the present moment is a trademark of Shaykh Umar's rhetoric and the master symbol that bridges this polarity is once again the Qur'an.

At the point this citation begins the Shaykh has just been elaborating upon the following Qur'an verses:

> And recite to them the tiding of him to whom We gave Our signs, but he cast them off. And Satan followed after him, and he became one of the perverts. And had We willed, We would have raised him up thereby; But he inclined toward the earth and followed his lust. So the likeness of him is like the likeness of a dog: If you attack it it lolls its tongue out. Or if you leave it it lolls its tongue out. That is that people's likeness who cried lies to Our signs (7:174–77).[13]

The Shaykh has seized upon the nearly obscene image of the dog lolling its tongue and he embellishes it. Subsequently, he will draw upon the Sura of Resurrection for his chiliastic vision—as always, with considerable dramatic finesse:

> So this is a picture for you, showing the condition of unbelievers in all their ways, for there they are lolling their tongues in falsehood [*bāṭil*], they loll their tongues in their lies, they loll their tongues in their thieving, they loll their tongues in their corruption and crime always and forever, in God's night, in God's day, in God's wisdom, in God's grace, in God's truth, in God's falsehood. I portray this for you so you will feel inner disgust at unbelief [*kufr*] and the unbeliever, at any error [*ḍalāl*] or any of those in error, to

establish you in truth so you won't loll your tongue as liars and
unbelievers loll their tongues. Here's the way the Qur'an portrays
for you the people of Paradise and the people of Hell: "Their faces
on that day shall be radiant gazing at their Lord and on that day
faces will be scowling; you would think some tragedy had been
wreaked upon them" (75:22–26).

It gives two pictures. One is radiant, white, dawn-like; in it is
beauty, in it is glory, in it is splendor, in it is light, in it is radiance,
in it is brilliance. This is the picture of believers, the people of oneness [*tawhīd*] the Muslims, the people [who] worship at the glorious throne, a picture of the people of the Qur'an, a picture of the
people of belief [*imān*] a picture of the people of Islam. Their "faces
shall be radiant gazing toward their Lord," toward the Sublime,
toward Beauty, toward the Perfect, toward Glory, toward the
Secret, toward Wisdom, toward Greatness. For their faces shall be
clothed with beauty from beauty, their faces shall be clothed with
glory from glory, their faces shall be clothed with the light of
God's light, their faces shall be clothed with the perfection of God's
perfection, and from the magnificence of God's magnificence,
because for them it is magnificence, beauty upon beauty, perfection
upon perfection. They shall have no weariness or care, "their faces
shall be radiant, gazing at their Lord."

They shall see none other than Him, nor gaze on any but Him,
for He is more knowing than any knower, greater than any great
[one], bigger than any big [one]. There is nothing lacking in Him,
nor will they want for anything with Him, nor do they have any
worry, for the whole world is theirs and they are before God
because they believe in God [*amanū billah*]. The whole world is
theirs without exception because they gaze at the Lord who is the
owner of all things. This is the picture. It gives you security
[*amāna*] in your thought, as you are purified in your recollection,
your word, grateful in your righteousness. You will be [part] of
this picture so full of honor of which God says: "Enter you among
my servants, enter you my paradise" (89:27–30).

And you can imagine the Prophet with you, next to your Lord,
there before you. You imagine your friends and you imagine the
Prophets in this picture, and if only you would imagine all your
friends in this picture, for their "faces will be radiant, gazing to
their Lord."

And the second picture, "on that day faces shall be scowling,"
arrogant, darkened, blackened, dismal, "you would think some
tragedy had been wreaked upon them" depravity, wretchedness,
terror, no one to bear it, no guardian, no patron, no *qibla* [the indicator of the direction of Mecca], no finish, no purpose, because

what they undertook in this world had no purpose, had no usefulness [*ṣalāḥ*], had no morality, had no religion [*ʿaqīda*], had no
meaning [*maʿna*], had no name, had no honor. They live without
God because their god is falsehood and there is no God but God,
and they live without a book because all their books are false
[*bāṭila*] and there is no book but the Qurʾan, they live without religion [*dīn*] for there is no religion except Islam and no religion with
Islam, they live without belief [*imān*] because there is no belief
without Muhammad, prayers and peace of God upon him.

Here then is an vivid expression of the pattern we have remarked in
Shaykh Umar's preaching from the beginning. He characteristically aligns
contrasts such as good and evil, truth and error, piety and baseness, security and terror. Quite unlike the case of Shaykh Muhammad, there is no
impression of a progression between security and belief, for these two categories share one semantic moiety over against their elemental contraries,
insecurity and disbelief.

The more one listens to Shaykh Umar, however, the impression of a
morally discriminating binary worldview shows curious cracks. His predication of abstract constructs like truth and error, trustworthiness and
betrayal begins to betray definite social contours amounting to a form of
we and *they*. Moreover, the dynamism in Shaykh Umar's paradigm is not
located among the *we* but among the *they*, the enemies, the agents of
moral disfiguration whom the Shaykh is constantly reacting against,
implicitly or explicitly. In specifying the identity of these foes and defining the nature of their threat, the Shaykh reveals once again that blend of
extremes, the immediate and the eternal, the militant and the withdrawn,
the warrior and the saint. And again, he seeks to establish the credibility
of the Qurʾan symbolically as the still point at the center of the storm.
Here are some illustrative remarks from the sermon delivered on January
5, 1979, in which the Shaykh is denouncing those who would place any
hopes in the achievements of modern science. As seen earlier in the discussion of *al-duʿāʾ*, the implication is that dealing with what is intermediary and provisional amounts to the error while the summit of perfection
has already been revealed and is immediately accessible.

And this is what we see in this age which some people call the age
of light [*nūr*] and science [*ʿilm*], but how is this age of light [or] of
science? For if science leads to falsehood [*bāṭil*] that science is a
detriment, and if that light leads to immorality [*fasuq*] that light
is a detriment. For if knowledge is true, it leads to truth [*ḥaqq*] and
if light is radiant, it points unmistakably to the presence of the
Lord of heaven and earth. And if science does not lead to that and if

light doesn't lead to that, then this is not the light we want nor the science we desire, for "he whom God does not enlighten has no light" (24:40).

We see in these days strange phenomena which have never happened before, nor have we ever heard of such things before. These phenomena began a couple centuries ago and have worsened, and they will continue to worsen as long as we are in a state of utter division [*mufriqan mufriq*] and utter fragmentation [*mumziqan mumziq*] and in the state of ignorance as to what we have in our hands. For falsehood does not come from our hands nor from what stands behind them. We see in our day, and we hear it here and everywhere onslaughts [*hajūm*] upon the truth of Islam and its light. Nor do these come from the common people, but from those who consider themselves the elite [*khawās*] who sit upon their thrones in universities. They are the ones who lead, they govern, they direct the affairs and they announce that they guide [people] into any path. It seems too that they have not studied Islam, for had they studied Islam in truth and if they were trustworthy in their understanding, they would not smear it with disgrace. They would prefer Islam to anything else because it is the religion that has raised all of humanity to the greatest heights of ideas in life that is true [*al-ḥayāh al-ḥaqqa*] whether in politics, society, economics or culture and all other areas that have anything to do with civilization. For without Islam it is not possible for mankind to know anything at all!

From here, Shaykh Umar goes on to quote remarks which he says were recently made by President Carter in America. Carter, he alleges, said that in America only the poor are imprisoned and only the rich get medical care. This purported statement, upon the American President's own authority, is held up by the Shaykh as proof that America, supposed beacon of freedom and peace, "the greatest country in this era," in his words, is far subordinate to Islam. For did not the Prophet command impartial treatment of great and small? And did not the Prophet say in a well-known *ḥadīth* that rank could not win impunity? And here the Shaykh quotes: "If Fatima the daughter of Muhammad has stolen, indeed, Muhammad himself will cut off her hand." At this climax, the congregation responds with a loud chorus of "Allah, Allah," and other devout expletives something like the "amen" and "hallelujah" shouted back to a preacher at a revival.

The above passage demonstrates from several viewpoints that what the Shaykh tells us is a social, economic, political, and military struggle, is also, and for him quintessentially, a war of words. By holding up Carter's purported remarks about inequality in America beside the alleged remark of Muhammad declaring judicial impartiality, Shaykh Umar symbolically condemns the whole modern era as failing to measure up to the age of Muhammad. But at the same time, the Shaykh reveals the logic of his argument. He is not, in fact, comparing societies or eras; he is setting up a lopsided duality by means of two representative figures, Muhammad and Carter. It is not that the Shaykh is intent on persuading his listeners that America is an oppressive plutocracy; on the contrary, it is because America occupies the opposite image that the Shaykh employs it as a club with which to beat local advocates of the "modern era" whom he supposes must be embarrassed by what he claims to be Carter's words. For instance, if the Shaykh were seeking to compare the ideals of Islamic morality with those of American justice, he could easily have cited a phrase from the American Constitution or some ennobling remarks about Carter's human rights policy, for this idiom might approach the lofty words of the Prophet. But the reason the Shaykh uses America as his foil is not because it is well known as a sink of oppression and regression, but rather because it occupies in the minds of his listeners an image of advancement toward "security" by means that confound the fundamental definition of truth, goodness, and security insisted upon by the Shaykh. In fact, America is an ambiguous term, associated in Upper Egypt with superior technology, material abundance, highly sought-after food exports (lately American frozen chicken had appeared in the market, causing a small sensation), tourists dripping with money, and, of course, its stunning military might as mirrored in Israel. Moreover, Sadat at the time was in the habit of speaking of Jimmy Carter as "my friend" and promoting all manner of comparisons between Egypt and the United States, inevitably recommending that the former should be imitating the latter. It is because an image of America which is "inconceivable" is perceived as rationally undeniable that the Shaykh seeks to transfer one pole of the comparison, that of Muhammad, out of the world of experience and into the world of belief. Then, by making it into a war of words, it is the Shaykh who now has the most powerful weapons and the invincible stratagems, for he is armed with God's word. Indeed, if he can reframe every attack as an attack upon that word, he will never be bettered.

The Qur'an Surpassing Human Limits

We have already seen how Shaykh Umar symbolically compresses the eternal and the instantaneous into a single image, but we should add that this freedom over time also applies to geography. The following passage, from the same sermon of January 5, 1979, demonstrates this usage and combines it with an unusually bold trope, where Shaykh Umar puts words in the mouth of God. The ensuing monologue opens with the introductory phrase *ayyuhā al-nās*, which is typically Qur'anic although what follows is neither a Qur'anic citation nor a paraphrase. The figure Abu Jahl, whom he mentions, was one of the leaders of pagan Mecca and an implacable enemy of the Prophet. Here he functions as the leader of Islam's enemies who are enumerated in an admirable jumble of centuries and continents.

> God challenges [those liars] and he says: "Oh people, oh enemies of Muhammad, oh enemies of Islam, oh enemies of the Qur'an! Whoever among you thinks that he can defeat Muhammad or hinder him or lower his voice, extinguish his religion or surpass what he has decreed. . . .
>
> "Come on, if any of you are able to devise such things. Come on, the earth is wide and the heavens are open. Come on, Abu Jahl of the first century! Come on Abu Jahl of the middle ages! Come on Abu Jahl of the twentieth century! Come on Abu Jahl of the thousandth century, the twenty-first century, the thirtieth century, the thousandth century, up till the Day of Reckoning!
>
> "Come on, any of you who think you can defeat Muhammad as either individuals or groups, then defeat him! Try it, individuals or groups, Jews or Christians, Persians, Byzantines, nations or peoples; armed with your tongues, armed with your teeth, armed with your reason, armed with your talk, armed with your money, armed with your good repute."
>
> They have surrounded [*ḥaṣarū*, that is, "blockaded, encircled, confined"] Muhammad by sea and by air, all of Europe has surrounded him. America, Russia, Belgium, Holland, France, Spain, Portugal, England, Italy, Austria, the Balkans, all of them have surrounded Muhammad. On the west coast of Africa, on the southern coast of Africa, on the eastern coast of Africa, on the southern coast of India, on the coast of the Pacific Ocean, and there in Spain and there in Japan; they have surrounded him here in Egypt and in North Africa and in central Africa and on the coasts of Africa and in central Asia, in every place they have surrounded him.

This passage clearly illustrates Shaykh Umar's sense of an extreme lack of security in the modern world in a geopolitical sense, just as his taunting indicates a kind of confidence, a belief that is not based on political independence or economic well-being. Although he has omitted little of the known world in the above summary of Islam's enemies, he will later single out national figures. The Shaykh upbraids President Sadat and his ministers for failing to apply the Qur'an and then, in unusually sharp, mocking language, he lashes out at Pope Shanuda III, the current leader of the Coptic Orthodox Christians in Egypt. Hence, while the Shaykh maintains on one level a seemingly static and unperturbed partition between what is self-evidently true and self-evidently false, on another level he admits to combat on a global scale.

In the following passage, from later in the same sermon, he gets still more particular about the source of his anxiety. Once again security and belief are under attack because the Qur'an is not accepted. But here Arabic as a language and Egypt as a homeland [*watan*], right down to the village, are under siege. Note that in the rhetoric, the causes of these problems are never historical or social events, but they are tied up with the devious and immoral use of language. Thus, the enemies of Islam employ their most pernicious trick when they dupe by trading names, that is, calling something what it is not, or more precisely, calling it by its opposite. Of course this accusation only emphasizes that one of the chief strategies of Shaykh Umar is to control the semantics of such terms as truth, reason, knowledge, justice, trustworthiness, etc., lest the value of these terms as Qur'anic symbols become inflated or relativized.

> If we go from one country in the world to another, we see them only in darkness while light is with Islam. We find there only oppression while happiness is with Islam. We find there only tyranny while justice is with Islam. But these have no wish that there be light, happiness, and justice in the world. What they want is that *they* should live, that *they* should prosper, that *they* should exist. Let the world crumble so long as *they* are happy and can live.
>
> In the shadow of this disgraceful way of thinking, we see that Egypt is disgraced. In our own day, there is Zionism here, just like there is Zionism there. They are at hand with their religion. They hide it under their cloaks, and they say what should not be said and they do [things] that should not be done. For the Torah vilifies the Qur'an and scorns it; sometimes it vilifies the Prophet and scorns him; sometimes it vilifies Islam and scorns it; and sometimes it vilifies Muslims and scorns them.
>
> Among these phenomena, we hear that the Arabic language is inadequate and we have to join with it other languages. Or that Muslims are a people that arrived here [*wafadū ali ḥunā*] and that they should get out because this country is not their country [*watan*]. We hear such things these days, and the government hears them too. People hear them just as we hear them, but we don't want to plunge into these matters now for they cover a wide scope.
>
> We even hear such things from young men and young women in the villages, children, boys and girls, such things as this country is my country and it's nobody's but mine. Egypt is my Egypt and

it's nobody's but mine. Islam is false and Muhammad, prayers and peace of God upon him, is not a Prophet, nor does he have any miracles [*laysa lahu mu'ajazāt*] that he is not mentioned in the books of old and that Islam is a religion of lust [*shahawa*] and a religion of tyranny and a religion of the sword, and that the Qur'an is not a miracle either in its expression or in its meaning. . . .

And I have seen and heard a great many young people who are in confusion and anxiety [*faza' wa qalaq*] because of this wicked disgraceful campaign [*hamla*] which they are waging upon Islam, its Prophet, its nation [*umma*] and I tell them: "Don't look and you won't see!" [*lā turā wa lan turā*].

For God, exalted be He, lays down the challenge and history pronounces, and after the challenge of God, there is no challenge. After the proof of history, there is no more speaking. . . .

God guides whom He wishes and says: "How many a city was stronger in power than your city which cast you out and we destroyed them and they had no helper" (47:13). God, exalted be He, challenged those enemies of the Prophet, of the Qur'an, and of Islam, one by one, and they were giants.

But these in our era were not like those, never, neither in their character, nor in their vision, nor in their understanding, nor in their awareness. The encounter with the Qur'an is an unambiguous [*sariha*] encounter. They say that the Qur'an guides to truth [*haqq*] but we don't want truth, that the Qur'an guides to oneness [*tawhīd*] but we don't want oneness [*tawhīd*], that the Qur'an guides to justice, but we don't want justice, that the Qur'an guides to freedom but we don't want freedom. . . .

As for the people of this age, they call polytheism the oneness of God [*yasammu al-shirk tawhīdan*]. . . . They call disbelief [*kufr*] belief [*imān*]. They call disobedience Islam. They call falsehood truth. They call lying trustworthiness. . . .

These are their traits from of old, they introduce deviations, they are liars who destroy by sabotage [*mukharribīn*].

This passage brings together a panorama of the threats to security seen by the Shaykh. The threat of the Jews revives, in many ways, a precedent that is as old as the Qur'an itself, although here the Shaykh abandons any pretense of Qur'anic allusion where they are referred to as *bani isra'īl* and speaks plainly of "Zionism." Obviously, the years of confrontation between Egypt and the modern state of Israel allowed Qur'anic themes that are hostile to Jews to gain popularity as subject matter for Egyptian preachers. Then came the peace initiative of Sadat, which encouraged unbounded optimism that improvements of Egypt's staggering domestic problems were in sight. But many were wary of these such promises.

Some preachers quickly adjusted their commentary on Jews to match the new circumstances, blaming them no longer for military aggression, for instance, but for obstructing and stalling the peace process. But such refinements, reflecting a close following of current events, are rare in the rhetoric of Shaykh Umar, just as they have little relevance to the Upper Egyptian peasant and worker to whom he speaks.

The assault Shaykh Umar attributes to the Jews is specified not in any state or nation but in the Torah. It is the Torah, symbolically, that is associated with the undermining of the Arabic language and the claim that Muslims are strangers in Egypt. Such outright identification of the Arabic language and Egypt with Islam is another feature of Shaykh Umar's rhetoric that plays freely with history and demography. It ignores the fact that a relatively small percentage of the world's Muslims are Arabs (roughly 25 percent) and the disproportionately large role Christian and Jewish Arabs have played in medieval Muslim civilization as well as in the modern *nahḍa* or Arab Renaissance. Likewise it overlooks the disproportionately large numbers of present-day Copts in Egypt, who are represented in the professions, arts, commerce, finance, education, and, in Upper Egypt, landownership. The reference to talk that Muslims don't belong in Egypt, which the Shaykh implies the government should put a stop to, has its basis in a deadly logic which the Shaykh leaves aside as "matters too wide to plunge into." He is touching on an analogy between Israel and Egypt that occasionally surfaces in vulgar sectarian polemics. The premise that the Jews are wrong because they took the land of the Palestinians by force of arms may be turned by Copts on their Muslim countrymen, who likewise began their "occupation" of Egypt by conquest. Hence the same legal ground for objecting to the Jewish state applies at home to the presence of Muslims.

The background for his comments on the notion that the Arabic language is "inadequate" also has a complicated history. The question is only simple because it has been transformed into a symbol for the *us* against *them* mentality that so permeates Shaykh Umar's social vision. The fact is that over the last three decades, while education on all levels, but especially elementary education, has increased enormously in Egypt, penetrating even into remote villages, foreign language learning has suffered relative to its once prominent place. And even though English and French are widely included in the curricula of secondary schools, the extremely poor quality of instruction is a byword among informed Egyptian educators.[14] Before the late 1950s, Minya had an international character which has now utterly disappeared except for the crumbling facades of Italianate mansions and the sagging evidence of British imperial architecture of dilapidated public buildings. The European community, numbering about 5,000 prior to its exodus, had also established schools which educated not only their own children but provided some opportunity for a European language education for local Egyptians. The elite Arabic language schools in Minya also enjoyed the presence of native Europeans as teachers. Understandably perhaps, the Copts as a group were more eager for the benefits of modern education and they had earliest access to foreign language education via missionary schools. (In Minya, American, British, and French mission schools were represented, aside from the large Greek school). Copts were also in the forefront of those who used these language skills as a means of brokerage and upward social mobility. President Sadat's "open door policy," which has sought to lure Western capital back into Egypt, has once again made competence in foreign language, especially English, virtually synonymous in the provincial mind with participation in the new prosperity.

Apart from foreign language as a symbol of collaboration with non-Muslims, Shaykh Umar also treats it as a symbol of foreign domination. In another sermon he tells a story of his childhood when he was selected to greet a visiting minister of the Khedival government and he had to learn a Turkish phrase for use in the ceremony. He comments on this as a sign of the great outrage of imperialism, and again, as another attack on Arabic, for it makes little difference, apparently, that the Turks are Muslims. What we are seeing here, therefore, is an argument that links the "security" of the Arabic language with security of the nation and ultimately the security of Islam in a way that is not unlike the linkage we saw in the case of Shaykh Muhammad between "security of nutrition" and "security of industry"—that is, material well-being and independence—and the fullness of religion.

The third way that foreign language learning symbolizes a threat to security for Shaykh Umar is that it is emblematic of modern secular education in toto. This point, which comes out explicitly in other sermons, would meet with sympathy from an audience that lacks the benefits of formal modern education or lacks the golden opportunities that such an education was supposed to deliver. Failing all else therefore, the school should at least be a place for religious learning. In addition, these rebuttals register a note of rebuke aimed at those who seek to gain power, wealth, and position by means of their education rather than by respecting traditional values where careers are usually subordinate to family interests and related loyalties. Here too, an attack on education amounts to a protest against the immense size, inefficiency, and wastefulness of Egypt's public sector, the overbearing bureaucracy, which one functionary I knew called "the octopus." For Shaykh Umar, the incursions of this regulatory officialdom is epitomized in the fact that one now needs a permit to build a mosque! Educational institutions that are the training grounds for bureaucrats are also the centers for modern "science." This combination cannot help but outrage the Shaykh because here is the seeming alliance between those who "disfigure" Islam and those who assume authority in the name of something other than the Qur'an, namely the state. From this point of view, he speaks with the voice of the restless and frustrated underling regardless of his age and education, who has little to hope for gain from the growing domination of an impersonal and compartmentalized civil service characterized by Egyptians as *al-naẓām,* "the system."

Traditional patterns of solidarity diffuse personal responsibility to the group and likewise diffuse anxiety and insecurity. Modern circumstances tend to individualize responsibility and the guarantees of security are elevated to the higher abstraction of "community," the state, and its agencies rather than proximate personalized groupings. The formulation of a consensual ideology at the level of the state has been a major problem since the 1952 Revolution.[15] Shifting tides of national interest and international alliances have been matched within Egypt by a deluge of often contradictory official claims that are supposed to be the basis for mobilization of the masses. It is hardly a wonder that amid this babel of short-lived political promises, Islam should be asserted as the irreducible solution. It is because so much ideological discourse has been justified in the name of religion that Shaykh Umar attempts to rescue the sacred language: "they call falsehood truth, they call disobedience Islam." But as we saw in his juxtaposition of Carter with Muhammad, the Islam he expounds does not exist in an empirical world, it exists in a text. Contrarily, when he says, "there is no book but the Qur'an," he means that no other worldview is permitted this enthronement as a sacred text. All others must be subject to the world of history, of limits, and of changing fortunes. The maintenance of these two dimensions is a central feature of his whole rhetoric. It is not, as one might be tempted to conclude, that he fails to distinguish between the "ideal" and the "practical"; it is rather that he bases such a distinction on interpretive criteria that would deny any polysemy to those multiple abstract terms he constantly sets up for contrast. Thus Islam is always what the "text" says it is, while every other use of the same language must be interpreted by the "context." To this degree, Shaykh Umar's argument is based on the selective application of two complementary modes of determining linguistic meaning. He claims, in effect, that the lexical symbols that sociolinguists call "shifters" occur only in man's speech but not in God's.[16] These symbols in the Qur'anic text are singularly "semantico-referential," as they consist of pure propositions while in all other texts the same terms must be understood as denoting "pragmatic" reference since their meaning is always principally carried by external situational factors and not by what is literally "said."

This duality is demonstrated neatly in the maxim that Shaykh Umar says he gives to young people who come to him confused by what they have heard in the campaign to defame Islam: "Don't look and you won't see!" This advice as a practical response suggests two readings, one the soldierly bearing of a disciplined ascetic and the other the retreat of the proverbial ostrich. But it takes on a different significance if it is understood not as a prescription for action, but as a principle for interpreting the sacred text. Those who "lie to God's signs" are those who would attempt to understand His language employing the same pragmatic factors that give meaning to all ordinary uses of human language. But for the Shaykh, since these Qur'anic terms are God's language, they cannot be understood in reference to experience, nor can their "real" meaning be transferred from the sacred text to the created world without a loss, indeed a reversal, of their authentic meaning. This is another sense in which we can speak of Shaykh Umar's mode of expression as metonymic, because this-worldly notions of truth, goodness, trustworthiness, security, and so forth, are not called such because they are similar to their "real" counterparts; they are called such properly only when they correspond however partially, to the one and same "real," that is, otherworldly truth, goodness, trustworthiness, security, and so forth.

Predication, in terms of Aristotle's characterization of metaphor, can only rightly be made in the move from genus to species and from species to genus, but it cannot be made from genus to genus or from species to species or by analogy.[17] Aristotle made a distinction based on form when he said that "poetry is more philosophical and higher than history, for poetry tends to express the universal, history the particular." But for Shaykh Umar the appropriate manner of interpretation depends on the source, that is, the speaker, not on genre. It is the Qur'an's presumed universality and unique semantic integrity that exempts it from being interpreted as analogy, for there exists nothing of equal stature. It alone is "poetry" in Aristotle's sense, and all the rest is history derived from it in various degrees of corruption.

The Qur'an and the Bible

There remains one final feature of Shaykh Umar's use of symbols, mentioned briefly above, which deserves fuller and more explicit exposition. We have noted how Shaykh Umar labels as evil those who imply that any this-worldly quality (knowledge, truth, security, etc.) can claim the dignity of such terms which belong only to God's book. Those like himself are right who use them in their religious sense, that is, as metonymic expressions of extension rather than as the predication of similarity between separate entities. We noted, too, that security for Shaykh Umar is compressed into a question of defending the text. Hence his move from security to belief is represented in a theory of semantics. The lengths to which the Shaykh draws out this presumption are shown when he projects his own theory of a sacred text into its supposed rival, the Bible.

On December 8, 1978, the day that President Sadat was visiting Minya, and while he was worshipping at al-Fuli mosque and hearing the sermon we analyzed earlier, Shaykh Umar was giving his listeners an answer to those who attack God and His book. At the very end, the Shaykh told his audience that before the day was out he was going to demand of Sadat why he did not govern according to the Qur'an, but the bulk of the sermon was preoccupied with still more heinous enemies. Among his opening remarks he says: "God sent down this book, and in the examination of it, there is everything that is good, in it are wisdom, knowledge, reason and conclusive judgment. Whoever conducts himself according to its method enjoys peace, deliverance, and success, and whoever differs from it perishes in regret and has no share with us." The key term for the rest of the sermon is given above as "differ" (*ikhtilaf*), a word that connotes not only to "differ from" but to "introduce differences in." From of old, says the Shaykh, the enemies of Islam have sought to protect their worldly power by slandering God's word, which they do by suggesting that within the Qur'an itself there are inconsistencies, contradictions, and points that diverge from other points. Specifically, it is the Christians and Jews who purposefully engage in this business, and note here that he refers to Christians as "Crusaders," a term with a clear militarist innuendo. He then singles out a figure whom he refers to as ibn Naghdala, a Jew, who was a minister of state in Muslim Spain, who, according to Shaykh Umar, was the author of a book pointing up "differences," that is, contradictions, in the Qur'an. This book, says the Shaykh, is the handbook of all missionaries and slanderers of Islam right up to the modern day.

The man Shaykh Umar mentions here, otherwise known as Samuel Ha-Levi, was a man of extraordinary intellectual gifts and diplomatic talents who served Badis, the Berber king of Granada (A.D. 1038–1073). Despite Shaykh Umar's remarks, there is little accepted historical evidence that this man of distinguished learning, who made noteworthy contributions to both Hebrew and Arabic scholarship, was himself ever a party to virulent religious polemic, although the enemies of Badis did occasionally resort to anti-Jewish sentiment to incite others to join them in their designs on his kingdom in Granada. According to R. Dozy, preeminent historian of Muslim Spain, the attack upon the Jews of that principality at the end of the eleventh century had little to do with Jewish meddling but much to do with Berber-Arab rivalries, for there was a great deal of tension and distrust between what he calls "les petits souverains."[18] Thus while there is scant ground for laying charges of anti-Islamic polemic against Samuel Ha-Levi, for nothing of such a character exists in his surviving writings, nonetheless there is evidence that he was accused with whatever veracity during his lifetime of criticizing the Qur'an.[19] The period sources, however, leave another impression, as the discriminating Nicholson points out: "In their admiration for his extraordinary accomplishments the Arabs all but forgot he was a Jew. . . . Samuel, on his part, did not scruple to employ the usual Muhammadan formulas, 'Praise to Allah!' 'May Allah bless our Prophet Muhammad!' and to glorify Islam quite in the manner of a good Muslim."[20]

Although such scrutiny of historical details is not irrelevant to an analysis of Shaykh Umar's rhetoric, it is plainly far beyond the horizon for virtually all his listeners. Here a populist preacher is merely appropriating an obscure medieval figure to serve as a pillory, both here and in other sermons, and to symbolize those who attack Muslim Scriptures. Needless to say, Shaykh Umar never takes up the specific arguments which are supposedly found in this alleged book written by ibn Naghdala, but, in listening to his sermons, it is clear that it supposedly points out differences between the Qur'an and Judeo-Christian scripture and then expounds upon contradictions within the Qur'an itself. These, at any rate, are the charges that he sets out to defend the Qur'an against.

What is interesting about Shaykh Umar in this regard, and for it his listeners deem him a man of learning, is that he does not limit his attacks on Jewish and Christian scriptures to those points which have long since become cliché, such as the Trinity, the Incarnation, or the Crucifixion; instead he sets out to convince his listeners that just as the Qur'an contains the proof of its divine origin and authority in its internal consistency, so too *al-injīl*, "the Gospel," and the Torah are shown up for inauthenticity by their inner contradictions. Of course, the central premise of this polemical exercise is the well-known Muslim claim, to which Shaykh Umar refers frequently, that the texts that the Jews and Christians venerate in their respective scriptures are not, in fact, the texts that God "sent down" upon the Prophet Moses on Mount Sinai and upon the Prophet Jesus on the Mount of Olives. This notion of "sending down," *al-nazūl*, represents, of course, a projection of a Muslim theory of revelation into the Bible, a theory which neither Christians nor Jews hold. Likewise the presumption that these texts are forgeries precludes any possibility of a genuine comparison, for it is only the Qur'an which can be believed in the first place.

As we examine a few of the concrete examples Shaykh Umar presents to his audience in this sermon, it is useful to recall again that his idiom is not the scholarly lecture but preaching. Hence it is his use of symbols, not his exegetical acumen as judged by academic standards, that interests us. One Biblical episode the Shaykh mentions here, and he has used it in other sermons too, is from 1 Kings 8:9, which he quotes giving chapter and verse. He sets the context first, paraphrasing freely. The scene is at the conclusion of the dedication of the temple built by Solomon. There, before all the assembled priests and elders of Israel, the King of Israel is transferring the Ark of the Covenant to its place of honor, and the words describing the contents of the Ark are seized upon by the Shaykh: "There was nothing in the Ark except the two tablets of stone that Moses had put there at Mount Horeb." This verse, the Shaykh expounds, is proof from the Old Testament that the Torah was lost and that the book now called the Torah was later fabricated by liars to take the place of the revealed book. Of course, the Shaykh never goes into any details which might suggest that something called the Torah should have been in the Ark that Solomon was dedicating, as if this Biblical quote indicates something that should have been, but was not in the Ark. But even beyond this oversight, the Shaykh is apparently oblivious to what the two tablets referred to in the verse consist of. These are, of course, precisely the stone tablets upon which, according to the book of Exodus, God himself wrote the Law for Moses.[21] Ironically enough, in the entire canon of Judeo-Christian scriptures, this is probably the single instance where God "came down" and dictated His own word by a process of revelation that suggests the directness of divine inspiration which Muslims traditionally hold with regard to Muhammad and the Qur'an. If there is any passage in the whole Bible where the text presents "God's word" as having literally "come down" and having been preserved (in stone), it is on these two tablets in the Ark. What Shaykh Umar believes these tablets to be, in his apparent naïveté, is not further indicated. But there seems little doubt that he altogether misses the significance of Biblical verse regarding the tablets which are, if anything could be so called, the Torah which he claims is here reported to be absent.

This carnival of confusion wherein Shaykh Umar misconstrues Biblical reference and sequence on the simplest level of the narrative itself is a pattern that recurs in his more usual manner of citing Biblical episodes, which is by paraphrase. In a sermon given on February 23, 1979, the heart of the discourse consists of a litany of alleged Biblical statements that the Shaykh considers to be outrageous. He attacks the anthropomorphism of God encountering Adam as He walks in the Garden, or Jacob, who is presented as wrestling with God. Curiously, the Shaykh claims the Bible says that Abraham married his sister and that Moses married his father's sister. He also objects to the suggestion that David as a prophet could ever sin. Hence the story of Bathsheba is denounced as slander [2 Samuel 11:2–27]. Likewise he rejects the authenticity of any text that presents Jesus disapproving of the strict enforcement of the law as when he prevents the stoning of the woman taken in adultery [John 8:3–11]. Shaykh Umar also includes in this list a number of stories of the Israelites and of Jesus whose origin I cannot identify except to say they are neither Biblical nor Qur'anic. The issue here, however, is that even if what he presents as Biblical references are occasionally jumbled or apocryphal, they are not without their logic and their rhetorical purpose, for each is meant to emphasize a contrary statement in the Qur'an. For this reason, the fact that Shaykh Umar relates many stories incorrectly on the most rudimentary, literal level, quite apart from the open question as to whether any of his listeners would notice the discrepancies, is quite secondary. The underlying claim that the Bible is already a forgery seems to encourage the polemicist to compound the argument by taking some further license in rendering an already twisted story.

In their service as symbols, elements from Judeo-Christian scriptures are treated with the same motivated distortion and purposeful disregard for detail that we have already noted in the Shaykh's treatment of history, politics, and geography. This deserves noting because while balanced scholarship on twelfth-century Spain is obviously impossible to find in Minya and current up-to-date insights into world affairs may also be unavailable to an amateur preacher, there is surely no practical difficulty in obtaining the text of an Arabic Bible, if indeed one was genuinely intent on studying it.

But here once again the sharp contrast between the liberties Shaykh Umar takes with the Bible and the constraints of his literal reading of the Qur'an is not accidental. It flows from the essential premises of his dichotomous logic. His refutation of charges that there are "differences" in God's word and by consequence in His world and among His believers is another way of reaffirming that divisions, anomalies, and contradictions of their nature belong to *them* whereas in the same way, harmony, integrity, and wholeness define *us*, regardless of appearances.

Here too the force of this ritual rhetoric as metonym is revealed from another perspective, for this Shaykh's remarkable capacity to engage his congregation does not derive from his role as a mediator between structural polarities. The excitement he arouses originates rather in the intensity of his partisan participation in the *we* of the socially marginal for whom and to whom he speaks. But it also relies heavily on the liminal properties that symbolically create the exceptional climate of a religious event. For this reason the great popular appeal of his preaching is deceptive since it seldom leads to anything except superficial involvement in meaningful social action outside of the mosque. Pierre Bourdieu has described well the character of what is lacking in this close collusion of the part and the whole, a condition that easily causes the fervor generated during the sermon to dissipate once the spell cast by the extraordinary orator has been broken: "The belief of everyone, which pre-exists ritual, is the condition for the effectiveness of ritual. One only preaches to the converted. And the miracle of symbolic efficacy disappears if one sees that the magic of words merely releases the 'springs'—the dispositions—which are wound up beforehand."[22]

Displaying Qur'anic Reasoning

On certain occasions, Shaykh Umar may address very specifically the principles that must be followed in order to correctly interpret the Qur'an. Such principles in no way compromise his fundamental postulate that the Qur'an is clear and unambiguous in its meaning, but they are given, says the Shaykh, "to increase your belief [*imān*]." On one occasion he delineates three such criteria. The first is to take into account the circumstances in the biography of the Prophet as to when a particular revelation was received. The second, which is likewise drawn directly from classical Islamic theology, is to interpret the Qur'an in the light of comments that the companions contemporaneous with the Prophet made concerning it. The raw material for this research consists of numerous collections of biographies and the *ḥadīth*. Scholarly competence in either of these sophisticated disciplines requires training leading to expertise as well as adequate bibliographic resources. As one might expect of a provincial town, such genuine academic pursuits are cultivated locally by a rare few, of whom Shaykh Umar is not one. As a matter of fact, this whole field of studying the words and deeds of the Prophet, which have normative status for Muslims, has grown in recent decades to be an area of considerable controversy. The major issues center around the degree of authenticity that may be accorded to reputed remarks of the Prophet as they have been transmitted through successive generations until they were codified a few centuries after his death into various canonical collections.[23] The weak foundation for a number of *ḥadīth* has led some reformers and modernists to question the credibility of any of them, leading some to dispute that they have the value as a source of Islamic law which has traditionally been assigned to them. Of course, Shaykh Umar in his preaching never gives the slightest hint that controversy surrounds these materials.

Finally, the third principle, the one the Shaykh expounds with the most vigor and confidence, is to interpret the Qur'an, as he says, "in the light of science, knowledge, and reason." This is his own favored method and, by default one might say, the only one within the reach of his relatively untutored listeners for whom serious investigations into ancient and medieval lore is frankly inconceivable. Although the Shaykh never gives a reflective definition of what he means by "science" and "reason," his meaning is easy to deduce both from the way he uses the terms and by alluding to leading contemporary Muslim thinkers who take a similar position. His argument, like that of the renowned Muhammad Ali of Lahore, is that "Islam conforms to the activistic, evolutionary, Weltanschauung of modern science and cultural philosophy."[24] In other words, the Qur'an should be interpreted along the lines of what one perceives as orderly, understandable, and based on good sense. Although this reasoning may resound with the same vocabulary as the zeitgeist of progress and enlightenment, we must not forget Shaykh Umar's condemnations of the modern era. It is useful to recall the insights of Durkheim and Mauss, who explain how the classifications that come to be regarded as religious and enshrined as reasonable derive ultimately from categories of social experience, although not perhaps with a simplistic isomorphic structural correspondence. The point here is that reason and science are not critical reflective procedures for the Shaykh; they are instead invoked as circumlocutions within the same defensive ethos he has repeatedly exemplified.

Shaykh Umar presents a number of cases where reason and science are evoked to prove once more that there are no differences or contradictions in the Qur'an. We can let one instance stand for many. In the sermon of December 8, 1978, he introduces the discussion in familiar terms, but the following passage demonstrates how he transfers the "reasonableness" of the Qur'an into his view of the cohesiveness of psychological and physical reality.

> Come to the Holy Qur'an and to what God sent down on the Prophet, prayers and peace of God upon him, and you will find what is well-coordinated [*tanasiq*, "symmetry, harmony"] combined together [*tarabaṭ*] and in harmony [*tawā'im*] in every way.
>
> For I reckon my body, my reason ['*aql*], my soul [*ruḥ*], my tongue, my eyes, my ears, my mouth and my understanding, all with Islam and the Qur'an. Here is rest for the conscience, tran-

quility for the heart, peace for the soul, calmness of spirit, because belief [*'aqīda*] harmonizes with the truth, and worship [*'abāda*] harmonizes with belief, and truth and morality and conduct harmonize with worship, belief, and truth and the Islamic world harmonizes with worship, morality, belief, and truth and the spirit of Islam harmonizes with morality, worship, belief, and truth, and all is "like a tree firmly rooted whose branches reach to heaven and which gives fruit in due season by the leave of its Lord" [14:24].

This is our Islam, this is our religion, well-coordinated, combined together, and in harmony. But our enemies do not want coordination, combination, and harmony. They want it to be divided, differentiated. They build upon lies and differences [*ikhtilāf*]. Oh, if they would only lie about something other than God, or other than the book of God, or other than the Prophet of God! But they introduce differences into what is most trustworthy of the trustworthy [*ṣidq*], what is most truthful of the true [*ḥaqq*], most good of the good [*khayr*], most just of the just [*'adl*] and that is God, His book, His religion, and His Prophet, to sow doubts among you and fragment your hearts so that you will not be Muslims in truth, but Muslims in name and appearance only.

But God, exalted be He, has met their skillful ploys in the past, and he meets their skillful ploys in the present and until the Day of Reckoning. By God's leave, He will meet their skillful ploys and they will clearly be the losers in their lost cause, for Islam is truth [*ḥaqq*] and God gives victory to truth, and there is no doubt that to Islam is the victory.

Therefore, when you see Islam and the Qur'an, you see harmony, connectedness, and coordination, just as in the universe, its sun and moon, its earth and sky, its night and day, its water and air, its cultivated land and its open country, all of it proceeds in accordance to the order of wisdom [*al-naẓām al-ḥakīm*] realized by the Lord the worlds, majestic is He, God, knowing and wise. Such is the Qur'an and Sunna, and such is the Prophet in his words and deeds.

The Shaykh then takes up what he pretends is one of the charges of the "liars" who claim the Qur'an contradicts itself. The example he chooses takes up the four different terms which, says the Qur'an in various places, were the basic material from which God fashioned man: *al-turāb* (dust, dirt), *al-ṭīn* (mud), *al-hama al-maṣnūn* (fetid mire or sludge), and *al-ṣalṣāl kal-fukhkhār* (clay like a potter's). The Shaykh goes on, at length, to demonstrate that no contradiction is present in these different references because the Qur'an is describing the same thing only in different ways. It is not a "difference" in the matter, but it is a question of various "states" (*ahwāl*), "intervals" (*aqwāt*), and "conditions" (*atwār*). It started with dust, he says, then when water was added, it became mud. Mud in time grows into fetid mire until finally it becomes like potter's clay. What should be remarked first about this exegetical exercise is the selection of the example. Of all the controversies touching on law and doctrine that surround contemporary discussion of the Qur'an, various expressions for the *materia prima* for the creation of man probably rank among the least compelling. This is also the case for the second example the Shaykh selects, which deals with varied Qur'anic expressions for the "expanse" or "surface" of the earth. But beyond that, in both the selection of these expressions and the way he handles them, he reveals again the dualistic pattern of rhetorical predication we have remarked repeatedly.

Admittedly, Shaykh Umar is not a sophisticated scholar of Qur'anic interpretation. However, he has clearly been exposed to some degree to the vast literature that deals with the Qur'an, its style and rhetoric. Parts of this literature also deal extensively with figures of speech in the Qur'an, of which classical authors tend to distinguish several types. T. Sabbagh, in his groundbreaking study, *La Métaphore dans le Coran*, explores this classical scholarship; he catalogues the usage of various kinds of metaphors in the Qur'an. He gives the metonym, which is his translation for *majāz mursal*, as one of four major types. The other three types he calls comparison, metaphor, and paraphrase or euphemism. Although it is not always easy to determine precisely to what category every prediction belongs, he makes a general distinction in that metaphor is based on the resemblance of certain features whereas "in the metonym, two objects are different but tied intimately to one another (*mais liés intimement l'un à l'autre*)."[25] What interests us at present is that Shaykh Umar has not only chosen a Qur'anic example that hardly qualifies as a point of controversy or even as a figure of speech (Sabbagh, in his extensive listing of Qur'anic figures, never even mentions this use of different expressions for dirt and mud) but that he interprets it in a patently metonymic fashion. The principle of transference he formulates and exemplifies for use within the Qur'anic text corresponds to the way he visualizes, in symbolic expression, the relationship of the Qur'an as a whole to everything else that would claim to be true, trustworthy, good, secure, and so forth. His presupposition that every Qur'anic expression is in harmony and interrelated requires that the believer find a principle of reconciliation between seeming contrasts, and in this sense it might be more accurate to render his use of the word *'aql* not as "reason" so much as "rationalization."

In contrast to his solicitude for the inner consistency of the Qur'anic text, we should briefly note the opposite tendency which he extends toward a non-Qur'anic text. In the following passage, from the same sermon, one notes how the Shaykh ignores the context of a metaphorical statement in order to indicate what he considers "contradictions" within the Gospels. Whereas he insists on a strict "semantico-referential" interpretation of the Qur'an, note in what follows how he supplies doctrinaire contextual or "pragmatic" interpretive factors to a verse from John's Gospel:

> So, then, I have inspected the so-called Gospels in the hands of the "Crusaders" and I found differences [*ikhtilāf*], one with the other, one with some of the others, and all of them between each other, concerning the sayings they attribute to Jesus, upon him be peace, concerning his message, concerning his nature, concerning his preaching, concerning his statements.
>
> As I told you last Friday, it suffices to read something from the Gospels, such as John's Gospel, chapter 10, verse 9, a saying attributed to Jesus, upon him be peace. It is not possible for reason [*'aql*] to maintain that such a remark could come from Jesus, for he is a Prophet from among the Prophets, and the inspiration of God was upon him, and all of them [i.e., Prophets] have one religion, and in all of them is faithfulness [*amāna*], in all of them trustworthiness [*ṣidq*], in all of them redemption [*wafa'*], in all of them knowledge [*'ilm*], in all of them blessing [*baraka*], in all of them honesty [*'iffa*], in all of them sweetness [*'adhaba*].
>
> Yet they say that Jesus said in that verse: "All who came before me are thieves and brigands." Is there any reason [*'aql*] that can believe [*yuṣaddiq*], even in its imagining [*wahm*, "fancy, self-delusion"], that one like Jesus said this about those who came before him from among the Prophets and Messengers?

Following his familiar pattern the Shaykh has pulled this quote out of a longer discourse on the "Good Shepherd," which is a richly imagistic passage; but the meaning of the particular phrase he seizes upon is at least suggested only a few verses earlier in the same chapter. This chapter of John's Gospel opens with Jesus' remark, "I tell you truly whoever does not enter the sheepfold by the door, but enters by some other way, he is a thief and a brigand." A few verses later he says, "I am the gate of the sheepfold." Then comes the remark cited by the Shaykh in part, "All those who came before me are thieves and brigands, but the sheep do not hear their voice." Without entering into details about what may be meant theologically by this overlay of personifications, one can at least note that on the level of symbol use, the reference to predecessors as thieves and brigands occurs under the metaphorical constraints of the "sheepfold" analogy, by which shepherd and non-shepherd are contrasted. There is no indication whatsoever in the gospel text that "thieves and brigands" refers to prior "Prophets and Messengers," as the Shaykh paraphrases the verse, and the Shaykh's leap to this conclusion is vividly out of character with what we have seen in his stringent metonymic method in regard to the Qur'an. To reach this conclusion he not only disregards, indeed violates, the sequence of metaphors given in John's text, but he gives "reason" (*'aql*) as the source of the objection.

To reiterate, one must understand that the Gospel functions here as a symbol for a social force. It is the perceived anti-Islamic motives of Christians that the Shaykh has straightforwardly redirected and attributed to the Gospel verse. But the discovery of such an apparent non sequitur in his interpretation of the text is only jarring if one assumes that he is actually discussing the texts themselves. What we have been demonstrating, however, is that the Shaykh's fixation on texts, both the Qur'an and the Bible, is not founded upon a reliance on "inner religious mood" or a proximity to the source of Prophetic charisma such as we spoke of earlier as *Gesinnungsethik;* it is based on a rationalizing orientation. From a structural viewpoint, therefore, the Qur'an in Shaykh Umar's mode of expression is a secondary representation presented as an end in itself. It is an instrument of justification rather than a source of inspiration. Belief is not the result of an encounter with the text, but belief is first brought to the text. Security is not seen as the basis for prosperity, achieved through economic productivity and political cooperation, but as the single-minded defense of an attitude toward the Qur'an based on "reason" and "knowledge." Such reason and knowledge, in turn, very closely resemble the group-centered, honor-based authoritarian ideology which characterizes the social foundation of village life in the Upper Nile Valley.[26] For Shaykh Umar, the movement from security to belief is not a process of social transformation of society from what "is" to what "ought to be." It consists mainly in overcoming the lies and the liars who oppose security and what, from his perspective, is wholly true, good, and reasonable.

It is because the Qur'an serves as the master symbol of all idealized desiderata, that we could say, in the terms of Stephen Pepper, that it served for Shaykh Umar as both the cognitive grounds and as the content of belief. The social implication of this logical puzzle has now been more or less exposed. The Shaykh's insistence that the meaning of the Qur'an is literal, unambiguous, and perfectly reasonable (that is, that it is not "symbolic"), does not encourage its study as what Malinowski called "a pragmatic charter of primitive faith and moral wisdom"[27] but it enhances its status as an oracle. The elimination of a creative aspect in its interpretation is a way of undermining threats to group solidarity that make appeals in the name of anything except religion. Finally, by rephrasing all perceived rivalry and hostility as a question of religion, and all attacks upon Islam as essentially malicious distortion of a text, it channels social and political statements into a religious idiom. Once this rhetorical maneuver is accomplished, such a strategy tends to make the triumph of an unchallengeable symbol, namely the Qur'an, rather than structural reform the immediate or even the final object of action. In this sense one can say that the preacher whose mode of predication consists of metonym may be the victim of his rhetoric as much as its master. By failing to acknowledge a categorical distinction between the text and the social order, that is, by fusing them without a copula, he denies himself a conscious point of leverage, a position of mediation, an intermediary step in which the transition between differing human circumstances can be systematically accessed and application of divine principles can be more realistically pursued. This mode may be contrasted to a mode of preaching that is more properly metaphoric, toward which we now turn our attention.

7 Security and Belief

The Transformation of Social Status

The deployment of *amn* and *imān* as symbols which bind the sacred and the social occurs in still another pattern distinct from those discussed above. In formal terms, this pattern resembles the metaphoric mode exemplified by Shaykh Muhammad of al-Fuli mosque because it posits security and belief as different universes of discourse which must be "translated" one into the other. Hence some agent or process of "translation" becomes a central preoccupation. In this usage, however, security is not identified with material self-sufficiency or military-industrial independence; instead it is figured as a quasi-civil transaction, as an interpersonal, or more precisely an intergroup transformation of status from one social category to another.

What is meant by "status" in this regard is most overtly illustrated in the social organization of traditional tribal or feudal societies, where the constellation of rights and duties, that is, the aggregate elements of citizenship, are inseparable from membership in the corporate unit, usually expressed in terms of kinship, based on blood, marriage, or ritual bonds, often overlaid by various strands of patron-client interdependencies. In the terminology of Henry Maine, for whom it carried a heavy juridical connotation, this assignment of rights and duties in virtue of group affiliation understood as "status" stands in contrast to the more articulately specified and individualized bonds that are established by "contract." Thus, theoretically, in the case of a tribal society, if a person loses his good standing within his own group, whether he abandons it, or it abandons him, and no other group adopts him, he is held to have no status, meaning that he is effectively disenfranchised as a social being. In principle, this nonmembership not only bars one from participation in religion, social, political, and economic activities, but it leaves such an individual defenseless, for the structure of the social order and consequently the entitlement to respect is premised on the relatedness of each actor to a larger group. The group, in turn, is related to concentric circles of other allied groups which guarantee the protection of their members by the threat of revenge upon any particular infringement.

Among the ancient Arabs, generalized rights and duties were conferred basically in virtue of tribal identity supplemented by quasi-feudal ties to landholders, warlords, or merchant aristocrats. The mechanism for the distribution and maintenance of rights and duties according to customary law was closely tied up with the concept of *amn* for one who was granted "security" was said to be in a condition of *amān*. The importance of *amn* as it arises in the Qur'an where it refers to aspects of tribal law has been described by Dr. Muhammad Abdul Rauf as a cardinal factor in the establishment of Islam as a replacement for prior legal arrangements.

> It is clear that the fear of insecurity was the major stumbling block against the faith in the early days; and there was need to counteract this disadvantage. A substitute for the tribal protection against insecurity was a necessary solution. . . . The bond established by Islam was the common ideology of monotheism and related beliefs. This bond gave rise to mutual rights and obligations equivalent to those obtainable in a tribe. This arrangement assured the would-be convert of protection of life and provided him with all that he expected from his tribe under the old system.[1]

To this insight into the semantics of the Qur'anic usage of *amn*, one might add that the notion of *amn* did not then disappear with the rise of formal Islamic institutions. Rather, it was retained and reshaped into an important juridical principle which in the medieval period provided the legal basis for a wide range of contractual relationships between Muslims and non-Muslims.

> The practice of *amān* greatly facilitated the growth of diplomacy and commerce between Islam and Christendom, and made possible the emergence of resident communities of European traders in Muslim cities. It provided the main legal basis, on the Muslim side, for peaceful contacts and communications with Christian states, until, from the late Crusades period onward, these were to an increasing extent regulated by European commercial and diplomatic practice.[2]

It has been noted earlier that reference to the theme of security has a certain seasonal appropriateness during the Muslim month of *dhu ḥajj*, which commemorates the rejection of Muhammad by his townsmen in Mecca and his emigration to Medina. The sermon we shall examine presently was delivered in this month, on December 1, 1978. It was preached by a schoolteacher, now retired, just as was Shaykh Umar. However, this preacher's training included attaining a degree in history from the prestigious Cairo University. He then went on to a career in one of the elite secondary schools in Minya. Shaykh Umar's formal education, on the other hand, never went beyond the equivalent of a high-school level teachers' training academy and his teaching was restricted to the primary grades. This preacher, Shaykh Abu Bakr, regularly delivered the Friday sermon at an oratory located within the local School Teacher's Club where a large room on the ground floor had been converted into a plain but well-furnished mosque. The Club's facilities consisted of a large building that had been an enormous and elegant mansion in Egypt's prerevolutionary days. This mosque had no staff, although, as is often the case, a couple of old men more or less attached themselves to it and the maintenance personnel of the Club generally saw to its practical details.

Shaykh Abu Bakr began his sermon by emphasizing that Muhammad's journey from Mecca to Medina, although carried out in secret, did not constitute flight or escape. Rather it indicated courage and steadfast fidelity. It was only after two oppressive setbacks had occurred in the preceding year, during what he calls the "year of sadness" (*ʿām al-ḥazn*) that the Prophet is compelled by dire circumstance to relocate. Both of these setbacks the preacher describes as losses of security, *amn*, prompting grievous trials. The first involved the death of Abu Talib, Muhammad's uncle, who had consistently resisted the growing opposition to the Prophet's expanding ministry. Abu Talib had continued to support his nephew, not out of regard for the message, for he himself never became a Muslim, but because Muhammad was a member of the lineage group of which he was the head. Muhammad, of course, had been orphaned as a child. This uncle resisted pressure to curtail the Prophet's preaching, which was incurring the opposition of Mecca's leaders and giving rise to social disruptions. The second incident was the death of Khadija, who had been the wife of the Prophet and his first convert. She was a widow of means who had originally employed the young Muhammad in her caravan trade. By marrying her, Muhammad had gained a modicum of leisure which had enabled him to turn his attention increasingly toward spiritual pursuits. These preoccupations culminated in the revelations which called him to become a Prophet at the age of forty.

With the death of Abu Talib, says Shaykh Abu Bakr, the Prophet lost one kind of security, his "external protection," *al-ḥamāya al-kharajīya*.

"Protection," *ḥamāya*, is a familiar term, which has not been singled out but has already appeared alongside of *amn* in the preaching of Shaykh Umar. For practical purposes it functions as a near synonym for *amn* with the difference that it carries a strong connotation of "defense" with the coloring of military or other physical conflict, whereas *amn* embraces a broader realm of moral integrity and personal well-being, including that of harmonious sentiments and peace of mind. Thus, while Abu Talib's death brought an end to the Prophet's external protection, the death of Khadija, says the preacher, spelled the collapse of his "internal security," *al-amn al-dakhalī*. In linking these two concurrent tragedies, and elaborating their effects upon Muhammad, the preacher soon replaces the term *ḥamāya* with *amn* when describing Muhammad's "external security," thus confirming their semantic convergence in this context. In doing so he likewise explicitly evokes the traditional category associated with the status conferred as *amān*.

With the death of Abu Talib and the change of clan leadership, Muhammad's standing in his own tribe a vis-à-vis the hostile Meccan aristocracy was severely challenged. At the instigation of the elite of the Quraysh, the tribe that dominated Mecca, a social and economic boycott was imposed upon Muhammad and his Muslim followers. Pressure on his clan's new chief led to a withdrawal of the earlier unconditional support. Active persecutions also began. Muhammad, finding himself in desperate straits, then decided to leave Mecca and bring his mission elsewhere. He departed for Ta'if, a nearby city in the Hejaz. The preacher explains that Muhammad chose to go to Ta'if because his uncle named 'Abbas owned land there and had commercial relations with certain local craftsmen and traders. On account of this avuncular connection Muhammad hoped for a positive reception, that is, at least to win the security if not the success that had been denied him in native Mecca. So the Prophet approached the notables of Ta'if and was allowed to preach there for ten days. But he was not able to gain their support. "They closed their ears," says Shaykh Abu Bakr, "and said to [Muhammad]: 'If you were trustworthy [*ṣādiq*] in what you say [the "sayings" of Allah, that is, the Qur'an] your own tribe would follow. Go to your own tribe first. Guide your own tribe first, then come to us.' " In other words, the Shaykh notes, the people of Ta'if disbelieved Muhammad's message not on its own merits. Instead, they rejected it and Muhammad with it on the testimony of his kinsmen whose rejection implied that they did not hold him to be trustworthy. Here belief, *imān*, is not depicted as the assent to moral dictates and doctrinal tenets. Belief has "trustworthiness," *ṣidq*, as its precondition. The notables of Ta'if declined believing because they were not prepared to assume that one who has been excommunicated from his own group and therefore lacks *amān* can offer them the substance of *amn*.

This connection between security as category of legal status and belief is developed even more strikingly in a further episode related later in the same sermon. Shaykh Abu Bakr describes Muhammad as departing Ta'if in great anxiety, uncertain about which direction to take, whereupon God sends down the angel Gabriel to instruct him that God has put the "king of the mountain" at the Prophet's disposal. The reference here is to the "jinn," incorporeal creatures, usually living in the desert, which are known to exercise certain supernatural powers. They may assume the shape of various animals and birds and can possess humans. Some are bad and some are good or, as it is said, some are Muslims and some are not, and they are depicted as the agents of benefit or mischief accordingly. Such creatures appear commonly in Arabic folklore and they are mentioned at several points in the Qur'an. Shaykh Abu Bakr goes on to relate that this king of the mountain then approached Muhammad and offered to cover his enemies with two great mountains of sand. But Muhammad recalling that God had sent him as a Prophet of mercy, declined the offer (here the Shaykh quotes the Qur'an, 21:107). The Prophet then wanders into a lonely wadi where he begins to recite verses from the Qur'an. The jinn who hear him are profoundly moved at the recitation and they begin to believe on the spot, thus becoming Muslims. The exact statement of the Shaykh is worth citing:

> [Muhammad] sat down in the wadi and he recited the Qur'an. A party of the jinn [*nafar min al-jinn*] heard it and went to tell their tribe [*qawm*]. They informed them that Muhammad had been sent [from *rasala*, that is, he was a *rasul*, "messenger"] and that guidance had spread throughout the land. If disbelief [*kufr*] still cloaked the earth, then the jinn of heaven would grant security to Muhammad [*f-inn al-jinn fī al-samā' qad amna bi-Muḥammad*].

Here, interestingly, Muhammad is seen as gaining from the society of spirits what the society of flesh and blood had refused him. In Muhammad's dealings with the jinn, belief leads to security while for the people of Ta'if, lack of security, that is, the absence of the status of *amān*, had been the grounds for disbelief.

The preacher then goes on to relate how a powerful relative of Muhammad finally agreed to protect him thus taking a decision that permitted his return to Mecca. This man, Mat'am ibn 'Adi, together with his seven sons, armed to the teeth, met the Prophet in the wilderness and escorted him back into the city. They were defying the Quraysh and attempting to break the boycott. The climate of hostility and intimidation remained, however, for the powerful in Mecca were by no means well disposed to the preaching of Muhammad. It is just at the critical point in the story that members of two feuding tribes from an oasis called Yathrib make contact with Muhammad. They seek him out to request that he come join them as an arbitrator to assist in the settlement of their cycle of bloody disputes. He meets with them outside the city and eventually he agrees to come upon certain conditions, notably, that they recognize him as God's Prophet, thus converting to Islam. While the arrangements for implementing this accord are being negotiated over the next year's time, the enmity of the Meccan establishment toward the Prophet's mission continues to grow. Finally, on the very night that the Quraysh, having concluded their plot to assassinate Muhammad, decide to mount their attack, he makes his escape. He flees to Yathrib to join those who have promised him security and to whom he has pledged his services as peacemaker. Shortly thereafter, their oasis settlement is renamed Medina, or, to give its full name, *madinat al-nabī* or "city of the Prophet." It is from this new base, of course, that Muhammad soon redirects his mission, taking the offensive against his opponents and within a decade defeating them.

The progression of status changes represented in this sermon closely parallels the paradigm of symbolic stages set forth in Arnold van Gennep's classic study, *The Rites of Passage*. The preacher is describing a movement on the part of the Prophet through a series of social transformations. This advance follows a pattern of steps that may easily be restated in terms of van Gennep's three famous phases: separation, liminality, and incorporation.[3] Moreover, the focus of the preacher is largely concentrated on the intermediary stage, the liminal or "non-structural" phase which is dramatized by the Prophet's experiences in the desert, marked by his encounter with the jinn, who grant him security, and later his negotiations to settle in Medina and then the actual emigration. Muhammad is not portrayed here as perfectly unruffled and unfailingly triumphant, statuesque in the face of mock adversity. He is clearly a sensitive and vulnerable man, deeply distressed by familial loss and political isolation. Furthermore, he depends utterly upon arranging social relations both for his personal safety and for the success of his prophetic mission. In this drama, the Prophet does not assert the "reasonableness" of the Qur'an as proof of its authenticity, nor does he rely solely on its promises as the assurance of his ultimate triumph. Rather, with considerable skill and determination, he engages in the concrete use, even the manipulation of, the available social institutions. His confidence in God and in his mission, his *imān*, is mediated by a realistic management of his social options and the innovative, opportune pursuit of the most advantageous circumstances possible—those that afford him the most security to conduct his mission. The Prophet moves from divinely assured security, which is *imān* or belief, to a politically assured security, which is *amn*, through a period of liminality during which he wanders, negotiates, and finally flees for his life making the most of ingenuity and taking risky initiatives.

Status Reversal

In a sermon delivered in another mosque, by another preacher, during this same month, a similar van Gennepian framework appears which turns in a different direction. This sermon was preached by the head of a *jamʿīya*, or benevolent society, called *ʿilm wa-imān* (literally, "science and belief"). This preacher is a man in his mid-forties who had been a schoolteacher, then an inspector, and who currently occupies a prominent post in the upper ranks of the provincial educational administration. Shaykh Uthman has served as a lay preacher in many local mosques over the years, and has only lately taken over as the *imām/khaṭīb* at the mosque sponsored by this association which his father founded and led until his recent death. This *shaykh* similarly plays heavily upon *amn* as a quasi-juridical process by which status changes are brought about. In this sermon, however, the Prophet is not depicted as seeking security; rather, he is dispensing it to others.

Presently a rich narrative segment from this sermon will be offered which presents an unusually dense weave of allusions. But a few linguistic remarks must preface this citation to enable an appreciation of certain rhetorical devices that enliven this passage and that are typical of this gifted preacher. One of the distinctive features of Shaykh Uthman's oratory is a nimble use of a pronounced stylistic technique which relies on what is known as "code-switching."[4] Of course, technically speaking, some measure of code-switching is almost unavoidable in a diglossia context, such as one finds with Egyptian Arabic, but Shaykh Uthman has developed his application of this pattern in a systematic fashion. He does this by adopting a sort of second voice as he preaches, taking the form of inter-linear comments, inserted in rapid-fire colloquial, in the midst of the rotund and cadenced statements spoken in *fusḥa*, that is, "high," "classical," or "standard" Arabic, which comprise the "real" text of the sermon. Since Friday sermons are supposed to be delivered in the standard language, Shaykh Uthman is able to combine the august authority associated with the Qurʾan and the classical tradition with the familiarity, concreteness, and creativity that are usually available only in the local patois. Sometimes, with a certain streak of pedagogy, even ostentation, Shaykh

Uthman frequently indulges in rhetorical affectations which he might well comment upon or freely reinterpret in a following statement, a sort of undertone, given in the colloquial language. While Shaykh Uthman is unmistakably an accomplished speaker of *fusha*, which is an art in itself and implies no small measure of scholarly accomplishment, he does not possess the ease and grace of an Azhari *shaykh*. Indeed, a number of Shaykh Uthman's expressions, although dressed in the proper vocabulary and spoken with the correct phonetic adjustments and changed word order, ring more as neologisms or deliberate archaicisms leaving the impression of a self-conscious mimic or even hypercorrection.

Here is an example, quite trivial in itself, but illustrative of the "switching" Shaykh Uthman engages in for various effects. It so happens that Shaykh Uthman would often address me in *fusha* rather than the colloquial language, which I normally spoke to him and to everyone else for that matter. On one occasion, we happened to pass one another going in opposite directions along an uncrowded street, and the Shaykh called out what is an acceptable greeting on the byways of Upper Egypt. He said *taruh fayn*, which translates literally as "where are you going?" The actual interrogative value of this salutation is analogous to "how are you?" in that it is a conventional form and not a serious inquiry into one's destination and purpose any more than the other expression is a sober query into one's health. For a response, it suffices to make a brief allusion to some general direction or any vague errand and then the banter of exchanges that comprise the greeting ritual proceeds. On this occasion, however, after calling out the greeting, the Shaykh crossed over to me, reached out to shake my hand, and repeated the greeting, but this time put it in impeccable classical form: *ayna tadhhab*, "where are you going?" The incongruity of this linguistic elevation brought a smile to his lips, and when I responded, with similar theatricality in pure classical Arabic, his grin broke into a chuckle. The playfulness of Shaykh Uthman's code-switching is amusing when it rides such a distance from low to high but has its more common use in the sermon where it introduces lightness and familiarity by moving from high to low.[5]

In the following sermon segment, delivered on December 28, 1978, I will note this code-switching, at least its most blatant cases, by putting the colloquial side comments into parentheses and translating them with a ring of the slang they have in context. In the dialogue that occurs in the narrative the Shaykh relates, he habitually changes his register, volume, and tempo to mark a quote. One is not sure, however, if he is exactly quoting the text from which he has derived this story, that is the *Sira* (biographical material on the Prophet's life), or whether he is paraphras-

ing, which, of course, would mean that he is inserting still another inter-
pretative step.

The books of *Sira*, oh Brothers, tell of a certain Sufwan ibn
'Umayya, one of the catastrophes who belonged to the Quraysh, so
long as he fought in battle against the Prophet, prayers of God and
peace upon him. He was a polytheist [*mushrik*] so long as he
fought in the ranks of those who know no God or Lord, fighting
the Prophet, prayers of God and peace upon him, and against the
words "there is no god but God, Muhammad is the Messenger of
God." But truth endures everlasting and the word of truth must fill
the world until God brings it to inherit the earth and all that is
upon it.

The Prophet, prayers of God and peace upon him, entered Mecca
as a conqueror [*fātiḥan*] and he rejoiced when he saw this accomplished for he conquered them by his patience. Sufwan ibn
'Umayya, this remarkable man, a polytheist, he thought that
Muhammad was like the Arabs in that he would not forget evil,
that he would harbor hatred and act treacherously, so he
approached 'Umayr ibn Wahb, who had been his friend, and he
whispered in his ear saying: "By heaven, there is no security [*amn*]
in the wrath of Muhammad, and there is no rescue for me but the
sea. I'm going to go and throw myself into it [sea]." So spoke
Sufwan ibn 'Umayya.

'Umayr ibn Wahb was a man whose heart God had filled with
light, even though he was late in coming to belief [*imān*] and
Islam. He immediately went up to the Prophet, prayers of God and
peace upon him, and said: "Oh Prophet of God. Indeed Sufwan,
who is, as you know, the chief of his people, he requests security
[*amn*]. Will you grant him security [*fa-hal ammantuhu*]?" The
Prophet, prayers of God and peace upon him, replied: "Indeed, we
grant him security [*āmmanāhu*]." And so he hurried back to him
[Sufwan] and said: "The Prophet of God has granted you security."
Whereupon Sufwan said: "By heaven I won't return with you until
he makes some public gesture [*'alān*] in my regard." (Hey, there,
what ya' afraid of?) The measures taken by the Arabs do not accord
with the measures of Islam or those embraced by Muhammad. (By
George, will you look at the special treatment he's after! He wants
some public gesture for Pete's sake!)

'Umayr ibn Wahb returned to the Prophet, prayers of God and
peace upon him, and said: "Oh Prophet of God, prayers of God and
peace upon him, he requests a public gesture." (Now look here, any
half-way normal man would have just told him, "why do you keep
bugging us? Now we've got plenty of good tough guys so just get

out of here. Fancy that, we give him something and then he wants more!") But the Prophet, prayers of God and peace upon him, as the books of *Sira* relate (what do you think he's gonna give him?), indeed, he gave him his turban.

Some of the Companions say that [Muhammad] took off his outer garment and rolled it up and gave it to ʿUmayr ibn Wahb as the public gesture for him to present to Sufwan ibn ʿUmayya until he was certain that the Prophet had granted him security [*qad āmmanahu*]. (Here ya' are, buddy, take it, it's yours!) ʿUmayr ibn Wahb went with it to Sufwan ibn ʿUmayya—the turban that [Muhammad] had on when he entered Mecca as a conqueror, which he now bestowed as a public gesture so that the ranks of his followers would treat [Sufwan] as a guest, in order that God might open the heart of such a man, so that he might take a place among his people and be one of them. (Here ya' are, my good man, it's yours.)

[Sufwan] looked at it, and it seemed to him like this was too much, and he said: "Is this the real one?" (What? Do you think he's sent you a fake or phony? No, this is the real McCoy!) At that, he immediately went to the Prophet of God, prayers of God and peace upon him, and the chronicler says that he was riding his horse while the Prophet, upon him prayers and peace, was praying.

Now turn this over in your hearts—[Sufwan] did not yet embrace the belief [*imān*] because he made no move to dismount from the saddle of his horse. (Because he figured he might walk on something and get his cloak muddy.) He continued to bear the conceit and arrogance of the Arabs, for he stayed on his horse while the Prophet was under his feet at prayer. (He didn't care what was going on.) The Prophet continued his prayer until he had finished with the *salām* whereupon he looked up and said: "Sufwan ibn ʿUmayya?" And our fellow replied: "Yes." Then he said in unadorned Arabic, "Oh, Muhammad" [*yā muhammad*] just that bare [*hakidha jāf*], "Oh Muhammad, ʿUmayr ibn Wahb claims that you have issued me an invitation." (What a pretext! Who does this guy make himself out to be? He claims he just sent him an invitation, while only a few minutes ago, he was saying "help me" and was about to throw himself into the sea!) "Verily, ʿUmayr ibn Wahb has come to me and claims that you have issued me an invitation." Whereupon, the Prophet, prayers of God and peace upon him, at once replied in speech both sweet and gracious.

[Sufwan] had said, "Oh Muhammad," but [Muhammad] says: "Get down, Abu Wahb." Muhammad says "Abu Wahb," he doesn't say, "Oh Sufwan." (*Sufwan* in Arabic, look it up, it means rock or stone. He doesn't want to say to him, "Get down, Oh Sufwan," like some kind of rock with dirt on it, so he says "Get down, Abu Wahb.") He even points out the way, "Get down, Abu Wahb, welcome, welcome." At that, he dismounts and the Prophet of God, prayers of God and peace upon him, grants him security [*āmmanahu*].

At this, our fellow asks: "Will you not honor me with two months?" (He's after a pledge!) "Will you not honor me with two months?" (If Muhammad had been any half-way normal man, he would have told him, "listen, buddy, come off it, get out of here.") "Will you honor me with two months?" [Muhammad] said: "We will grant you four!" (Take them, my good man.) Four months. (Four months or whatever you like.) Oh the wisdom of the Prophet, prayers and peace upon him.

The books of *Sira* tell that the Prophet engaged in severals raids and campaigns in this period and some of the books say that Sufwan ibn 'Umayya gave his own armor to the Prophet and that he fought with it.

The chronicler says that once when the Companions of the Prophet, prayers of God and peace upon him, were returning with sheep of those whom they had defeated [that is, booty] the Prophet was riding on a horse and beside him Sufwan ibn 'Umayya was on his mount, and he had not yet accepted Islam. Sufwan looked there at the narrow lanes of Mecca and upon the sheep. The Prophet saw his feelings and that something was urgently pressing upon his heart, and he said, "Oh Sufwan ibn 'Umayya, do you like that lane?" He said, "Yes, oh Prophet of God." He said, "Do you like what's in it?" He said, "By God, yes [*allahuma na'am*]." He said, "All that is in it is yours." All at once, Sufwan said, "By heaven, no one bestows in this conciliatory manner except the soul of a prophet. I testify there is no god but God and I testify that Muhammad is the Messenger of God."

The Prophet, prayers of God and peace upon him, he didn't have time to get angry at anyone, because he is the herald, for he is great of soul and great of zeal. He wants to win someone over to his ranks every day. As he told to 'Ali ibn Abu Talib when he was departing for Yemen, words to the effect: "Better than the world and all it contains is that you bring guidance to one man." Prayers of God and peace upon you, oh my master, Oh Prophet of God.

This story, occurring at the Prophet's triumphant entry into his old community and the most influential city in Arabia, makes both a distinction and a fusion of the idea of security as social and political "status" and security as belief in God and His Prophet. Although the two converge symbolically at the end, the Prophet suspends the isomorphism as if to contrast the ways of Islam with the ways of the Arabs. As histories of these great events indicate, Muhammad pardoned virtually all of his former enemies in Mecca. As one modern biographer, Emile Dermenghem put it: "The victor's soul was drunk with pardoning. There, in his birthplace, realizing his desires, he only dreamed of winning over the hearts of his people through generosity as the Koran had imposed. He was, moreover, too intelligent not to take into account that reprisals would have been absurd."[6]

Upon the capitulation of the city, his army entered it without force, and although a few specific murderers and slanderers were not spared, he had it announced to the general population that there were two choices, if they meant to stay: they must either profess faith and obedience to Allah and his Prophet or they would be killed. Practically all converted, for henceforth all benefits would come from that quarter. However, some of the Muslims who accompanied Muhammad in this great hour of his triumph were not as inclined to forget old feuds and uneven scores. Hence even the Muslim histories acknowledge incidents of "unauthorized" slayings of Meccans by the Muslim victors. Needless to say, Shaykh Uthman in his sermon does not refer to such blemishes in the history of Islam, although an awareness of such realities makes Sufwan's apprehensions and anxiety for a "public gesture" quite a bit more reasonable. Shaykh Uthman's ridicule of Sufwan, who was a cousin of the Prophet on the maternal side, and apparently a self-centered old aristocrat, ignores the psychological realism in the episode, in order to emphasize the open-handedness and liberality of the Prophet.

Symbolically, this story dealing with the triumph over Mecca can be seen as the reversal of the *hijra,* or flight to Medina, which results in the transformation of Arab tribal solidarity into an egalitarian Muslim community founded not on *amn,* but upon *imān,* faith. Muhammad had earlier been ostracized because he refused to acknowledge their particularist deities. Now that he is master, he dispenses security even to a pagan as a sign of the bounty of his universal God. Furthermore, the story encodes the transformation of the basis of security from worldly might to spiritual right. In the first place, the victor's turban, emblem of political and military supremacy, is donated to a vanquished chief as a token of submission. At their first encounter, Muhammad, who grants security, is at prayer while Sufwan is martially mounted. Note that Sufwan in a posture of dominance is told to dismount and he obeys the Prophet who had been "under his feet." Then second, we are told that the Prophet wore the armor of Sufwan. Finally, in a most significant exchange which results in the conversion of Sufwan, Muhammad presents a gift and the old chieftain accepts it. It is not simply that Muhammad demonstrates his superior authority by giving, and Sufwan acknowledges it by receiving. Rather, the utter contradiction to the old social logic is that Muhammad gives booty that belongs to the captors to an "outsider" who not only had no hand in winning it, but is himself in the category of an adversary.

It is interesting in the presentation of this narrative by Shaykh Uthman that he draws this transformation of security into faith out of a social and political idiom and he makes it into a parable to encourage good manners. This is seen in the consistent character of his side comments, in the "moral" he states at the end (the advice to 'Ali) and finally by the way he magnifies the use of terms of address at the first encounter of the two principal figures. Note the way the preacher calls attention to the supposed civility and graciousness of Muhammad's word and the supposed "bare," even rude address of Sufwan. We have remarked, however, that the use of "Oh Muhammad [yā muhammad)" as a vocative in the recounting of episodes from the Sira or in other "dramatic" presentations is neither unusual nor necessarily disrespectful. In other sermons by Shaykh Uthman such a form of address has even been put in the mouth of Muslims with no indication whatsoever of any impropriety. In the Sira itself, from my own cursory reading of Alfred Guillaume's translation of ibn Ishaq's Sirat Rasul Allah (which is usually known by the name of its editor, ibn Hasham), I have noticed a pattern which confirms that "Oh Muhammad" is a form of address used by non-Muslims, whereas Muslims either use no form of address or, as was seen in the sermon, they use the form, "Oh Prophet of God."[7] The formulaic phrase "prayers of God and peace upon him" is a semantically frozen refrain which is freely added by the preacher after any mention of Muhammad, even when technically it mixes persons. For instance, in the above sermon, this formulaic is put in the mouth of 'Umayr ibn Wahb when he is directly addressing the Prophet, in which case the formula should be changed to "prayers of God and peace upon you" but this is never done.

The preacher holds up the Prophet to the admiration of his audience because he uses the kunyā, that is, a teknonymy, "Abu Wahb" (literally, "father of Wahb") instead of the proper name "Sufwan." Interestingly, only two weeks before, in the sermon of December 15, Shaykh Uthman was relating from the Sira the conversion of Khalid ibn al-Walid, another Meccan who had been an aggressive enemy of Islam. The Shaykh there makes a similar fuss over the use of a first name. In this instance, however, the Shaykh praises the Prophet's use of the expression "Oh Khalid" (the exact parallel to "Oh Muhammad" or "Oh Sufwan") because, says the Shaykh, this directness shows the Prophet's great openness, familiarity, and mercifulness. The preacher attempts to justify the Prophet's nonuse of "Sufwan" by indicating that etymologically the word means "stone" hereby implying that a name has some kind of literal link to the man. But if the Shaykh were consistent here, he could only rightly commend Sufwan by the same token because "Muhammad" is etymologically linked to the word for "praise," one of the central attributes of God. Hence, the whole point here is not really the etymology of names. (Interestingly, in other sermons, I have heard the Shaykh refer to Mcʿawiyah, another Meccan aristocrat who came late to Islam and the first Umayyid Caliph. The Shaykh had nothing but good things to say about him, with no comments on his name, which means, etymologically, "howling bitch.") The Shaykh's apparent interest in language has other motives than description, for he is making the terms of address a symbol for his principal point about civility, manners, and politeness.

From a sociolinguistic point of view, the different naming terms used in the brief exchange that he is apparently citing from the *Sira* can be most immediately interpreted as signaling social distance. While "Oh Muhammad" is a perfectly proper vocative in the mouth of a non-Muslim throughout the *Sira*, the *kunyā* "Abu Wahb" is clearly a term of familiarity and closeness, a sort of *tutoiement*. One unmistakable indication that the Shaykh's point about the use of names is superficial and forced comes later in the narrative in the second exchange between the two figures. Whether the Shaykh is quoting a text from the *Sira* or dramatizing the passage *ad libitum* is not clear, but note that in direct address the preacher cites the Prophet as calling the man "Oh Sufwan ibn ʿUmayya," a term which the Shaykh told us a few minutes earlier would imply that the man was a "dirty rock." Likewise, note that at the end of the episode the Shaykh puts the usual greeting of Muslims into Sufwan's mouth: "Oh Prophet of God." In other words, the Shaykh's point about naming terms set forth in a nutshell what the rest of his side comments confirm, namely that kindliness, patience, and pardon are superior to social rank, wealth, and Arab dignity. Security in the sense of protection and well-being appears in this paradigm as a preparatory stage, an interstitial category that culminates in belief. Once again, it is not the text of the Qurʾan in its inimitability, its "reasonableness," or its knowledge that achieve conversion but the Prophet's effective use of social institutions. Security is mediated by the Prophet; it does not derive unmediated by belief (*imān*) in the Qurʾan, as depicted by Shaykh Umar. For Shaykh Uthman, whose sermons tend often to be drawn from the *Sira*, it is the reconciliation of hostile groups that epitomizes the unity of Islam, while for Shaykh Umar, whose sermons are steeped in the Qurʾanic text, it is a matter of bringing together "differences" of verbal expression.

At the end of many of his sermons, Shaykh Uthman turns to a discussion of current events or local topical issues, sometimes responding to letters from listeners, sometimes drawing upon news items, and sometimes giving personal reflections on recent events he has observed in the community. Sometimes such applied comments are included in the body of the sermon itself and sometimes they occur more as comments given after the stylized prayers which always conclude the Friday sermon in any mosque. Those listening remain seated, of course, for the actual ritual worship, *al-ṣalāh*, only follows thereafter. In the case of the sermon already cited, delivered on December 29, 1978, Shaykh Uthman continued after the sermon proper with a host of such comments, including remarks dealing with what he called *shāriʿ al-amn* (literally, "security street," the idiom glosses "in matters of security"). He lists different kinds of security, such as "political security" and "security of nutrition," noting that there is much clamor about such topics, and he wants to translate the highblown rhetoric into practical terms for what he calls "the man on the street." These are his remarks:

> Today we hear much about matters of security, but what does the citizen [*muwaṭan*] want? The ordinary person, the man on the street, he wants to be assured of a good piece of bread [*lughmat al-ʿaysh*] first of all, and to be assured of security [*amn*] so he can live in peace [*amāna*]. For the Prophet said: "Whoever is secured in his home is unharmed in his country and he has his daily provision, it is as if he owned the whole world."
>
> So the first thing the citizen wants is a good piece of bread, and after that security in his house and on the street, and after that, hospitals and health units. If these are assured to the citizen, and the citizen is assured of these, he won't want for anything. He will sleep in peace and worship wholeheartedly. I was talking to you recently about some of our brothers who visited Port Said or somewhere, and how they said that there a person who sells sugar cane juice keeps the sugar cane right outside his shop, and the carpenter leaves his wood out in the open in front of his shop, and people feel at ease to pray outside their homes.
>
> By Heaven, prayer is always linked to security, my Brothers, the security of nutrition, the security of the homeland [*waṭan*], political security, all kinds of security. As soon as the citizen feels that security, he can say: Oh Lord, to God the King be praise, Oh Lord.

From here the preacher goes into a detailed discussion about the prices of essential food items and household needs like kerosene. Prices are a source of immense popular anxiety and constant preoccupation in Egypt, where the government has until very recently controlled both the flow and the retail of virtually all basic commodities. Due to numerous economic factors, usually associated with Sadat's "open door" policy, creeping inflation had topped black-marketing as the way for shopkeepers to anticipate the new prosperity which all hoped would follow from Sadat's peace initiative with Israel and his budding friendship with America. Clearly from the above remarks, Shaykh Uthman has a very concrete notion of security: food, shelter, health care. But to this he adds immediately that security is linked to prayer, referring here to the obligatory ritual prayer, *al-ṣalāh*.

When Shaykh Uthman ties prayer to the concrete necessities of daily life, he is not merely using this religious ritual as an image of the fullness of the social order. For him, prayer has quite as pragmatic a purpose as the more physical conditions for security, for he portrays it as the mainstay of good mental health. He has made this point in a number of sermons, but he made it most straightforwardly when he appeared, for the first time, on national Egyptian television, on a weekly religious talk-show called *hādha huwa al-islām* (This Is Islam). The host and the other guests had been discussing questions relating to security and Islam, when this question was put to Shaykh Uthman:

> Is the mosque a link between the spread of security [*amn*] and reassurance in the souls of Muslims?

Shaykh Uthman answered as follows, although unfortunately it is not complete because there was (as is fairly common in Egypt) a breakdown in transmission. Nevertheless, his point is clear:

> In reality, if we are to say that there are factories for the production of security and belief [*amn wa imān*] then the mosques of good Muslims are those factories. The requirements of security are to be considered as among man's natural needs. The guarantee of Islam is a good guarantee and it is bound to the mosque because it makes the sons of the prayer-mat (if you'll permit the expression) always peaceful and secure. For the Prophet says: "If one is sad or in difficulty, let him resort to prayer."
>
> It is enough to say that once when inspiration was delayed, the Prophet clung to the Kaʿba and day and night, God's word descended:
>> In the name of God, the Merciful, the Compassionate.
>> By the white forenoon, and by the brooding night. Thy Lord has neither forsaken thee nor hates thee and the Last shall be better for

thee than the First. Thy Lord shall give thee, and thou shalt be satisfied. And the rest of the Sura (93:1–5).

It is enough to cite the splendid and illuminated *ḥadīth* and all
the sayings of the Prophet, prayers of God and peace upon him, are
splendid and illuminated when he says: "Whoever is secured in his
home is unharmed in his country and he has daily provision, it is
as if he owned the whole world."

And if people in our day—and this is the tax of the era we live
in—if they sometimes miss tranquility, and they sometimes lack
the security of their inner selves, and people are closed up within
themselves, Islam gives them a place. [transmission interrupted]

We find that the Prophet gives a noble example of this, for the
mosque always imparts peace. He used to find a certain Abu Hammam, as it is related by Abu Saʿid al-Khuduri, and Abu Hammam
he found always in the mosque even at times not specific to the
prayer. And he said to him, "You, Abu Hammam, why are
you continuously in the mosque? What does this mean?" [He
answered:] "I am full of anxiety and debts, and I cannot pay them."
The Prophet said: "Shall I tell you some words that if you say
them, all your troubles will leave you, and all your debts will be
settled." The Prophet then said: "Abu Hammam, say, 'I take refuge
in you, Oh God, from anxiety and sadness. I take refuge in you
from incapacity and lethargy. I take refuge in you from cowardli-
ness and shame. I take refuge in you from the enormity of debt and
the subjugation to men.'"

Oh Abu Hammam! The Prophet ordered him to take refuge in
God, for people take refuge in different shelters. Oh sons, the
mosque has taken the place of the person of Muhammad who had
dispensed *amn* so liberally, even to his old enemies.

Just as man no longer needs protection from feuding tribes, so security
no longer consists in a "status" transformation. Today, the enemy is anxiety and economic distress, problems like those of Abu Hammam, and so
security must involve protection from these new enemies. It is perfectly
consistent with this preaching that the benevolent society of which
Shaykh Uthman's mosque is a part is extremely active in a variety of
social, commercial, and educational programs. Shaykh Uthman takes seriously the role of the mosque as engine of security, and with its limited
resources, he encourages use of these facilities to reassure those who need
a community and a visible institution as the symbol for the security which
is otherwise only the words they profess to believe.

8   Morality and Religion in
Ideology and Action

From the outset we have stressed that the role of the Islamic preacher in Egypt cannot be adequately described by any single model drawn from classical socioreligious theory. Attempts to reduce this role to what is arguably its historical norm, its primitive prototype, or putative cross-cultural equivalents are only partially satisfying. Similarly, efforts to define one master category as the basis of all others have also tended to elude or ignore the remarkable variety of social structures and ritual patterns that constitute this continuity and simultaneity of forms. The fluidity that surrounds the indigenous concept of the *shaykh* or more formally the *imām/khaṭīb* stems in part from the relative underdevelopment of research and reflection regarding this position. But no less important is the fact that the role itself is currently undergoing uneven changes in regard to its function and authority due to multiple disjunctures in the society at large.

It has been noted that today many if not most educated Muslims, especially those who are politically active, leaning toward the left or the right, are outspoken in their rejection of any notion of vested religious authority. But this widespread view is premised upon two contrary visions, secular modernism and religious fundamentalism. Hence, its proponents converge on an ideological claim rather than on social description. Nevertheless, at practically every level of empirical observation, there continue to exist today, as there have existed virtually from the days of the Prophet, certain individuals, and even culturally articulated classes of individuals and families, who enjoy privileges, exert influence, and perform functions in virtue of superiority in matters construed as religious, appealing to authority understood implicitly or explicitly as based on divine selection, inheritance, talent, knowledge, achievement, or some other criteria.

In an effort to reconcile the alleged ideologically conceived null set of persons possessing religious prerogatives with the indisputable reality of variously accredited authoritative figures, we have formulated a threefold typology of preachers depicted as specialists in three approaches to transformation of charisma into everyday living. Similarly, each of these types of preachers has been associated with a particular form of social institution that constitutes a version of a mosque community. Each displays its own set of attitudes and its proper orientation toward social involvement, thus reflecting patterns of the sort Weber described as "roads to salvation." Each type of preacher follows a characteristic pattern which validates his identity and largely accounts for his effectiveness within some particular setting. All three types, each in its own way, seek to gain recognition and then to maintain it through the implementation of their ritual role. In doing so, each also necessarily articulates, however incompletely or insignificantly, a formula for extending this symbolic performance, asserted as his legitimate right, into the history of the actual community.[1]

In the case of pre-modern urban, literate Muslim civilization, the most widely recognized formal religious specialists were designated as the *'ulamā'*, who formed a discrete class of what even the magisterial H. A. R. Gibb scarcely scruples to describe as a "clergy."[2] Nor is such a characterization restricted to those who might be regarded as lax, ethnocentric, or narrow in their perspective. For example, Edward Said, in a recent literary work treating nineteenth-century India, glosses the term "mullah" without qualification as a "Muslim priest."[3] Nor is such terminology objectionable within the framework of comparative social science, since the *'ulamā'* did in fact constitute a privileged, hierarchized, essentially urban corps that typically occupied the middle ground between the ruling elite (often composed of a military aristocracy) and various elements of the indigenous population. Through their virtual monopoly over legal and educational services, with ancillary functions as advocates, arbitrators, administrators, and ritual specialists, and while maintaining their nearly autonomous economic base as overseers of the vast properties designated as *waqf*, these clerks and doctors were the primary agents of systematization and rationalization in their societies. Increasingly in modern times, however, these positions have been taken over by centralized secular bureaucracies. Although some *shaykhs* carry on the tradition of the formal *'ulamā'*, as they continue as teachers, legal consultants, and administrators within the shrinking confines of those venerable institutions still operated under religious auspices, the duties of most such figures are now centered around activities directly related to ritual leadership and instruction within the mosque. Thus their "clerical" character in the contemporary religious sense of this term may be said to be more pronounced today than it was several centuries ago.

The Preacher as Image and Actor

In addition to the literate realm of the *'ālim,* or scholar, the popular culture of Egyptian Muslims, both urban and rural, has long tended to understand religious authority as centered in the *walī,* or saint. Whether living or dead, this figure is widely believed to possess supernatural powers that enable him, or less frequently her, to act as a miracle-worker, a clairvoyant mystic, and an intercessory patron. Such a holy man is normally closely associated with Sufi fraternities whose constituency often cuts across potential lines of social fragmentation, especially among the peasant and proletariat masses whose primary bonds were expressed as family, tribe, neighborhood, village, or craft guild.

Alongside these two types is the figure of the *mujāhid,* or divinely inspired warrior, who also stands as a perennial representative of religious authority, but whose influence inevitably rises in times of turmoil and struggle. For this term, derived from the noun *jihād,* resonates with the summons to repeat the glorious early conquests of Islam and the victory over the medieval Crusaders once more in the face of European imperialism and neo-colonialism. But this concept also points inward toward the overcoming of domestic obstacles. It has wide currency as a reference to militant efforts to bring about societal reform or to stir up consciences to mobilize opinion to combat against internal corruption as well as external aggression.

The mythic appeal as well as the political force of these types of religious roles reappear in contemporary Egypt in varied combinations. Different historical periods or isolated classical achievements that portray each of them apart from the others as preeminent are, not surprisingly, often selectively recounted and extolled by the participants in each case. Thus the preacher serves not only as an image, that is, a ritual icon mediating within a given constellation of social realities and idealized aspirations, but also as an actor, dramatizing the historical processes that impress the stamp of divine order upon human chaos. The preacher gives form and direction to the multiplicity of expectations and bewilderments that are born of the believer's resolve to submit to God's law. Symbolically the *khaṭīb* steps into the breach between the eternal word and the changing world. He reinterprets the confusion that may result when what is held to be the sum of goodness and truth seems to be vanquished by alien invaders. This he may do by creative adaptation as well as by persistent imitation of canonical dictates, by explanation and assertiveness no less than by silence and inaction, all the while recasting the significance of immediate particulars into, as Geertz's famous definition of religion states it, "conceptions of a general order of existence."[4]

In the last two chapters, we have analyzed sermon rhetoric for the quality of linkage predicated between the concepts of *amn* and *imān*. Within the framework of three types of preachers we depicted two general modes of semantic conversion designated by an analogy to poetics as metaphor and metonym. As a heuristic paradigm, this framework sought to suggest a procedure for framing the conversion of symbols characteristic of the rhetorical styles that mark specific types of preachers. At the same time, the analysis of sermons in their contexts has also provided an invaluable point of entry for a survey of the general range of topics that preoccupy various preachers who in turn are responding to the social personalities of the mosque communities which they lead.

As we continue to focus on the sermon as the nexus for investigating the authority of the preacher, we will shift our emphasis toward the preacher's relationship with his audience and with the wider society. Hence, the starting point here will not be the exploration of stylistic patterns that disclose rhetorical strategies, but rather the design of the overall reference system whereby a preacher alludes through the sermon to the order of social, political and economic action external to the ritual setting. In doing so, we expand our interest in symbols beyond the Geertzian "problem of meaning" to reflect directly on the second dimension of what Abner Cohen has called the "two dimensional man."[5] Many have convincingly argued that Cohen's own elaboration of this dynamic process suffers from oversimplification.[6] Too often he seems to divide his theoretical capital into mutually exclusive opposites, leaving a framework that verges on a caricature of Herbert Marcuse's "one dimensional man." As a result, Cohen's two master categories of "power" and "symbolism" exercise a sort of reductionist tyranny over all concurrent modes of representation. In the same fashion, Cohen's argument is also hampered by his unfortunate reliance of the concept of "mystification" to describe the capacity of symbols to bridge conflicts over cultural values and to reshape, even regenerate, social relations in constructive ways.[7] Nevertheless, he has provided a clear and useful demonstration of how symbols make "visible" the form and function of "invisible" organizations which underlie and subdivide formal social structures in an urban African context that has many common features with Minya.

By stressing the Weberian principle that never loses sight of the fertile distinction between power and authority, that is, between coercion and legitimacy, it is hoped that Cohen's basic insights when applied to an ethnography of Islamic preaching will again prove fruitful. With this provision, then, we turn to the procedure to be used in approaching sermons and preachers not simply as the occasions for the symbolic redefinition of religious moods and motivations but also as arenas for active, if indirect, participation in the social, cultural, and political confrontations that define the fundamental character of the encounter between creature and creator.

Salām *and* Islām: *Transformations of Morality and Religion*

The Arabic terms *salām* and *islām*, which form the second couplet of the widely repeated slogan already cited, shall provide the theme for this further exposition of the sermon. Through an examination of this contrast we hope to advance from the speech and its speaker to those whom he addresses. As "key symbols,"[8] the two terms, which are available for almost unlimited application, unmistakably represent enduring, diffuse, and central values. Their range and intensity exceed that of *amn* and *imān*, which we glossed rather conventionally, so much so, perhaps, that it is tempting to press their conceptual content still further in the direction of a double abstraction that would link them closely with the twin perfections indicative of the profane and sacred realms. Our initial purpose was to chart underlying patterns of rhetorical transference of meanings by way of symbols. With this demonstrated, we now adopt another tactic, designed to pursue a related but different interest, one more properly committed to "pragmatic" rather than "semantic" analysis. To signal this new direction a less literal translation of these two terms is also desirable. We prefer therefore not to resort to the transparent English cognates of "peace" and "Islam" but rather to propose another sort of idiomatic interpretation. In this light a more accurate gloss with respect to the native point of view would be to render these terms respectively as "morality" and "religion."

The motives for introducing this broader translation are manifold, but before detailing them, it is helpful to note certain linguistic parallels that link these two terms in the same way as was the case with the earlier pair, *amn* and *imān*. First, *salām* and *islām* are morphologically derived from a single trilateral root. Their usage as fixed nouns with more or less frozen semantic content invites one to treat them as quite separate lexemes. But their common etymology includes a number of related connotations. A partial lexicographical illustration suffices to demonstrate this:

salima *salām:* to be safe and sound, unharmed, intact, secure; to
be unobjectionable, blameless, faultless; to be certain,
established, clearly proven; to be free, to escape.

aslama *islām:* to forsake, give up, betray; to hand over, to turn
over; to leave, abandon; to deliver up, surrender, expose;
to commit oneself; declare oneself committed to the will of
God, become a Muslim, embrace Islam.[9]

Drawing solely upon such dictionary definitions clearly does not provide
the specific English terms we have just suggested. On the level of context-
free reference, that is, lexicography, the term "morality" would be better
rendered by the plural form *akhlāq* and "religion" would probably be
given best as *dīn.* The interest here, however, is not to shrink these concepts of *salām* and *islām* to their thinnest English correspondences but to
select terms that indicate their broader scope as pivotal cultural categories
at the heart of public ritual rhetoric. In order to proceed effectively in this
examination, moving beyond a literal translation to the registering of
their social significance, it is helpful to encode the stated methodological
intention in terms that reflect the cultural implications that are invisible
on the level of an abstract text.

Nevertheless, there can be no disputing that the noun *salām* denotes
"peace" and even though this word abounds with a rich array of religiopolitical resonances, as does its most common English translation, certain particularities of the Arabic should not pass unremarked. Clearly in
both languages, the respective terms convey a sense of harmony and security, the presence of solidarity and absence of hostility, with its beneficial
consequences for personal and public affairs. But for the Arabic-speaking
Egyptian, several additional associations accompany this expression that
would not ordinarily occur to the speaker of English. For one thing, the
Arabic term is embedded in the conventional Muslim greeting, *al-salām
ʿalaykum,* a phrase which is recommended for use by Muslims in the
Qurʾan itself.[10] Moreover, not only is this phrase consecrated as the
proper form of salutation, but one form of the verb derived from this same
root includes among its meanings the idiomatic expression "to greet" or
"to give one's regards to someone." Also, there are multiple uses of *salām*
in formal worship and other ritual settings. It appears most prominently
at the conclusion of the daily ritual prayer when each person praying uses
this formula twice, first turning to the right and then repeating it, turning
to the left. This liturgical rubric is known as *al-salām.* Likewise, this
greeting is formally prescribed as the opening statement of a preacher
which he addresses to the congregation when he climbs the pulpit for the
sermon at the time of the Friday noon assembly.[11]

Another standardized use of the term appears as part of the pious exclamation that is uttered, especially in ritual settings, after any mention of the name or even a title of the Prophet Muhammad, *ṣalli allah ʿalayhi wa salim*, that is, "God bless him and grant him peace." An abridged form of this eulogy is also attached, although less frequently, to the mention of other Qurʾanic prophets, *ʿalayhi salām*, that is, "upon him be peace." As a substantive, *salām* is also included as one of the ninety-nine beautiful names of God and the male name ʿAbd al-Salam, literally, "servant of the peaceful one" is quite common in Egypt. On still another level, not unrelated, the term is often heard in the form of a colloquial expletive, such as "*ya salām*," giving voice variously to feelings of relief, surprise, delight, shock, outrage, or disgust. In this sense it is roughly akin to such English expressions as "for heaven's sake" or "My God!" although it does not seem to carry the undertone of imprecation which is sometimes perceived as slightly irreverent if not blasphemous.

Allusions of *salām* referring to events and conditions in the social order are also very frequent. Apart from its free use in local parlance as the opposite of feud and anxiety, its use as a national policy signal, especially since Sadat's historic initiative to Jerusalem in 1977, has greatly inflated the relevance of the expression in Egypt. Overall, the term has acquired a positive valence conveying patriotism and even nationalist fervor. During the initial period of research when these sermons were collected, the term *salām* came to preoccupy the media. In the build-up to the signing of the Camp David Accords and especially after Sadat was awarded the Nobel Peace Prize together with Menachem Begin, in 1978, the Egyptian state-controlled media freely acclaimed the nation's leader not only as *baṭal al-ḥarb* (the hero of war), a title originally bestowed after October 1973, but *baṭal al-salām* (the hero of peace). As a slogan it seemed to permeate all areas of public life. Just as a new café or shop opened in the mid-1950s might still bear the name echoing the era of its foundation, such as "Independence Bookshop," or, if it was established a few years later, "High Dam Café," or "Unity Furniture Store," so too at the end of the 1970s one could observe new facades with labels such as "Peace Hardware Supply."

But even apart from the anticipated prosperity that was loudly promised as the principal benefit of reconciliation with Israel, *salām* conveyed the view that Egypt would return to its self-declared central position in regional affairs as leader of the Arab world. Remnants of ʿAbd al-Nasir's radical policies calling for mass mobilization, which had encouraged uprisings abroad and had threatened numerous conservative Arab monarchies which he had dismissed as "reactionaries," were still lingering. But from the mid-1970s onward the soaring price of petroleum had made a number of these states, especially in the Gulf, magnets for long- and short-term emigrant labor from Egypt. Thus *salām* also suggested a relaxing of the political tensions that continued to complicate and obstruct the flow of an eager Egyptian labor force to enormously lucrative jobs in oil-rich Arab states. Especially after his peace initiative, Sadat's regime encountered increasing resistance to cooperation from these wealthy neighbors. But even before this, serious problems remained unsettled, as was clear from the border skirmish between Egypt and Libya in August 1977. Sadat frequently commented on the alleged shortcomings of leaders in various Arab states, making remarks that were echoed by preachers. But Libya's unpredictable Qaddafi, certainly his favorite *bête noire*, was openly accused of supporting Egyptian dissidents and even terrorists in an effort to overthrow Sadat as the prelude to the unification of Egypt and Libya, supposedly under Tripoli's leadership. Moreover, reports of clandestine financial aid from hostile foreign governments smuggled to Islamic student extremists were, in fact, assumed to be true by most residents in Minya, who therefore longed for "peace" in their streets as a direct consequence of improved regional cooperation.

It must not be overlooked, too, that under the banner of *salām* Sadat, and to a lesser extent his successor Mubarak, took decisive steps on several occasions to coopt or to muzzle political opposition. One of Sadat's preferred techniques for countering unacceptable challenges to his firm hold on power was to call for a popular referendum, supposedly to elicit citizen response to his fairly autocratic decisions. The campaign for such support conducted in April 1978 presented *salām* quite baldly as a choice to be either accepted or rejected. In addition, on the same ticket voters were asked to endorse the removal from the media of anyone who held so-called atheistic ideologies and to approve the banning from public office anyone who had "corrupted political life" prior to the 1952 revolution. As was typical of such exercises, the government subsequently claimed a 98.29 percent "yes" response, with 85 percent of the electorate responding.

Traditionally most mosque preachers in Upper Egypt have seldom involved themselves directly in explicit political contests on the national and international levels. This reluctance stems not only from the quite reasonable fear of potential reprisals, but also because they, like their congregations, seem realistically aware of their exclusion from the mechanisms of policy formation and decision-making which would render efforts to influence government officials as futile. But this is not to say that shifts in matters of national and international political and economic policy do not engage their attention, nor that they are exempt from feeling the effects of such policies enacted in their name. For they, again like their congregations, are generally quite conscious of their vulnerability in the face of resistance to official action. But even if immediate engagement in political affairs on this high level is unusual, the assessment of such activity from a moral perspective is quite common. Moral judgments are not constrained by the limitations imposed on practical politics and morality as a field of discourse is not the subject of restrictive laws such as those that carefully hedge about the range of explicitness permitted in matters of parties, platforms, and the selection of candidates. One result of this political marginalization is an amplification of the symbolic potency of moral pronouncements. Governing is seen not simply as a secular task but also, perhaps even primarily, as a sacred performance. The preacher as actor is easily compared to the president, who is also another preacher. Sermons, therefore, may be seen as emanating from the mosque pulpit as well as from the Parliamentary dais although the implications of what is perceived as comparable rhetoric is rarely the same in these distinct institutional settings. Thus just as the idiom of morality may be exploited to serve political ends within the arena of power and its distribution, so too the concrete particulars of local politics may serve as the vehicle for pronouncements upon morality deriving from the imperatives of religion.

This distinction between domains of discourse suggests both the continuities and disjunctures between the social meaning of *salām* when used, for example, by the president and when used in the course of a sermon. Although everyone may speak in favor of *salām*, this apparent unanimity on one level may at the same time express contrary intentions to different groups and in different settings. Nor does this double dimension necessarily always imply fruitful grounds of confusion. For it is often precisely through artful leaps between the layers of such opposed contexts that a given preacher maneuvers to give the term various shades of meaning. Finally, the need to reckon with the contradictions as well as the consistencies that link rhetoric to action justifies the converting of *salām* into a concept that more definitely embodies both the obligation and the freedom conveyed by the term morality. *Salām* therefore may be seen to embrace all aspects of mundane experience, as the essential quality that brings harmony to conscience and to society.

The second Arabic term, *islām*, although instantly recognized as a self-evident loan word in English, must also be reviewed lest surface similarity lead to distortions of cultural content. In English, when written, where capital letters provide it marking as a proper noun, Islam, together with its derivative adjective, Islamic, is universally reckoned to denote a vast but specific object. In Arabic, however, where there are no capital letters and no sharp conception of common versus proper nouns, the term lacks such a boundary. Moreover, Islam for Muslims themselves represents something lived that claims a range of empirical and idealized references extending immeasurably beyond the pale of its deceptive anglicized homonym. In English the term evokes a clouded notion, reflecting a long and ambiguous history of largely competitive, often hostile relations between two neighboring civilizations. But its usage in Arabic, among those whose culture is unimaginable apart from everything associated with the word, is still more nuanced.[12] As a gerund within an Arabic sentence, *islām* does not necessarily refer at all to religion but may, theoretically at least, designate the idea of "surrender" and "resignation" or "commitment" quite apart from any suggestion of a divine will. The contextually marked usage, however, has all but displaced this abstract meaning so that some scholars have argued that *islām* is in effect an ellipsis for "surrender to God."[13]

But for the Arabic-speaking Muslim of Egypt, the elasticity of the term and its polysemy hinge not so much upon the ambiguity of "surrender" versus "surrender to God," as upon an indeterminacy as to how the term applies to those many different settings where it is indistinguishably applied. Unlike the English tendency, the term does not allow for an easy reduction to a bounded set of discretely identifiable images, ideas, persons, places, events, and activities. Islam is rather a global and diffuse concept, an ethos and a worldview touching upon the totality of experience with a center of gravity in primordial symbols that forever resist easy delimitation or straightforward definition.

We have already observed that *islām* in the context of the sermon does not translate as "creed" or "worship" or even as an ethical code. It conveys rather an authoritative and all-embracing way of life, valid not only for those who assent to it and take it as their model, but for all humanity at all times. Thus conceptually it is not equated with limited groups, to certain times, rites, buildings, legal systems, or intellectual disciplines. It is, as objective reality, the substance of divine order encompassing all history. It is, in short, religion. Certainly many of the Muslims we describe are quite aware that *islām* has rivals to its claims, and they may realize that their declarations about its universality and its monopoly on truth are not recognized or even demonstrable elsewhere, but these outside views are, in local cultural terms, largely rejected as either partial or distorted. By elaborate ideological manipulations, it is always possible to reaffirm that *islām* alone is absolute and everything else whether sacred or secular achieves a measure of legitimacy insofar as it imitates or resembles it. This sentiment is especially strong among the fundamentalists who often go so far in their enthusiasm as to deny the right of any competing views to be formulated or tolerated. Their appropriation of the term *islām* as modern ideology, that is, as an all-embracing explanation and justification for political domination, has lately inflated the semantic range of the term. Doing so has also pushed the term "religion" to its extremes, causing a sort of shrinkage of its versatility. But what is lost as a basis for historical and theological reference reappears as it is applied often narrowly to all phenomena in the light of a monolithic and utopian scheme just beyond the brink of full and active participation.

9 Formalization and Structure

The Preacher as the Affirmation of Traditional Authority

The sermon delivered by Shaykh Mustafa on May 18, 1979, and reproduced in Appendix A represents a local version of the most common type of preaching heard in government mosques of Egypt. On the surface, the selection of sacred symbols and their relevance to social institutions admits a minimum of specific reference. Following the pattern of a mosque of the *'ālim* in which it was preached, the sermon tends toward the classical standard. It displays what would seem at first inspection to be zero-marking, that is, it is devoid of eccentric features and decidedly unoriginal in its stylistic externalities. However, this initial impression is deceptive, especially when one explores its rhetoric in the context of its preacher's social identity and the moral climate that prevails in the community represented by the congregation. The text is rich in circumlocutions, qualifications, and paraphrases, to the point that one might detect the existence of an unacknowledged "crib" as its model, although it is skillfully dressed with proverbs, explanatory asides and bits of folk wisdom that seem to betray a colloquial Upper Egyptian component woven into the whole. The central theme of the sermon, including the main Qur'anic verse around which it is built, is quite familiar; in fact, the verse is among the most commonplace of citations in all of contemporary Muslim religious rhetoric. Yet it would be myopic to conclude from this that the message of this preachment suffers from an excess of stylization that impinges seriously on its meaningfulness. Rather, in this case it is precisely through what Maurice Bloch has described as "formalization" that this preacher achieves his overall effect.[1] To account for the impact of such a sermon, therefore, one must go beyond a mere examination of what is

194

actually said. The symbols employed derive their full force from the broader social factors that are understood only when one attends as well to the "rules of use" appropriate to this discourse.[2]

Thus, before embarking on a commentary on the *shaykh's* remarks themselves, the underlying force of certain cultural values should be made explicit and several sociolinguistic preliminaries should be provided. But first, a technical detail touching on the shape of the received text should be noted. The actual tape recording of this sermon was done by a young Egyptian acquaintance to whom I entrusted my equipment more on the basis of his eagerness to help and his familiarity with the mosque than upon his ethnographic aptitude or engineering skills. On this particular day, after leaving him with the tape recorder, I departed to attend the Friday sermon in another mosque, delighted that modern electronics could provide at least this measure of bi-location. Such conveniences, however, are not without risks, for as I found here and in many instances all manner of slippage is to be expected, although one often discovers something unexpected in the process. In short, the sermon on this tape is slightly flawed in that the very beginning and the very end of it have been cut off, and in their place, my helper has recorded Qur'an chanting.

While such unwelcome and unsolicited editing tends to frustrate an anthropological researcher in search of untampered raw data, it nevertheless poignantly illustrates a set of well-formed assumptions in the mind of this native. What he has done was an attempt to reproduce the framing of the weekly sermon broadcast live on the state-controlled radio where such Qur'an chanting precedes and follows the ritual oratory. On the air, of course, it is performed by professional chanters and it never cuts into the text of the actual sermon. However, the portions that are missing here from Shaykh Mustafa's sermon are almost certainly the most predictable and formalized elements of the speech. Because of this, it plainly occurred to the lad who make the recording for me that these parts of such a sermon were worthless or of negligible value compared to the Qur'anic recitation. In the case of this *shaykh,* it is quite doubtful that this minor loss of tape footage would significantly add to or subtract from the sermon's content, for I have heard the Shaykh on numerous occasions and he repeats virtually the same beginning and ending formulas whenever he preaches. But their absence from the text as given in the appendix is misleading, since their presence in the actual event contributes no small part to the weight of formalization which is key to an understanding of the rest of what is delivered from the pulpit. Therefore, the readers must take into account that this translation, taken unabridged from a transcription of the tape, opens and closes with an abruptness that was modified by a formulaic preface and conclusion that are missing here. Apart from this trimming, the acoustic quality of the recording was good enough to assure that its rendering here may be considered complete.

Second, as regards the perennial difficulties of translation, not only from Arabic to English, but from oral performance to written text, a few orthographic conventions have been adopted to preserve, however inadequately, some of the oratory's expressive qualities. It is quite impossible, of course, to approach anything of the range and variety of elocutionary particulars that make up the total effect of a skilled delivery. But the use of punctuation, capitalization, and division into sentences and paragraphs is designed to contribute visual clues to suggest some echo of the aural modulations. Among other aids, citations from the Qur'an have been set in quotation marks. Also, in a faint effort to simulate their authoritative voice and intrusive effect as the sacred text, the English translation usually employed here is that of A. J. Arberry, whose free verse and archaic English usages makes some attempt to carry over from the Arabic a certain poetic structure from the original Qur'an.[3] Following each citation, I have supplied the number of the chapter and verse to allow for easy tracing of the context of the phrase since what comes before and what follows an isolated segment of text from the Qur'an are often familiar to the listeners. Hence unstated allusions are often conveyed by this proximity, in ways that may strongly color what is understood by the use of a mere token phrase. Seldom if ever does such a preacher himself give such numerical references and he may not even indicate clearly that he is citing from the Qur'an. When he does verbalize this source, a preacher may do so with a stock introductory phrase such as "The Lord says . . ." or "It is written in the Book of God . . ." which are retained in the sermon's translation. Likewise, quotation marks are used to set off utterances from the *ḥadīth*, the non-Qur'anic but authoritative words and acts of the Prophet.

Third, a brief profile touching on certain distinctive features of Shaykh Mustafa's social identity must also precede an examination of the sermon itself. At the time of this sermon, he is a young, quite affable man, scarcely over thirty, and a product of the traditional educational system, having started as a child in the Qur'an school, or *kuttab*, and continuing through the religious schools to its pinnacle, and having finished the basic degree of the prestigious Azhar University in Cairo. He is every inch a professional *imām*, who at all times wears the distinctive ankle-length coat and head covering of the traditional *'ulamā'*. Only recently appointed head of al-Qushairi Mosque, an important institution near the city center, he is widely respected and viewed as having a promising future career. Interestingly, later, in the mid-1980s, he obtained a good post at a mosque in

Saudi Arabia, which is further testimony to his abilities. In addition to these admirable professional qualities, Shaykh Mustafa also takes care to conduct his household affairs in conformity with the traditional standards of separation between public and private space. He and his family occupied a relatively small apartment in a large, overcrowded block of flats housing mostly other young families, many recent urban immigrants from the countryside. Here he made it a point to seclude his own quarters by installing a somewhat clumsy but serviceable partition on the common balcony in order to effectively isolate his dwelling. He was a most gracious host both at the mosque and at his own home, but he observed conscientiously the formal code of decorum with regard to the mixing of sexes. Once, for instance, he asked me to take some photos of him and his family which I did. Then afterward, he requested that I not show the pictures of his wife to anyone. As an official representative of established religion, Shaykh Mustafa is commonly accorded the various gestures of traditional deference or calculated indifference by others who see him primarily in terms of his office.

Another important factor defining Shaykh Mustafa's public character is his origin, for he is a native of the region, born and raised in a nearby village. Although he resides with his young family in Minya, his contacts with kin remain strong and frequent. One of his younger brothers serves as a low-grade clerk in the local directorate of the Ministry of Religious Endowments. This matter of local ties stands out because it is quite rare among Azhari *shaykhs* in Minya, almost all of whom are originally from Lower Egypt. The advantages that flow from this distinction of being a native son of Minya include a recognition of the scarcity of Azhar graduates among Upper Egyptians, and appreciation of the fact that such success has not carried him off permanently to the fleshpots of Cairo, but has led to his return to the provinces. Moreover, among those Azhar graduates who do return to Upper Egypt, very few take up work as mosque preachers. Most seek positions as schoolteachers, an occupation that is less politically exposed, less socially confining, more prestigious, and far more lucrative if handled correctly. Indeed, the denigrating anti-clerical barb that a preacher only works on Sunday has its Egyptian Muslim variant. But Shaykh Mustafa is an exceptionally active figure among his colleagues and in addition to his post at the mosque he has a regular part-time teaching post in a Coptic grade school, for Arabic instruction is closely conjoined with religious education.

This biographical fact of Shaykh Mustafa's local origins suggests yet another dimension of his personal and professional life which is perceived as his stability, solidarity, and ultimately his credibility. Egyptians gener-

ally and Upper Egyptians most of all tend to consider the continuity of
residence and the proximity of relatives as a prerequisite to a normal
healthy life. Today, however, given the complications of employment
within the nation's enormous bureaucracy (to which mosques and schools
belong), not to mention the impinging problems arising from chronically
under-financed and uncoordinated policies, there are countless functionaries, including preachers, whose postings have scattered them far
away from their homes. Then, because housing is in such desperate short
supply and money for travel is also extremely limited, such working men
not only reside, often for years, in makeshift lodging, but also are often
forced to postpone marriage, and even after that to endure long separa-
tions from their families. The ordeals caused by this displacement comprise a familiar theme in modern Egyptian film and fiction where they
have become synonymous with massive expense, inconvenience, and
unhappiness. These adverse conditions bring with them not only the personal hardships of isolation and alienation but also inevitably result in
poor job performance exacerbated by disregard for local circumstances and
a lack of sustained attention to longer-term issues.[4]

The mood of dissatisfaction and unrest with shades of depression
among the young professionals working in government service who are
caught up in these conditions seems especially hard on mosque preachers
posted far from home. Their highly public religious identity excludes
them from partaking inconspicuously in many of the leisure activities
that are available to their professional colleagues in other fields who
might share their incommodious exile. In Minya itself, as well as in several of the surrounding villages, there are a number of these preachers
from the Delta assigned to work in mosques, men of roughly Shaykh
Mustafa's own age, although none of them possesses the quiet confidence
and the unmistakable approachability of this native son whose exceptional religious credentials seem to set him not so much apart as ahead of
his fellows.

Formalism as a Rhetorical Tactic

Turning then to the sermon itself, several blatant structural features stand
out which mark this text as a token of the ʿ*ālim* type. These include its relative brevity, the absence of digressions, and its relatively tight thematic
development, which is essentially the elaborate reworking of one simple
Qurʾanic injunction, the "bidding to honor and forbidding dishonor."
Certain ostentatious linguistic elements that disappear in translation also
define the scholarly character of this sermon. Although this preacher does
occasionally slip into the colloquial speech, usually by way of a quick aside

or a paraphrase, overall the preachment is manifestly a discourse in classical Arabic. Word choice, pronunciation, and syntax all combine to display the deep roots of traditional learning and the professionalism of the practiced pulpit orator. These stylistic traits are recognized in this case as authentication of his training and not as academic artifice or affectation. What is communicated by this exploitation of the higher language in this diglossia culture is not lofty dramatics, in the sense of "stage English," but rather the close identification of the speaker himself with the values represented by his speech. Shaykh Mustafa's homiletics exemplify a provincial version of extreme formalization wherein content and form are solidly fused. Since the Shaykh himself and his mosque are likewise identified with this classical heritage and manner, the effect is a harmonious concentration upon what is understood and publicly affirmed as the handing down of the core ideals of the great civilization of which they are a part.

Earlier, reference was made to the insights of Maurice Bloch with regard to the social function of formalization in political and religious oratory. This theory applies in different ways to all the preachers discussed but it serves to illustrate the case of Shaykh Mustafa most clearly. Bloch's principal argument is that when a speaker addresses himself to concrete empirical events in a prescribed and fixed oratorical mode, he gains authority but he loses the advantages of specific reference. By the adoption of the "sacred" code, an orator elevates the level of communication by evoking the most diffuse symbols ascending to a plane of discourse that rules out dissent. Likewise, the orator who articulates the relation of daily life to divine revelation by resort to a culture's great commonplaces tends to diminish his participation in factionalized interest groups as he takes on the symbolic persona of the unified collectivity. Bloch speaks of this process of "merging" as having many consequences, two of which are of special relevance for these Islamic preachers:

> The move towards the formalized therefore becomes a move in the direction of unity. . . . The tendency towards unity via unspecificity means that specific issues cannot efficiently be tackled since if the formalized oratory is a form of social control within a set of fixed norms it cannot deal with individual (hence divisive) innovative action. . . . It removes the authority and the event from the speaker himself so that he speaks when using formalisation less and less for himself and more and more for his role. This explains the inability of the speaker to manipulate his power for strictly personal ends.[5]

Similarly, Bloch elsewhere pursues another side to this question and carries the relocation of authority from the speaker to the role even further. He suggests that as formalization crystallizes and tends toward greater fixity and predictability, and as the acquired skill or the legitimate access to its use is more elaborately safeguarded, such utterances progressively cease to serve active functions in political affairs at all; they evolve into what is more accurately described as religion.[6]

Of the three preachers whose sermons are examined in this section, Shaykh Mustafa demonstrates by far the highest degree of formalization. It might be tempting to cast him, by pushing Bloch's theory only a little further, as a representative of the unchanging primordial worldview that is often set in opposition to the modern world of increasing differentiation, rapid change, and centralized interdependence. But moving in a direction that would equate the Azhari with a stereotype of timeless conservatism is both superficial and premature. To do so assumes a single standard of formalization and one fixed role identity, neither of which are easily demonstrated in this instance nor necessarily implied by Bloch's hypotheses. In fact, the validity of his theory seems to follow equally well where there may be a shifting definition of religious roles.

The key to understanding the social message in this sermon turns on what is signaled by the potent and oft-repeated Qur'anic phrase, the "bidding to honor and forbidding dishonor." As the Shaykh's allusions suggest, there exists a considerable literature that explicates the meaning of this phrase which occurs numerous times in the sacred text. In fact, many contend that it stands as the phrase that best summarizes the preeminent moral charge given by God to the Muslim community. This is a phrase which has stirred up a formidable history of controversial interpretations, going back to the day of the four Rightly Guided Caliphs when it was seized upon by the schismatic Kharajites. Later it was a pivotal issue in the doctrinal disputes of the rationalist Mu'atazilites, eventually condemned as heterodox. At their defeat it was taken over as a fundamental maxim in the systematic theology, or *kalām*, of the high middle ages where it was seen as embodying the essential moral principle guiding political and social life. The degree to which this injunction was to be publicly enforced was an issue at the heart of Muslim theories of governance which have undergone constant and often conflicted cycles of reformulation. Louis Gardet has summed up both the contents and the sentiments that are evoked by this verse:

> The bidding to honor [*al-amr bi l-ma'rūf*] stands then at the heart of the Muslim polity as a constant principle of reform. It has provided the grounds, over the course of history, for no little abuse including the justification of political revolts. For its part, the central power has also all too often channeled it in the direction of its

own vested interests. But it stirs the feelings of peoples no less profoundly. Indeed, the absence of the power of the caliph . . . has perhaps increased the vitality it has for the conscience of every Muslim and his personal accountability.[7]

Given then the indisputable centrality of this phrase for the legitimation of moral action, it is hardly surprising that it was adopted as the virtual charter statement of the Muslim Brothers.[8] More recently, it has been echoed across the Islamic world stage when it was preached and shouted as a reproach to the Shah in Iran and a call to arms for those who would replace his tyranny with an Islamic state. This same Qur'anic phrase was also frequently voiced in Minya, especially among the youthful followers of the *Jamāʿa Islāmīya*, for whom it served as the seal of their own zeal to implant an Islamic order as they saw it in their own society. In brief, the phrase reappears constantly in the pamphlets and sermons of fundamentalists such that they have almost come to claim it as their own slogan. Others, however, including Shaykh Mustafa, as demonstrated in this sermon, are not at all prepared to surrender the phrase to them. While the history of its recent use has colored its interpretation with the intolerant aims and sometimes violent methods of those who use it most often and most insistently, this preacher redirects the interpretation of this phrase back toward its traditional understanding as subordinate to legal institutions.

Given the prevalence of the phrase as a popular justification among Islamists, it seems plain earlier in the sermon that Shaykh Mustafa's choice of this topic and his interpretation of the phrase have ethical pedagogy as well as doctrinal explication as their motives. Around the time this sermon was preached, in May 1979, local tensions in Minya had grown quite hot, fueled by a series of provocations and occasional clashes between civil authorities and Copts on the one hand, and Muslim extremists on the other. The preceding months had seen a steady rise of incidents supposedly justified by moral imperatives. Police and university officials had finally responded decisively only to meet still greater dissidence and unrest. Feelings on all sides continued to run high at the time as reports of sectarian violence, misguided fanaticism, government crackdowns, and international terrorism threatened to snowball. By his focus on this phrase, Shaykh Mustafa seeks to reclaim for those who share the perspective of the official religious establishment the traditional values of order and harmony under law that form the classical reading of this highly charged catch-word.

It is precisely by an alignment of clichés and formulaic attestations that Shaykh Mustafa initially frames his presentation. But this is not to deny dramatic movement. Note how *ḥadīth* are introduced that prompt the expansion of the Qur'anic phrase from a this-worldly moral imperative (paragraph 3), to a precondition for God's assistance (paragraphs 8 and 9), until it is finally advanced as the criterion for the Last Judgment (paragraph 17). Furthermore, Shaykh Mustafa makes it clear from the outset that the scope of the phrase must extend to every facet of private and public life (paragraph 4). This generalizing assertion rebuts, if only in passing, the standard accusation of fundamentalists that Azhari *shaykhs* restrict Islam to the mosque. He follows this universalization with a particularization on another plane, for he singles out the Muslim community as the elite of "all mankind." In reciting the Qur'anic verse, "You are the best nation ever brought forth to humankind" (paragraph 5) he is giving the first stanza of a larger passage that repeats the familiar charge "to bid to honor and to prohibit dishonor" immediately after this line. Here, Shaykh Mustafa is addressing his listeners as members of that superlative community of chosen ones who were faithful to the Prophet in his early trials. It is also worth noting that this designation of those who "bid to honor and prohibit dishonor" as the "best nation" is itself no random or eccentric declaration. Once again, it is a commonplace to which deep sentiments are attached. Jacques Jomier has remarked that this phrase, which opens verse 110 of the Sura *āl-ʿAmrān*, "is perhaps the single [verse] in the entire Qur'an that is most frequently cited by preachers."[9] Nor is it coincidence that this same Qur'anic citation about the "best nation" is inscribed in large elegant calligraphy high on the walls of the magnificent Assembly Hall at the Arab League headquarters in Cairo.

Thus, after recalling to his listeners their election as "best nation," Shaykh Mustafa enlarges on the theme by applying two other Qur'anic appellations, both of which appear in conjunction with verses elsewhere that repeat the charge to "bid to honor and forbid dishonor." In both these cases, he introduces the noun forms *al-falāh*, "happiness or prosperity," and *al-nasr*, "assistance or victory" (paragraphs 6 and 7), and after elaborating upon them freely, he quotes the actual Qur'anic verses where the terms appear in verbal form. His exploitation of these terms depends heavily on a semantic shift between their different morphological forms and, more important, between classical and colloquial connotations in their usage. These associative leaps are very common in preaching, and upon this polysemic scaffolding he begins his grand rhetorical sweeps. Unfortunately, most of the subtleties of this progression are lost in translation, so it might be helpful to dwell momentarily on the following example.

The two nouns at issue, reflecting modern Arabic usage, are glossed in the sermon as "happiness" and "victory." As Qur'anic terms, however, these same words do not have this same flavor of broad application. Instead they convey a narrower and more restricted meaning, which is preserved by Arberry in his translation. The participle whose modern noun form connotes "happiness" is rendered "prosperers" and the finite verb of the noun form that today denotes "victory" is given, with philological accuracy, as "[to] help." One need not pursue this point further to recognize how easily the historical transformation of semantics illustrated by these terms gives them an unusual latitude. Taking advantage of this verbal play, a skilled orator can easily breathe new life into otherwise obsolete Qur'anic references by grafting them onto contemporary cognates which have wider and more immediately felt meanings, registering a much higher rate of emotional voltage.[10]

The Sharī'a *as the Whole Law*

In exploring the social implications of this sermon which seeks to interpret the summons to implement moral obligations, one may follow a rhetorical progression from a specification of "who" to a delineation of "where," "when," and "how." This movement emerges, beginning in paragraph 8, with a Qur'anic citation, which is then elaborated and supported by a passage from the *hadīth,* and followed finally by a brief legal and doctrinal exposition. The culmination is with the *sharī'a,* which is projected as the ultimate vehicle for the movement from morality to religion. Already in paragraph 3, however, there were indications of this orientation exhibited in the emphasis on the ritual duties of Islam. Thus "bidding to honor . . ." is recast as including at the forefront compliance with the more strictly religious features of the *sharī'a* rather than stepping quickly over this dimension to stress the need to apply it to areas of purported civil and criminal jurisdiction. These opening references to the *sharī'a* leave little doubt about their point of departure, since they deal specifically with prayer and alms, two of the five pillars of Islam, to which a third is soon added (paragraph 13), the *hajj.* In all cases, the emphasis reverts steadily to the injunction "bid to honor and forbid dishonor" as an imperative equal in stature to the pillars but also as applying to their practice.

Interestingly, in the etymological exercise of paragraphs 10 and 11, where the Shaykh pretends to define what is glossed as "honor" and "dishonor" by punning on their morphological stems, the supplied direct object of this "honor" is once again the *sharī'a.* The Shaykh plays on the root *'arif,* meaning "to know, to recognize," and similarly on the root *nakar,* meaning "to disown, to be ignorant of," suggesting that the latter refers to knowledge or ignorance of the *sharī'a.* As classical Qur'anic exegesis, such an interpretation is groundless and quaintly anachronistic, since the *sharīʿa* as it is propounded and understood did not exist at the time the Qurʾan was revealed. It is rather the product of a later movement that arose in response to abuses of power. It sought to establish norms based on the sources of law and on the precedents of those who had been closest in time and space to Muhammad. But even so, scholars commonly acknowledged that custom, *ʿurf*, could override the stated law.[11] But a contradiction on the level of history and doctrine may have a more harmonious meaning on the surface of contemporary ideology. What is being asserted, as the allusion to Muhammad ʿAbdu (paragraph 13) confirms, is the sacred status of the *sharīʿa* as the only legitimate expression of revealed imperatives for modern daily life.

The points Shaykh Mustafa has incorporated into his sermon to underscore this divinization of the *sharīʿa* are quite conventional. Even the linkage of the *sharīʿa* as the elliptical object of *ʿarif* and *nakar* is a cliché, and at least as old as the great Qurʾan commentator, Baydawi, who died in 1268.[12] Likewise, the *ḥadīth* prescribing that the reform of evil should first be attempted with the hand, then, failing that, with the tongue, then finally with the heart is equally trite. It is an often-cited recollection and it appears in the great Summa of al-Ghazzali (died in A.D. 1111) in conjunction with a study of applications of moral law.[13] But trite phrases, standard recitations, and repeated textual citations are the fundamental stuff of formalization, and it is by displaying fixed phrases and proverbial expressions that Shaykh Mustafa achieves his impact and identifies his role. Conveyance of new information or a fresh analysis or any reflection that implies a personal point of view or active rationality would only detract from the impression of a unified and comprehensive tradition that persists in the health and vigor of the preacher.

As an Azhari and an *imām* in a mosque under state supervision, the Shaykh's promotion of the *sharīʿa* expresses what Muslims idealize as the sum and substance of religion and morality. Simultaneously, he places himself at religion's center as the bearer of this tradition, its loyal advocate, and its faithful interpreter. The very absence of ego references or local allusions only serves to magnify his image as a disinterested, indeed, almost impersonalized authority. He represents the letter, without which there is only a tenuous spirit. He does not call for specific action both by reason of his detachment from immediate issues and by reason of his attachment to the sacred *sharīʿa*. Yet the role he is asserting by way of this sermon presupposes an entire social order to guide all facets of personal and communal life. The legal tradition he embodies includes attempts to spell out in endless intricacy internal and external variations to cover all imaginable cases. The most appropriate description of this posture is not "representation" but "impersonation" as the word is used in a positive sense in the Victorian era.[14]

Indeed, it is precisely because the *sharīʿa*, quite unlike modern civil and criminal codes, extends into the seeming incidentals of ritual, intimate matters of personal hygiene, as well as unenforceable areas of motivation and intention that it occupies such a special place in Islamic rhetoric. It is declared to be both hopelessly impracticable and utterly irreplaceable, sometimes by the same person depending on the frame of reference. It continues to embody an ideal despite the fact that it has long since ceased to function and hence ceased to evolve until for all practical purposes it has become antiquated and ossified, except in the limited domain of personal status law, especially inheritance.[15] Formerly, the very flexibility of juridical procedures, what Weber in his stereotypes referred to as *Kadijustiz* (*qāḍi* justice)[16] had allowed the *sharīʿa* to flourish, for it provided a mechanism for the unsupervised adaptation of the "law" to local circumstances in the polyglot, segmented, stratified, and largely illiterate premodern imperium of Islamdom.[17] But these erstwhile virtues serve now as obstacles to its incorporation into modern juridical and legislative protocols.[18]

Ostensibly, Shaykh Mustafa is advancing the cause of the *sharīʿa*, but it is vital to notice that he does this by assuming its value and by an elucidation of its principles. Other preachers, as we shall see shortly, omit any discussion of what the *sharīʿa* prescribes, preferring to pour out demands that the government "adopt" this enormous corpus of uncodified scripture and opinion as "laws" in the modern sense. Shaykh Mustafa, in other words, does not objectify the *sharīʿa* or confuse its character with righteous demands that it be "enacted."

When Shaykh Mustafa begins his exposition of the "attributes"[19] of "bidding to honor and forbidding dishonor" (paragraphs 16–24) following his definition of a hierarchy of obedience and counsel (paragraphs 14 and 15), he is once again indirectly expounding on the *sharīʿa*. He imparts the impression that what is called the *sharīʿa* with all its associations of authenticity and justice is not reducible to what is found in the ancient volumes, but that it exists primarily as living and malleable knowledge in those, like himself, qualified to pronounce in the name of this tradition. Such an authorization, which is formalized among Shiʿites as the *mujtahid*,[20] is not made explicit, but the implication is unmistakable. By neglecting to elaborate any rationale for his mightily implied claim, apart from the formality he himself incorporates, the Shaykh merely reaffirms it. By refraining from anything resembling commentary upon local turmoil, by avoiding any trace of defensiveness, or polemic against the use that militant fundamentalists have made of this key phrase, the Shaykh has engaged in an invisible but cogent rebuttal and counter-thrust. By way of what seem to be the merest clichés, he boldly reasserts the priority of traditional authority, and by a display of impersonality together with staid oratorical competence, he not only reaffirms the values represented by the order of the mosque and the society as constituted, but he reestablishes his own role of preacher as the legitimately enfranchised and properly trained functionary who possesses both the charge and the skill to pronounce upon "honor" and "dishonor."

Shaykh Mustafa stops short of displaying an inclination toward favoring restoration of the classical structure of Muslim society upon which the *sharīʿa* was premised, as he declines to include in his sermon the classical prayer for the ersatz Caliph, the religiously approved leader. Nevertheless, through a wealth of other officious markings, Shaykh Mustafa does make his own role and the social meaning of his sermon quite evident. He identifies with traditional order and structure over against innovation and irresponsibility, or, as it is perceived from his point of view, against ignorance, chaos, and adolescent rebellion.

Before leaving this example, it is helpful to restate that not all cases of formalization and impersonation, even while they serve the same purpose, are quite as abstract, contained, and unengaging (at least on the surface) as this one. As we have suggested, the inherent tendency to claim the middle is here so pronounced because of certain extreme factors, notably the stress of civic disturbances; and perhaps the relative youth of this preacher has made the situation more transparent. Yet the general contours and implications remain even when topics range widely to cover ritual observances, seasonal celebrations, or are framed as appeals to develop such fundamental virtues as patience, charity, or honesty.

As an indication of this potential range of specificity that may be expressed in a sermon which nonetheless bases its authority upon the exploitation of formalization, we end with a few paragraphs from a sermon delivered by Shaykh Muhammad of al-Fuli mosque. His topic here is the virtue of sincerity, *akhlās*, a most familiar sermon theme which appeared as the third "attribute" in the list expounded by Shaykh Mustafa. In terms of strict linguistic description and of formal indicators, Shaykh Muhammad's sermon differs very little from the one just presented, although the critical bite of his preaching, even as it comes through in translation, is not as bookish or distant from immediate experience. Nevertheless, the strain of moral obligation and societal editorializing performed here does not exceed similar "sermonizing" that occasionally appears in political speeches or the semi-official press.[21]

Servants of God, pardon me when I say it, but in these days of
ours, corruption has become a beacon-light and what is repulsive
has become, in our time, the normal thing. To show many different
colors [that is, play chameleon] is counted as wisdom and turnings
and reversals in our midst have become the sum of politics. No one
cares for you except for some profitable advantage [*muṣlaḥa*].

If he needs you, he lifts you up to the heavens, but if he can do
without you, he drops you and lets you fall to the ground. If you
happen to be rich or the boss, you get favored treatment, but if you
are poor or in distress, you get only scorn. For that reason, communication between us has been cut off and we have come to find
that no one can be trusted. A friend is no longer a sincere counselor
and there is no power or strength except in God, the exalted.

Indeed, there is an evil afoot that is aimed at the community, to
cut off the souls of its citizens from the spirit of sincerity. A wave
of egoism [*ananīya*] is overwhelming the community with its love
of money, its love of high standing, its love of power, its love of
preeminence. These are lethal germs in the body of nations that
cause blood to spill and strength to be sapped. When they take
over, nothing remains but the dead carcass.[22]

10   Creativity and Adaptation

*The Preacher as Advocate of
Religiously Inspired Modernity*

The second sermon reproduced in its entirety, in Appendix B, was delivered on Friday, December 15, 1978, by Shaykh Uthman. His exposition of semantic conversions dealing with security and belief have already been described. There he served to demonstrate the rhetoric strategy associated with metaphor. As was seen, this technique, based on the presentation of extended allegories and aided by nimble leaps of code-switching, produces the calculated transfer of properties from the sacred to the mundane. He accomplishes this interpolation, moreover, in a manner that fully recognizes the essential gap between these domains. Consequently, he also exemplifies the need for recognizing a self-conscious interpretive agenda to bring them into meaningful conjunction.

A brief biographical profile of Shaykh Uthman has also already been given. But in exploring the links he forges between morality and religion it is necessary to expand upon this sketch. The unusually high credibility this preacher enjoys, especially among the local educated class, owes much to his compound social identity and his relatively broad cultural orientation. His effective articulation of multifaceted symbols within this local setting cannot, therefore, be easily separated from his ability to fuse the different strands of his personal and professional relationships into the voice that defines his ritual role as mosque preacher. The result, suggested in the title, "advocate of religiously inspired modernity" reflects a considerable measure of innovation and adaptation.

Hence this *shaykh*'s preaching, combined with other ritual expressions, offers elements that tend to be less predicable, seemingly experimental, and sometimes idiosyncratic as compared to the established formalism of an Azhari preacher such as Shaykh Mustafa. Likewise, his efforts to carry over Islam from the pulpit to the streets allow for a greater flexibility and a more dialectical interaction with the everyday happenings of the world outside the mosque than is usually found among Islamic militants. The treatment of morality and religion in the rhetoric of this fundamentalist mode (examined in the following chapter, as typified in Minya by the fulsome oratory of Shaykh Umar) follows a basic model displayed in the performances of well-known figures as 'Abd al-Hamid Kishk or the Ayatollah Khomeini.

Nevertheless, Shaykh Uthman's originality does not verge toward solipsistic eccentricity of a sort that isolates him or distances him from the congregation. On the contrary, he constantly seeks to diffuse the aura of solemnity that surrounds ritual authority. On some occasions, for instance, he goes so far as to eschew the pulpit, which in the case of his mosque is already of a very simple "low church" design, and he preaches, with the aid of a microphone, while seated on a small podium with a book of the *hadīth* in front of him. Thus, he acts as an individual, although the behaviors that express his distinctive personality as preacher are not directed toward an enhancement of the role itself but toward a diminishment of the ceremonial constraints to straightforward communication. In other words, it belongs to this particular type of preacher as actor that personalized qualities follow him into the pulpit. There, they are publicly displayed as the basic elements from which he composes his customized image as a religious authority. The particular sermon which has been selected for analysis here is an unusually elaborate version of his typical rhetorical procedure. It is built around a story that features a series of incidents from the life of the Prophet. This narrative structure forms an elastic frame device for multiple allegorical extensions that connect, often with forceful emotional overtones, to concrete situations his audience would easily recognize.

In the city of Minya and throughout the surrounding region, Shaykh Uthman is widely known and respected by virtue of two separate and highly prominent social identities. One derives principally from his professional achievements. Having distinguished himself as a schoolteacher, then as an administrator, he was recently appointed to the prestigious post of Public Relations Director at the provincial office of the Ministry of Education. His academic field was the teaching of English, and he is a fluent speaker of the language, which is by no means true of all English instructors in the region. But this skill, plus his winning personality, have made of him a great asset as a translator, not only within his own ministry, but elsewhere, including the governor's office, in the hosting of distinguished foreign visitors.

The other dimension of this preacher's pronounced social identity derives from his family. He is held in high repute, especially by devout local Muslims, because he is recognized as the successor of his late father, who was revered as an exceptional religious leader. Shaykh Uthman has one brother in the city who has also distinguished himself in the field of education, specializing in Arabic literature. But in matters of religion, there is no doubt that Shaykh Uthman alone has assumed the mantle of this father who died only in January 1978. This familial connection stands behind the preacher's impressive professional competence to endow Shaykh Uthman with his distinctive claim to authority, not only as a ritual leader but as a spokesman for the renewal of Islam and its application to a troubled modern world in a way that both preserves tradition and welcomes change.

Shaykh Uthman's father grew up in a small village not quite an hour's walk from Minya. With little more than a primary education, which centered on the memorization of the Qur'an, he began teaching school in 1925. In addition, he was an active participant in the community affairs of his day and he was reputed to have been among the first in the area to join the Muslim Brotherhood, probably in the late 1930s. This national and later international association, founded in the Canal Zone in 1928, and later based in Cairo, did not have a widespread following in Upper Egypt; it was virtually absent from rural villages there.[1] Soon he emerged as one of the group's leading members in Minya. Sometime in the late 1960s, he founded what started as a small wayside mosque on land that had become a rubbish dump close to a railroad yard beside Ibrihimiya Canal not far from the city center. The site was gradually cleared as it eventually grew into a flourishing *jam'iya* that included not only a large mosque but workshops, offices, classrooms, a clinic, and a student hostel. Shaykh Uthman's father's affiliation with the Muslim Brothers led to his arrest and imprisonment during each of the four waves of government repression that outlawed the society and then moved against its followers and sympathizers. First incarcerated briefly in 1945, and again in 1952, then for two years in 1954–1956 and finally once more in 1965, he acquired the reputation of a martyr among his local followers. During this last round-up of dissidents, the youthful Shaykh Uthman and his brother were also arrested along with their father and all three were detained for about a month in Cairo's infamous Turah Prison. In 1975, Sadat announced grandly that he was commemorating his own "corrective revolution" of a few years before by closing this old colonial prison compound which had become a symbol of official repression against Islamists. Shaykh Uthman's relatively brief tenure there is well known in Minya and he occasionally refers to it, usually obliquely, in preaching, as a sort of credential.

It was only shortly prior to the beginning of my research in Minya that Shaykh Uthman's father died. Shaykh Uthman himself had already begun establishing himself as the new head of the *jam'īya*, which included serving as its regular weekly preacher. To some degree, it might be observed that the charisma of his father had passed to him as he took over these tasks, although by this time Shaykh Uthman had gained considerable experience as an occasional preacher in a number of normally unstaffed mosques in the area, including frequent duties at the mosque of the local Teacher's Club. The old Shaykh had been widely esteemed for his strict Islamic observance and his moral zeal as a reformer and generally members of this *jam'īya* mosque community regarded Shaykh Uthman as a devoted son displaying updated versions of the same qualities. In an earlier era, it would have been quite likely that upon his death, Shaykh Uthman's father would have been interred within the mosque itself or a domed shrine would have been constructed adjoining it to honor him. For such was the tradition of the *walī*. But in the spirit of modern reverence he was buried in the cemetery of his native village. Nevertheless, on the day after the end of Ramadan, when it is customary for Muslims to visit the graves of the family, Shaykh Uthman led a sizable contingent in a sort of religious procession to visit the tomb of his father. They originated and concluded their veneration of the founder at the mosque itself. This small pilgrimage is one of many indications of the continuity and development that were observed as Shaykh Uthman assumed the leadership of what was unmistakably the most active and prominent (although in terms of buildings, not by any means the largest) of all such religious societies in the city.

Another mark of this continuity of authority of which Shaykh Uthman spoke freely involves his taking over of his late father's residence as a place of study, spiritual retreat, and private consultation. In the last years of his life, the old Shaykh had acquired a simple one-room apartment on the roof of a building just across the street from the mosque of the *jam'īya* he had founded and continued to lead. This sparsely furnished cell was now used by his son, who left it largely intact as a sort of shrine with all its books and fixtures in place. Shaykh Uthman even said that he had initially hesitated to touch such incidental items as the twelve piasters that happened to be left on his father's writing table at the time of his death. Typically, Shaykh Uthman was in the habit of spending time in this room before going to the mosque to deliver the Friday sermon and lead the community prayer.

Shortly after his father died, Shaykh Uthman remarked on how he liked to sit in his father's chair and use his books to prepare his sermons. But as the months passed, it became evident that the son was not only taking possession of this spiritual and intellectual patrimony, but also was appropriating still more visible emblems of his inherited position. This further adaptation most visibly involved certain significant articles of clothing which conveyed symbolically this same creative approach to the demonstration of his authority.

Several months after his father's death, Shaykh Uthman began to adopt an unusual garb which he apparently reserved for wearing to religious rituals such as the Friday prayer or for the public dawn prayer on the occasion of the *'īd al-aḍhā*. It consisted of a heavy, voluminous cloak of off-white wool that resembles a wide poncho or chasuble. It is apparently a garment made in Tunisia or Algeria for ceremonious occasions and it belonged to his father, who had received it as a gift. It had no sleeves and reached from the shoulders to just below the knees. In the context of Upper Egypt, this is a strange garment, although it communicates a certain exotic elegance and unspecified ceremonial suggestiveness. Nothing like it is to be found in the traditional wardrobe of Minya and it is quite out of keeping with Shaykh Uthman's normal attire of suit and tie or the tailored ensemble of trousers and jacket that are the standard summer apparel of middle- and upper-echelon functionaries in Egypt. Together with this distinctive overgarment Shaykh Uthman also began the practice of carrying a most extraordinary walking stick of extremely gnarled form, although handsomely sanded and lacquered. This stick was his father's although, like the cloak, it is not at all clear whether the old Shaykh ever used it. By these unusual accoutrements Shaykh Uthman expressed the same adaptation discernible in his sermons. It also made manifest his personal and professional vision of the link between morality and religion.

The significance of this cloak and stick, plus the important fact that Shaykh Uthman remained without any head cover, lies in the way it blends the traditional Islamic religious garb and that of the modern Egyptian city. The outer garment in no way approximates the familiar *galabīya* worn by traditional men in the region, although the stick, known as an *'aṣaya*, is a common fixture in the region, although rarely is one seen that is so outlandishly shaped and ornate. In rural areas, peasant men often carry a stick that is normally longer, straighter, and clearly serviceable as a staff. It is also used as a weapon. This same stick is the stave frequently seen in folk dances. Among the gentry a stick is also carried, but of another sort, being short, sleek, and often capped and tipped with silver. Furthermore, peasant men normally wear a brimless head cover, some modified turban, a *taqīya* or skull cap, or a knit hat. However, increasingly since the 1950s, the fashion among urban men has been to appear bareheaded, like 'Abd al-Nasir.

The other basis of contrast for Shaykh Uthman's self-chosen ritual dress refers to various sets of recognized religious garb. The traditional Azhari uniform, a sort of long dark coat over a distinctive white caftan, differs considerably and the red tasseled tarboosh with the white band is always present. Shaykh Uthman's dress likewise bears no resemblance to any defined apparel identified with the Sufi tradition. Finally, and no less importantly, it stands out as quite distinct from the usual range of white garments that have been adopted by local members of the Islamic Society as the public statement of their commitment to what they contend to be a purer practice of Islam.

Shaykh Uthman, as noted earlier, is an outspoken critic of red tape, tokenism, and hollow display. On various occasions, when challenged by fundamentalists, I have heard him defend his lack of demonstrative Islamic emblems, and notably the absence of a beard, on the grounds of their superficiality. Furthermore, he is an ardent promoter of "natural" products over artificial substitutes, as shown in his ostentatious consumption of pressed sugar cane juice rather than bottled soft drinks. What he accomplishes in the occasional wearing of this highly personalized ceremonial attire is, evidently, a compromise between the tacit expectations of the Muslim community with regard to a preacher, increasing pressures from the youth who themselves seek greater religious visibility, and his own modern convictions. He therefore concedes a periodic appearance in a sort of religious garb that imitates none of any defined ideological camp. He dramatizes his mix of peasant origins and urban upward mobility with a most singular walking-stick that is quintessentially natural and utterly functionless while being an heirloom recalling his father's memory.

The fact that Shaykh Uthman rejects standard religious garb while playing lightly with possible substitutes also fits together with his entirely secular education and his career choice. He is a product of that liberal era that regarded the ignorance and backwardness of Muslims as the major obstacle to progress toward an Islamic Order that would incorporate the science of the West into the spiritual culture of Islam. Shaykh Uthman is quite articulate about his resistance to the traditionalism of the Azharis and the Sufis as well as the mimicry of the alleged apparel and presumed mannerisms of the Prophet that preoccupy many fundamentalists. He justifies his response on the basis of a distinction between *sunna al-'adāt*, that is, "customs" which are human and subject to change, and *sunna al-'ibāda*, or "worship" which is divinely ordained and eternally valid. It is only matters of doctrine and ritual which fall into the second category. Moral principles that guide behaviors belong in the first category which requires responsible adaptation. To bring this point home, he is fond of addressing a *reductio ad absurdum* to those young enthusiasts who insist on supposedly total compliance with what is held to be the Sunna of the Prophet. He suggests, for instance, that they should complete their absolute conformity by rejecting all innovations, including abandoning modern medical care, eyeglasses, telephones, radios, automobiles and mechanically printed Qur'ans. They should ride camels, wear hand-woven cloth, and restrict their diet to food imported from the Hejaz.

Clearly, Shaykh Uthman's views on Islamic fundamentalism are mixed and nuanced, in contrast to the enthusiasm of Shaykh Umar who has put his considerable oratorical skills perhaps opportunely at the service of the new wave. But an important difference between these two preachers must also be seen in the extra-ritual identity of Shaykh Uthman, notably, the measure of authority and prestige that he has, in effect, inherited from his saintly father. His rational, realistic, and moderate stance on practical matters clearly diverges from the strains of hagiography and miracle that often abound in the stories he relates in his sermons. But this contrast is not perceived as a contradiction in his case. Given his solid social, political, and personal credentials apart from the sermon, his role has become one of mediation between the generation of his father and the generation of his own sons.

Shaykh Uthman's own schooling also bears its influence upon his approach to religious leadership. His secondary education was at an elite teachers' training college in Asyut. Thereafter he went on for a diploma at the British Institute in that city, which, he laments, has long since been closed. In speaking of his religious education, Shaykh Uthman describes himself as an autodidact who is utterly devoted to reading. He tells of extracurricular attendance at the local Qur'an school as a boy, but most important were the books which he read in his father's library. He drew my attention especially to the modernist classic of Muhammad Husayn Haykal, *The Life of Muhammad*. Haykal, who was one of the most influential writers of his day, was a novelist and essayist as well as a historian. He was also in 1922, the founding editor of *al-Siyāsah*, the journal that served as the organ of the Liberal Constitution Party. His *Life of Muhammad*, published in 1934, is regarded in some circles as the first biography of the Prophet by a Muslim to apply critical historiographic techniques. As such, its admirers acclaimed it as a "creative synthesis" of secular liberalism and Islam, and thus as the cornerstone of a new progressive ideology.[2] Such a bright movement failed to appear, however, and subsequent intellectual historians have exposed the "romantic proclivity for the epic quality of early Islam" that preoccupies Haykal.[3] This same tendency underlies much of Shaykh Uthman's preaching, including the sermon presented here. His preaching correctly reveals what is either a disinterest or a lack of familiarity with classical religious sciences; even his incorporation of Qur'anic citations is seldom more than ornamental. He speaks rather as a sensitive and well-informed man of the world who is enchanted by the dramatic qualities of the canonical literature no less than he is respectful of its legal and credal implications.

I have suggested in foregoing comments that Shaykh Uthman's appropriation of his father's role as preacher was in the process of transition during the time of my field research. Another indication of this new direction is the fact that Shaykh Uthman was just beginning to show a talent for popular religious writing. In March 1979 he had an article published in a major journal for the first time. It appeared in a glossy, colorfully illustrated mass-circulation monthly, richly subsidized by the government of Kuwait. The magazine is called *al-Waḥī al-Islāmī*, "The Islamic Inspiration," and it offers an assortment of pieces dealing with issues of Islamic history, doctrine, and morals, plus more general topics discussing the geography, art, and literature of Islamic lands and popularized reconciliations of science and religion.[4] Shaykh Uthman's article occupied three pages and was accorded a handsome line drawing of a muezzin calling to prayer over a skyline of minarets and domes. It appears under a creative writing rubric which is a regular feature, called "Islamic Stories." His brief story bore the title, "Their World and Our World," and in it he portrays an extremely romanticized Caliph 'Umar ibn al-Khutab governing humble and polite subjects with utopian equanimity and divine simplicity. He ends the extended allegory with the rhetorical question: "This was their world. . . . Where is our world from that?" The publication of this article, as soon became evident, represented for Shaykh Uthman a certain introduction to the national religious scene in Egypt. Shortly after it was published he was invited to appear on the television interview program "This Is Islam" which we discussed earlier. He was later invited back. At the same time, he managed to get the host of the show, a national celebrity of sorts, to visit Minya and to preach in his mosque at a Friday prayer service. Naturally, such media attention and this association with fame increased his stock among many local people.

Crafting the Summons to al-Daʿwa

In the actual text of the sermon, the first sign of the creativity that Shaykh Uthman brings to his role as preacher appears in his highly unorthodox introduction. Here is an immediate and, to the traditional listener, a jarring departure from the conventional prelude of a *khuṭba*. The standardized formulas, notably the profession of faith and blessings upon the Prophet and his family, are simply left out. Such an omission would be unthinkable in the sermon of an Azhari preacher and perhaps even more unlikely for the fundamentalist who tends, if anything, to be hypercorrect in these details, sometimes to the point of near parody.[5] At this opening of his sermon and later in paragraph 35, where the second part of the sermon begins, at which point similar eulogistic attestations are normally repeated, Shaykh Uthman simply substitutes an introduction of his own devising built upon a sequence of Qur'anic verses. One might also note that as the sermon continues such a concentrated use of the Qur'an never recurs. As is seen in other sermons, he is also fond of another equally unconventional variation on this prelude, in which he strings together rhapsodic verses of classical devotional poetry. Both of these versions, although unconventional, leave the impression of a carefully worded set-piece whereas normally the body of his sermons, including this one, are often marked by digression and chatty improvisation.

Nevertheless, this introduction is thematically coherent with what follows, as it contains the germ of the central issues that will be developed later. Initially, as the narrative elements of the sermon first appear, one may sense that Shaykh Uthman is skipping randomly from one detached episode to another, as in the anecdotes about Khalid (paragraphs 4 and 5) and Safina (paragraph 6) or toward the end of the excursus on suicide (paragraphs 36–39) and "routine" (paragraphs 40–41). But this judgment derives from a classical norm for composition which is only partially applicable. The structural integrity of Shaykh Uthman's sermons can only be appreciated when they are understood as responses as well as proclamations. In these seemingly disconnected introductory sections, as well as the elaborate narrative of Khubayb, the Shaykh is drawing upon this material to serve as something like parables that allow him to comment upon contemporary issues that touch upon different portions of his audience. In other words, one might depict such a sermon as one side of a two-, three-, or four-sided exchange. His listeners who have become aquainted with this style of veiled editorializing are aware of this diversity of audiences. They understand that some elements of the sermon are designed specifically for certain segments of the community, while others carry a general relevance for everyone, although not always in the same way or to the same degree. One device that reveals this interactive premise directly is a rubric Shaykh Uthman presents about every third or fourth week in which he publicly reads letters from listeners from the pulpit at the end of his ordinary sermon. These letters are presented anonymously for no names are mentioned, and they can be quite pointed in their comments, including reactions to the Shaykh's sermon content. After reading each letter, the Shaykh gives a verbal reply, invariably treating the remarks with respect, although his ready wit enables him to skirt delicate issues with a touch of humor.

It is certainly going too far to suggest that all the symbols employed in such a sermon are ciphers for persons or events known to his congregation. Nonetheless it is clear, here and elsewhere, that Shaykh Uthman, more than any other preacher under consideration, aims his remarks purposefully at locally identifiable references. His fundamentalist colleague Shaykh Umar, on the other hand, is certainly more explicit, especially in his denunciations. But his targets, such as President Sadat or the Coptic Patriarch, belong to a stratosphere far removed from the ordinary experience of his listeners. Frequently enough, Shaykh Uthman too alludes, sometimes at length, to national and international issues and events. But for him, the interpretive tilt of this topical commentary inevitably redirects the attention of his hearers back toward essentially local interests and related practical attitudes. Given the character of the tensions stirring in Minya and throughout Egypt at this time, therefore, it comes as no surprise that the focal point of this sermon deals once more with "youth." By connotation, he is speaking of the organizations that offer young activists, many of whom are in his audience, a mode of participation by way of religion in the larger affairs of their society and the world. It is the growing prominence and the increasing militancy of the student-based Islamic Society that Shaykh Uthman is dealing with in this sermon. However, note that he spreads his repudiation of extremism freely to other quarters too, by adding, in passing, a few reproaches against the compromises of official religion and the excesses of Sufi brotherhoods. He accomplishes this by circumlocution rather than direct specification, although the object of this criticism is unmistakable. In fact, with only the rarest exception, this *shaykh* never mentions the Islamic Society by name any more than he singles out a particular Sufi brotherhood or the Azhar. By avoiding such specificity, he conforms to the protocol of traditional sermons.

One of the first challenges that Shaykh Uthman raises to the fundamentalists consists of his opening statement on the validity of "differences." The contention surrounding this term was discussed earlier in the light of Shaykh Umar's refusal to allow for any "differences" in the Qur'an as an assault upon the unity of Islam. Here, however, the preacher flaunts his essential disagreement with hard-line fundamentalists who use the doctrine of unity to justify an alleged privileged place for themselves as judge and enforcer of what they consider the proper interpretation of Islam. Interestingly, Shaykh Uthman does not intone the principles of pluralist secular nationalism in his response. He seizes instead upon a Qur'anic verse often cited by the young fundamentalists as the basis for their supposed interventions against immorality, which often rely on open intimidation and vigilante tactics: "Oh you who believe, if you should quarrel on anything, refer it to God and the Messenger" (4:59).

Since the Islamic Society designates itself as the only proper representative of God and the Messenger in an otherwise corrupt society, it suffices in their own context to advance this verse as proof of their righteousness. By manipulating this phrase and adding the surrounding verses of the Qur'an, however, the preacher reinterprets this legitimating text in a way that disallows any implication that God and the Messenger can be identified with a particular group. He detaches the right to judge and hence to govern (and thus the self-appointed duty to police) from any definite social referent. He insists that its real basis lies only in an attachment to "faith" (*imān*) and "submission" (*islām*).

As was demonstrated in an earlier chapter, Shaykh Uthman's notion of faith implies a reflective consciousness, that is, a personally appropriated responsibility for the translation of religious imperatives into social obligations. The faith that he depicts as the arbiter of values, and which, as we shall see, is closely tied to his notion of reason, is distinguished from blind loyalty to traditional custom as well as conformity with any new group.

The term *al-da'wa*, which he calls "the best of words" (paragraph 2) and which he uses repeatedly, is an important symbol in Shaykh Uthman's preaching and one that identifies him as a reformer. It is a highly charged expression, drawn from the Qur'an, that conveys the sense of a call, a bidding, a summons, a demand, or an invitation. In its original instance it consists of God's call to mankind to obedience. But its general meaning today includes a strong sense of a Muslim's obligation to bring this call to the attention of sinful humanity. When employed in a religious context, the most appropriate translation for the term is "Muslim missionary activity," which carries overtones of moral urgency. An altogether different expression is used for Christian missionary activity, that is, *tabshīr* (properly, "evangelization") that derives from the root meaning to announce or proclaim.

But the term *al-da'wa* has a still more particular reference, especially in conjunction with Shaykh Uthman, because it is also the title of the famous monthly magazine that was published by the Muslim Brothers before their suppression. And, since 1975, although the Society of the Muslim Brothers has remained officially outlawed, this magazine has been allowed to recommence publication. It was subsidized by funds from Saudi Arabia and it was under the editorship of 'Umar al-Talmasani, one of the old guard who was imprisoned during most of ʿAbd al-Nasir's regime. This monthly magazine frequently tended to publish provocative articles highly critical of government policies, which resulted several times during the late 1970s in issues failing to appear because they were, reportedly, confiscated by the authorities. Eventually, in the early 1980s, its publication was once again suppressed. But at this time Shaykh Uthman occasionally promoted this magazine from the pulpit, an extraordinary gesture accorded no other periodical. Regardless of whether his listeners followed his recommendation, such open support of *al-Daʿwa* telegraphs this preacher's firm though moderate stance rooted in these ideals and those who struggled and died under its inspiration. This link to the old Muslim Brothers will be made even more explicit shortly.

In the light of this background, the meaning of the opening remarks about Khalid ibn al-Walid (paragraphs 4 and 5) may be understood as introducing two points reiterated and developed later in the sermon. The first is conveyed simply by the heroic military associations evoked by this name. He is reputed to have been one of the greatest battlefield geniuses of Islamic history, outstanding both for his technical abilities and for his personal qualities. He is popularly credited with the leadership that led the Muslims to their swift successes against the Arab tribes that apostatized after the Prophet's death, and later with organizing the victorious campaigns against the Byzantine and Persian armies. Khalid has therefore come to serve as the *mujāhid* par excellence. In a sense he serves as a patron to the militant fundamentalists who envisage their own struggle as parallel to that of Khalid's day, both in its uneven odds and in its eventual divinely ordained triumph. But it is noteworthy here that Khalid ibn Walid does not appear in his usual character as tactician and conqueror for the cause of Islam. He is presented rather as a docile and self-effacing convert who begs forgiveness, who regrets his godless past, and who is, as the preacher summarizes, "recalled to reason."

The second point drawn from the allusion to Khalid reverts to an item discussed earlier with respect to Shaykh Uthman, and that is his penchant for elaborating upon terms of address and the etymology of names. Earlier it was pointed out that the many surface contradictions in these digressive commentaries suggest that what he offers as sociolinguistic analysis is perhaps better seen as a convenient opening for his moralizing upon the importance of self-restraint, civility, and good manners, especially with respect to dealings with authority.[6] Much the same motive recurs here under this related camouflage. For example, in paragraph 4, the preacher amplifies his argument based upon forms of direct address to stress the courtesy, kindness, and gentleness of the Prophet. The obvious contrast is with the tendency toward intolerance on the part of many of the fundamentalists that easily erupts into belligerence when they confront those with whom they disagree.

The similarly exaggerated interest in the name of Safina (literally, "ship"; paragraph 6) reveals a related motive which follows the slightly different turn of that story. But both instances show that consistency is subordinate to the effort to elaborate upon his moral. In this same sequence the preacher evokes the aura of modern science in advancing the importance of ritual prayer. This argument relies largely on the manipulation of symbols belonging to the overlapping vocabulary of these distinct conceptual realms. In brief, a review of Shaykh Uthman's statements in these adjacent paragraphs reveals that he commends the Prophet decorously as the model of politeness because he addresses Khalid by his first name. In a parallel instance, however, in the sermon fragment discussed earlier, Shaykh Uthman asserted that the Prophet's behavior was exemplary because he explicitly avoided the first name and used the teknonymous form known as the *kunyā*, that is, *Abu* plus the name of the eldest son. According to the *Sira*, Khalid ibn al-Walid was otherwise known by the *kunyā* Abu Sulyman.[7] But the *shaykh* never mentions this name. The other alternative suggested by the preacher is a sort of no-naming. The Prophet's behavior is celebrated as the paragon of politeness because he calls his visitor "Khalid" instead of saying "Oh you there."

The fact that Shaykh Uthman bends his own principles of interpretation from one occasion to another in order to deliver the same moral is pointed out here in order to stress once more the creativity of this preacher. On the one hand, he adopts the role of a teacher bringing to life the persons and events of an ancient text. But the manner in which he does this demonstrates a second purpose, for he recasts the literature into a morality play. One of the elements of effective moralization is to bring the significance of the action portrayed in the story within the reach of those who hear it. The problem is that the epic exploits of those who shared the company of the Prophet are hardly available for imitation for today's ordinary Muslim. So, by extricating from these rich stories that most familiar and valued traditional virtue of *adab*, or "proper respect" and "courtesy," the *shaykh* manages, in effect, to bring the practice of authentic Islam within the grasp of everyone, whether peasant, worker, civil servant, professional, or student. At the same time he is undercutting the implied case for their superiority on the part of the militant fundamentalists, including Shaykh Umar, who identify their religious legitimacy with traditional values of honor, utter loyalty to the group, and the ability to defend and impose authority.

The Shaykh presents *al-daʿwa* not only as a call to God, therefore, but as a call to civility and personal responsibility, and in the episode on Khalid he equates it with a call to "reason" or *ʿaql*. It is this faculty of judgment and discrimination that he returns to most insistently in his reproaches. For the charge of unreasonableness serves not only to expose the shortcomings of the Sufis and the Azharis, but it also deflates the grandiose self-image of the student extremists.

The episode about Safina ibn ʿAmar (paragraph 6) opens, as noted, with another of Shaykh Uthman's extrapolations regarding the name and its meaning. His point is to explain how a Muslim could bear such an unlikely name, for the word means "large ocean-going vessel" or "ship" and it apparently does not occur as a name normally, either in ancient times or the present. Presumed in this context is another detail often remarked in Shaykh Uthman's preaching, which is that the Prophet often changed the name of a person upon their conversion from a pagan or "bad" name to a new Muslim name. The ambiguity here is that Safina rings in the ear like one of these "bad" names used by the ancient Arabs. Hence Shaykh Uthman sets out to demonstrate that it was not only a "good" name, but that the explanation of how he got the name reveals that force and compulsion fail where kindness and liberality succeed. In the process, he embarks upon still another tangent that builds upon his appeal to "reason," and evokes the prestige of modern psychology to support his explanation for the peculiar name. Here the reference is shorthand for a favorite notion of his that will be elaborated further in paragraph 38. It touches on the assertion that Muhammad was the master psychologist who anticipated all of the so-called modern scientific discoveries and whose teaching is the best of therapies. But note that Shaykh Uthman has his own way of presenting this familiar view of the comparability of science and religion, fairly devoid of the exaggerated boasting and irate defensiveness seen in such preachers as Shaykh Umar.

Lessons from Tales of Islamic Heroism

From here we move on to the sermon's most elaborate story, that of Khubayb, extending from paragraph 7 to paragraph 30. It also contains a number of intermittent digressions, seemingly unrelated to the story, but their motive is more clearly seen once again by the logic of moralization. The greater length of the story adds a certain complexity that enables a view of Shaykh Uthman's cumulative effect, but his techniques are constant. Once again, we must assume that his audience is familiar with the basic characters and events in this piece of well-known hagiography, for it is one of those stories that everyone has heard before but which comes to life again in varied retellings. Hence the Shaykh is free to highlight and extemporize without detracting from the drama of the plot and he can rely on at least the better-informed listeners to draw conclusions from his innuendo and ellipsis. For those who regularly listen to such a preacher any one sermon is like a middle chapter of a longer book, whereby points developed in prior weeks are now considered to be firmly in place and incomplete suggestions are held in abeyance for later. All of this results in a mature style that allows for a greater adaptation of the abstract symbols of Islamic religion to local and contemporary circumstances. This preacher is less constrained than the others we have featured in terms of formal oratorical language and reference, for his constraints are pictures closer to those which impinge upon ordinary daily reality.

In paragraph 7 where Shaykh Uthman sets up what he calls "the *ḥadīth* for today" he emphasizes once again that this story has special relevance to youth. This includes both an appeal for the young to listen well and a signal to everyone that what follows is chiefly motivated by the confusions that are leading to the various social discomforts, notably civil unrest. Along with his introduction, he cites his sources, giving a bibliographic reference in a way more characteristic of the lecture hall than the pulpit. Although we have seen Shaykh Umar refer to titles, these are tracts and fundamentalist pamphlets that have an altogether different standing than the *Sira*. This specification of Shaykh Uthman evokes a familiarity with forbidding obscure tomes that has an inviting and demystifying effect. He often colors such references to canonical literature with a pedagogical motive, encouraging his listeners, especially young people, to study these texts for themselves.

After the story is introduced, but before the narration actually begins, there is a series of comments that serve to give this episode a certain continuity with other sermons and with current issues. The apostrophe on "people of *yasr*" ("ease, affluence, abundance") repeated at the end of paragraph 7 refers to another well-known incident from the *Sira*. During the early persecution at Mecca, Muhammad promised paradise to those who suffer for the sake of Islam, using this term as his epithet for the community of his followers.[8] Similarly, the short allusion in paragraph 8 to the man "who was sawed from head to toe with a saw of iron" refers to the passion of a martyr for Islam. Both of these incidents had been spoken of in detail in other sermons and these briefest allusions serve merely to recall them as stories in the same genre as the one that is about to follow.

What appears in paragraph 9 is different in that it is not a lesson from the *Sira*, but a trite Arabic proverb, which we have translated literally: a "crooked pole casts a crooked shadow." This folk maxim is used to mean that the home is the breeding ground for character, and hence children can be presumed to have a sound or unsound moral character depending on the training given by their parents. The preacher presents this cultural assumption categorically, and then turns it interestingly into a criticism of views on the emancipation of women. Remembering, of course, that his audience consists almost entirely of men, this insistence on the traditional place of the mother in the home is not, as it might initially seem, a reprimand from the traditional quarter that disapproves of women in school and in the work force. Shaykh Uthman is by no means a reactionary on this question, but rather a strong promoter of female education, including adult education, and there are a good number of activities organized at his mosque for the participation of women, such as sewing classes, sessions on hygiene and home maintenance, and religious instruction. His point in these remarks seems rather to be a call to young men to seek in a wife a strong and virtuous character, the stuff of which good mothers are made. And then he calls upon married men to take seriously their domestic responsibilities of overseeing the mother's care and taking upon themselves the discipline of their children when needed.

Appended to this ratification of home life is a curiously modern metaphor used with reference to the ritual recitation by the father of the *shahāda* in the ear of a newborn baby. The preacher mentions the power and effectiveness of this religious custom as though it works in the fashion of a magical charm, as he compares it to a message set down on a tape recorder that will thereafter remain fixed.

Even after these preliminaries, when the narrative finally seems underway in paragraph 11, the Shaykh once again interrupts his explanation of the irresistible spread of *al-da'wa* to recapitulate, in paragraph 12, his emphasis on youth. Note that he gives his remark the full weight of the *ḥadīth*, referring explicitly to Bukhayri, the most authoritative of *ḥadīth* collections.

In paragraph 13, there follows a circuitous reference to the weapons carried by Khubayb and his companions. This exposition sets Shaykh Uthman off into a tangled commentary that gets so strained he eventually drops it, apologizes for it, and then recovers the thread, only to lapse back into another explanation. The phrase in question, *asliḥa al-da'wa*, which we have glossed "arms of the call," has a certain poetical quality that could imply spiritual rather than material armaments. St. Paul's use of images like "helmet of salvation" and "breastplate of truth" certainly has its resonance in Islam.[9] Nevertheless, there can be no doubt from one's knowledge of the anarchical character of the Arabian desert at the time, when Mecca and Medina were at war, and more patently, from the way the story unfolds, that Khubayb and his companions were armed physically and were warriors. In the description of the subsequent ambush and skirmish, the Shaykh can hardly suggest that the Muslim party was ill-equipped, although they were certainly caught off guard. But the preacher hedges flamboyantly on this point as if to cover over the obvious implications of violence immediately associated with the resort to weapons.

The reason Shaykh Uthman goes to such lengths to reinterpret this allusion to the carrying of arms is clearly to discourage the use of weapons in the local context. In the region of Minya, especially in the countryside, knives and guns, including pistols are a very common item. The "cowboy" ethos of the area is famous throughout Egypt and use of these weapons in fights and feuds, as well as occasionally in banditry, is a factor every traveler must reckon with.[10] In the course of the past months as sectarian tensions were periodically exploding and mounting generally, and the Islamic Society was growing more assertive both in the city and in the countryside, the number of incidents involving weapons, beatings, stabbings, and shootings had increased alarmingly. The Coptic grapevine was my prime source for these reports, but even granting a certain exaggeration that reflected their legitimate anxiety, it was clear that religious extremism had combined perniciously with the code of vendetta justice and male bravado to escalate into a number of isolated assaults and some enduring and fatal confrontations.

Moreover, the resort to violence in association with fanatic Muslim groups had already made a vivid impression in the public mind. While it outraged peaceful citizens and civil officials, such tactics were appealing or at least justifiable to those who sympathized strongly with the cause of the new fundamentalism. Everyone was aware of the existence of various clandestine groups that would occasionally stage violent symbolic assaults in the name of Islam or that would prompt the government to well-publicized mass arrests and announcements of the official discovery of caches of arms or bomb factories. During the summer of 1977, the nation had been spectator to the trial of the leadership of one such group, known as *al-takfir wa-al-hijra*, which had been found guilty of the kidnapping and assassination of the former Minister of Religious Endowments, Shaykh Hussain al-Dhahabi. Although the crime and the eventual trial occurred in the environs of Cairo, the youthful ideologue of this extremist group and all key members were from Upper Egypt, some from Minya. Added to this was the new enthusiasm for "revolution" sparked by the current events in Iran.

Shaykh Uthman's ploy in paragraph 13 appears to be not so much an effort to deny the fact that Khubayb and his men carried weapons and used them as to divert the listeners' attention elsewhere. First he throws out allusions to Egypt's great housing shortage. Then he leaps to the need for better transportation. From that he jumps to the hope that the state, because it seeks to follow Islamic principles, will someday have a program of publicly supported financing for the purchase of such expensive items. He then retreats from his cul-de-sac and appeals to the authority of the experts in Islamic law (note that he uses the term *fuqahā'* rather than *'ulamā'*) to affirm that only one who is utterly sound (*salīm*) himself is permitted to "raise his voice."

It is only in paragraph 14 that the preacher finally takes up the story, at which point he displays, with an explicitness we have not yet seen, a manner of dramatization that is special to him and another indication of how he presents himself as preacher. He is particularly fond of presenting a visual *mise en scène* that is a self-conscious emulation of cinematographic sequence. He starts with a broad panorama and proceeds to zoom into close-ups that catch the heart of the action. He even goes so far, as we see in this paragraph, to invite his listeners to imagine that they are picturing what he describes on television. Another verbal clue to this movie consciousness recurs later in paragraphs 17, 18, 24, and 25, when he introduces new sections of the story as "scenes" (*mashad*), the same term used in the theater. What makes these references so singular is on the one hand the implied vulgarization of the lofty oratorical idiom to the level of a movie. No other preacher we have seen would compromise his formalism to this degree. Furthermore, movies have been and continue to be associated with loose morals and Western decadence both by Azhari traditionalists and even more vehemently by fundamentalists. In Minya, no one who considers himself a good Muslim and who wishes to be thought of by others as such would ever go to a movie theater! Television has somehow escaped this stigma, but insofar as it shows many of the same things that appear in films, it too is suspect in the eyes of many. Video technology was only to arrive several years later, but it too quickly brought condemnations from fundamentalists.

The second feature of this imitation of a cinematographic format lies with Shaykh Uthman's artful delivery, a feature that is impossible to preserve in the reduction of this oral performance into a written and translated text. While it would not be accurate to say that this preacher is exceptionally gifted as a raconteur, he is nevertheless capable of shifting effectively from one character to another and then back to a narrator's voice, throughout all of which he sprinkles his own freewheeling interpolations. Some of this is done to overcome the potential obscurities due to diglossia, but no little part of his interlinear commentary displays familiar editorial motives, sometimes subtle, but more often blatant.

When the preacher comes to speak of the capture of Khubayb, he pauses significantly to accentuate that the details of this part of the story differ from one teller to the other. We have already indicated the political signals that are contained in such a statement as we find here—"differences are good"—but we can now elaborate on his grounds for making a statement so readily disturbing to the ultra-orthodox.[11] The character of Shaykh Uthman's tolerance stems in large part from the model of the open classroom where there is a place to examine everything, but the professor is the most qualified to give pronouncements. Here it is accepted that there may be more than one version of a story, just as there may be more than one version of a movie, while the essential core, the lesson it communicates, can remain unchanged. This sense of moderation and balance between fanatical extremes is the important identifying element. He opposes those whom he calls "fools and crazy men" by which he means those who are Sufis or who follow the cult of miracle-promising saints, just as he opposes the irresponsible righteousness of the headstrong and bellicose fundamentalists. It is presumed that reason is the shared norm and that deviance can be corrected by persuasion without recourse to threats. The affirmation of the right to differ is not a weakness that an enemy could take advantage of, as with Shaykh Umar, but a sign of confidence and individual conviction.

The discussion of Khubayb once he is in custody, beginning in paragraph 19, involves certain miraculous happenings that force Shaykh Uthman to clarify his position concerning the possibility of such phenomena. The first is the discovery that Khubayb has grapes to eat when grapes are out of season, and the second is the inexplicable nocturnal illumination of Khubayb's cell. The Shaykh has already prepared the audience for his handling of these events by his recollections in paragraph 17. Here, he refreshes their memory about the main point of the sermon delivered the week before, December 8, 1978, which dealt almost entirely with a rebuttal of the claims to miraculous power on the part of holy men. These ideas are not of themselves new but it is helpful to reinterpret them in this new setting. The expression that served as the leitmotif of the earlier sermon fuses two categories that are revealing indices of whom it is that Shaykh Uthman confirms as the normative Muslim. The first term, which we gloss as "ritually pure" (*al-muwaḍa'īn*), describes in its broadest sense a person who conforms to the traditional *sharī'a* in the relevant matters touching on diet, bathing, fasting, and so forth. But in its more narrow sense, and it is thus that the term is ordinarily used in speech, it refers to those who perform the ritual washing before the *ṣalāh*, or prayer. Hence the term implies a broad moral compass, but is specifically associated with fidelity to the five obligatory daily prayers. The connected phrase, "sons of the mat," we have already noted, but we can add here that it contains a coloring of "those who are well instructed," for the "mat" emblemizes wisdom and equanimity as well as devotion and regularity. The final word that Shaykh Uthman offers on miracles is that they are only to be lent credence when they occur at the hands of one who is "ritually pure and a son of the mat" in which case it can be explained as "reasonable" but "from a heavenly perspective."

After thus disposing of any claim to Khubayb as a "saint," that is, a *walī*, the Shaykh steers the story back to the penultimate episode, which he will exploit as a gentle but firm rebuke of those who would act with force or violence in the name of Islam or religious reform. His high praise for Khubayb's heroic restraint and his refusal to harm the little boy of his captor who brought him the razor clearly reiterates the same lesson we have seen before. The superiority of this persistent kindness in the face of oppression and imminent death is then confirmed by the supposed spontaneous conversion of Mawiya, the slave in charge of the prisoner.

In this section of the story, paragraph 20, we note that the preacher returns to the idea of *al-daʿwa*, this time in connection with Khubayb's recitation of the Qurʾan. On one level, this remark alludes to the power and feeling that pious Muslims sense in the chanting of the Qurʾan, a ritual that belongs in every important social occasion (weddings, births, funerals, dedications, holidays, and prayer, of course, where the chanting is an integral element in the cycle of prostrations) and is frequently broadcast on radio and television. But on another level, it is apparent that the preacher means to specify that just as the chanting of the Qurʾan cannot be stifled even in "the darkest prison cells," those who are persecuted for their belief in the Qurʾan are still participants in the spread of *al-daʿwa*. By this sort of remark this preacher indicates, once more, that for him the active pursuit of religion is not to be equated with exterior form or politicosocial involvement but can include religious acts in utter isolation as well. There is also an unmistakable autobiographical ring to this mention of the Qurʾan in a prison cell which, though brief, would not pass his listeners unnoticed.

The Shaykh's emphasis on the interior quality of Islam, which we have linked to Weber's *Gesinnungsethik*, is articulated admirably here in the way the preacher presents an image of the Qurʾan not so much as a text but as an attitude. In speaking of Khubayb's recitation, he notes that the people learned to hear for "[Khubayb] in carrying his heart is carrying Islam, even if it is not apparent to anyone." In a kindred statement in another sermon, Shaykh Uthman cited a memorable remark claiming that every Muslim should be "a Qurʾan walking about the earth."

Another set of intriguing allusions that accompany this section are more immediately related to the question of the legitimacy of violence. For instance, in paragraph 21, the preacher pretends to supply Khubayb with a justification for taking the life of the little boy, and he puts the words in the mouth of 'Ashmawi. This is the name of the fabled executioner, the hangman, in Cairo, whose name cannot help but evoke memories of those who have suffered at his gallows. The mention of Farid Shawqi in paragraph 23 calls forth the world of this dramatic movie hero. Shawqi is a popular Egyptian actor who approximates a combination of John Wayne's rugged dignity and the honorable pugnacity of Clint Eastwood. Later, in paragraph 26, the Shaykh cites the name of Hindawi Sayyid Ahmad Duwayr, which is a reference of another order. This man, originally from Minya but long resident in Cairo, was a leading figure in the Society of the Muslim Brothers and was implicated in the plot to assassinate 'Abd al-Nasir in 1954. He was tried and executed, but partisans of the Society, including Shaykh Uthman, clearly venerate him as innocent and a martyr.

The moralization featured in paragraph 22 centers around hostage-taking, which in recent years has become almost institutionalized, especially in the Middle East, as an underdog tactic. On the international stage, it was employed by Palestinians who hijacked airplanes, or kidnapped diplomats. Obviously Shaykh Uthman is lashing out at those who would glorify this conduct and legitimate it in the name of Islam. The reference at the end of this paragraph to a "sugar field" alludes to the well-known practice in rural Upper Egypt of using fields of sugar cane as places of refuge for fugitives, for criminal hideouts or for holding someone hostage. Here is an interesting example of an ideologically motivated act that is thrust into the same category as the local gangster maneuver by the same name. Both are equally condemned.

However, the rhetorical character of this condemnation is curious, especially the repeated phrase that there is no hostage-taking "in Islam." This usage, "there is no x in Islam" is a set idiom that apparently encodes the most absolute possible rejection. It occurs again, in exactly the same form, when Shaykh Uthman condemns suicide while moralizing upon the holocaust of Jonestown in paragraph 38, and again when he attacks the "ogre of routine," or red tape, in paragraph 47. Obviously to say that such and such a behavior does not exist "in Islam" is to assert that "Muslims" are never permitted to act in such and such a manner. But in this reification of Islam there emerges an important ambiguity between the social and the ideological definition of a Muslim.[12] Definitive declarations about what is and what is not "in Islam" form part of the standard vocabulary of the fundamentalists, which is not to imply that they therefore can agree among themselves. However, in their case, this locative metaphor is simple to understand: being *in* or being *out* of Islam is effectively equated with being *in* or *out* of their self-defined community of Muslims. For the saint and the Azhari, each in his way, it is also prevalent, but in their usage, it is taken as an abstract pronouncement, the statement of an ideal which will be altered and tempered in application. Shaykh Uthman creatively adapts the formula by borrowing strains from both of these more fixed positions and then adds another dimension. For him, it is possible to level an apodeictic judgment in the manner of traditional authority while at the same time embracing change by respecting a realistic social base.

He accomplishes this mixture of sociological and ideological validity by his discerning use of the term "sons of the mat." The phrase avoids the swift identification of "us" against "them" by its generality while it nevertheless indicates a certain social entity. But the operational element in this symbol so central to Shaykh Uthman is not doctrine, in terms of an intellectual or even emotional assent, nor is it political, in terms of an active and public commitment to a certain definite program of reform; it is *ritual.* In other words, the preacher has devised his own meaning for the forceful axiom "in Islam," a meaning that wrests it away from the either/or absolutism with which it is characteristically associated. By framing ritual in its broadest sense as the authentic mark of the Muslim, he refutes those who ultimately insist on the measure of a person's "Islam" by any external criteria, whether it be "right action" or "right declaration." It is rather some more interior and hence inaccessible quality that is the basis of any judgment.

This reading of Shaykh Uthman's remarks on this subject is reconfirmed when he reiterates the same formula used with hostage-taking on the subject of suicide:

> In the history of Islam and of the Muslims, there is absolutely
> never suicide. You'll never find it! It's impossible to find an inci-
> dence of suicide except among fools and crazy people who have
> never prayed to God, glorious and majestic, so much as a single
> prostration, who have never sat beside a wash basin or the canal to
> make the ritual ablution, saying: "In the name of God, the merciful
> and compassionate." They have never stood before the *qibla* and
> said *Allah akbar.* (paragraph 38)

Taken literally, the Shaykh categorically denies that any Muslim has ever committed suicide. This is nonsense, of course, for an occasional Muslim, however irrational, does take his own life. The Shaykh revises his remarks admitting this sad but obvious fact shortly thereafter: "and as for suicide, well, that's their own business. You hear about people committing suicide. So you take some fools from among Muslims who have never sat upon the mat. They find themselves in some tight spot, so they kill themselves, and may the Lord forgive them" (paragraph 40).

The Shaykh then alludes to an event still fresh in the public mind, the suicide of "that minister of health." Still more vivid, but politically much more volatile, is the suicide of General 'Abd al-Hakim Amir, who grew up in Samalout, the next town north of Minya, where his family still retains great land holdings and considerable influence, although they are not in favor with the current regime. General 'Abd al-Hakim Amir was 'Abd al-Nasir's chief of staff, and thought by many to be his heir apparent. To some extent, he was also a political opponent and rival of Sadat under 'Abd al-Nasir. Blame for the 1967 defeat at the hands of Israel was pinned on Amir, and he took his own life in September of that same year.[13] The Shaykh's failure to specifically mention this local and well-known incidence of a public suicide is itself noteworthy, for he avoids throwing out a red herring while he asserts by innuendo that 'Abd al-Nasir's government was headed by godless men who for the most part came to the end they deserved.

Religion Unmasking Worldly Deceits

In the course of his comments on prayer in paragraph 38 the preacher elaborates further on the "psychological" benefits of the Prophet's religion, a point we called attention to earlier. He lets an elliptical remark suffice for a whole line of thought that he had often presented and with which his listeners are presumably familiar. The quotation, "Let us take our rest in it, oh Bilal . . ." refers to Muhammad's request to Bilal, the first caller to prayer, to call the assembly to prayer at times of trial. This is a standard illustration for Shaykh Uthman when he presents prayer as a psychological panacea, especially to anxiety-ridden youth.

His comment that "British friends" have shown that prayer restores a person to security (*amn*) and peace (*salām*) is a reference to an incidental piece in the British press that was picked up and given great play by the Muslim media and has been still further celebrated by the fundamentalists. The article reported that a team of British doctors had determined that the *ṣalāh* had a certain therapeutic value for cases of stress. What Shaykh Uthman and others make of this, of course, is that here is scientific verification for still another facet of traditional Islamic practice. Other kindred claims based on the same "medical materialism" are frequently heard with regard to the avoidance of pork, alcohol, carrion, or the health benefits of fasting.

Another telling use of the symbol of "science" and "religion" in the West among Muslims is articulated in the preacher's interpretation of the bizarre tragedy of Jonestown, which was a headline story a couple of weeks prior. In paragraph 37, he sets America up as a foil in order to unfavorably contrast it with Islam. Hence, he describes it as the supposed pinnacle of "progress in culture and science" while it is "zero in the realm of the spirit." The actual facts and circumstances of the Jonestown events interest him very little, of course, and the few particular remarks about the cult are meaningless generalities. The point he wants to make, however, is clear, namely that America knows nothing about religion, for Jonestown is supposed to stand for something typical.

Rather soon, however, he leaves behind the complexities that surround the Jonestown events and he moralizes at a level that his listeners can more easily grasp and judge. In paragraph 40, he generalizes freely to suggest that Americans commit suicide casually, in any and all tight situations, but most readily as the result of amorous disappointments. One cannot help but hear in this declaration an implied condemnation of the disapproved mixed-sex companionship of young people that is perceived locally as an "American" style. The noteworthy contrast with Shaykh Umar here is that Shaykh Uthman deploys "America" as a symbol of materialism, emotional immaturity, and self-indulgence and not as a superpower, a master image of greed and hence of colossal political oppression and economic dependence. Shaykh Uthman, typically, does not permit the massive inflation of his symbols but rather seeks to tie them to some element within the manageable experience of his listeners.

But even while Shaykh Uthman consistently avoids playing upon the collective excitement that is aroused by appeals to primordial and sacred values, and thus avoids the debilitating dualistic worldview of the fundamentalists, he cannot avoid participating in the tension of religion and politics and still be considered as a serious preacher. His subtlety makes the difference. One might think, for instance, that presenting Khubayb's unjust slaughter at the hands of idolaters would be an excellent opportunity to stigmatize the current government as effectively guilty of the same outrages. This is an easy and obvious parallel, so much so, in fact, that Shaykh Uthman's failure to make it explicit might itself be thought to be worthy of note. Nowhere in the whole sequence on Khubayb's death (paragraphs 25–30) is there any visible indication that the analogy of this persecution extends to the contemporary regime.

This impression of neutrality is quite illusionary, however, for a more alert analysis of the images used by Shaykh Uthman reveal not only the character of his opposition, but also the authority upon which he bases his judgments. Note, for instance, in paragraph 25, the way he develops the meaning of the word *khashab*, a general term meaning "wood" or "timber." To make this unspecified archaism meaningful, the preacher immediately explains that what is referred to is a torture device, much like one called "the maiden" that was in a Cairo prison. The instant association, in context, is the infamous maximum-security prison where so many of the Muslim Brothers were incarcerated. In the text of the *Sira*, this vague reference to a device called the "wood" is made definite in a way that utterly belies any historical basis for this association with the modern "maiden." Although Shaykh Uthman entirely avoids mentioning it, the instrument is referred to in a relevant passage of the *Sira* as "Khubayb's cross"[14] and the verb used in the *Sira* is likewise the unambivalent expression for "crucifixion."[15] The preacher's manipulation of this symbol represents an effort to divest this martyr's death of its aura of Christian imagery and frame it affirmatively as a version of modern state suppression.

Another passing allusion that smuggles in significant political commentary follows in this same paragraph 25 with the "man in Yemen . . . in that backward system of theirs." There are two probable barbs in this comment. One is a backhanded reminder of 'Abd al-Nasir's disastrous military adventurism in this remote land in the name of Arab Nationalism. His boastful aid and his alliance with leftists cost Egypt money and lives and even then failed to achieve its objectives. The second is the worn cliché of Yemen as a poor and almost chaotic society, half of which was then controlled by atheistic Marxists.

Again, in paragraph 27, a double entendre is worked into the description of the one who is taunting Khubayb and urging him to curse the Prophet and renounce Islam. The preacher uses the term *qazam*, a term usually glossed as "midget" or "dwarf." This is the derogatory nickname that Sadat used in public rhetoric as an epithet for Mu'ammar al-Qaddafi of Libya, who claims, loudly and defiantly, that 'Abd al-Nasir designated him as his successor to lead the Arab World, and who has developed an elaborate quasi-religious ideology of his own, set down in the multiple volumes of his "Green Book." The preacher's remark about this "midget" attempting to "brain-wash" Khubayb is a fairly straightforward slight against the propaganda campaigns so typical of the official Libyan media.

Another instructive recasting of this last section of the Khubayb episode involves a slight but significant readaptation of the narrative itself. In paragraph 27, the preacher makes a great fuss over the martyr's final words and his nobility in the face of mockery and death, summarized by his riposte: "By God, I wouldn't want Muhammad to even be pricked by a thorn and I am sitting in my house." These are well-known words, associated with this story, but according to the text of the *Sira* it is not Khubayb who speaks them, but another member of his party named Zayd ibn al-Dathinna.[16] Khubayb himself is depicted as having feelings of a much more righteous, vindictive, and menacing character. According to the *Sira*, the last utterance on his lips is: "Oh God, reckon them by number and kill them one by one, let none of them escape."[17]

Furthermore, this cry of Khubayb for vengeance is usually one of the most resonant features in classical accounts of the episode,[18] where Arab honor and affirmation of the Qur'anic "eye for an eye" formula are centrally depicted.[19] Immediately following the chapter on Khubayb in the *Sira*, a number of panegyric verses are recorded as is the convention, and in these are several references to "Khubayb's curse," for it was believed that all who took part in this crime paid for it later. In fact, there is mention of one of those present at this execution who later became a Muslim, but even then he suffered dizzy spells that were attributed to the residual effect of "Khubayb's curse." Finally, there is specific mention later in the *Sira* of the Prophet himself leading a raid against the perpetrators of the deed, the motive for such a raid being, in the words of the *Sira*, "to avenge his men killed at al-Raja', Khubayb ibn 'Adiy and his companions."[20] Moreover, the telepathic message about Khubayb's death sent to Muhammad, which the preacher speaks of in paragraph 30, is relayed in the *Sira* in direct conjunction with the martyr's call for revenge.

Given all we have said, there is no need to restate the reasons Shaykh Uthman has for diverting the audience's attention from the many strains of this story that ratify and recommend holy revenge. But even while he strives to discourage the local feud mentality that has been conflated into sectarian tensions, he stops short of expressing anything but token confidence in official institutions. While aiming criticism at the far right and the far left of Muslim groups, he takes care to point out abuses and problems on the civil and national level as well. This preacher's effort to meet a broad range of opinion and to reshape it without causing offense includes a special attitude toward local officialdom. He knows, of course, as everyone does, that informants of the secret police, *al-mabāḥith*, can be expected to listen and report on any insulting or seditious comments. But more than that, he is himself unavoidably identified with the state bureaucratic elite, and hence it would undermine his own prestige and position to make wholesale negative criticisms of those who occupy local offices of authority.

The manner in which Shaykh Uthman voices his disapproval of a topical event, a decision, or some practice that touches immediate political sensibilities can differ slightly from his treatment of religiously marked opponents. His favorite resort is, again, that technique of using *Sira* as a device for drawing implied parallels. One good example of this occurs in the sermon of December 29, 1978. Earlier that week, Yusuf Saba'i, editor of *Al-Ahram*, the semiofficial newspaper of the Egyptian government, had been taken hostage along with a hijacked plane to Cyprus. For a few days the Palestinian terrorists holed up in the grounded plane while various negotiators attempted to arrange a settlement. At the height of this stand-off, Sadat ordered a group of Egyptian commandos to stage an Entebbe-like raid in the hopes of rescuing the hostages. A wild shoot-out resulted that senselessly cost the lives of dozens of soldiers, hostages, police, and airport workers. The fiasco greatly embarrassed Egypt and it led to the immediate severing of diplomatic ties with Cyprus.

Shaykh Uthman, making indirect editorial comments in the course of his sermon, approaches this crisis of conscience with an elaborate account of how the Caliph 'Umar ibn al-Khutab came to decide to engage the Byzantine forces in what became the first naval battle in Islamic history. The preacher carefully elaborates the precautions taken by the Caliph beforehand, his laborious consultations with other Muslim leaders, his collaboration with experts in strategy, and his foresight regarding all the necessary preparations. Most of all he stresses the Caliph's constant solicitude for protecting the lives of his soldiers, even that he ordered that only volunteers would be allowed to participate.

Discerning the Enemy Within

On another occasion, in the sermon given on May 4, 1979, shortly after Sadat's autocratic dismissal of the Egyptian Parliament and the ordering of another national referendum to ratify his call for new elections, and various measures to curb political opponents, Shaykh Uthman again centered his sermon around the Caliph 'Umar ibn al-Khutab. In this case, he strings together a series of seemingly unrelated anecdotes all of which illustrate the Caliph's virtues of personal humility, generosity, his tolerance of dissent, his sensitivity to complaints, his accessibility to his subjects, his scrupulous accountability with public funds, his paternal solicitude toward the poor, women, and children, his distaste for any privilege or trapping of luxury, and his insistence that provincial governors follow his example.

Another example of Shaykh Uthman's style with a most interesting twist came at the end of the sermon preached on December 7, 1978. He is commenting upon reports of a bizarre and suspicious disturbance that occurred at the Bulgarian Embassy in Cairo. It received sensational, front-page coverage in the national press, in a way that clearly indicated that the Egyptian government sought to exploit the minor incident for political advantage. Allegedly there were a number of threats, beatings, and even some shooting on the part of Embassy officials and employees directed at certain residents who occupied apartments in the same building as the Embassy. One Egyptian woman who worked at the Embassy was supposedly presented with a gun as a gift. Exactly what happened and why was always a bit foggy, but the Shaykh is not interested in the details anyway. He begins some remarks by reciting, for comic effect, the funny-sounding foreign names of the Bulgarian diplomats, adding his typical denunciation of violence. He follows this by remarking that one can expect such immoral conduct from "reds" and then he appeals to the Egyptian government to tighten security around communist embassies and to increase surveillance of these untrustworthy diplomats.

Then, in an extraordinary aside, Shaykh Uthman interjects a slow and deliberate remark that has the quality of being confidential while it is utterly forthright and public. He says, "I know what I am saying will be transmitted and I want it to be transmitted in all its exactness." The word we gloss here as "transmit" conveys the notion of word being passed on in a somewhat officious way from one agency to another. It is impossible to take this reference, curious as it is, to mean anything but a call to the secret police, *al-mabāhath*, who are always presumed to be listening attentively. But this bold direct address is effective not only as a way of demonstrating that he is aware of their presence, but as a way of implying that they should be checking up on communists instead of Muslim preachers. There is also a hint of a certain collegiality on the part of Shaykh Uthman with his invisible counterparts in the service of the nation.

This adoption of responsibility by one who is a respectable functionary as well as a concerned preacher is another characteristic of Shaykh Uthman's self-conscious presentation of self, and the first prominent example of it in the December 15 sermon occurs in paragraph 32. Here, after describing the scandalous behavior of certain young people whom he typifies as "hippies" (paragraph 31),[21] he tells his listeners that he means to call these things to the attention of "our dear friends, the police." He then reaffirms this call for a stricter official curtailment of youthful frivolity by adding, impressively, that he himself plans to look into the matter as to whether any school was involved in that raucous and mixed-sex picnic he noticed. He assumes, as he says, that no "sons of the mat" would ever be involved in such an affair, and he ends with a witty allusion to their drum as their "weapon," a remark that goes back to his earlier digression on the "weapons" of *al-da'wa*.

The final segment of this sermon, from paragraph 41 until the tape from which it is transcribed ran out, shifts to another topic, but what it illustrates, for our purposes of analysis, is continuous with the rest of the long sermon. He opens this section by declaring that Islam condemns bureaucratic red tape and ceremonious brouhaha, which he calls the "ogre of routine." Behind this remark are two points. First there is an appeal to see practical decision-making power vested in local authorities, what he calls "the ones closest to the problems of outlying areas." Second is the demand that officials do not satisfy themselves with ceremonies and show, but that they involve themselves in the real daily affairs that confront them in their respective departments.

The need to overhaul and reinvigorate the massive and insufficient octopus of Egypt's national bureaucracy is a common theme everywhere in public life, including Sadat's own speeches. Such discussions include the call for decentralization, to the extent that one of Sadat's major political platform items at this time was the alleged autonomy of each provincial administration. Each provincial governor (*muḥāfiẓ*), it was constantly repeated, was to be like the president (*ra'īs*) within his province. What Shaykh Uthman has done is to take this slogan one step further, to recommend that genuine authority be given over at an even lower level of officialdom, in fact, at the very grass-roots, the level of the *markaz* (roughly, "town" or "township").

Shaykh Uthman's encouragement of initiative and his promotion of administrative self-sufficiency in social and economic matters extends to his idea of religious authority as well. He once expressed these remarks below in a sermon delivered on February 2, 1979. They contain a special insight into just what he means by this pattern of local autonomy. Since it touches centrally on what seems his most basic concept of his own role as preacher, these remarks are worth reviewing carefully. Toward the end of that sermon, the Shaykh is commenting at length upon the recent sudden death of one of his colleagues at the Provincial Ministry of Education. In the midst of these sundry reflections he makes the following assertions. Once again he is leaping freely between quotes, paraphrasing, and supplying editorial comments on a story from the *ḥadīth*, much of which involves subtle shifts between classical and colloquial Arabic. The stylistic clumsiness of this sermon segment is partially due to a looseness of expression on the preacher's part, and partially due to an effort to preserve the effect of the many meanings that are compressed in the term *wajib* (that is, to obligate, to enjoin, to owe, to be necessary, to be incumbent).

> The Prophet, prayers and peace upon him, said in a long *ḥadīth:*
> "Whomever you praise for goodness, I enjoin paradise upon him."
> That's how the *ḥadīth* reads, or in other words, by walking in a

funeral procession, we are praising the goodness of a person. Indeed, the Prophet, prayers and peace upon him, when speaking on the subject of what he enjoins, has also said: "By walking in a funeral procession, we commend a person for evil." That's the expression in Arabic. Thus the Prophet, prayers and peace upon him, spoke of what he enjoins. But then we ask: "Oh Prophet of God, what are you speaking of when you speak of enjoining in the first case and in the second?" And he told them its meaning: "Whomever you praise for goodness, I enjoin upon him paradise; and whomever you commend for evil, I enjoin upon him hell-fire. You are the witnesses of God upon earth." Now take note, to whom is he referring? He is talking about good Muslims, the ritually pure, the kindly. Don't get the idea that he is referring to just ordinary people! No, not at all! He means *you!* Yes! "Whomever *you* praise for goodness." That is *you*, who sit on the mat, oh ritually pure, and kindly ones. *You!* Whomever you testify to in Islam for goodness, he is good, and whomever you commend as otherwise, then that case is otherwise. This saying came to mind, oh brothers, after the funeral last Wednesday.

This statement about the judgment of the dead is an adequate metaphor for what I believe to be Shaykh Uthman's view of the basis of his authority as preacher. It depicts the Prophet handing over the right to evaluate good and evil to the company of the living, who declare their verdict by their willingness or unwillingness to march in the ritual of a funeral procession. But, the Shaykh insists emphatically, it is not a power entrusted to ordinary people, but rather to the "ritually pure . . . sons of the mat," that is, to those who like himself seek to creatively adapt their religion and morality. The highest arbiter of right and wrong is not the traditionally affirmed *walī* or Azhari, nor the fundamentalist who bases his authority on direct and immediate relationship to the Qur'an and so-called primitive Islam; it is the community grounded in reason and faith. Shaykh Uthman claims his authority as preacher not on the basis of any inherent superiority, but as one who presses each believer to assume responsibility for his personal integration of the call of God in the modern world.

11   Unity and Commitment

The Preacher as Apologist for the Ideology of Islamic Fundamentalism

This third and final unabridged sermon, again reproduced in Appendix C, was chosen to exemplify that type of preacher who legitimates his function by assuming the culturally constituted duty of "struggle" or *jihād*. It was delivered by Shaykh Umar on April 6, 1979, shortly after the first series of arrests in Minya had shown that official patience with the provocative actions by religious extremists had run out. As was explained earlier, illegal and disruptive demonstrations of many forms had escalated enormously in the preceding months, fueled by a growing sense of frustration as Sadat was rushing ahead with his treaty with Israel while proving in the eyes of many to be evading the promised prosperity that was to accompany the new era of peace. It was the local Islamic activists, specifically those operating under the banner of the student Islamic Society, who had assumed the leadership of this public opposition. Their rhetoric was couched in the usual religious and moral rebuke that was widely perceived by their opponents as a facade for political accusation and even revolutionary counter-measures. Their enthusiasm over what they trumpeted as the triumph of Islam over Western Imperialism in Iran continued unabated, as their slogans made plain. Their rejection of the Camp David Accords signed in Washington two weeks before the delivery of this sermon was presented as a position that had the vigorous support of the rest of the Arab world which was furious about the separate peace and was already implementing measures designed to isolate Egypt.

Earlier, when Shaykh Umar's pattern of rhetorical conversion was considered in some detail, his central mode of expression was characterized as metonymic. The penchant for literalness indicated a purported unmediated application of the Qur'an, carrying over its dictates and imitating the Sunna of the Prophet without passing through an intervening historical heritage. In the present discussion, we shall elaborate on how this metonymic mode functions as a rhetoric of social participation. Morality and religion are presented here in this symbolic idiom by a preacher who draws his authority through his projection of the cultural archetype of the *mujāhid* or "warrior."

A noteworthy parallel to the analysis proposed for this sermon of Shaykh Umar is given in an intriguing study by David Parkin on the rhetoric of government bureaucrats in rural Kenya.[1] He found it useful to draw the analogy of "ideology" and "plan" as related in a manner similar to "symbol" and "sign." While Parkin does not assign to these terms the highly technical force they sometimes bear in semiotic studies, he develops a useful distinction which assists in the description of this preacher. Parkin qualifies ideology as emotive, effusive, and elastic, and then gives what he calls its "practical implications" as follows: "The emotional force of an ideology engages attention; its polyvalent messages or exhortations reach out to the widest possible audience, though obviously at the cost of depth in each of the messages; and its scope for creativity allows leaders and ideas to come and go quickly, though at the cost of commitment to the ideology as a whole."[2]

He depicts "plan," on the other hand, as the move toward implementation involving the matter-of-fact organizational details regarding the execution of a given task for which adequate motivation has already been aroused: "The plan presupposes a hierarchy of officers who make decisions and delegate tasks. Leaders cannot be easily moved. Indeed they are likely to constitute an exclusive clique. The plan has no room for redundant idioms. Action is of the essence."[3]

In terms of Parkin's scheme one might suggest, however, that what Shaykh Umar, rousing orator that he is, often presents as a call to direct action is better redefined as ideology in the guise of plan. Thus a qualification which might be added to Parkin's framework is to consider how differently structural roles interact with rhetorical display to assist in the construction of cultural configurations of authority which may lack the presuppositions of reward and enforcement that give a bureaucracy its effectiveness. Because Shaykh Umar occupies a position of ritual precedence, but has no substantial institutional influence external to the mosque and indeed does little apart from preaching there, it might be observed that what he may present as plan constitutes in reality a mimic plan rather than a concrete scheme awaiting implementation. This tendency is especially pronounced when he casts his speech into an apocalyptic frame. In this mode, the preacher soars to bold and sweeping proclamations demanding the direct application of religion to morality which he backs with threats of divine retribution. To this degree he masks the effusiveness of his message, which is essentially ideological, with imperatives that focus on intention rather than actual performance. Nevertheless, there are others involved with this same local movement who doubtless do have plans for action, notably the staging of political protest and the mobilization of dissident opinion. Such activists as these may not hesitate to exploit the Shaykh's highly emotive and diffuse proclamations for their usefulness in prompting demonstrations, rallies, even riots in which "action is of the essence" although a visible "hierarchy of officers" behind the plan may not themselves be directing the operations.

The final preliminary remark to be made with regard to this preacher is to distinguish the apologist from one who possesses genuine charisma. According to the argument offered here, Shaykh Umar exemplifies the apologist because his vision is essentially closed, defensive, and static. This evaluation is not based simply on an examination of his preaching alone, but as a holistic review of his performance throughout the community over a period of time. Charismatic leadership necessarily includes the ability to synthesize and articulate the ideology of a movement, but the presumption underlying this attribution is that the charismatic leader is also the creator or revealer of this message. Ralph Nicholas summarizes this point neatly: "The connection between the leader and the ideology is so close that it is difficult to disentangle the loyalties of the adherents. Followers often tend to merge the physical person of the leader and his ideology, attributing divine or superhuman qualities to both."[4]

In the case of Shaykh Umar, it is important to point out that neither the ideology he proclaims nor the tropes he employs are by any means original to him. In fact, for those who have read the classic polemical essays of such authors as Sayyid Qutb and Muhammad al-Ghazzali, or who have listened to any extent to the strident fundamentalist line of Shaykh ʿAbd al-Hamid Kishk, whose sermons on cassette recordings are widely played and ubiquitously available, the contents of Shaykh Umar's sermons can be recognized as trite, often vulgarized, and colorfully exaggerated. Thus not only is his material derivative, as those seriously engaged in the ideology of Islamic fundamentalism would immediately discern, but, more detracting, Shaykh Umar, as a public personality, emits the air of a lonely lion, unattached to the affairs of a burgeoning movement. Nor does he acknowledge his colleagues even as he permits himself to indulge in tangents that imitate the topicality of other recognized ideologues whose judiciousness and insight in political affairs he can in no way reproduce. These features of his rhetoric cause him to lose the respect of those who have an intellectual as well as an emotional investment in the movement of Islamic fundamentalism.

To identify Shaykh Umar as an apologist also has roots in his personal history, although such facts would not necessarily be of deep interest to everyone, notably among the socially disadvantaged youth who are most drawn to his sermons and who are the quickest to regard him as one endowed with superlative authority. As was already indicated, Shaykh Umar is a retired primary schoolteacher whose oratorical gifts brought him to prominence in the 1930s when he became a prominent figure in the teacher's union. Under 'Abd al-Nasir, he was a leading spokesman for the cause of the 1952 Revolution throughout this region of Upper Egypt. One Azhari *shaykh* who had grown up in Minya told me that Shaykh Umar was for a time regarded as *khaṭīb al-thawra* or the "mouth-piece or preacher of the Revolution" in this area and as such he shared the podium with many visiting dignitaries, was assigned many quasi-official tasks representing the regime, and was favored with several trips abroad. Shaykh Umar had never suffered arrest or imprisonment during this era that was so hard on those who shared the ideology he now identifies himself with and propounds with such ferocity. Many older *shaykhs* did not hesitate to imply, therefore, that he has made a career of loaning his formidable oratorical skills to a succession of popular movements, despite the inherent contradictions within them that led to the removal or the decline of the real leaders of these respective movements. Of course, as the autobiographical disclosures in the sermon demonstrate (paragraphs 8 and 9, in particular) Shaykh Umar strives to present his past as utterly consistent with his present. It is perhaps because there are many who remember his earlier 'Abd al-Nasirist reputation that he provides these self-justifying anecdotes such as we have not seen in any other preacher.

Dividing the Moral Universe

Turning to the text of the sermon itself, I must note a slight lapse in the recording from which this sermon was transcribed. An initial introductory paragraph was recited before the one given in the appended text which has been marked paragraph 1. As in the case of Shaykh Mustafa, my helper, whom I had entrusted with this task, only engaged the tape recorder after the stylized formalities were ended, which Shaykh Umar repeats before every sermon. It is important to point out, however, that this ritual framing-device is a consistent feature of Shaykh Umar's preaching, whereas its omission is a noteworthy marker of Shaykh Uthman. Furthermore, it is not surprising that the particular introduction that Shaykh Umar uses is still longer and more embellished than that of any Azhari traditionalist. Such ostentation in sermon oratory is consistent with similar exaggerated displays of symbolic affiliation in this Shaykh's affectations in his dress, his bearing, and even his conversation.

In the two Qur'an citations that Shaykh Umar selects for recitation at the opening of the sermon proper (paragraph 1), he intones in embryo the form and content of all that follows. In terms of form, the citations constitute a duality, a complementarity, and, as the rest of the sermon demonstrates, this preacher is constantly advancing his points by means of highly categorical dualisms and mutual oppositions. In terms of content, this pairing results from his cardinal principle of religion, which is to "obey God and his Messenger," and its central consequence for morality, "You have a good example in God's Messenger." The first encodes a divine imperative and a warning that those who failed to obey saw their "power depart" and were defeated. The second phrase sets up the standard for God's pleasure as imitation of the Prophet.

After elaborating on these citations with characteristic fire and brimstone monitions, he crystallizes their meaning into one all-embracing and ultimate question. Pronounced with a highly dramatic flair which is only meekly reflected in the written text of paragraph 4, he sets up the suspense and then and poses his startling interrogative: "Do you [singular] want to please God?" Behind it is the second and only slightly less apocalyptic tocsin: "Do you have anything that can protect you from God?" The keynote of threat, risk, and ultimate decision rings out unmistakably everywhere in this presentation, but in the immediate local context the obvious correlative to this proximity of judgment is the recent arrests and curtailments of fundamentalists by civil officials. The Friday before this sermon was delivered, in fact, the large *jam'īya* mosque where Shaykh Umar is here preaching was forcibly closed by police and no public prayer service was held. This direct intervention into a mosque is extremely unusual and it had caused widespread anger and protest among fundamentalists who feared that such crackdowns were only the beginning. Shaykh Umar's tone of confrontation, therefore, is inspired not only from traditional themes, but is in direct response to specific persons and events. Note, for instance, how the preacher at many points throughout the sermon lists by occupation the various parties upon whom he calls to face the decisive question he poses in the name of God. It occurs in paragraph 3, again in paragraph 4, and most instructively in paragraph 7 which includes, "government employee . . . a teacher, a supervisor, a judge, an engineer, a clerk, head of a department, a police officer, the governor of the Governorate, the chief of the secret police." Needless to say, this patent preoccupation with agencies of law enforcement and the official maintenance of civil order communicates quite clearly whom he is hurling his menacing questions at.

Those whom Shaykh Umar singles out in these references to social and political positions—and we shall see this reappear on an international scale later in the sermon—provide a sort of mirror for an understanding of what he assumes to be the basis of his own social and political legitimacy. Here and throughout the sermon, Shaykh Umar seems to be addressing, by apostrophe, the powerful and influential of the world rather than the essentially powerless and marginal Muslims who in fact constitute his audience. He is challenging their authority and claiming to admonish and judge them in the name of a still greater authority. This pattern has certain characteristics that have been widely observed in many other movements and its implications have been identified. The claim to speak directly in the name of God implies the overriding of any temporal authority or scientific knowledge and it elevates the conceptual level altogether out of the ambiguous everyday world and into a transcendental realm where ideas gain in clarity what they lose subtlety. By evoking symbols in their most pure and most abstract form, everything is graded as black or white without intervening shades: "Whatever the ultimate ground of authority in a culture, the general tendency in ideology is to draw an absolute antithesis between the prevailing secular authority and the authority on which the movement is based, between absolute evil and absolute good. Manichean imagery is a common feature of ideologies; it endows an ideology with absolute authority by demonizing its opposition."[5]

This penchant for absolute dichotomies is not only prevalent in Shaykh Umar's sermon rhetoric, it might even be said that it is the basis for it. The pattern not only reflects in the whole tenor of the translated text, but it also emerges clearly in the deliberate prosody, tempo, volume, and even the phonetic qualities of the sermon as it is delivered. The most simple and forceful contrast, and the one repeated most frequently, centers around the two terms *ḥaqq* and *bāṭil*, which we gloss roughly as "truth" and "falsehood." But the Shaykh is not always so plainly symmetrical in his staging of oppositions. At times one positive object is counterposed to a long list of negative items, or vice versa. Or some Qur'anic phrase will be presented in contradistinction to an entire anecdote.

In order to illustrate the breadth and versatility of this technique which at the same time is a way of summarizing the meaning of the sermon, we present here in synoptic form a partial listing of the binary sequences that fill this preacher's oratory. All of the elements are proposed in association with the positive or negative response to his earlier question: "Do you want to please God?"

Paragraph Number	ḥaqq/"truth"	bāṭil/"falsehood"
3	belief in the day of resurrection	serve the hand of falsehood
5	desire to please God	desire to commit falsehood
6	desire to please God	to obey the president
6, 7, 13, 19, 63, 64	desire to please God	to protect one's job, gain wealth
8	Arabic	Turkish
9, 10	truth	imperialism and its profit seeking
3, 10	the Book, Sunna, Islam	opportunism, submission to idols
11, 12	to die for the truth	to commit falsehood
13	peace and security	tyranny and falsehood
14, 15, 17, 23	servant of God and Truth	servant of the president, of orders, of Satan, of the government
16, 21, 31, 34, 37	reliance on God	reliance on creatures, on wealth, on governments, on non-Muslims, on non-Egyptians
16	the after-life	this world
18	my God-given independence	independence of the nation
18	God speaks/preaches	the president speaks/ proclaims
19	the recording angel	the government clerk
20	unity of the Arabs	disunity, misery, poverty
21	God's supervision	government supervision
22	free before God	answerable to the government
23	God's ownership	the government's ownership
24, 25	Egypt	Syria, Iraq, Libya, Yemen
26, 27	Qur'an as inspiration	music and national anthem as inspiration
28	freedom, love, justice, mercy	dollars and profits

Paragraph Number	ḥaqq/*"truth"*	bāṭil/*"falsehood"*
30	listen to God	listen to idols
32	Qur'an	technology
37	Muslims	unbelievers
38, 49, 50, 51, 52	Qur'an as constitution	man-made constitutions
38	obey God and his messenger	trust in the power of nations
40, 41, 42	unity of God, of the Qur'an, of Islam	Pharaonic monotheism, Amon Ra, paganism
45	"bond of God"	political parties
47	Qur'an	law of the people
47	God	the nation
48, 49, 51, 52	Qur'an, Book of God	authority of teachers, professors, generals, party commissars
55	Muhammad	sufi *shaykhs*, sufi fraternities
56	unity of the Book of God	divisions, differences, deviations
57, 58, 59, 60, 61	Muhammad as perfect man, ruler, teacher, military leader	defeated earthly leaders, tyrants, teachers of falsehoods
65	religion exemplified by Muhammad	material prosperity, food
66	the education of Muhammad	worldly knowledge, progress

From this schematic listing of some of the explicit themes in the sermon under discussion, the pattern of simplistic conceptualization and reduction to primordial values is easily discerned. The distinction between a religious principle and its moral application is erased in the process, since the social world is no longer treated as a forum for action but as a kind of parable. At times, this effort to pair some religious truth to its supposed nonreligious falsehood can approach the ridiculous, but such hyperbole is a form of mockery that is an accepted convention in this idiom. His contrast of the Qur'an with the national anthem, for instance, is meant to ridicule not only the government and the idea of music with its immediate associations of Western corruption, but the cyclic replacement of the old anthem with a new one as though it reflects a capriciousness in policy as well as in symbol use.[6] Similarly, his contrast of the Qur'an with the radio play dramatizing ancient Egyptian mythology achieves its effect when he pretends to regard the broadcast as a kind of catechism whose intention is to proselytize.

In examining the symbols of this sermon as a code of social as well as cultural reference, the most basic formula that emerges is, as we mentioned earlier, the opposition of "us" and "them." How the "us" assumes different configurations depending on the "them" is reminiscent of the way classic segmentary lineage systems are said to be activated according to the level of structural opposition. Thus at times it is "us" as servants of God against "them" as servants of Satan. Then it can become "us" as Muslims against "them" as non-Muslims. This can be reduced to "us" as true Muslims and "them" as corrupt or false Muslims. Later, it becomes "us" as Arab Muslims against "them" as Turks. This is further refined to "us" as Egyptian Muslims against "them" as Libyan, Syrian, or Yemeni Muslims. He then can speak of "us" as against the government and against the people and the nation. He also elaborates his position as "us" against "them" as local civil authorities, functionaries, Sufi fraternities, and generally those with power, property, and education.

In the midst of this architectonic dualism built upon the division of "us" and "them," intoned with highly inflated moral righteousness, one may also detect a prevailing asymmetry in the contrast of these two categories. The "us" signals all the richness of familiar, complex social relationships, spanning generations and incorporating a broad spectrum of particular persons, whereas the "they" is depersonalized and flat by comparison. It seems to epitomize the salient features of homogeneity, typification, and anonymity which Alfred Schutz identified as the foundation of the "they-relation [in which] my partners are not concrete and unique individuals but *types*."[7] This lack of depth on the part of the "they" may also help explain the pattern of extreme reversals which are another feature of Shaykh Umar's sermons. Not infrequently, he leaps suddenly from an ascendant rhetoric of confident bravura and triumphalism to stinging assertions of self-rebuke and desperate realism. The most vivid instances of this flash from one plane to another allude to issues of primal insecurity, namely the loss of one's job or the need for food. Here Shaykh Umar intersperses his rousing denunciations with graphic concessions to the very real and very proximate fears of his audience. With a mixture of shared shame and sympathetic commiseration, illustrated in paragraphs 10, 16, 18, 32, and 34, he announces in almost accusatory language that the failure to keep God's law and therefore to achieve His victory results from the groveling for a "crust of bread."

This stark evocation of the problem of hunger, echoing the issue of "food security" heard in other sermons, easily shatters the fragile image of moral heroism. It rings with immediacy in the ears of the large proportion of landless or near landless peasants in Upper Egypt for whom the "crust of bread" functions as a proverb excusing all manner of lapses from ideal behavior. Caught between the bleak official monopoly of the state agricultural cooperatives which appeal to their higher motives as good citizens and the cycle of indebtedness that turns them into clients of the richer peasants, the poor and vulnerable cultivators almost invariably attempt to bypass the state's system to direct their surplus production toward the private hands of their local patrons who give considerably more attention to their sustenance than do Ministry of Agriculture bureaucrats. When questioned about this preference for traditional dependency over modern contractual arrangements, the explanation for this lack of faith in progress often comes in the form of the numbing question: "From where are we going to eat?"[8]

One might add that this link between hunger and moral compromise is not always passed over so freely, nor regarded as inevitable. In analogous settings elsewhere, other preachers have adopted the opposite course by depicting conditions of hunger and oppression more as opportunities for moral heroism than as grounds for embarrassed exculpation. Instead of skirting an acknowledgment of this wretchedness, a preacher may affirm or even celebrate it as the springboard for a rebirth of confidence and resolution. In his famous sermon "A Knock at Midnight," Dr. Martin Luther King, Jr., cited a stanza by the African-American poet Paul Lawrence Dunbar presenting an image of the human predicament that, once faced, can inspire one to accept further sacrifices and sufferings for the sake of change:

> A crust of bread and a corner to sleep in
> A minute to smile and an hour to weep in
> A pint of joy to a peck of trouble
> And never to laugh when the moans come double.[9]

As Dr. King employed them, these lines refer to circumstances of affliction parallel to the deprivation of the Egyptian poor. However, the undercurrent flowing through these lines, which Dr. King raises to the surface, concentrates on the tiny portions of hopefulness, the smile and the joy, rather than the great mass of desolation. The "crust of bread" here is not a symbol of shame but a token of relief and the promise of eventual emancipation. The condition of being a victim is not treated disparagingly, as though it reflected a hidden guilt. For Dr. King, the abundance of trouble does not obstruct an admission of possible complacency, confusion, or lack of courage. Granting, of course, the considerable differences between American and Egyptian society, this glance at the late preacher of the civil

rights movement nonetheless offers an instructive contrast. For characteristically, Shaykh Umar seldom dwells on discomforting evocations of mis-
ery. Rather, he hastily shifts the weight of responsibility for all such conditions off to a distant "them" who control resources, markets, banks, and
bureaucracies.

The Preacher as Judge

Another interesting pattern that emerges from Shaykh Umar's references
to "them" while it indicates certain features about himself can be seen in
the specific named persons he singles out for his political condemnations.
In general, when he assails the superpowers his categories are simply
"America," "Europe," and "Russia," but when he surveys the Arab world
he gets more specific. He cites either by name or by office the leaders of
Iraq, Yemen, Syria, and Libya, all of whom are military strongmen. He
fails to mention any Arab states that are relatively more stable and whose
governments are monarchies or republics, such as Jordan, Saudi Arabia, or
Morocco. Likewise, in railing against Sadat's cabinet, the only figure he
singles out apart from the Prime Minister is the Minister of War (see
paragraph 61). To this, one can add that his one extended image on the
failure of Western models as compared to Islam is couched in terms of
Muhammad's military success despite his lack of professional training
while modern generals are given a thorough military education and they
are still defeated. Shaykh Umar places himself implicitly in this company
of warriors.

While Shaykh Umar in various ways associates himself with the ranks
of those who symbolize force and power, he is also very ornate in his dis-
association from any of the institutionalized forms of civilian or low-level
participation in the political structures that are available. Even in a country which enforces universal conscription for young men and where one
gets the impression from seeing so many uniforms that an enormous percentage of the young men are soldiers of one sort or another, no one takes
the idea seriously of a septuagenarian's involvement in anything like the
army. But, since there is the "party," namely Sadat's newly constituted
National Democratic Party which invites popular membership, the
Shaykh goes to great lengths to denounce participation at this level. In
paragraph 49, he goes so far as to declare that the only party he could join
would be the "party of God," which is a way of further specifying his
claim to divinely ordained superiority and detachment from contingent
political realities.[10]

This pattern of distancing himself from any particular social structures
in any positive sense has its climax in that quite striking passage of para-

graphs 22 and 23 when Shaykh Umar declares his personal freedom, although the theme reappears elsewhere. What he means by his ringing reply to official propaganda, in shouting, "No! I'm the master of my own freedom. I give freedom to myself so I am *free!*" is not only that he refuses ideologically to accept their terms, but also that as a preacher, he resists any genuine social involvement apart from his services as orator and symbolic head of the community in ritual prayer. This freedom of Shaykh Umar derives, therefore, from the special properties of *communitas* and hence it is a freedom maintained only in potential, never in actuality, for it belongs to the liminal moment and not to dynamics of structure.

But the final comment to be made regarding Shaykh Umar in his role as preacher lies not in deductions from his designations of "them" nor from his self-separation from the social entities to which his cultural analogies would join him, but from the underlying implications of his "us." We have already indicated the dimension of exclusion in his usage, which reaches its highest pitch in his extended pronouncements of his freedom. But there is also a dimension of inclusion in this process by which the personal *ego* of the Shaykh as "I" is symbolically extended and expanded in most significant ways. We discussed earlier the remarkable rhetorical trait of Shaykh Umar by which he assumes the first person singular of God, not only in paraphrase of scripture, but in elaborate tropes such as the one found in paragraph 18, where the preacher adopts the voice of God in a rebuke of Sadat as "the president." This is an extraordinary technique and would be considered near blasphemous by some orthodox Muslims.

But even beyond this unabashed identification of his authority with God, Shaykh Umar occasionally rises to another stage of inclusion wherein he expands his "us" to include a vision of the whole world. Such a disclosure occurs in the closing paragraphs of this sermon (67, 68, 69). There, he proclaims that it is the "community" *(umma)* that must "become the judge/arbiter between East and West, between America and Russia, between America and Europe and Russia, between heaven and earth." If we interpret this appeal as a statement about Shaykh Umar's understanding of his own role as well as an image of how he imagines the ultimate shape of the Islamic victory, two important consequences follow. First, in appropriating the Qur'anic term "midmost nation" in this almost van Gennepian sense, he indicates in a curious way an awareness of the power that resides in the nonpossession of power. In fact, it is precisely this authority to judge the world that he claims. This implies governance, of course, but the authority of arbitration differs considerably from the authority of administration. Second, however, Shaykh Umar has made a revealing statement in the light of our discrimination about the difference between the "closed" and the "open" society. With this image of his own role and the social character of the community as fixed in-between rather than encompassing in some way, he has raised to the level of ideal the static morality which sacralizes its own social bonds and turns inward away from participation in a greater society. This identification of Shaykh Umar with the entire community signals an ultimate form of metonym as the leader in the form of the warrior and apologist overreaches the implications of transcendence and all but substitutes ideology for religion.

Conclusion

Over the last two decades the image of Islam has undergone a dramatic transformation, not only in the eyes of outside observers, but also for countless Muslims. The overthrow of the Shah of Iran, the assassination of Sadat, and the seizing of the Grand Mosque in Mecca in three successive years or, more recently, the rising appeal of HAMAS at the expense of the PLO in the Palestinian national movement and the overwhelming election victories of the Islamic Front in Algeria are all examples of events that have urged this change of perspective. But Islam's revival as a popular political force did not spring forth unheralded from an empty desert. It had already displayed its considerable vigor earlier in this century at the creation of Pakistan, for instance, as well as in scores of other initiatives whose purported minor significance at the time afforded them little exposure on the stage of world affairs. Instead, the reins of destiny in the Middle East were seen as having passed to the hands of strong secular nationalists like Ataturk, Bourguiba, and 'Abd al-Nasir. The future, it was said, belonged to them.

The field research conducted in and around Minya which has been presented here dates from just this period of transition. It was a time of rapidly spreading new awareness epitomized by the triumph of the Ayatollah which prompted wildly varied responses ranging from shock and exuberance to bewilderment, terror, and nervous, tentative curiosity. For most Egyptians, who were then still preoccupied with the uncertainties of their lot after concluding a separate peace with Israel, such regional eruptions betokening a revolutionary Islam only hit home the following year. On October 6, 1981, their president, garbed in the regalia of his office as commander in chief of the nation's armed forces, was gunned down by some of his own soldiers before television crews who caught the action live. He was surrounded by representatives of the international diplomatic corps and members of Egypt's civilian and military elite, all gathered to celebrate the anniversary of what had been the most decisive act of his presidency, the declaration of war against Israel in October 1973. It would be difficult to imagine a better calculated setting than this to demonstrate the full symbolic intent of his assassins, for whom this killing was an act of righteous tyrannicide committed in the name of religious duty. Khalid Islambouli, who led the squad of attackers, gave voice to this vision, shouting "I have killed the pharaoh" as he finished firing into the center of the reviewing stand.

Since that day, the vulnerability of Egypt to severe domestic upheaval and the possibility of an Islamic *putsch* has been the subject of widespread study and speculation by all manner of journalists, scholarly experts, and policymakers. Most of this concern, sometimes verging on preoccupation, has not, however, been motivated by disinterested curiosity. Rather, a sizable portion of the reporting and analysis trained on Islamic militancy in Egypt has viewed this upsurge as a dangerous "security dilemma" which had to be understood precisely in order to be controlled or eliminated.[1] Some have viewed the entire Islamist trend in Egypt solely through the lens of the Iranian paradigm, presuming the basic question to be whether Cairo will go the way of Teheran or why "Islamic fundamentalism" there has "failed to show the kind of growth in power, size or influence which many observers had expected."[2]

This approach, which assumes the Islamist movement is essentially a struggle for political domination, while useful in some cases, has nonetheless often led to a narrowing of the general focus on the study of Egypt's Islamic institutions. It has caused attention to be concentrated heavily on a relatively small extremist element within a broad, complex, and diffuse society. It has also frequently resulted in simplistic, shallow generalizations about its composition and thought based largely on selective and prejudicial data obtained at a considerable remove from direct observation, through prison interviews, trial transcripts, underground pamphlets, and reviews of arrest lists.[3] Thus estimates on the numbers of those involved may vary widely, from a few score to tens and hundreds of thousands, while concepts of membership and the criteria for distinguishing between militants and gradients of dedicated believers often go begging. Clearly, too, a great deal of this vagueness and speculation stems from the illegal and clandestine character of many of the groups concerned. Typically, as was true of the original Muslim Brothers, their seeming transparency may be deliberately deceptive, leaving many even within the organization ill-informed about its full character. Often details surface only afterward, and then are frequently distorted by rationalization and justification when the outcome of operations is no longer at risk.

Having become well acquainted with Minya's preachers in the late 1970s while residing in the city, I was naturally eager to follow up after I left to return home. It was by no means clear then what direction events would take. A great tentativeness prevailed following the chain of local crises of 1979 as the government finally began to move forcefully against the growing assertiveness of swaggering Islamist activists. Early that summer, the *jamā'a islāmīya* had been banned by presidential decree, but the core of the group was clearly not about to simply disband upon these orders. Locally, the movement had suffered a severe blow to its organizational structure and its public image because of its poor showing in confrontations with the authorities. Among the activists themselves, these setbacks and the resulting slights upon their reputation had led to a process of fragmentation.

It appears in retrospect that the relatively small size of Minya and its utter lack of a developed university context that initially provided the *jamā'a islāmīya* with an open field eventually also served to undermine the group's capacity to persist in defying official edicts generally supported by public opinion. Instead, the older university in Asyut, located seventy miles to the south with three times the number of students in a city double the size of Minya, began to emerge progressively as the center of gravity for Islamist activism in Upper Egypt. This fragmentation had three immediate effects which would prove significant for the course of the organization over the next decade. First, it stigmatized the corporate action of the members as overtly political to a heightened degree. The clannish character of the group, notably its inner circles, became even more pronounced. While their insistence on the importance of reclaiming religious legitimacy was still heard in Minya and to some degree acknowledged, the vigilance of the police acting to contain their activities and to suppress public demonstrations inevitably isolated them from others who were not willing to share the often unspoken signs of suspicion if not reproach cast by the conservative solid citizens and the occasional harassment of police which they drew by their distinctive beards.

Nearby Asyut, on the other hand, offered a larger pool to swim in and because of its much better established student subculture, a more hospitable environment for continuing to mobilize what they perceived as the vanguard of a new Islamic order in Egypt. In Upper Egyptian terms, it is an unparalleled metropolis, at once more sophisticated and more rudimentary. Also Asyut, like Minya, had a disproportionately large and prominent Coptic minority which provided the Islamic Society militants with immediate targets for their provocations and campaigns.

But no less important was the toleration, if not the tacit support, of their activities by a highly placed patron. It so happened that the governor of Asyut Governorate at this time was 'Uthman Muhammad Isma'il, a man with close personal connections to Sadat and exceptionally favorably disposed toward Islamist organizations. It was he who had, in the early 1970s, played a key role in encouraging and coordinating these groups in their earliest days by enlisting them to act as a counter to the entrenched socialist and 'Abd al-Nasirist cadres which had long dominated campus politics. As organization secretary of the country's only legal party, the Arab Socialist Union, he had prepared and directly supervised the violent attacks of many Islamist squads against the foes of Sadat's nascent regime.[4] This occurred at a time when Sadat himself was struggling against the odds, as many insiders believed, to consolidate his hold on the government. The unleashing of such Islamist forces had been designed to win the new president the support of those who regarded religion and the direction of the nation as going hand in hand. Plainly the governor's early and close ties to Islamic groups had brought him to see them as allies and he was reluctant to apply in Asyut some of the same strict measures that were being enforced to a greater extent in Minya.[5]

Second, on the ideological level, this fragmentation led to a hardening of lines and a radicalization of positions on the nature of the Islamist mission. A steady drift occurred toward the revisionist doctrine of *jihād*. This concept would soon receive international attention as the creed of those who succeeded in killing Sadat, but at this time it was a newly forged synthesis. It built on the earlier teaching of such mythic figures as Hassan al-Banna, Sayyid Qutb, Salah Sirriya, and Mustafa Shukri, all charismatic theoretician-militants, whose stature as martyrs enhanced their credibility as uncompromising fighters in the struggle to establish an Islamic order.

In brief, the doctrine went beyond earlier views in that it declared not only the illegitimacy of the regime but the infidelity of those who governed. Thus it provided a legalistic justification for the killing of those deemed to be falsely ruling in the name of religion while they themselves were preventing its full application. Finally, it insisted that *jihād* was "the missing duty" a sixth pillar of Islam, to cite the title of a soon-to-be-famous underground tract by 'Abd al-Salam Faraj, chief ideologue of the *Tanzīm al-Jihād* (Jihad Organization). This meant that struggling against infidel leaders came to be construed as a primary task for all believers.[6] The social implications of such a doctrine not only increased the separation of its advocates from the wider civil society but also widened the gap within the Islamist movement itself between the growing moderate center and an emerging extremist wing.

The third major consequence of this fragmentation was that it forced those who would remain committed to the cause to devise new strategies to affirm their identity and validate in action their heady theories. Their expulsion from the facilities that had been available to them in Minya had, at least for the moment, severely restricted their activities there, although it had not eliminated them. Some chose to relocate to Asyut, joining the movement there not as unknowns but as seasoned pioneers whose experience was welcomed. Others stayed in and around Minya continuing their efforts on new fronts.

One tactic was to attempt to sabotage the legal institutions to which they were now subjected. For instance, in June 1980, the prominent leader of Minya's *jamā'a islāmīya*, Sayf, mentioned earlier, was placed on trial in the city. During the several days that it lasted the government made a very strong show of force. Over a thousand troops were brought in to patrol the city and all the streets surrounding the court building at the center of town were closed to civilian traffic. Under such surveillance the city remained calm, but inside the courtroom Sayf created a sensation by his attempts to turn the trial upside-down. He declared loudly and repeatedly that Islam was in the dock and he insisted on posing questions and responding with explanations quite out of keeping with expected behavior. Among other things, when the call to prayer sounded at noon on the first day, Sayf demanded a recess so that he and others might pray. It was reported later that not only did the exasperated judge grant his request but a number of the gallery and even some minor court officials joined in the prayer at which Sayf served as the *imām*.

Ultimately, Sayf was found guilty and sentenced to prison where he would remain, intermittently (for he escaped at least once and was hunted down with the help of a nationally televised alert) for the next few years. Because of this confinement he missed participating in the climactic events surrounding the week of Sadat's death. His fortunes changed for the better, however, in the mid-1980s. He took a good position with Sharif Plastics, one of the largest companies in a growing manufacturing and commercial network which formed part of the economic component of a spreading Islamist subculture. When I asked about him in the summer of 1991, I was told that he had just won a seat as a delegate in the Parliament in the elections the year before. He could now be seen coming and going through the city's most posh neighborhoods in a large chauffeured automobile. Such a rise as this personifies, in local terms, one pattern of the accommodation between moderate Islamists and the Mubarak regime. In his pursuit of the "politics of ambivalence" Sadat's successor has certainly widened the democratic umbrella to include as much as he can of the religious right. But witnessing the ascendency of Sayf, looking from the bottom up, gives ample grounds to wonder, as many do, whether the shoe is on the other foot.[7]

Striking a Fateful Blow

The second tactic followed by the *jamā'a islāmīya* stalwarts after the shattering of their organization's base in Minya was to intensify an existing familiar pattern of provocation and escalation. This type of insurgency, which seems to match the strategy of some other parts of the Islamist movement in Egypt, has been treated in numerous sources and need not be recounted again here.[8] But several noteworthy features, less often treated, pertain specifically to the participants from Minya and deserve attention.

For instance, virtually all accounts of Egypt's 1981 "autumn of fury" point to a steady deterioration of civil order, punctuated by a steep rise in the number and the gravity of "incidents," starting in the spring and summer of the preceding year. It reached a climax in June when fierce sectarian clashes broke out in al-Zawiya al-Ḥamra, a new, already overcrowded, lower-class neighborhood in northern Cairo. These highly publicized disturbances involved several days and nights of burning, shootings, and beatings, primarily between Copts and Muslims. The dispute that set off the violence was the disposition of a vacant lot belonging to a Copt which some Muslim residents wanted to appropriate for the building of a mosque. It is not insignificant that a local Coptic priest pointed out later that a distinct regional factor was involved, noting that "most of the trouble began after the arrival of rural migrants from Minya."[9] Exactly who he is referring to remains unspecified but the timing of the appearance of the troublemakers does follow closely after the dispersal of the Islamic Society from Minya University. At any rate, Islamic groups from Cairo quickly sent burly delegations to join in the dispute on the side of the mosque builders as did the local leaders of the ruling National Democratic Party.

Meanwhile, back in Upper Egypt, a few months before the widely published collisions of al-Zawiya al-Ḥamra, a similar case occurred involving some of Minya's fundamentalists. It seems that a contingent from the truncated Islamic Society decided to join in an on-going feud in a rural village not far from Minya where the antagonists happened to be a Muslim and a Coptic clan. Their entrance as a self-appointed Islamist militia into this dispute, whose origins remain unclear and by this point irrelevant, threatened to precipitate a major escalation of the fighting. It immediately prompted a chain reaction bringing Christian allies to the excited support of their outnumbered co-religionists, thereby provoking the Muslim party to call upon more of their fellow believers. News of this confrontation, a familiar cycle of vendetta that had suddenly mutated into a sectarian conflict exceeding all normal proportions, quickly came to the attention of officials in the city. But when the district police, usually charged with overseeing the settlement of village disputes, proved helpless, the headquarters of the Central Security Forces in Minya sent in troops to quell the disturbances. The authorities dispersed the largely peasant partisans and then arrested the leadership of the Islamic Society interlopers. Included among these latter was Karam Zuhdi, a particularly aggressive student activist from Minya and a lieutenant of Sayf, who had come to occupy an increasingly influential position in the fragmented organization.

But the same dynamics of clan honor that had originally been upset when the Islamist youth first joined in the fight were now to operate once more, this time in their defense. For matters had reached such a pitch that now instead of diffusing the tension, this belated intervention by the security forces threatened to widen it as the conflict moved from the village into the city of Minya. Immediately, a crowd rallied before the police station consisting of Islamic Society comrades, sympathizers, and relatives of the detained along with Muslim villagers involved in the original feud. They all demanded the release of the arrested youth. The temper of this mob protest mounted into an unruly siege, and at one point the police headquarters was set on fire. Finally, as the stand-off threatened to explode into an open battle, since feuds in Upper Egypt are conducted with guns, a hurried compromise was reached. Local authorities, in touch by phone with Nabawi Isma'il, the powerful Minister of the Interior in Cairo, obtained permission to release the militants in exchange for a dispersing of the crowd and a return to order.

While all this was happening, Sadat himself was out of the country on a state visit to the United States, working out details of the Camp David process which was proving increasing delicate and problematic. Upon his return, he learned of the events in Minya and he immediately overruled the Minister's deal and ordered that these Islamic Society activists be re-arrested in addition to others who had been involved in recent confrontations at the universities of Minya and Asyut. This forceful response came almost exactly one year after Sadat had delivered a speech before the university faculties of Minya and Asyut in which for the first time he had openly raised the question of "religious extremism" on the campuses. He had also sounded stern warnings of the wrath to come if such disturbances continued.

So, the police made their sweep, but it was too late. Already a number of the leaders, including Zuhdi, had slipped underground. Nevertheless for the moment, this relatively small and localized crackdown succeeded in quieting the situation, at least on the surface. But instead of working toward a resolution of the tension, Sadat's reaction only confirmed the Islamists' convictions about his despotic character while it fed their suspicion of his collusion with Copts and Americans. To all of this was added, on the score of traditional morality, the dishonorable conduct of a government that had retracted its word and so had revived a blood feud after it had been settled. Karam Zuhdi escaped to a safe house in Cairo where he stayed in hiding. There, several weeks later, with the help of his confederates, he was introduced to ʿAbd al-Salam Faraj.

It was this meeting that soon led to the establishment of the *Tanzīm al-Jihād* as a national organization, now including an Upper Egyptian branch having Zuhdi himself as its *amīr*. But the original Cairo group and this newly appended Saʿidi wing were by no means always in full harmony. In fact, Zuhdi later testified at his trial that he was not especially impressed by Faraj, purportedly the brilliant theoretician of the *jihād* doctrine, and that he had learned nothing from him that he didn't already know. Furthermore, Zuhdi added, he disagreed with Faraj on one major issue. According to Zuhdi, *jihād* had first to be waged against the Copts and only later against the government which he considered to be under their control. "The way I see it," he said, "the Christians are concentrated in Minya and Asyut and they take advantage of their numbers to hold demonstrations of strength and superiority. They have arms, and this is what encourages the Muslim youth to react forcibly against missionary proselytism in order to put an end to the Crusaders' manifestations of superiority."[10] Note the pique of offended honor ringing through allusions to demonstrations of "superiority."

The prominence of these staunchly sectarian views, blended with a mentality of clan rivalry and supported by a penchant for the use of violence were distinctive elements that Zuhdi and his comrades brought into what had been until then a fairly refined urban-based secret cell. But even more interesting, by most accounts, it was Zuhdi who some months later was responsible for introducing ʿAbd al-Salam Faraj to First Lieutenant Khalid Islambouli. This young officer was the linchpin of the ultimate strategy for he brought the readiness, competence, and most of all an instant opportunity for the realization of the verdict at the center of the *jihād* doctrine.

Khalid Islambouli was also a native son of Minya, having grown up in Mallawi, a small town just south of the capital city. He was from a religious family that was prominent in public affairs, his father being a lawyer, an uncle a judge, and another relative Hussain Islambouli, the district head of Abu Qurqas, a sizable village about halfway between Minya and Mallawi. Moreover, two of the other assassins were also from Mallawi, Hussain 'Abbas and 'Abd al-Hamid 'Abd al-Salam. The fourth gunman was a childhood friend of Faraj's from his native Bahara governorate in the Delta. These affiliations illustrate once again an overall pattern in recruitment, especially among the Upper Egyptian contingent where bonds of kinship, friendship, and village solidarity rather than ideological appeals define fundamental loyalties.

Likewise, when Islambouli stated his own motives during his trial, he gave three reasons for his action, one lofty but two ringing with the logic of retribution: "I did what I did, because the Shari'a was not applied, because of the peace treaty with the Jews and because of the arrest of Muslim 'Ulama without justification."[11] He leaves out, however, a fourth more personal reason which was attested to by several members of his family, namely his outrage at the midnight arrest of his one brother Muhammad during Sadat's purge of mid-September 1981.[12] In other words, here too, complementing but also colliding with justifications for Islamist violence that cite Qur'anic verses and obscure medieval legal opinions are the contours of another familiar pattern of cultural ideals known as the code of honor. It is an ethos whose adherents "view as ultimately moral the bases of greater status, control over resources, and such control as people can exercise over others" since "the supreme virtue is autonomy."[13] In fact, one Egyptian researcher has remarked on how frequently the families of the defendants at the *Tanẓīm al-Jihād* trial spoke of it as *qaḍiyat al-sharaf*, "a case of honor," and how such language was also widely reflected in the rhetoric of their defending attorneys.[14]

Of course, Zuhdi and his colleagues were not in Cairo the day Sadat was murdered. The had returned to Upper Egypt to begin readying their own move which was to match the supposed seizure of the radio-television center in downtown Cairo, from which, supposedly the Islamic Revolution would be proclaimed. The great call (*da'wa*) would be issued to the Muslim masses who would theoretically rise up in arms to greet it. The plan for Zuhdi and his comrades was to occupy the police headquarters in Asyut, which they attacked early on the morning of October 8. It was a gratuitous display of violence that shook the city profoundly but the event was hardly noticed by a distant world still reeling in shock after witnessing the bloodshed on the reviewing stand. The siege in Asyut lasted for several days and was finally only reversed by a virtual invasion force, including paratroopers, leaving a death toll among the policemen alone that counted over eighty. After order was restored, trials followed and Zuhdi among others received a life sentence. But these later contrary events, born in large part of the fragmentation of the Islamic Society of Minya, once again did not bring the association to its end. Rather they helped nurture the roots of a persistent countercultural community that would adjust to the times and continue to thrive.

One of the first gestures made by Husni Mubarak after his election as president was to attempt a reconciliation between the government and those elements of the Islamist movement that were willing to accept participation in an expanded multi-party democratic process in exchange for a rejection of violence and open anti-regime agitation. In part this strategy has worked although parliamentary government in Egypt is still hobbled by widespread corruption, an autocratic executive branch, and essentially a state party which refuses to surrender its prerogatives to become a mere ruling party. In the election of 1984 Islamists won 7 seats out of 450 and again were still more successful in 1987, taking 38 seats; some Islamist deputies have been elected under the transparent rubric of an opposition party fronting for them since religious parties as such are illegal.[15] But in the election of 1990, the maturing Islamic Alliance together with all opposition parties, except the tiny leftist National Progressive Unionist Party, boycotted the election to protest a lengthy chronicle of unattended objections to presidential high-handedness and government-sponsored election chicanery.[16]

Behind these protests against the government's unabashed manipulation of democratic processes which gave the boycotting parties grounds to declare the elections of 1990 illegitimate since under half of the electorate went to the polls, there lurks the conviction that given a fair race, the nation would choose altogether new leaders. It would support those who would govern in a manner far more responsive to what is perceived as the authentic popular will. For Islamists, of course, the alternative for which the nation longs is the one they promote as a divinely blessed agenda. For this reason they have resurrected the old Muslim Brother slogan "Islam is the solution" and they have seen it resound deeply with the populace at large. Furthermore, the Brotherhood's new political organization, the Islamic Alliance, has worked assiduously not only to distance itself from the extremists but to dispel the fears of Copts. The Alliance has declared its unequivocal affirmation of national unity with full rights and duties for all citizens. To demonstrate this, the Alliance placed several Copts on its constituency lists. In fact, the only Copt actually elected (rather than appointed) to the 1987 Parliament was on this Islamist ticket.

   This steadily growing appeal of a maturing Islamic center presents by far the greatest challenge to Mubarak's regime as it capitalizes on the frustration, discouragement, and alienation that have marked almost two decades of controlled liberalization and limited democracy. Indeed, Saad Eddin Ibrahim has gone so far as to suggest that for the 1980s "religious popularism is proving to be the functional equivalent to Nasser's national socialism."[17] But this rather rosy portrait of Islamism coming of age is still very rough around the edges. Periodic press reports along with surging rumors of arrests, pockets of upheaval, and not uncommonly shoot-outs between police and Muslim groups have continued in a steady stream, especially in Upper Egypt. Closer to the front pages, a formidable list of politically motivated attacks and killings have occurred in Egypt over the past several years, leaving Americans and Israelis as well as prominent Egyptians as victims.

   In 1987, for instance, attacks were perpetrated on, among others, Hassan Abu Basha, former Minister of the Interior, and Nabawi Isma'il, who was the last to serve in that post under Sadat. Makram Muhammad Ahmad, editor of the popular weekly *al-Muṣṣawar* and an outspoken critic of political violence, was also shot from a moving car. In October 1990, Rifa'at Mahjub, Speaker of the Parliament, was killed in an ambush. Then in June 1992, Faraj Foda, an articulate and persuasive advocate for a secular order as the best future for both Islam and the nation, was gunned down in front of his house.[18]

   But later this same year Islamic militants stepped up their violence and in the process introduced a unprecedented tactic. Not only did they continue to target their non-Muslim countrymen, their intellectual detractors, and political foes, but they began assaulting European tourists in Egypt. Bombings and shootings suddenly became a major factor in Egypt's most profitable foreign-exchange-earning industry. Virtually overnight the Mubarak regime responded to these highly publicized operations with wave after wave of raids leading to mass arrests and detentions. Islamist militants, including many who recently returned to their native Egypt after serving with the *mujāhidīn* in Afghanistan, then vindicated the government's fears by greatly increasing their own attacks on numerous fronts. In the months following the murder of Faraj Foda, the tempo quickened steadily so that by June 1993 the number of persons killed in fundamentalist-related violence during the previous year was given at over one hundred forty, of which roughly a third were suspected extremists. About three hundred others have been listed as wounded. The courts too were abandoning mercy. In June 1993 a military tribunal sent Sharif Hassan Ahmad to the gallows, the first person to be executed for a religiously motivated political crime since the assassins of Sadat were hung in April 1982. Moreover, twenty-two others who had been convicted on similar charges had also received death sentences over the previous six months, all of which were ratified.

Clearly the Mubarak regime had decided at last to bring the Islamic movement to heel. Or had it? In fact, this new resolve for all its bloodshed seems disturbingly selective in the eyes of some. It has brought out a new level of anxiety among Egypt's Copts, who were quick to notice that the state only took these draconian measures when militants began to seriously threaten the nation's lucrative tourist business. They lament angrily that very little of this solicitude for security has been directed toward their protection. Antoun Sidhom, editor and publisher of *al-Waṭani,* a weekly Coptic newspaper, describes the chilling message many Christians detect in this response: "It is as if the Government is telling everyone, 'It's O.K. if you munch on little Copts, but don't touch the tourists.' "[19]

A Still Harder Road Ahead

It seems then that the fusion of utopianism and righteousness that produced the Islamic Society of Minya and elsewhere during the late 1970s no longer persists. Rather, for some time the movement has been dividing and the polarization of two contrasting approaches to Islamization becomes increasingly evident. One element has accepted the political "rules of the game" in exchange for a place, however underrepresented and restless, in the councils of state. The other has institutionalized its exclusion from the ordinary conventions of civil society, choosing to construct an alternative separate community. On the furthermost fringes of this second group are the real extremists who have opted for terrorism. Only those following the first of these two directions qualify for the label "Islamic-oriented protest groups" which Maha 'Azzam has recently suggested to replace "Islamic fundamentalists" as the most suitable descriptive term at the current stage of the movement.[20] Those belonging in the second camp, however, who have taken the leap or been pushed over the brink, are apparently determined to stop at nothing until they bring about the establishment of an Islamic Egypt. Nevertheless, given the steady drift toward intolerance throughout the society encouraged by official complicity aimed at coopting the Islamist center, some have called into question the real substance of even these differences over the long run. Milad Hanna, a prominent Copt and former Minister of Housing, shares the view that "the government is selling fundamentalism in the hope that this will stop the fundamentalists overthrowing it. But they don't need to overthrow the government because they can Islamicise the police, the army, the ruling party, everything, from within."[21]

Returning to Minya in the summer of 1991, I observed two conspicuous developments that might serve as emblems of this uneasy split. First, on a side street, just off the main square, a new mosque has been opened, called *masjid al-tawḥīd*. This name, which denotes the assertion of the "oneness" of God, is significant for its echo of Wahhabi puritanism as well as Khomeini's absolutism as applied to a state ruled by God's elect. More specifically, the doctrine of *tawḥīd* commonly serves in the Islamic movement as the basis for refuting the legitimacy of a secular political order and as a taunt to Christians who are depicted as Trinitarian polytheists. But this mosque of itself is extremely small, consisting of barely a storefront. It could not possibly accommodate more than twenty persons crowded tightly inside. However, in observing the mosque, it became evident that its function is not just to serve as an enclosure for prayer. Rather it provided a base for a small more or less permanent bazaar set up on the nearby sidewalk selling religious publications, articles of clothing, and other assorted merchandise indicative of participation in the Islamist movement. Furthermore it marked the frontage before which ritual performances are conducted outside in the middle of the main street every Friday at noon. Unmistakably it is the very central and strategic location of this vest-pocket mosque more than any other quality that has made it the favored site of fundamentalist activity.

As I observed a Friday prayer gathering and listened to the sermon, broadcast at high volume over a speaker that carried the message for several square blocks, I could not help but remark how highly stylized the ritual at this Islamist prayer service had become. Totally gone was the fertile angularity of the early days, the jagged edges and unrehearsed possibilities inherent in an excited, eager, and defiant assembly that feels no boundaries separating it from its uncharted potential. Nor was the modest crowd particularly youthful. It was made up mostly of bearded men in their thirties or forties, some of whom had brought their small sons with them. All, almost without exception, were dressed, as though it were a uniform, in the white unbelted caftan or *gallibīya*. Likewise all also wore the proper head covering, again mostly white. By such garb, of course, they were following what they claim to be the specifications of the *Sunna* which recommends this attire and this color. At the prayer service and while interacting casually afterward, they left the impression of a group with a highly marked collective identity, like the members of a club or at least a distinctive subculture. Their behavior illustrates a pattern which was implicit but never so blatant among the typically more open and populist Islamist congregations of Minya a decade and a half before.

But just on the other side of the city center one's eye is caught by a very large and striking new building. It stands on the site of the old headquarters of the Central Security Forces. It is an oversize structure, out of all proportion to the surrounding buildings, a colossus reaching some ten stories high and protruding into the skyline without a rival. It has a sign on top of it. Written in tall clear lettering quite visible at a distance one reads: Ministry of the Interior. This superstructure is designed, it seems, not only to house the administrative particulars of Minya's regional directorate of this ministry (controlling movements, issuing residence permits, registering vital statistics, investigating crimes, overseeing police, and the like), but also to assert itself as a public declaration of the strength and solidity of the state as the enforcer of law and order. In addition, its squared modern lines end in a flat roof studded with a webbing of antennae, cables, and electronic communication dishes of various shapes and sizes, tilted upward at knowing angles. They quietly bespeak a convergence of invisible powers at centers of control.

As I reflected on these two uneven architectural innovations in the city I wondered what relationship one might suggest between such poles. I recalled, for instance, remarks from the compelling conclusion of Habib Boularès' farsighted book, *Islam, the Hope and the Fear*, in which he calls upon Muslims to emerge from their frightened isolation and to search for new Islamic answers suited to the modern age rather than flee to the hollow but reassuring slogans of a faith that is inherited but not truly adopted. There he declares, "Muslim society cannot resign itself to living in a state bordering on schizophrenia. . . . It cannot at the same time impose on social life the requirements of the traditional and submit material development to the demands of the rational."[22] Posed so starkly, and taking concrete shape in the contrast of an ultra-modern security apparatus overshadowing a determinedly traditionalist congregation, this dilemma may seem to portend that the alienation between the Islamist movement and the government will only continue. In fact, it will very likely worsen as a new generation faces the same tide of disappointments, frustrations, and abuses that their fathers struggled largely in vain to overcome.

But this dark view, while it reckons rightly with the potential for antagonism and violence on the part of both contenders, is by no means complete. It omits an important third dimension which insists that the essentially political contest reflected in this dichotomy is itself part of a larger domain of coherence. What is missing from this reduced perspective of two almost schizophrenic realms is a largely unnoticed process of transformation that has affected the mosques of Egypt over this same last decade and a half but which is not so easily seen in the current strained context of ideological divisions and competitive power relations.

One of the frequently overlooked measures announced by Sadat in that famous diatribe of September 1981, after which the news of mass midnight arrests seized the headlines, was the announcement of plans to incorporate all the private mosques of Egypt into the government's system. Plainly his motive was to curtail the use of free pulpits and more generally the character of mosques as sanctuaries, for many had come to provide opportune platforms and meeting rooms not only for dissident preachers but for critics of all sorts, sometimes even those who were not Muslim. This taking over of private mosques by the Ministry of Religious Endowments was already a long-standing practice. It had been happening as a matter of policy for much of this century although the task had begun to resemble the labor of Sisyphus. The recent explosion in the rate of mosque construction made it simply impossible for the state treasury to accommodate all these institutions under the terms understood to define a government mosque. Hence, an entirely new and streamlined procedure was introduced. The new rules would not concentrate on mosques in their totality, with all their expensive physical needs of expansion, maintenance, and repair. Instead, the interest of the Ministry would extend principally if not solely to their preachers.

Figures in recent years on the numbers of mosques in Egypt have varied considerably, even in official sources. Speaking before the Parliament in 1979, for instance, the Minister of Religious Endowments gave the total at roughly 33,000, of which he said only one in five was then incorporated into the government system.[23] Two years later, Sadat, in his fulsome address of 1981 spoke in round figures of 40,000 private as opposed to government mosques.[24] However, in 1984, Egypt's Ministry of Planning published a report numbering only 26,110 private mosques in the country as compared to 4,993 in the government system.[25] But by 1986, when the process was officially completed and a basis for the old distinction was strongly qualified, the total number of mosques was registered at 60,000.[26] Whatever the real figures may be, the galloping increases readily indicate the impossibility of the Ministry's task of placing salaried *imāms*, even part-time, in anything but a fraction of these mosques. Nevertheless there have been efforts in several quarters to increase the size and improve the quality of the nation's corps of professional preachers which had been declining for many years.

For instance, in 1977, a new college devoted exclusively to the training of preachers for mosque service, the College of Missionary Service *(Kulliyat al-Daʿwa)*, was founded at the Azhar. But the school has not been as popular as its patrons had hoped. In order to attract reluctant students it offered exceptionally attractive financial subsidies and then added still more incentives when the initial package was apparently not sufficiently appealing. Also its standards of admission were notably lower than at the more prestigious religious colleges of the Azhar. Thus the real fulfillment of the Ministry's mandate to staff pulpits was not done by expanding the number of full-time preachers under its supervision. It has been accomplished rather by, in effect, sanctioning the services of free-lance local volunteers who had, for the most part, already been performing them sometimes regularly, sometimes occasionally, in response to their congregations' needs. The major concern added at this point was to assure that all preachers were subject to the scrutiny of the existing mosque inspection bureaucracy. In the overwhelming majority of cases, little or no intrusion occurred, for changes were only sought where a preacher habitually indulged in political commentary or incitement in his sermons.

This expansion of the Ministry's apparatus undoubtedly did serve to rein in some scattered prominent dissidents. In fact, a few independent mosques noted for their pronounced Islamist posture initially refused to submit to these procedures and were subsequently forcibly taken over and were assigned a government preacher as their new *imām*. But for the most part, this absorption policy had minimal effect on most private mosques, since needless to say the most radical elements ignore and evade it. But these changes have had a definite broadening impact on the overall practice of mosque preaching, including in government mosques. By this quasi-official recognition of these amateur preachers, among them doctors, engineers, teachers, and other professionals, the Ministry has also validated their non-classical credentials in ways that had not commonly been done in the past. The 1980s therefore, while wracked with religiopolitical tensions, was also a time of remarkable vitality and diversity for mosque preaching in stylistic terms as well as in an expansion of the sermon's content. It was not only the mosque pulpit that enjoyed a sort of renaissance; this broadening of authorization for non-professional preachers reached into other arenas as well.

These same years also saw the flourishing of a curious genre of officially sponsored public religious meetings at which representatives of various Islamic orientations would engage in a "dialogue" (*ḥiwār*). Held outdoors in packed tents and auditoriums, or before live studio audiences, the meetings brought together representatives from the Azhar, from the unofficial Islamic intellectual establishment (often leaders of jamā'ya mosques), and perhaps sometimes a spokesman for some milder shade of Islamic extremism. The speakers would hold forth and interact with the audience in exchanges of questions and answers touching on issues of ritual, doctrine, morals, and social justice. Such discussions were not uncommon fare for prime-time television programming in Egypt during the 1980s and the press too reported on the contents of such open discussions. The purpose behind these officially sponsored dialogues was to allow the Azhari *shaykh* and some responsible lay preacher to set out the issues properly for the benefit of those confused or ill-informed Muslims who might have come under the unhealthy influence of fanatics. At such gatherings, it often happened that youths would rise at the finish to declare their gratitude and profess rather conventionally that they now understood the errors of their past ways.

One effect of convocations of this sort and the overall leveling out of mosque preaching has been an erosion of the barriers that traditionally divided the *ʿālim* from the *walī* and the *mujāhid,* although the first and last of these types are most in evidence. To the extent that earlier institutional polarities separated them sharply with regard to training and the nature of their institutions, they have come to share much more of a common ground and a common language. Interestingly, this growing cooperation of preachers, official and lay, was formalized in 1987 when Dr. Muhammad ʿAli Mahjub, the Minister of Religious Endowments, announced the establishment of a new body called the Supreme Council for Islamic Preaching *(Majlis Aʿla al-Daʿwa al-Islāmīya).* It was charged with bringing together the leaders of the largest *jamʿīyas* and senior government preachers under the direction of the Shaykh of the Azhar.

Over a century of successive encroachment by a relentlessly centralizing secular state on the traditional prerogatives of a once nearly autonomous religious establishment might invite one to entertain deep suspicions at such an announcement. Could it spell an attempt by the government to curtail the *jamʿīyas* which have established their distinctiveness to a degree the state feels it can no longer tolerate? Such action has happened often enough in the past. But in the present era, characterized by unprecedented demands for public accountability, mounting pressure for wider popular participation, greater equality, higher living standards, backed by a growing impatience over the lack of effective integration between aspirations and instrumentalities, such an old-fashioned supposition may be missing the point. More than this, perhaps far more, may now be at stake. Such a council could in fact signal the opening of a rare channel of direct communication from the bottom up.

The calibrated ambiguity that has stamped President Mubarak's cautious domestic governance through a game of counterbalancing or "market politics" has perhaps recognized the need to open up contacts with the new force represented by these leaders. Can it be a coincidence that in March 1993, as raids and arrests of fundamentalists accelerated, Mubarak, never known before as a particularly devout Muslim, made the pilgrimage to Mecca?[27] It would be stretching the case surely to suggest a comparison between this council and the classical *diwan* of head muftis who for centuries played the legitimating function for the Ottoman sultans and for Mamluk emirs before them. But the establishment of such a group may nonetheless signal the inching forward across a symbolic threshold that has been so gradual in its approach that it might almost have been forgotten. This move which, for all practical purposes, recognizes these lay preachers as a new "clergy" is occurring at what appears to be a decisive juncture in Egypt's modern history. It represents a formal inclusion of a type of religious authority that may not necessarily reflect so much an atavistic revisiting of the past as it does a respect for the achievements of these societies of which the Islamic Society is only one quite atypical example. It also acknowledges their potential as agencies of religious and moral influence.

In the history of religiopolitical relations in contemporary Egypt, 1905 marks the close of an era. In that year the elaborate hierarchical structure which had evolved into the distinctive attitudes and institutions that defined nineteenth-century sufism came to an official end with the formulation of the so-called Internal Regulations under direct state supervision.[28] Could it be that just as the major pattern of Islamic mystical piety saw its official demise shortly after this century began, so too the future pattern of Islamic activism is being formulated just shy of the next century's start? To that extent, the *ʿālim* of the Azhar seems, as always, wholly dedicated to a middle ground. But the winds of change seem to say that the tilt now points resolutely toward the engagement of the *mujāhid* in the secular city just as the world was once so close to the heavenly city of the *walī*.

Appendixes

Sermon of Shaykh Mustafa
May 18, 1979

1

al-Salām ʿalaykum!
The topic today is the "bidding to honor and forbidding dishonor." May God's prayers and peace be upon the Prophet, his family and those related to them, and those protected by them, on his companions, his followers, and whoever follows them in virtue until the Day of Judgment.

2

Indeed, the most faithful of all the books of God, may He be exalted, and the best guidance is the guidance of Muhammad, the son of ʿAbdullah, and the worst of things is any innovation, for every innovation is heresy [*bidʿa*], every heresy is error, and all error leads to hell-fire.

3

Oh brothers, believers, friends of the Messenger of God, the summation of divine statutes, taken in its ultimate form, is the bidding to honor and the forbidding of dishonor. The Prophet, prayers and peace of God upon him, wanted to establish a firm foundation, and regarding the Islamic *sharīʿa*, he said: "Look with understanding, walk in justice, answer with peace, and bid to honor and forbid dishonor." This is the foundation, this is the obligation about which you can be certain. When he spoke of this foundation, it was so that it might serve as a guiding light to those who would be guided.

4

The bidding to honor and the forbidding of dishonor is not something peculiar to the streets, nor is it restricted to the home or to local milieu;

rather it is the essential foundation for all mankind. The people of Israel who preceded Islam, God put upon them a curse, disgrace, lowliness and poverty. Why? Because their convenience led them to dishonor and they followed it. Islam came to bid to honor and to forbid dishonor, and this is a fundamental pillar of the life of Muslims, on the streets, in the home, in the nation, and for all creatures on the face of the earth.

5

This activity is the cause for the general good which God, blessed and exalted be He, accomplishes in fullness for all mankind. But goodness is accomplished only by those who bid to honor and forbid to dishonor. Why? God says concerning this goodness: "You are the best nation ever brought forth to humankind" [3:110]. The goodness is in you. This goodness comes forth from your hands and from under your feet. "You are the best nation ever brought forth to men, bidding to honor. And forbidding dishonor, and believing in God" [3:110].

6

Happiness [*al-falāḥ*] is the goal of all mankind. Happiness is what all mankind desires. But our Lord, exalted and praised be He, makes happiness the crowning result of the bidding to honor and the forbidding of dishonor. "Let there be one nation of you, calling to good, and bidding to honor and forbidding dishonor; those are the prosperers" [3:104].

7

The victory [*al-naṣr*] over self, over enemies, and over everything that confronts mankind with wrong, from whence does this victory come? It comes from the bidding to honor and the forbidding of dishonor. "Assuredly God will help Him—surely God is All-strong, All-mighty— who, if we establish them in the land, perform the prayer, and pay the alms, and bid to honor and forbid dishonor; and unto God belongs the issue of all affairs" [22:40–41]. We also want to please our Lord, and that begins with His help; "assuredly God will help him who helps Him, surely God is All-strong, All-mighty."

8

We want to know from where such power [*al-quwa*] comes, and whose place he establishes here in the land; "perform the prayer, and pay the alms, and bid to honor, and forbid dishonor." Those who are established in the land, bid to honor and forbid dishonor, they perform the prayer and they pay alms. And our Lord, exalted and praised be He, informs us in a holy *ḥadīth*: "Anyone who petitions God, or who supplicates God in prayer, if he would find an answer, or would desire help near at hand or understanding, let him bid to honor and forbid dishonor."

9

It is related that our great Prophet, prayers and peace of God upon him, said in a holy *ḥadīth:* "Bid to honor and prohibit dishonor before you make your petition or I will not grant it to you. Call upon me or I will not answer you. Help me or I will not help you."

10

What is meant by "honor" [*ma'arūf*] and what is meant by "dishonor" [*munkar*]? What is the meaning of the bid to honor and the prohibition of dishonor? Honor is that which men know [*mā 'arafahū al-bashir*] because in it is what is loved and sought for from the wisdom of the *Sharī'a,* for this is the bidding that God loves and which the Prophet of God receives generously, and which corresponds to the *Sharī'a* of God, and the guidance of the great Prophet. For that reason it is called honor. There is no doubt that people will acknowledge [*yata'arif*] it because it is from the wisdom of the *Sharī'a,* that is, it is the object of God's bidding, and the bidding of the Messenger of God, prayers and peace of God upon him.

11

As for dishonor, it is called dishonor because the *Sharī'a* disowns it [*yunkaruhū*], nor is it pleased with it, for the *Sharī'a* disapproves [*yunkaruha*] every alteration and discrepancy [*mukhalafa*] and it does not want to make it known [*ya'arrifuha*] to anyone. For that reason, we find that sins and offenses and departures from it are both internal and external, for in it is bidding and forbidding. The wisdom of the *Sharī'a* urges us to cast off sin of the exterior and sin of the interior, and to cast off the exteriority of sin and its interiority.

12

And perhaps people will ask, who is it that bids to honor and forbids dishonor? All believers are responsible before God for bidding to honor and for forbidding dishonor. They are responsible for this obligation because God has made it an "individual obligation" [*farḍ 'ayn*]. The obligation to bid to honor and to forbid dishonor is a judgmental obligation that admits of no exemption or exception at any time whatsoever. The *imām* himself is not exempted from a single such obligation, for they apply to everyone.

13

The Imām Muhammad 'Abdu, may God be pleased with him, said: "Indeed, the obligation of the *ḥajj* is not like the obligation to bid to honor and to forbid dishonor. The obligation of the *ḥajj* is incumbent upon those who are able, while the bidding to honor and the forbidding dishonor is an obligation that extends to those who are able and unable." The Prophet, prayers and peace of God upon him, said: "Whichever of you sees dishonor, let him correct it with his hand, and if he is not able, let him correct it with his tongue, and if he is not able, let him correct it within his heart, but that is the weakest of faith [*imān*] and after that, there is not the smallest part left."

14

Under all circumstances, in every setting, the believer must prohibit dishonor, he must disown disobedience, and he must bid to honor, for this is the job [*wazifa*] of every Muslim. As our Lord, praised and exalted be He, says in His great Book: "And the believers, the men and the women, are friends one of the other; they bid to honor, and forbid dishonor; they perform the prayer, and pay the alms, and they obey God and His Messenger. Those upon them God will have mercy" [9:71].

15

"And the believers, the men and the women, are friends one of the other." And the companions of the Prophet, prayers and peace of God upon him, relate in their manner an exact *Sira*. At the starting point of any meeting or assemblage where they gathered to counsel one another in truth [*haqq*] and patience, they would begin by reciting the Sura, "Afternoon": "By the afternoon! Surely Man is in the way of loss, save those who believe, and do righteous deeds, and counsel each other unto truth, and counsel each other to be steadfast" [103:1–3].

16

For the attributes of bidding to honor and forbidding dishonor are among the attributes of the believer in truth, for which it is necessary that he study. He needs knowledge that he might be farsighted in his aims, that he be clear in his giving of evidence [*dalīl*]. Knowledge [*'ilm*] is the first of the attributes of bidding to honor and forbidding dishonor. For a person cannot bid to something when he does not know the reality of the thing [*haqiqa hadhā al-shay*], nor can he forbid what is dishonorable. Hence the first attribute of the believer is that he be knowledgeable in what is bidden and what is forbidden.

17

Second, he must be actively engaged in what he has learned, because he who has learned something and does not act upon it can only end in disaster and God help us. The Prophet, prayers and peace of God upon him, says, in a *hadīth* to this effect: "On the Day of Resurrection, it will be for man as it is for a donkey walking on sand, his feet will slip and slide. The people of hell will say to him: 'You charged us to bid to honor and to forbid dishonor, so what has brought us to this?' And he will say: 'I bid you to honor and to act upon it, I bid you to honor but you didn't do it. I forbid to you dishonor and its actions.' "

18

And thus Abu Dara, may God be pleased with him, relates that the recompense for one who has not learned is one measure, but the recompense for he who has learned but does not act is seven times greater. So one who has knowledge is punished sevenfold. The reason for this is that the Prophet of God, prayers and peace of God upon him, used to teach his companions knowledge with action.

19

You will die, but He who is eternal will not die. Act as you will, as though you had a debt to pay. It is also said that all sons of Adam are sinners and that the best of sinners is the one who repents. I have spoken what I have to say and may God forgive you and me.

20

Praise to God, Lord of the worlds, whose reward is for the righteous, nor does he have any enemy except evil-doers. I bear witness that there is no god but God, no associate with Him, and to Him be sovereignty and praise—He brings to life and he causes to die and over all things He is the almighty—and to our great master and beloved, our professor, Muhammad, Messenger of God. May the prayers and peace of God be upon this prophet, upon his family, his wives, his descendants, his companions, his followers, and their followers in goodness until the Day of Judgment.

21

And so, dear brothers, we found that the attributes characteristic of bidding to honor and forbidding dishonor can be defined as knowledge and then action. Then comes a third attribute, sincerity [*ikhlās*]. Indeed, to be sincere in counsel, and to be sincere in bidding to honor, it is essential that the final purpose of this bidding be kept in sight, and that it be something desired in truth, and that the desire be for something specific.

22

One must also be faithful [*amīn*] in his bidding and forbidding. He must not tell lies to anyone, for those who lie to God are unbelievers. The Messenger, prayers and peace of God upon him, said: "Whoever deliberately lies about me will occupy a place in hell-fire."

23

Once, our master Abu Bakr, may God be pleased with him, had a man come to him and ask him about a verse in the Book of God, for he did not understand its meaning, and he said: "Let heaven afflict me and earth scorch me if I speak out on the Book of God on something I do not know about." For a man must be faithful to the Book of God, and the Sunna of the Messenger of God, and the Call to God for the bidding to honor and the forbidding dishonor is the Call to God [*da'wa*].

24

Then comes the last of the attributes of bidding to honor and forbidding dishonor, and that is to be gentle [*laṭīf*], to be friendly and cheerful in the bidding to honor and the forbidding dishonor. One must not be rude or impolite, whether by grouping people together or by splitting them apart, and paying no attention to what is said. Our Lord, praised and exalted be He, said to His Messenger, prayers and peace of God upon him, as follows: "It was by some mercy of God that thou wast gentle to them; hadst thou been harsh and hard of heart, they would have scattered from about thee" [3:159]. Tenderness [*līn*] and friendliness [*rifq*]. Such friendliness as the Prophet, prayers and peace upon him, refers to when he says: "What matters except that which adorns, and what do we remove except that which detracts, and of all things, the greatest is the Call to bid to honor and to forbid dishonor."

25

God, may He be praised and exalted, is the All-gentle [*laṭīf*]. "God is gentle, he loves gentleness in all things." Once a man who was ill came up to the Messenger, prayers and peace of God upon him, and he was rude in his speech, rushing to say all sorts of things upon being told to bid to honor and to forbid dishonor, and the Messenger, prayers and peace of God upon him, said: "Be at ease and do not be in difficulty. Be happy and do not get into any conflicts."

26

For this religion is "easy" [*yasr*] and there is nothing in it that makes for difficulty. So if a person wants to bid to honor, it is necessary that he be at ease, for this is the short-cut to avoiding disobedience and to action according to the Book of God and the Sunna of the Messenger of God who bids to honor in his glorious book.

27

To bid to honor and to forbid dishonor is piety and fear of God. And what is man if he is not pious and he does not fear God for himself, for his people, and for his religion? And if this is the case, then listen to no word of his, but tend first to yourself, reform your own affairs and then reform the affairs of others. I ask the Beneficent, may He be praised and exalted, to make us bid to honor and to forbid dishonor. [The tape ends.]

Sermon of Shaykh Uthman
December 15, 1978

1

Praise to God, the strong, the mighty, the glorious, the victorious, who made nations [*ummum*] out of many customs that they would be different [*takhtalif*]. People were all one community [*umma*] and they were differentiated. But God, may He be blessed and exalted, made believers out of many customs so that in their differences they would refer the matter to Him, praised be He and exalted, so that the matter would be referred to Him and His Messenger: "Oh you who believe, if you should quarrel on anything, refer it to God and the Messenger" [4:59]. Man is never at fault because he differs, but man is at fault when he differs and so strays from the path. God, may He be blessed and exalted, showed the way for believers and He made differences that He might solve them, and make such ones return to Him, to God, blessed and exalted, and His Messenger: "Oh you who believe, if you should quarrel on anything, refer it to God and the Messenger" [4:59]. He made faith [*imān*] to be based on preconditions [*sharūt*] so that reason might be the judge except that the more it did so, the more reason would go astray; so that desire might be the judge, and yet the more it did so, the more it would be destroyed; so that inclinations might be the judge, except that the more they did so, the more they would be lost, for indeed He made faith from preconditions so that every matter might be entirely referred to God, blessed and exalted be He, and to His Messenger: "But no, by thy Lord! they will not believe till they make thee the judge regarding the disagreement between them, then they shall find in themselves no impediment touching thy verdict, but shall surrender in full submission" [4:65].

2

He made the best of words the summons [da'wa] to God, blessed be He and exalted, in sincerity and true righteousness. He made this one of the preconditions of Islam also, for among the best of words is the call to God and works of reform. He said: "Surely I am of them that surrender" [41:33]. He made life that it should not widen out to differences, nor should it widen out to divisions [firqa] nor should it widen out to sadness or to squandering: "Not equal are the good deed and the evil deed. Repel with that which is fairer and behold, he between whom and these there is enmity shall be as if he were a loyal friend" [12:34]. Then He made it that results should follow for the one who endures patiently, who bears with it and who fights [yujāhid]: "Yet none shall receive it, except the steadfast; none shall receive it, except a man of mighty fortune" [41:35]. God made us from among His servants, to be those that are patient and steadfast. He has set us on the path of his followers, oh merciful, oh compassionate, oh Lord of the worlds.

3

We testify that there is no God but God, He alone, no associate with Him, and that His beloved and His chosen one is the master of those who call, the mediator [wasīṭ] of their delegation and the best of them, our master Muhammad, prayers and peace of God upon him. [He is] the smiling one, the engaging one who opened his heart greatly to his brothers and he opened his heart greatly to those who were not his brothers.

4

Khalid ibn al-Walid said: "Each morning they referred matters to the Prophet, prayers and peace of God upon him, and repeatedly he expounded Islam." It seemed that Khalid was hesitant, and yet it was said that Muhammad never refused to admit anyone to come before him. It seems that Khalid did a great deal of what he did during his ignorance and you know what Khalid did during his ignorance [fī jahalīyatihi]. Khalid came repeatedly to the Prophet, prayers and peace of God upon him, and he put one foot in front of the other. Khalid said: "I came no closer until he smiled at me, and he continued to smile at me until I stopped in front of him. I greeted him, and he answered me with an open face. He didn't answer with a snide remark. He didn't say, "Heaven help us, you're the one from the skirmish at Uhud"—far from it. The Prophet, prayers and peace of God upon him, didn't say that. "He continued smiling at me until I stopped before him." He said: "Oh Khalid," for he called him by his name. He didn't say, "Oh you there" or anything like that, but he said "Oh Khalid, I consider you a reasonable man, and I want only that you be guided to goodness." He recalled him to reason. He didn't recall his past, for should the Prophet have pointed to the past, he would have done offense to Khalid and his feelings. He recalled him to the goodness that was in him, if it was his reason that guided him at Uhud, or that didn't guide him to what all of you well know. But the Prophet, prayers and peace of God upon him, began to explain Islam and goodness to [Khalid] from the time of his arrival. "Oh Khalid, my son, I take you for a reasonable man and I only wanted you to be led to goodness."

5

Khalid was the one who broached the topic. He said: "Oh Prophet of God, pray to God that He will forgive me for [holding] to those many positions where you have seen me. Indeed, after all that had happened, after you were wounded, oh Prophet of God, prayers and peace of God upon him, after you fell into the ditch at the battle of Uhud. You were wounded and you fell, and after all that, oh Prophet of God, you say to me what you say. I pray to God that He will forgive me, oh Prophet of God, for holding to those many positions where you have seen me." The [Prophet], prayers and peace of God upon him, said: "Oh Khalid, indeed, Islam cuts through everything that goes before it." Then he placed his noble hand upon Khalid's chest and said: "May God forgive Khalid all the positions he has held against me. May God forgive Khalid. May God forgive Khalid." And the Prophet, prayers and peace of God upon him, rejoiced greatly in the Islam of Khalid ibn al-Walid.

6

And another revered companion took notice of this loss—and this story is related by Abu Na'im in the *Hiliya*. Abu Na'im recounts concerning Sufyan ibn Bihman. He says, "I asked Safina ibn 'Amar"—Now watch out, 'Safina' was not a name. 'Safina.' Never in my life have I heard a name like 'Safina.' "I asked Safina ibn 'Amar about his name." What kind of name is 'Safina'? Where did you ever get it? A boat [*markib*]? Safina said, "Indeed, as for my name, he who named me was the Messenger of God, prayers and peace of God upon him. That's something, you mean they called people the strangest things. His name was "boat." "Indeed, as for my name, he who named me was the Messenger of God, prayers and peace of God upon him." Then he says: "He went out and with him were some of his companions. They loaded up their baggage, with each one carrying his own gear, carrying their baggage, and some of them carrying it with difficulty. It seems that the Prophet went out as each was carrying their possessions and he said to me: 'Unroll your [wrapping] cloth!' For it seems that Safina, before he was named Safina, used to carry a large cloth or a wide and abundant woolen cloak. The Prophet of God said to him: "Unroll your [wrapping] cloth!" And he unrolled it, as he had placed some of the provisions of the tribe into it. "Carry what is yours like a ship!"

When you're carrying all that, you're working like a ship. Our companion said: "By heaven, I carried instantly the load of a camel or two, yet it did not overburden me by the blessing of the Prophet, prayers and peace of God upon him." That's psychology for you. If anyone is carrying a quarter kilo, for instance, and he carries it because he is forced to, or if he is carrying something that he doesn't want to carry, and that happens these days, my sons, if someone buys a half kilo of tomatoes for example, he might feel as though he were carrying a whole mountain. That's psychology, so now for Safina ibn 'Amar—the Prophet, prayers and peace of God upon him, enabled him to carry the load of a camel or two and he proceeded to carry the load of a camel or two and he proceeded to carry it gladly by himself because Muhammad, prayers and peace upon him, is the instructor [*murabi*] and the teacher [*mu'alim*] but above all is the psychological cure ['*alāj nafsi*]. He makes love of goodness to blaze forth, and our companion was able to carry an entire mountain while his heart was light because the words of the Prophet, prayers and peace of God upon him, are radiant words.

7

After that, my brothers [we come to] the *hadīth* for today, an event from among the events as recalled in the books of *Sira*—sometimes called *Ghazwa al-Raja'* although sometimes the books are called by the long title, *Sira Marsadin ibn Abu Masadin al-Ghanawi*. And this *Sira* will strengthen your hearts for in it is something to support the youth. The youth of Muhammad, prayers and peace of God upon him, for he provides for them a wholesome abode. He trained them in religion, and you know well the manner in which he trained them in religion ['*aqīda*]. "My son, if you inquire, inquire of God, and if you turn to someone, turn to God, and learn that if the community [*umma*] agrees on what benefits you, nothing would benefit you except what God has written for you in the book, and if the community agreed on what would cause you harm, nothing would cause you harm except what God has written for you in the book." He had trained their capacity to resist and their capacity to endure in patience. People of *yasr*, he has supplied their shelter, their reward and their guidance, and this is not a simple matter. Be patient, people of *yasr*, for your appointed place is paradise.

8

He made paradise their appointed place and he gives it to them in accord with their endurance. He endears them to the great goal, and there is no great goal like paradise so that whenever any of them start feeling tired along the way—and excuse the expression—they will recover their resolution and once again carry their burden. In addition to the capacity of their faith, he empowers them with faith in Him, for no one feels this except the believers. It was accomplished among me in the past as the one who was sawed from head to toe with a saw of iron: "There is no enticement away from religion [*dīn*]."

9

As for the home, it produces children, and as the crooked shadow corresponds to the shape of the pole, so can we expect it there. If the pole is straight, so too the shadow must be straight, but if the pole is crooked, then what it produces is also crooked. A home that is not wholesome produces what is not wholesome. The Prophet, prayers and peace of God upon him, began education at the very foundation. I fear to say that he did not rear children in a nursery school, day-care center, or in a foster home. He determined that a child should be raised at its mother's breast. It is therefore necessary to choose a virtuous mother, for if a virtuous mother is chosen, virtuous children will result. The children will be born from a virtuous mother and then they will learn in Islam how they are bound by noble values, how they are bound by "there is no God but God" and by the Sunna of the Messenger of God, prayers and peace of God upon him, as it is announced in the ear of the infant as soon as he is born. As some might say, the tape of that tape recorder has nothing recorded on it yet, and the first thing recorded on the tape is not a corruption, an outcry, some backwardness or the like. The child is born in the shadow of Islam when it is announced in its ear: "God is greatest. God is greatest. I testify that there is no God but God. I testify that Muhammad is the Messenger of God."

10

That's the home. This home produces such things as I shall recall to you sirs regarding the raid of Raja'. Raja', then, was near Mecca, on the water of the Hudhayl, and the Hudhayl were a tribe from among the tribes of the Arabs. The raid of Raja' occurred at this place with regard to a number of wells of the Arabs that belonged to the Hudhayl in the Hejaz.

11

A delegation of the Hudhayl came to the Prophet, prayers and peace of God upon him—oh, that God would open your hearts in faith [*imān*] and in Islam [*islām*]—and all at once upon their arrival, all smiles and cheer, they said: "Oh Messenger of God, Islam is spreading among us, your call which began to illuminate in noble Mecca. A good breeze blowing from Mecca brought the call [*da'wa*] to them, and a good breeze is one that continues to blow and blow. As a result of that good breeze, we were appointed and we seek to be upright, for Islam is spreading among us. We request that some of your companions stay with us, that we might come to know Islam, that they might teach us our religion [*dīn*]."

12

So whom did he choose? A group from among the youth, the finest of youth who had been reared in a virtuous home. The *ḥadīth* as given by Bukhayri indicates that he choose six, or it is said ten, and at their head was 'Asim ibn 'Umar, and as their reciter [*qarā'*] and counselor [*muftī*] was Khubayb, about whom we shall speak this Friday. We ask God, blessed and exalted be He, for the best intentions and good resolutions. As for youth, and in the mosque these days, it's all young people, I trust that the youth will give heed and that the old will not be angry at the young people, and that He may guide us all.

13

Now pay attention to Khubayb, this is really something beautiful. This group set off, and their equipment was for the Call [*al-da'wa*]. No one carried anything except the arms [*asliḥa*, "weapons"] of the Call. Now someone's going to ask, what are the "arms of the Call." Well, in each age, one carries the arms of that age, and being up to date is one of the essential features of an individual in an Islamic country. One doesn't wear in summer what one wears in winter, when one needs a house, not a hut, nor a hovel, nor some leaning, flimsy, lowly place. It must be a house which is invigorated under the care of a woman, and it should be protected from the heat of summer and from the cold of winter. And one needs an animal for riding. By heaven, that's the greatest, to have among the rights of an individual in an Islamic country, an animal to ride. It's even possible that an Islamic country would provide for him something to ride, and to facilitate this for him. There might be bicycles on the installment plan, or motorcycles on installment, and if salaries went up, there could be automobiles on installment, and if that level were raised again, there might even be airplanes on installment. This is a big issue, but it is all by way of speaking, because some of the brothers will say, "what are you babbling about" so it's all by manner of speaking. Now some of the experts [*fuqahā'*] add that their arms were not for enemies, nor for fear of anyone or any such thing. This is an Islamic country which has fulfilled all of its conditions and there the individual Muslim is in his strength, and if he uses his arms against someone, or lifts his hand against someone, or even turns his thoughts against someone, then it is necessary that his thinking be sound [*salīm*] and that his tongue be pure, his hand too must be pure, and if you raise your voice, it is necessary that the shout be pure and untainted. And I hope that our brothers will understand this in its broadest meaning.

14

So everyone set off and had with him only that simple weapon until they arrived at the watering place of the Hudhayl. You can all picture the scene clearly, like on television, beautiful—when suddenly they stopped in the face of an ambush. On heavens! Suddenly, they found some of the Meccans, those who had lost their cousins or their sons or their brothers from among those who fought among the pagans at the battle of Badr. They suddenly found all of these assembled before them in ranks, for they had conspired to ambush them. What now? Whom are they going to seize? Those who are callers [*duʿāh*], for the one who calls has great importance to the Messenger of God, prayers and peace of God upon him.

15

They were stopped by an ambush. Then there appear some differences, and differences are good [*ikhtilāf hilwa*]. Some said: "By God, we shall not disgrace our religion ever." So those who seized them said: "Very well then, we'll take you to Mecca and sell you there." ʿAsim ibn ʿUmar had been set as leader of the party that said: "By God, we shall not disgrace our religion, and with us are our guests, so we must fight [*nuqātil*]." Khubayb, however, was in charge of the expedition and he said: "As long as I am in command, I command that we go to Mecca, for if our blood is spared, perhaps, by the help of God, we will leave Mecca again." ʿAsim ibn ʿUmar fought and was killed along with three or four other companions. The rest were brought into Mecca, where they would be sold, turned over to the strong nobles of the Quraysh, and finally relegated to those who had lost relatives at the battle of Badr.

16

It was a difficult situation, but Khubayb was a man strong in Call. Where did they put him? He was placed as a prisoner in the house of a man who had a stone for a heart and a stone for a name. This was Hujayr ibn Abu Ihab who had purchased him at a good price. He paid out fifty head of camel. Then he brought him home and announced to the whole Quraysh the time for the execution, and he spoke to the Quraysh to this effect: "Gather together your imbeciles, your children, your women, gather all of you because on such and such a day, we shall carry out the sentence of death on this Khubayb ibn ʿAdiy, companion to the Messenger of God, prayers and peace of God upon him, who took part in the battle of Badr and whom we hold in custody. We intend to keep him there until we display him after he has mounted the chopping block. We will slaughter him and all Mecca must be present at the killing of this Khubayb, may God be pleased with him."

17

The second scene [*mashad*] is a little strange. I spoke some about extraordinary deeds last Friday, and we said that accomplishments that go beyond the ordinary to defy cunning men are not at the hands of crazy people or fools, but they are at the hands of the good. Our expression was "those ritually clean from among the sons of the mat" [*al-muwada'īn min abnā al-ḥaṣir*]. God, exalted and blessed be He, gives them success in some of their affairs, and some people conclude that these are extraordinary matters, but from a heavenly perspective, they are ordinary, and there is no one who teaches the soldiers of your Lord [*junūd rabbika*] except He.

18

Enter Khubayb on the stage! They had him in custody and he was put in a prison cell by our friend [*sahibuna*], none other than Hujayr. Hujayr took matters in hand and he placed one of his female servants in charge. Isn't that good? One of his female servants! See that prisoner in the cell, watch out for Him! "You're in charge of him and your life is in exchange if he escapes." They put him in chains and kept him under close guard.

19

Then we come upon some extraordinary things, about which all the books of *Sira* write and I want you all to go back to them, my sons and my dear brothers. The prisoner was in the house of Hujayr ibn Abu Ihab. A certain Mawiya—she's the woman they put in charge of guarding him—she said: "One day, by God, I entered upon him and I found him eating grapes, and at that time there were no grapes to be had in the land." He was eating grapes! "Where did you get them, my brother?" Of course, someone would say to you—"What's this you're talking about?" But he recited the Holy Qur'an, recalling the word of God, praised and blessed be He: "Whenever Zachariah went in to her in the Sanctuary, he found her provisioned. 'Mary,' he said, 'how comes this to thee?' 'From God,' she said. Truly God provisions whomsoever He will without reckoning" (3:37). In other words, what's so strange about it? Why are you looking toward the earth, just lift up your face. Lift up your head to heaven and you'll see some very strange things. Just lift up your head and face to the sky.

20

Then, it is said, "By God, he used to recite the Qur'an." The people of the neighborhood listened to it, the women and the youth, they heard the Qur'an on the lips of Khubayb. Watch out for the Call to God [*al-da'wa ila allah*]. It can't be helped. It's just got to spread and spread. There can be no stopping it. Indeed the Call to God radiates even from the darkest prison cells. It must spread. It simply must spread! There you have everybody listening to our friend all night while he recites the beautiful words. They all gathered round, leaning to hear what Khubayb had to say, for if one of them is carrying his heart, he is carrying Islam, even if it is not apparent to anyone.

21

Then it says that during that very night, a light was seen emanating from the cell. Take note, it's the book of *Sira* that says so. The cell itself was illuminated. Then it says that he asked for an "iron" [*ḥadīda*] in order to put his things in order. And the term "iron" in the books of *Sira* means a razor. He knew he was about to arrive before God, blessed and exalted be He. Of course, someone might take him to task for this, like 'Ashmawi. "Okay, Khubayb, you're finished after a couple more days." But Khubayb was going to make himself ready to meet God, blessed and exalted be He, and how was he going to get ready? He asked for an "iron," that is to say, for a razor. "My good woman, Mawiya, if you please, could you get me a razor so I can put myself in order, for after a couple days I am to arrive before God, blessed and exalted be He."

22

Mawiya said: "I sent him an 'iron' with one of the servants of my Lord and Lady." Now take note, here comes a part that is beautiful and charming. There's the little boy. She takes the razor: "Here, son, take this inside to that poor fellow so he can put himself in order. It's something that means a lot to him because he says that our Lord [*rabbina*] is going to receive him in a couple days." So the boy goes off with the razor in his hand. But then, just after the boy has left, it suddenly hits Mawiya and she cries: "Oh dear, Oh dear, we've been tricked! We're destroyed! I've just sent off the boy, son of my master, to him, and with that razor. That's it, his end is at hand! Undoubtedly, Khubayb will kill the boy or will take him hostage [*rahīna*]." She doesn't know that there's no such thing as taking hostages in Islam. What's this about hostages? That's something barbarians do! There's absolutely nothing in Islam like taking a child hostage! Like taking a man hostage in the sugar field, or taking an old man/preacher [*shaykh*] hostage. This is never a way for Muslims, because Islam knows nothing of this whole business of hostages, because it is Islam and peace [*salām*]. There's no such thing ever!

23

She entered and there she found that Khubayb had the little boy seated on his lap and he was instructing him in the Call [*yuda'iha*]. He had the boy on his lap and was playing with him. She said: "Oh, my gracious me!" But Khubayb said: "By your father you are courageous. You feared some treachery from me because you wanted to kill me! See, you're afraid that I'll pull some dirty trick on this boy, that I'll put the razor to his throat like in some movie, like Farid Shawqi, and I'll say: 'By damn, if you don't let me out of this place, I'll splatter him all over!' " That's never the way. That's only in the movies! That's not the way for Muslims, or for the sons of Muslims. A Muslim never wars against anyone, never! That's crystal clear. That can never be. "You, Mawiya, you were brave, to send the son of your master with a razor, weren't you afraid that I'd finish him off, kill him?"

24

And then all at once, she said—watch now, here's where Islam comes on the scene—: "Oh Khubayb, by my lord Muhammad, I was sure you wouldn't kill him!"—my lord Muhammad [*rabbi muhammad*]! All of a sudden the word bursts out. The word is in reason [*'aql*] and in the heart [*bāṭin*] and it gets repeated. "My lord Muhammad!" And before that she knew utterly nothing of Islam or of Muslims, but here she's in its company, in association with it, and look: "By my lord Muhammad, I was sure you wouldn't kill him." That's the second scene.

25

The third scene is beautiful my brothers, although also a little terrifying. The whole Quraysh turned out and they brought Khubayb forward. Then the goodly narrator says that they raised him on "wood" [*khashab*]— "wood" like there used to be in the war prison from which no one returns, something called the "maiden" [*al-'arusa*] and may God prevent you from ever seeing one—they raised Khubayb on the wood. Yes, on the wood, right before everyone, and there's no leaving now, for it's just about finished. It's like the man in Yemen, as they tell it, when someone did something in that backward system of theirs, and may God forgive them, and just before the executioner was to make the blow with his sword, he would say: "One cut or two?" In other words, he asks for an opinion of the unfortunate as to whether he should administer one blow or two. And someone says, "Give him one blow and let's have it over with." In other words, strike him once and you'll make us feel better.

26

As for Khubayb, undoubtedly they proposed something to him just before they were to carry out the execution, for one of them comes up and says, and here is the quote: "Renounce Islam, and we will let you go your way!" He won't renounce, nor will he go. We can never set before us either betrayal or false gods. "Renounce Islam and we will let you go your way." And in our memory, there is one of our brothers, and he is Hindawi Sayyid Ahmad Duwayr from among the sons of Minya. That was said to him the day before he was taken into custody: "Do you such and such and we'll let you go your way." Then after that, they didn't let him go his way, but they threw him into prison, but there's no reason to go into all of that. "Renounce Islam and we will let you go your way." But he said, "There is no God but God. By God if I were given all the earth I would not renounce it!" But they wanted him to say something else.

27

Then one of them said—and it seems that even though he happened to be tall, he was more like a little dwarf [*qazam saghayr*]—after he walked up beside Khubayb, he said: "Don't you wish that it was Muhammad here in your place and that you were sitting in your house?"—No, how stupid!—Khubayb said: "By God, I wouldn't want Muhammad to even be pricked by a thorn and I am sitting in my house."—You don't want to make a big fuss now, you don't want to brain-wash him. It's all over. You'll finish him off and you can relax! But no, "Don't you wish that it was Muhammad here in your place and that your were sitting in your house?" "By God, I wouldn't want Muhammad to even be pricked by a thorn and I am sitting in my house."

28

Khubayb looked around him and said: "Permit me to pray two prostrations [*raka'ayn*] to God."—Oh yeah, that too?—And some books of *Sira* claim that this was the beginning of the tradition [*sunna*] of two prostrations before death. He originated the custom. So they let him pray two prostrations, and it occurred to him that they shouldn't be very long, so he hurried them and then he said: "If I did not fear that you would take me for afraid or weak, I would have made them longer. But I don't want to give you the impression that I'm looking for an opportunity to forestall dying, lest you think I'm afraid or something. So instead of lengthening them, I shortened them."

29

So he performed two quick prostrations and then he said, as it is related in some of the books of *Sira:* "I have not from the beginning submitted to any foe, nor have I reverted, for I am to return to God, nor did I hesitate to join on any Muslim side where the combat was in the cause of God." Now that takes nerves of steel. There's firmness!

30

Then, so say the books of *Sira*, when they placed Khubayb on the wood, he looked around him and said in a loud voice: "Oh God, I find around me none but the faces of my enemies. Oh God, bring to the Messenger of God, prayers upon him, my greeting [*salām*]." And all at once, the Messenger of God, prayers and peace of God upon him, who was seated in the midst of his companions, in that hour when Khubayb called upon him, at this call of Khubayb, so says the narrator, the Messenger of God fell into a slight faint and said: "That was Gabriel conveying to me the greeting of Khubayb. May the mercy of God be upon you Khubayb. May the mercy of God be upon you."

31

So brothers, that's on Khubayb. And now we turn to another type of youth, and an issue concerning youth that merits our attention these days. I was on my way to you a short time ago, walking near the railroad station, and I came across a group of young people. They were near the water, a good number of them, and astonishing as it may sound, there were some young ladies among them. They were carrying a drum and they were hippies of some kind [*khanāfis*, "beetles"]. It doesn't worry me a great deal, for those among the sons of the mat [*abnā al-ḥaṣīr*] reject such a business. And as for the sons of the mat, their mat serves to forgive them from a great many of their matters. But here is a gathering that is altogether wrong [*shirr*], quite forthright and recognizably sinful, a case of corruption, this group. And I don't know what school they're from, but I intend to follow this up tomorrow, and God willing, perhaps I can take upon myself personally, the responsibility for some of these people. A group of young people down by the water, blocking the street, with girls among them, and their "weapon" [*silāhuhum*] was a drum.

32

Moreover, there was a gentleman who came to us yesterday to say the following. And I'm referring this matter to our dear friends, the police [*ahbā'nā min rijāl al-amn*] and I am going to speak with them about it. One of the brothers came to say that there are some young men who spend time sitting under the new bridge that leads to the Engineering College, and they lift up their heads from under the bridge to see what they can as the girls, their sister students, are coming down the steps. As I say, I'm referring the matter to our dear friends, the police, and I'll tell them the story of the *Sira* of *Marsadin ibn Abu Marsadin al-Ghanawi*.

33

And in your hearts, all of you, see what a difference between some youth and other youth, and so I come back to say: when is the shadow straight and the pole crooked?

34

This is what I have to say to you, and may God forgive both me and you.

35

Let us praise God, be He praised and exalted, and take refuge in Him from the evil in our souls and in our works, and we ask Him, that he might make you and me among those who listen best to his word.

36

So there's the *ḥadīth* on Khubayb, a radiant and pure [*mutawaḍa*] *ḥadīth*. I forgot to mention in the process that Khubayb was guilty of no wrong either in his own mind or in the minds of his companions. Indeed, one of them killed himself with some kind of sword or something, and so he escaped from the predicament I spoke of because he believed that he was on his way to ruin anyhow. The Prophet, prayers and peace of God upon him, says:—it goes something like this, for I haven't quite memorized it—"Who ever falls from a mountain and kills himself, he is in hell fire, and there he shall stay forever." The *ḥadīth* goes something like that.

37

Oh what is the greatness of Islam, and what is there without it? All those people in America who have made such progress in culture and science [*ḥaḍāra wa ʿilm*] are zero in the realm of the spirit and in the virtuous values that link us with what is above. What happened with those wretched ones we all heard about a few weeks ago in that suicide event—they all committed suicide. Nine hundred people committed suicide everyone of them. And the strange thing about it was that their motives, they said, were religious [*dīnīya*]. Acting on the basis of religion! And why would they do it? To escape! They said they wanted to escape from the world to what they call—well, I don't know what they call their Kingdom. This is weakness and corruption, rottenness, and may God protect Islam from such evil.

38

In the history of Islam and of the Muslims, there is absolutely never suicide. You'll never find it! It's impossible to find an incidence of suicide except among fools and crazy people [*ḥamqāʾ wa majanīn*] who have never prayed to God, glorious and majestic, so much as a single prostration, who have never sat beside a wash basin or the canal to make the ritual ablution, saying: "In the name of God, the merciful and compassionate." They have never stood before the *qibla* and said *Allah akbar*. For the [Messenger], prayers and peace upon him, when he was pressed with difficulty or defeat used to take refuge in prayer, and he would say: "Let us take our rest in it, oh Bilal, let us take our rest in it, oh Bilal." And that is because prayer [*ṣalāh*], as I was telling you last

Friday, taking the words from some of our British friends, is shown lately to be an outstanding psychological cure that restores to a person a complete sense of security [*amn*] and peace [*salām*]. No, it's never possible!

39

Then there was that good man that [Harun] al-Rashid put in prison one day,—or maybe it wasn't al-Rashid, maybe it was someone else—and he said some beautiful and pointed things, oh Brothers. He said: "In this world, there has got to be both joy and sorrow. It's essential that we bear with what we don't like. If I'm imprisoned one day"—see the lovely things people of the past had to say—"indeed the sword must one day be returned to its sheath, and if I am absent from a place one day, still the sun must set, and if I find myself in a difficult situation someday, still that fire too must one day be extinguished . . . [inaudible]. And the fire in the flint dies out, but without striking it there can be no sparks, nor does it fear water. To be cast in prison for no evil deed is no shame, it is rather a beautiful home. When one who is gracious is imprisoned, his honor is restored, except if you fail to turn yourself to good account while in the guise of a slave. How many a sick man has been restored to health, while the physician and the one who came to visit him both died."

40

Look at these good people, and as for suicide, well, that's their own business. You hear about people committing suicide. So you take some fools from among Muslims who have never sat upon the mat. They find themselves in some tight spot, so they kill themselves, and may the Lord forgive them. Or like that minister of health who committed suicide, and I don't know who all who commits suicide, whoever they might be in places far from Minya, and praise the Lord. Look at Americans. Someone's girlfriend leaves him and he commits suicide. Her boyfriend leaves her and she commits suicide. They get into a tight spot and they commit suicide. They get into a dispute and they both commit suicide. This is never the case with good Muslims, because for Muslims, there is always life, for better or for worse. For the Prophet, prayers and peace upon him, said something to the effect: "I am surprised about the believer and his circumstances." Or, to the effect: "If the affair is good and the outcome felicitous, be thankful, for that is best for you. And if the affair is distressing, bear up patiently, for that is best for you."

41

The ogre of routine, my brothers, and the system of official procedures, will we never see an end to the ogre of routine in our day?

42

I was representing you at a meeting of good gracious people at the police headquarters [*al-amn*] and it all went very well. It was the occasion when the director of the Ministry of Agriculture in Minya, that is, the land reform, was saying farewell to become the General Director of the regional agricultural office in Beni Suef. A fine thing! Undoubtedly it will come to a good end, for the man is good and upright.

43

Indeed, everyone was invited to be present at the farewell of our gracious brother, that is, to attend the celebration of our gracious brother, and that includes the new governor of the Governorate of Minya, may God keep him from error. But we disagree with some of what was said before these two good sirs. Obviously, bestowing congratulations is a simple matter. Everybody bestows congratulations; all organizations congratulate, all factions congratulate, all companies congratulate, and this is fine. A happy outcome results when the hearts of the good turn toward their good brothers, for the Prophet says, prayer and peace of God upon him: "Whoever performs for you some honorable service, reward him, and if you are not able to do so, wish him well when he departs."

44

Thus we spoke at the police headquarters on the benefits of increasing education. But it is necessary to move from congratulations to the striving of everyone in every position, each striving in his own right to bring about good for the service of all citizens. The congratulations of organizations and groups and companies to one of our brothers is not sufficient, however much it is appropriate. Indeed, it is also necessary to move on to the step that follows the bestowal of congratulations, and that means to put one's hand out and set to thinking about the project itself in order to serve the citizens. For this truly adds both to those who congratulate and to those who receive congratulations.

45

We were present representing you, and to God, exalted and praised be He, be honor and power, saying that where matters of agriculture are concerned, they should be regulated at the local level [*markazīya*]. For where matters of the Governorate [*muhāfẓah*] are in the hands of the people themselves and are regulated by the local community [*markaz*], that is best.

46

We want to commend the people of the outlying districts [*abnā al-aqlīm*] for these are the ones closest to the problems of the outlying areas. We want to commend those who are near to the good people, since they should be the ones to solve their own problems, for they know them best.

47

The ogre of routine; Islam fights against it, my brothers. Oh how I wish all of us today, in whatever position we have, would set about doing something. Oh how I wish we would fight against routine. No paper should ever be late. And our dear friends, who are here present with us today, and among them are some of the great men of the community, and may God bless them and bring them to flourish, for their hearts are pure, how I wish. . . . [The tape ends.]

Sermon of Shaykh Umar

April 6, 1979

1

The Exalted has said: "And obey God and His Messenger, and do not quarrel together, and so lose heart, and your power depart; and be patient;
surely God is with the patient. Be not as those who went forth from their
habitations swaggering boastfully to show off to men, and barring from
God's way; and God encompasses the things they do" [8:46–47]. And the
Glorious and Majestic says: "You have had a good example in God's Messenger for whoever hopes for God and the Last Day, and remembers God
oft" [23:21].

2

These verses from the book of God, exalted be He, if all Muslims took
them seriously and placed them before them, they would not now be in
this shameful and debased condition. The first verse is the axis of every
move toward goodness and the glorious motive-force behind every truth,
and the source of dawn's light to everyone who watches for God, exalted be
He, whether in secret or in public. For without faith in the last day, in the
resurrection and recompense, there is no religion [*dīn*], no morality [*khu-
luq*], no truth, no justice, no goodness.

3

Those who live out their lives in such a way are mounts for any rider, fair
prey for any thief. And those are the ones who do not believe in the day of
resurrection or who think that the judgment is some kind of sport or game.
But what about someone who believes in the day of resurrection and

responsibility before God, exalted be He, and then permits himself to serve the hand of falsehood [*bāṭil*], whosoever's hand it might be that would urge to falsehood, even if it be that of a king, a president, a minister, the rich, the powerful, a father or a son. For if there is someone who believes in the day of resurrection, the rising, the judgment and the recompense, in heaven or on earth and he permits another, whoever that might be to direct him to falsehood, or to lies or evil, or who uses his tongue for anything of falsehood, lies or evil, the book of God confirms a fact about him when it says: "Assuredly thou art calling them to a straight path; and surely they that believe not in the world to come are deviating from the path" [23:72–73].

4

Indeed, I ask every one of you a question that you should put right between your eyes at this instant: Do you want to please God? For if you want to please God and you are a [government] functionary [*muwaẓaf*] or a worker [*'amāl*] or whatever happens to be your position, your place of work, whatever your job is, high or low: Do you have anything that can protect you from God? Is there anyone you can turn to to protect you from God?

5

If you want to please God, and you really believe that there can be no one to protect you from God, then why do you commit falsehood, or why do you do anything before you have determined whether it is truth or falsehood? This is the question that everyone must pose himself, day and night, so long as you want to please God. Then why do you do what God does not want? Do you really believe that there is no one who can protect you from God? Yet this statement is affirmed by the prophets and angels, for the Prophet said to his sons, "I cannot protect you from God." Moreover, the noblest of creatures, the consummate creature, the one closest to God, exalted be He, that is, Muhammad, prayers and peace of God upon him, said to his own daughter: "I cannot protect you from God."

6

Then why do you obey the president in a matter that angers your Lord? Put the matter before you and follow it through so that no one will be able to divert you to a lie or to falsehood or hypocrisy or evil. Indeed, this world is paltry, its pleasures slight, and its tenure short. Nor will its amusements help you. If you believe in the day of judgment and you are in any position or job, then take heed, take heed, lest you commit forgery, falsehood, or evil.

7

Someone asks, I'm a government employee in such and such a department, a teacher, a supervisor, a judge, an engineer, a clerk, head of a department, a police officer, the governor of the Governorate, the chief of the secret police. And what are you to do about the policies of the government when they ask you to arrest someone without any reason, be it true or false? This is the question I want to direct to everyone on the face of the earth.

8

And I've seen this from the time of my childhood, how the country [*umma*] follows the general opinion. When I was a child, in 1914, I was nine years old and they dressed me in a white *gallabīya* and a white cap so I could welcome the king's minister of agriculture. This was 1914 and I was in the Qur'an school [*kuttāb*]. I was to welcome the minister of agriculture and he was Egyptian, that is, Arab, from an Arabic country, but as minister of agriculture he was under orders of the Turkish viceroy [*walī*]. The Turkish viceroy! Now this Turkish viceroy didn't want anything to do with Arabic, he wanted things Turkish, and so they made us memorize Turkish phrases. Even today I remember the phrase and it goes like this: "kandig yash yob bysha." And so we memorized it: "kandig yash yob bysha" and we were just little schoolboys who didn't know if we were going east or west or up or down, because he did what he pleased. So instead of saying: "long live so and so, minister of agriculture" (in Arabic) —May God forgive them—we had to say: "kandig yash yob bysha." We were just schoolboys who didn't know any Turkish and our fathers in the village didn't either as we stood there to welcome the minister of agriculture. But why wasn't this carried out in the Arabic language? No, the ruler [*ḥākim*] wanted it in Turkish, and so Arabic was dropped for the sake of the ruler. Of course, I said it.

9

And later as a young man when we would shout: "Down with George V, King of England," everybody would get all excited as if the heavens were going to collapse upon the earth, and they would come out and arrest us in the village for calling for the fall of the British emperor on account of their imperialism over Egypt. The police would get all excited too, and the commissioner and the local garrison would be up in arms, and they would arrest us and accuse us of activity against imperialism. And that's what imperialism is all about; it commands these people. And these people are not believers in the truth, they believe in their profits [*muslaḥātahum*]. If their faith in the truth was like their faith in their profits, they would have stood by us [saying]: "Down with George V, King of England."

10

But they live according to their profits, and their profits shift and change according to the climate of profits. These profits were supported by imperialism and they took advantage of this support. But the support of truth did not need this support, and yet the problem was not one of truth or falsehood, it was a question of a crust of bread. There's the real profit, and the crust of bread is a problem well known to us. When I want to say something about the Book, the Sunna and Islam, they say, "Oh Brother, we need bread to eat!" If it happened that a calf came wandering into the village, you'd be groveling gathering grass and presenting it to him. If there was some profit to be made by you in dealings with a dog, you'd be saying, "My master." Isn't our Lord going to call us to account for the likes of this? Why? because we don't believe in the day of resurrection, because on the day of resurrection there will exist nothing but the Truth. The utter Truth in his Book of Truth and the Sunna of Truth of the Prophet.

11

Therefore we'll see on the day of Resurrection believers like the Imām ibn Hanbal in the conflict over the creation of the Qur'an. The Caliph brought him in and said: "Confirm that the Qur'an was created." He said: "No! The Qur'an is the word of God, exalted be He, uncreated." "I will torture you, I will imprison you, I will kill you!" He said: "No, I will not do it, for you are ordering me to commit a falsehood and I shall brook no falsehood ever, fearing God my Lord." So they tortured ibn Hanbal and put him in prison until the assistant vizier and a representative of the Caliph rescued him and said to him: "Oh your grace, Imām." He said: "Yes?" They said: "Affirm that the Qur'an was created." He said: "No. If it is decreed that I should die soon, I want to die for the truth and then I shall meet the truth with truth." Thus the youth [shabāb] of our master Ahmad ibn Hanbal and his truth defeated the falsehood of the Caliph. He was sent forth from prison and he cut the flesh from his body, for the flesh had died, though martyrs never die. After a few days they examined him and they found that his flesh had died, so his son came and said to him, "Oh father, pray that God will avenge you on those who tortured you and imprisoned you!" And he said: "Oh my son, may God forgive them. What will it benefit me if God gets angry at a Muslim and I am delivered from my anger. I do not desire God's wrath on any Muslim. I have pardoned all my enemies except the people of heresy [bida'], for God forgives them all, except the people of heresy." See how splendid this is! And then he said: "What can kings and presidents do to me? If they imprison me, prison is but my monk's cell. If they exile me from my country, exile is but a touring expedition. If they kill me, death is but a cure." Now isn't that the Islamic way! "And fear the day wherein you shall be returned to God, and every soul shall be paid in full what it has earned; and they shall not be wronged" [2:281].

12

But still more than that was Summaya who was tortured along with her father, her brother, and her mother in order to force her to pronounce in favor of disbelief [*kufr*] and paganism [*shirk*] and abandon the profession of Islam. And the verse descended upon the Prophet after he passed them that said: "Be patient, oh family of *yasr*, for your meeting place is paradise." And the verse descended which gave them permission to pronounce the words of disbelief with their tongues while he made their hearts all the more sure and calm in the profession of Islam. But Summaya refused and Abu Jahl came to her and said: "Curse Muhammad and cease believing in God and believe in the gods and the idols." But she said: "I testify that there is no God but God, and Muhammad the Messenger of God." So they made a fire and set an iron lance upon it and they brought it over to her and aimed it at that place between her thighs to kill her. And that's just how they killed her, but before they rammed that lance between her pure thighs—may God be pleased with her—they asked her again to curse God and his Prophet, but she grew firmer in her faith [*imān*] and her Islam to God and his Prophet, and she recited those famous immortal words: "By god, I will not corrupt my tongue with the word of disbelief after it has been purified with the word of faith." And why all of this? Because she wanted to please God. And what is it to please God, but to be in absolute Truth?

13

And if any government employee [*muwaẓaf*], any husband or wife, any ruler [*ḥākim*], any one at all places an order before you and gives directions, whether it be a president, a father, a brother, an uncle, a head of a company and he says, "Listen, do such and such." Say to him, "Does that please God? If it pleases God, I will do it, even though it is a minor thing." And if he says, "It pleases God," then you answer, "Give me the proof [*dalīl*]. Give me the proof from the Book of God, from the Sunna of His Prophet and the works of the righteous, for without that I won't do what you want, for I am the servant of God and I do what pleases God." And if we did this, there would never be tyranny, or discontentment, or any kind of hostility and we'd be living in real peace [*salām*] and security [*amān*]. Why? Because no one would do anything except what pleases God, and what pleases God is Truth, Goodness, and Justice.

14

There's nothing in a president who has a hundred thousand men come before him who say: "Give me an order, for I am your servant [*'abduk*]. If you tell me to kill my father, I will kill him to please your excellency." God is with us, and God is above us, and God surrounds us and brings us to die. You and I will be uncovered before God, exalted be He, and even if you don't want to please God, I certainly want to please God, so let us never abuse the Truth.

15

And what about those peoples who follow after the Americans who besiege us, and torment us, who dishonor us and bring us to sadness and ruin in the world with the enormity of their loans and consultations? They are worse than children who are treating as a game everything involved in governing a people, or between peoples and nations. Has Qaddafi stopped playing the game he's been at so long? Has Hafaz al-Assad stopped playing the game he's been at so long? And what about all the others? And that fellow in Yemen, did he call back his troops when they were striking Muslims for the sake of Marxism? Did the ruler of Afghanistan call back his troops when they struck Muslims? Did the ruler of Pakistan call back his troops when they were striking Muslims who were praying at the funeral of Bhutto? And why all this? Because soldiers are under orders. They say, "We have our orders," or, "We are servants of orders." You say, "Why are you doing this, my man?" And he says, "I'm the servant of orders." But God, exalted and praised be He, when he created you, did he say you were a servant of orders? He told you, "You are my servant, and I am your Lord!"

16

And so he says to you, "Okay, then, who's going to feed me?" But if there are in the world a billion human beings who eat at the price of their honorable work, there are also billions and billions and billions and billions and billions of creatures who possess no authority over their sustenance: animals, birds, fish, insects. Are these worrying about their sustenance? It amazes me that the insects of the world know their way to food better than people, when it's a question of the way to nourishment. And the Prophet, prayers and peace of God upon him, pointed this out, and Jesus himself, we recall, spoke of it in the gospel, drawing our attention to the birds. They go out hungry but return with stomachs full, and they spend no time worrying about bread, or the cheese bin, or the honey jar, or the oil jug, nor the refrigerator. All those people who spend sleepless nights worrying about the refrigerator and what's in it. But man is always leaving what is really sure for what is unsure, forgetting the afterlife for the world and forgetting God for ourselves.

17

My desire for all of you is that you might come to improve your situation to be independent. And what is independence? As we say: Complete independence or a violent death [*al-istiqlāl al-tām au al-maut al-zuʾām*]? Independence of what? The nation [*waṭan*]? Yes. Independence of the people? Yes. But what about independence for me? You know, the nation is independent and I am still a servant. Is that the end of it? The kind of independence that completes the independence of the nation is the independence of the human being. And there is no independence for man unless he is aware of the distinction between truth and falsehood. A man who doesn't distinguish between truth and falsehood is no man, nor is he anyone's servant! He is not even Satan, for Satan at least distinguishes between truth and falsehood and he chooses falsehood. Satan knows truth from falsehood but he chooses falsehood purposefully, even though he knows the truth. He says: "The truth, I want nothing to do with it, I'm choosing falsehood." The devil knows truth and falsehood. You follow falsehood and you make yourself the servant of Satan.

18

The ultimate independence of the nation, the ultimate independence of society, and the deepest meaning of democracy is this: The depth of democracy is that no one, neither my president, nor my wife, nor my father, nor my brother can come up to me and say: "Do such and such!" And if you say: "That's wrong." He says: "You're fired." "And I tell you, no, no, no, finished! I'll do whatever you want, sir. I'll do whatever you want, even if you want me to kill my wife, I'll kill her. Just leave me to eat my bread, sir, for God's sake." Is this the good citizen or functionary? No! The ultimate independence is that I can say to the president: "This is Truth, I accept it, and this is falsehood, I reject it." That's the deepest meaning of democracy, if that's what the president wants. Why? Because that same president is responsible on the Day of Judgment. Listen, you give a speech that lasts for three hours or four hours or five hours, and ears perk up to listen all over the earth. What do you want with your speech-making? Do you want what I want or do you want something I do not want? Our Lord, exalted be He, says I made your ears so that you could hear everything that is said. So did you listen to what I wanted or did you listen to what I did not want? I made your hands and your feet to take you to what I want, not to what I don't want. Well, then, did you strive for what I wanted or for what I did not want?

19

Ask yourself these questions: You, government employee [*muwaẓaf*], who take some action or decision [*tuktib taqrīr*] against your brother, some subordinate or your boss [*raʾīs*]. Do you care about what pleases God and what God wants, or did you see what your boss/president wanted and then you wrote it? Before you write, my friend, take careful note as to what is on your shoulder. There is a clerk there over you. You write, and he writes, you revise, and he revises. ". . . Not a word he utters, but by him is an observer ready. And death's agony comes in truth; that is what thou wast shunning! And the Trumpet shall be blown; that is the Day of Threat. And every soul shall come, and with it a driver and a witness. Thou wast heedless of this; therefore We have now removed from thee thy covering, and so thy sight today is piercing!" And his comrade shall say, "This is what I have made ready. Cast, you twain, into Gehenna every forward unbeliever, every hinderer of the good, transgressor, disquieter, who set up with God another god; therefore you twain, cast him into the terrible chastisement." And his comrade shall say, "O Lord, I made him not insolent, but he was in far error!" He shall say, "Dispute not before Me! For I sent you beforehand the threat! The Word is not changed with Me; I wrong not My servants" [50:18–29]!

20

Those are the verses. And if everyone put them before him, there wouldn't be events like those we're now in the middle of. There wouldn't be any animosity between husband and wife, between friend and friend, between one group and another group, between one nation and another nation, between one Arab and another Arab, or between citizen and citizen. Why? Because all would reckon with the account at the hands of the Lord of Lords, the overseer of righteousness, the one who parts the clouds. No, I tell you. Why is it that people have their quarrels? God is one! If we Arabs acted like that, there would have never been the contentions among us. This miserable situation, this painful poverty, about which I don't have to tell you.

21

And the proof [dalīl] that our Lord looks after me is in the way I was formed. Was it my mother who supervised all of that and who knew what was happening? Where did I come from, and there I was in her belly, in the path of her innards? Did she know about me? Understand me? Supervise me? Provide for my needs? There was One supervised me, One who was with me, One who supplied my needs. His hands were with me. He protected me in my mother's belly. He nourished me. He caused me to sleep. Then he said, "Go out, my servant, into my wide world." So how could it be that He who oversaw me in my mother's womb would not oversee me in the world? Doesn't He see me when I'm in bed? Doesn't He see me when I'm walking along a wall at night? Doesn't He see me when I'm standing in the field of eggplants or leading my oxen? Doesn't He see me when I'm sitting there writing? That orator [khaṭīb] who's speaking there, what is he speaking about? Is he giving out reports so they will have cause to arrest me? That functionary who is writing and making charges about me, saying that Islam is this or Islam is that. Make the charge against him! Does he know what he's writing about?

22

Shame on you [*'ayib 'alayk*]. Those fingers you're writing with, who is moving them? Your hands, who created them? The paper and the pen you are writing with bear witness against you. Shame on you! Be a man! Straighten up! Be free! Are you buying freedom? I don't need your freedom. I get freedom for myself, not from the government. Never! Because if I have to buy my freedom today, someone's going to come up to me and say, "No, that's not freedom. There's freedom for the party [*hizb*] but not for enemies of the party." No! I'm the master of my own freedom. I give freedom to myself so I am *free!* Free to speak, oh brother, before the face of God and not before the face of a creature. Free to reason and to understand before the face of God and not before the face of a creature. Free for doing good and not for doing evil before the face of God and not before the face of a creature. Free in heart and conscience, not to betray or cheat before the face of God and not before a creature. I speak the Truth and when you speak the Truth, I'm with you, and as for falsehood, if you speak falsehood, I'm not with you. That is the freedom that I give to myself.

23

I give freedom to myself before the government gives it. Go after the freedom that belongs to you and leave off with the freedom of government. We're not servants of the government, nor servants of the Nile, nor servants of Egypt, nor servants of the globe of the earth, nor of the heavens, nor of paradise, nor of hell-fire, nor of money, nor of a family, nor of women. We're servants of the One. His servants alone! "And fear a day wherein you shall be returned to God, and every soul shall be paid in full what it has earned; and they shall not be wronged" [2:281].

24

We live on what God owns, not on what is owned by the government. The government applies to God for its freedom, not to the people. Don't say you're a "son of the people" [*ibn al-sha'ab*]. What is this "the people"? Okay, so we see the people of Syria; they support their president. Or look at the people of Iraq; they support their president. If the people were free would the people of South Yemen support Marxism and a Communist lackey as their president? And look at that fellow in Libya who says: "I'm a prophet." And then he memorizes the Qur'an. I tell you it's a big fake! If the people were free they would have left him. What about us, then? As we've said before, and we'll repeat it, what about Egypt?

25

Egypt, the gift of Muhammad 'Ali! And before that it was: Egypt, gift of the Nile. And then someone tells you: "No, we're pharaonic." Someone else tells you: "No, no, we're Arabs." Then another one tells you: "No, we're neither pharaonic nor Arab, all of us are 'the people!' " Suppose someone tells you we're all Nahas, or someone tells you we're all Gamal, or someone tells you we're all Anwar. What is this anyway? Do we march under a different banner every day? Okay, we want no more of that. We say that we are God's glorious and majestic. None of the others. Is that forbidden?

26

Now take for example the fact that peace has come to the country, and then there's the national anthem. In 1914, there was a national anthem and we changed it. In 1922 there was a national anthem and we changed it. The revolution came so a song was made and we changed it again. Then a few days ago because of the peace treaty—and may God bring peace—we changed the anthem again. If it is for good, it is from God, if it is for evil, they would not act except by God's leave. And if it is for good, who brings it about? [Audience roars: God!] And if it is for evil, whose support do we seek? [Audience: God!] For national peace and a national anthem should be for the remembrance [*dhikr*] of God and not for the remembrance of any other except God! That's all there is to it. There's no need to change it for some past treaty, nor for a present treaty, nor for any future treaty, because the anthem is in the name of who? [Audience: God!] "In God there is no change ever, He exists eternal."

27

So what is it with this anthem, melody and music? They say that music is the language of God in the cosmos. Listen well to what they say about music. What will they tell you about music? Music, they'll tell you, is the language of God in the cosmos. Oh, dear Me! Music is the language of God? Then why didn't the Qur'an descend in musical form? Eh? Fa-la-la, fa-la-la. That's strange, are you laughing at me? That's the language of God, and why is that? Because it brings hearts together. Heaven help us! Are their hearts brought together, those in the movie houses listening to music? One has his heart set against the other. Why do we have this turmoil between East and West, between the North and the South, between the rich and the poor, between the large and the small, between Europe, Russia, and America, between the ruler and the ruled, between husband and wife, between son and father? If music could bring [them] together, our Lord would have said to Muhammad, peace be upon him: "Take this musical score and strike up the music with the lute or some other instrument. Sit down in Mecca and start crooning"; ". . . for He brought their hearts together. Hadst thou expended all that is in the earth, thou couldst not have brought their hearts together; but" *music?* Oh heaven, what a mistake [*yā salām ʿala al-taḍlīl*]! Our Lord said: "hadst thou expended all that is in the earth"—music, films, cinema, navies, armies, weapons, money, gold, silver, pearls, rubies, buildings, trains, automobiles, airplanes, all the wealth—"thou couldst not have brought their hearts together; but God brought their hearts together" [8:63].

28

They don't care about the Qur'an, instead they want to play music in order to take in how many thousands, how many millions of dollars and live from their profit. They don't hold to the Qur'an. But for me, it's freedom! My freedom is that I fly, I fly, I ffff-llll-yyyy, on wings of love and mercy and justice, gliding across the kingdoms of God and His glory and perfection, for I love Him. And what is it to love Him? I love to live according to his morals [*akhlāq*], piously, purely, and cleanly, in goodness.

29

When I listen, I listen only to Him, I hear only His call, glorious and majestic, as He says: "And when My servants question thee concerning Me—I am near to answer the call of the caller, when he calls to Me; so let them respond to Me, and let them believe in Me; haply so they will go aright" [2:186]. I turn to Him, there is none other than He. I call to Him alone, I don't call to any other than He. I live in His tranquility and security. Poverty doesn't concern me because I am with Him. I am satisfied and rich. Knowledge [*ʿilm*] doesn't concern me because with Him I have enough. Darkness doesn't concern me because with Him I have light. Fear and Terror don't concern me because with Him . . . [transmission interrupted]

30

Listen to what has been inspired, not to what clatters and pollutes. "Give thou ear to this revelation. Verily I am God; there is no god but I; therefore serve Me, and perform the prayer of My remembrance. The Hour is coming; I would conceal it that every soul may be recompensed for its labors. Let none bar thee from it, that believes not in it but follows after his own caprices, or thou wilt perish" [20:13–16]. Is there anyone who listens to him? What's he listening to? And when you leave him, he puts up an idol, because he listens to something apart from the Glorious and Majestic, and anyone who looks to him is blind unless he looks to none other than God, for after God there is nothing, with God there is nothing, before God there is nothing.

31

The verse is: "O believers, take your precautions; then move forward in companies, or move forward all together" [4:71]. You see the power, the weapons [*silaḥ*], the strength and power for defense. The Muslim is the weapon of Egypt, its mind, its goodness, its honesty, its piety, its women, its sons, its roads, its agriculture, its commerce, and its industry, all of this is the power for defense, which has one purpose and that is to defend the Truth.

32

In 1959, Russia invented her satellite and they sent it to the moon. America didn't have anything yet, so what did America do? They answered back and said, we've got to catch up with Russia and overtake them. So America and Russia started overtaking one another, each one wanting to outdistance the other. And as for us, we just sat. We sat and did what? We would take a little piece from the Qur'an and leave a thousand pieces. We take one verse from the Qur'an and leave a thousand verses. We take one piece of wisdom from the Qur'an and we leave a thousand pieces of wisdom. We take a part of the world [*dunyā*] and we leave a million parts. What is that? Is that any life? When we got ourselves lost and in financial straits, in order to eat, we've got to drink, and here we have agricultural land and irrigation water that's the best. And here we have working man's hands that are the greatest hands and the greatest workers of the world. And here we have minerals for industry with no mining and no industry. So a group goes to Russia and says: "Please, give it to us." The group stretches out its hands to America and says, "Please give it to us." The group goes to Europe and says, "O Europe, give it to us." And who are they? Our Lord tells us in the third verse: "As for the unbelievers, they are friends one of another. Unless you do this, there will be persecution in the land and great corruption" [8:73].

33

Come on now, what did Russia do for us when she was our friend in 1956? What did she do when she was our friend in 1967 and there were 17,000 Russian advisors here and they withheld spare parts from us? What did she do for us in 1973?

34

Come on, what about America? What's the latest thing happening in America? It's that the Aramco Company is after Saudi petroleum for their own advantage. They've set out to drill oil wells in Saudi Arabia and they've written into the agreement, a document from the hands of the members of the Senate of America, and clear in that document is that the

Secretary of State is to watch over it. He took it and is secretly putting it in action. In other words, for a little petroleum from Saudi Arabia, they get a crust of bread, while they're really out to destroy her.

35

And after that, as for the money that results from the petroleum, they have to destroy that too. Where does that money go? It goes to the banks in America and Europe. And who directs the banks in America and Europe? The Jews! Who takes the interest from the billions from the price of oil which belongs to the Arabs? The Jews! And what do the Jews do with the interest? They build up their settlements [*musta'amarāt*], they buy arms, they outfit their army to strike the Arabs.

36

And what else, my brothers? They want to develop some replacement for the oil that belongs to Saudi Arabia, Kuwait and the Emirates, so they can send them back to eating sand like they used to eat sand. Hence nuclear energy! They want to replace petroleum with nuclear energy so that afterward, they'll have reduced them again to poverty and they'll mock the world and say to everyone. "Oh, my servants!"

37

I tell you it's a lie. They're putting a lie before you. I'm the owner [*ṣāḥib*] of light, the owner of goodness, the owner of petroleum, the owner of nuclear energy, the owner of the day, the owner of the night. Trust in me and love one another, don't abandon each other; protect each other because you're all in danger if you start consuming each other. An explosion will destroy you and what will be your attitude when the sun and moon and the planets burst like bubbles? Where's your religion [*dīn*]? Oh you people of disbelief [*kufr*], oh you who pretend to be ignorant of the religion of Islam and are set against the people of Islam, to you I say: "As for the unbelievers, they are friends one of another. Unless you do this, there will be persecution in the land and great corruption" [8:73]. There you see, "persecution in the land" [*fitna fī al-arḍ*]! Russia is on guard against America, against Baghdad and Damascus and South Yemen. And Baghdad and Damascus and with them that small-fry [*ḥittat al-ṭifl*] to the West and that small-fry in South Yemen, they're set against Saudia, Kuwait and the Emirates. And all of them are warring against Egypt instead of Israel. In other words, instead of waging war against Israel, they wage war against Egypt. Instead of encircling Israel, they encircle Egypt. Instead of fearing Israel, they fear Egypt. Egypt has become the enemy of the Arabs while all the time, it's Egypt that is the professor to the Arabs.

38

If they were only halfway together in 1947, they could have finished this Palestine business once and for all. But the Arabs are not of one religion now, not of one opinion, nor of one constitution. Everyone has their own constitution and we've abandoned the Qur'an. Everyone has his god, we've abandoned God. Everyone has power [*sulṭān*] but not the power of God. Everyone has his aspiration [*raghba*] and has abandoned the aspiration of Islam, and for that reason, we're all impoverished. Why? Because our Lord told us this: "And obey God, and His Messenger, and do not quarrel together, and so lose heart and your power depart" [8:46]. You see, see, persecution! When we trusted in the power of nations and we presumed that the disbelievers were with us, we did not get ahead, nor did we obey God and His Messenger. We quarreled and we were frightened, we were held back, we were stricken, we were reduced to silence.

39

And so what has happened to the Remembrance [*dhikr*] of God, the Messenger, the Qur'an, Islam, and the Muslims, all the good women, the good children, the good teachers of Egypt about whom the government is silent? Why? I don't know. Is it pleased with this situation? I don't know. Is it possible to suppress virtue in a country, our country, that we call a country of faith and unity [*balad al-imān wa-al-tawḥīd*], even before they knew God? For the president in his speech yesterday said Egypt was the country of unity [*tawḥīd*] before God sent His Messengers. I don't know how the president could say such a thing. Our Lord does not leave any nation without a Messenger, and unity is an innate characteristic [*fiṭra*]. And the Egypt he's talking about didn't know unity that is the true unity [*al-tawḥīd al-ḥaqīqī*] until it came upon Moses, upon him be peace.

40

Before Moses, Heaven help us! There was Amon Ra. Who is this Amon Ra? The son of the Sun! And that man, the radio announcer! Last Friday there was a play broadcast about Hatshepsut and Tutmoses and Amon Ra. They told you: "I am God incarnate!" That was an announcer on an Egyptian broadcast!

41

He said that God was incarnate before Hatshepsut in the form of Tutmoses in order to father, by her, Amon Ra. I slapped my palms together and I said, Heaven help us! Where are our youth going to, and where are our old men [*shuyūkh*] going to, where are people going who don't know the Qur'an? God does not beget. He does not pay court. There is nothing similar to Him. He doesn't manifest Himself to spirit or to men or even to angels of heaven. As God says: "Whatsoever is in the heavens and the earth implore Him; every day He is upon some labour" [55:29]. And the Prophet says: "The angels of God make their petitions as you make your petitions."

42

That is unity! That is unity! That is Knowledge [*ʿilm*]! That is religion [*dīn*]! So why, oh why do they mix it up with things pharaonic, and things pharaonic from a moral and social point of view? What's more, things pharaonic are all tyranny and despotism. "Now Pharaoh had exalted himself in the land and had divided its inhabitants into sects, abasing one party of them, slaughtering their sons, and sparing their women; for he was of the workers of corruption" [28:4]. Where's your sense? What do we want with Tutmoses or his father Ramses, or Hatshepsut? Don't we have ʿAmar ibn al-ʿAs? Don't we have Khalid? Don't we have ʿUmar ibn al-Khutab? Don't we have someone greater than that? "You have a good example in God's Messenger for whosoever hopes for God and the Last Day, and remembers God oft" [33:21].

43

I testify that there is no God but God, He alone, no associate with Him and I testify that Muhammad is the Messenger of God, and my master, prayers and peace of God upon him, and upon his family, his companions, and on those who follow him until the Day of Judgment.

44

Now what is there to be said about ancient history, of which nothing remains except statues and stones? In point of fact, there is some knowledge in it, though not all of it is knowledge, whereas God has brought to us all knowledge [*ʿilm*], all wisdom [*ḥikma*] and all governance [*ḥukum*]. There was a man named Ahmad Mukhtar Pasha who wrote a book entitled *Approaches to the Qurʾan*, and in it he interprets with a mere seventy verses of the Qurʾan the entire universe. He finds that these seventy verses, which he explains from the Book of God, bring together all the hidden laws of the universe. Get this book and read it instead of saying yourself, or letting any speaker say it, or having it in some play, that God was incarnate, for that's a departure from faith, from Islam and its unity, in favor of the glory of the Pharaohs.

45

Indeed, we are an ancient civilization as a nation, and we have an urbane culture that is both humane and godly. But what of the Qurʾan and the highest of creatures, Muhammad, Messenger of God, prayers and peace of

God upon him, of whom God says: "You have a good example in God's Messenger for whosoever hopes for God and the Last Day" [33:21].

46

Get the book and see that it says: "And hold you fast to God's bond, together" [3:102]. Have you forgotten the bond of God? Have you forgotten the bond of God and the Prophet of God? Oh, if only the great men of the world would respect and teach these matters of which I'm speaking to you! If only! If only! That great gentleman of ours, our noble president, Anwar Sadat, he doesn't really embrace these matters, no, by heaven! And our distinguished prime minister, Mustafa Khalil, likewise doesn't embrace them. Why this is I can't tell you. Long live Anwar Sadat and Mustafa Khalil, long live both of them, the first among men in Egypt who are responsible before God, not before me, but before God!

47

Why isn't the Qur'an our constitution? Why isn't the Qur'an the law and "in the name of God" written beneath all the laws and statutes? And don't say, "in the name of the nation" [*umma*] or "in the name of the people." Yes, the nation is above all our heads because it is of us and we are of it; so too the people are above all our heads because it is of us and we are of it, but God is greatest [*allah akbar*]. God is greater than the prophets, the messengers, the angels and whatever is in heaven or on earth. God is greatest and to him be praise in heaven and on earth, and to him is the majesty in heaven and on earth.

48

When it comes to the nation, the Qur'an speaks of morals [*akhlāq*]. Okay, how many constitutions are there in Arab countries? Are the Arabs united or are they divided? How many leaders are there of Arab armies? Are they victorious or are they defeated? How many teachers are there among adults, youth, and old men? How many wise men? How many doctors at the university? Do they teach or do they not teach? How many? How many? What are they? What are they accomplishing? Nothing but division, defeat, immorality, rancor, hatred, lies, fallacious imported ideas to disgrace women, to destroy the decency of men, to lead the nation to ruin and the people to destruction.

49

Come to the Qur'an then. What does the Prophet say? "There will be persecution." And they said: "Oh Messenger, we have not departed from it." But look at the departures from it. By heaven, the Prophet says nothing of the Communist party, he says nothing of the National Democratic Party, he says nothing of the Socialist Workers Party—and, of course, I respect these parties because they are people, and I'm not against them—but there's something better than that, something more lively than that. There's a party better by a thousand times [Audience: "the party of God," *ḥizb allah*]! Yes, greater than any. Our Lord is Truth, there is only one way. God is one, one Lord, one beginning, one end, one creator. Shame on all of you, don't let yourselves be mocked! "There will be persecution." They said: "Oh Messenger of God, what is the way out [*makhraj minha*] of it?" What's the way out? He said: "The Book of God." The Book of God. The Book of God. That's all.

50

This *ḥadīth* is known in Syria, they know it in Iraq, they know it here, they know it everywhere. The way out of persecution is the book of God. Take this book and none other, all of you, and we have our way out. Study the book of God and you will see the way out of persecution. Take the constitution, you clever ones. Take anyone's speech, you clever ones. Take anything you like, you clever ones. Take the statutes of 1923, you clever ones. Take the statutes of 1953, you clever ones. Take the statutes of 1976, you clever ones. Take them all and what do you get but differences [*ikhtilāf*]?

51

But if only you took the Book! The Book, and apart from it, there is no book. The Constitution, and apart from it there is no constitution. The Method, and apart from it there is no method. The Truth, and apart from it there is no truth. What is the Constitution, the Method, the Truth, and the Book? It is the Qur'an! That's all. And why? I tell you, in it is the warning and the Lord's inspiration, the message of what went before you, wisdom about what is between you and prophecy as to what comes after you. So you should take heed, for it is the clear light, the penetrating decision, the bond of God, the straight path, what scholars never exhaust, nor is it ever exhausted with the wealth of opinions and responses, which was not created, whose wonderment never ends, which even the jinn could not refrain from listening to it as they said: "'We have indeed heard a Qur'an wonderful, guiding to rectitude. We believe in it, and we will not associate with Our Lord anyone'" [72:1–2].

52

Whoever speaks in the name of it is truthful [*ṣadīq*] and whoever works in its name is truthful, and whoever makes decrees in its name is just, and whoever commands by it guides to the straight path, and whoever desires guidance from anything apart from it strays from God, and whoever yearns for a glory other than what belongs to it, God will bring low. That's the Qur'an! Bring me the Book in which are the weighty matters for the benefit of the individual, the Muslim, the society, the nation, in the present and in the future, internally and externally, in reason and in the heart, for the tongue, for work, for aspiration, in the nation and in the whole world. Bring me the Constitution. In it are those weighty matters which are set forth in the Holy Qur'an.

53

Oh you youth, don't be misled, by bringing a lot of other books forward with the Qur'an. And you who belong to Sufi orders, who want to guide the community, you're deluded! Getting involved with parties and pleas is far from the Qur'an! And as for those who are forming a new party, what can we say about that? "O tribe of jinn and of men, if you are able to pass through the confines of heaven and earth, pass through them . . . NOT" [55:33]. "What, did you think that We created you only for sport, and that you would NOT . . ." [23:115]. Why do you take the verse and leave out the *Not?* Finish the verse! Why do you do such a thing, taking only parts and pieces of the Qur'an? The Qur'an was what the Prophet prescribed for recitation, nothing else.

54

I, in my freedom, I take up the Book of God as a call, a summons, a light, a guide, as my method and my conduct. I read it because our Lord said: "Whoever brings the Qur'an to bear on his problem, I will give to him what I have not given to those who petition me. Receive the recitation of the Qur'an." Read it and chant it, for as you chant it in the world so is your place with God in accord with the last Sura and verse that you read. Indeed, the Qur'an is a witness [*shahīd*] and intercession [*mushāfaʿ*]. When the Day of Resurrection comes and the seas and all civilization are overwhelmed, it will intercede for me.

55

So you Sufi *shaykhs* and you members of orders who come to tell me about the party of so and so and the party of this theory or that, or this policy or that—I have One party, One Lord, One master and Prophet and he is Muhammad, prayers and peace upon him.

56

So take up the Qur'an, and next Friday, God willing, I'll bring you the message of Qur'an on unity [*waḥdanīya*], on assembling [*jamʿīya*] and on divisions [*farqīya*] from the first Sura to the last, so you can see that the Qur'an is the party that belongs to you. And let me warn you in the gravest terms about letting your jealousies turn you to someone who calls to something other than the Book and the Sunna. Give the command to your children, to your women, to your men, to your youth, to your old men [*shuyūkh*], to those outside and to those inside regarding the Book and the Sunna, for any departure from the Book and the Sunna is error, deviation, and the broadest destruction. It's all up to you!

57

The Prophet, prayers and peace upon him, epitomizes all the virtues of the perfect man. There is none above him, none like him, none to follow him. "My Lord reared me with the best education." And God bears witness to him when he says, "surely thou art upon a mighty morality" [68:4]. He is supported in Truth, with no flaw in his love or his reason: "By the Star when it plunges, your comrade is not astray, neither errs, nor speaks he out of caprice. This is naught but a revelation revealed, taught him by one terrible in power" [53:1–5]. The successful teacher, in the words of one of his companions: "I have seen no teacher better than he, whether before him or after him." "It is He who has raised up from among the common people a Messenger from among them, to recite His signs to them and to purify them, and to teach them the Book and the Wisdom, though before that they were in manifest error" [62:2].

58

He is a teacher who is pious, sincere, having good counsel, successful, one who teaches Truth, not one who teaches Falsehood, one who teaches fidelity, not lies, a clear teacher, not deceitful, no impostor, a man confirmed, learned, rooted in Truth, not to be shaken, grounded in goodness, not to be toppled: "If they cry lies to thee, then do thou say: 'I have my work, and you have your work; you are quit of what I do, and I am quit of what you do'" [10:41].

59

He is the ruler [*ḥākim*] all-seeing, wise, who does not command rashly or with oppression, nor does he permit the tyrant to triumph, nor does he forsake the oppressed, for "surely We have sent down to thee the Book with the truth, so that thou mayest judge between the people by what God has shown thee. So be not an advocate for the traitors. . . . And do not dispute on behalf of those who betray themselves: surely God does not love the guilty traitor. They hide themselves from men, but hide not themselves from God" [4:105, 107–8].

60

He is the victorious leader. He didn't graduate from the Military Academy, nor from a College of War, nor from a College of Arts, nor from a

College of Engineering, nor from a College of Aerospace. And yet, he laid down, as you know, the civil, the criminal, and the military laws. He supervised the military activities in twenty-eight battles and he didn't lose a single one, and forty-seven expeditions, and he didn't lose one. But as for those other leaders, the leaders of Arab nations, leaders of European nations, leaders of Russian nations who have studied at military academies, how many times have they been defeated? How many times have they lost their soldiers? But Muhammad? Never was he defeated! "Surely We have given thee a manifest victory, that God may forgive thee thy former and thy latter sins, and complete his blessing upon thee, and guide thee on the straight path, and that God may help thee with mighty help" [48:1–3].

61

Come on, all you in the army, come on Muhammad al-Gamasi, the Minister of War, and all you Ministers of War of the Arabs, where did you study? Muhammad didn't study like you did in any military academy. Yet he conquered, first among the Arabs where he was never defeated, then among the Persians where he was never defeated, among the Europeans where he was never defeated, in the whole world where he was never defeated. Why? Because God, exalted be He, taught him. It was the will of God, not his own will, for the promise of God is more perfect than what you promised yourselves, and the knowledge of God is more perfect than what you have learned yourselves. "God has indeed fulfilled the vision He vouchsafed to His Messenger truly: 'You shall enter the Holy Mosque, if God wills, in security, your heads shaved, your hair cut short, not fearing'" [48:27].

62

Why then is not a pious and generous husband and a wise and gracious father the model for a husband and the model for a father, the model for a friend, the model for a neighbor, the model for a teacher, the model for a ruler, the model for a reformer? Why has this faded from the whole world? "Oh God, if the sun were to rise at my right hand and the moon to rise at my left hand, I would not leave this command until God appeared or I was destroyed without Him."

63

So come and listen to the discussion between him and his companions as it came up at the Battle of Hunayn, where there was a great deal of booty: twenty-four thousand camels, forty thousand sheep, four thousand measures of gold and silver. That's a tremendous amount. And to whom did he give all that? He gave it to the Emigrants [Muslims of Mecca who had followed the Prophet to Medina], and some of them were turning in their hearts. But he left out the Ansar [the early Muslim converts of Medina]. And the Ansar said, "Let's just leave him." This talk reached the Prophet, but he didn't get angry or anything; he told them: "Come on, you want something, here, I'll give it to you. Come on, take it. You're welcome to it. What do you think now? Don't you desire to give to those whose hearts are turning and to the poor some of the wealth of the world and its pleasure? Do you want to abandon your faith as well?" They said: "Blessing belongs to God and to His Prophet." He said: "Didn't I find you in error and enrich you with God's guidance? Didn't I find you poor and I gave you the booty of God? What do you have to say to that, Oh Ansar?" They said: "Blessing belongs to God and to His Prophet." He said: "By heaven, if you want something say it! You came to us banished and we gave you shelter, you came to us poor and we have made you rich, you came to us few and we have made you many. By heaven, if the people follow one path and the Ansar follow another path, I have followed the path of the Ansar and not that of the Emigrants. Affairs have been on the side of the Ansar. Oh God, have mercy on the Ansar, on the sons of the Ansar, and the sons of the sons of the Ansar." Then that group wept until their jaws ached. See their faith, see the way their hearts were turned! There is no book, there is no "I am Muhammad, Messenger of God who can destroy your houses!" No, he didn't wish them ill, but he said: "Oh God, have mercy on the Ansar, on the sons of the Ansar, and on the sons of the sons of the Ansar." And they cried until their jaws ached and said: "Blessing belongs to God and to His Prophet." And he said: "May it be enough for you that whereas people return from near and far to their camp, you return to the Messenger of God, for he is your camp." And they said: "Our pleasure is in God our Lord, exalted be He."

64

In Islam is our religion, and in Muhammad is our portion and our prosperity. Say with me: Our pleasure is in God, exalted be He, Lord. [Audience repeats.]

　　Our pleasure is in God, exalted be He, Lord. [Audience repeats.]

　　And in Islam, our religion. [Audience repeats.]

　　And in Muhammad, Messenger of God, our portion and our prosperity. [Audience repeats.]

65

There exists for you in the Messenger of God a good example. And for whom is this Message meant? For every Muslim on the face of the earth, and for every human being who ever was. Who is this example? Who is this model? Who is this method? Muhammad, Messenger of God! Why? Because he is the promise to anyone who would succeed. Listen, I say, success! And what is success? Success is training the spirit, reason, heart, conscience, feelings, morals. It's not magic, like the poet said yesterday, when he said, "your religion and my religion ['aqīdatukum wa 'aqīdatuni] is nourishment [ghadhi] and prosperity." That's changing the divine and unique religion to a religion of the stomach and plants and poetry. No, my friends. Nourishment and prosperity, bread and pure water is not religion, my friends. These are means. Our religion is: There is no god but God. Muhammad is the Messenger of God.

66

As for nourishment, prosperity, fruits, nails, electricity, rivers, dams, homes, villages, apartments, the Nile, all of these are means, my friends, something to be left behind. Religion is something else again. Listen to the Muhammadan religion, to the Muhammadan products, to the Muhammadan education. "Muhammad is the Messenger of God, and those who are with him are hard against the unbelievers, merciful one to another. Thou seest them bowing, prostrating, seeking bounty from God and good pleasure. Their mark is on their faces, the trace of prostration. That is their likeness in the Torah, and their likeness in the Gospel: as a seed that puts forth its shoot, and strengthens it, and it grows stout and rises straight upon its stalk, pleasing the sowers, that through them He may enrage the unbelievers. God has promised those of them that believe and do deeds of righteousness forgiveness and a mighty wage" [48:29].

67

You see what is produced? This product is prosperous, favorable, exalted, brilliant, expensive, lordly, divine, spiritual, angelic. This is the Muhammadan product, that belongs to the whole man, the one confirmed in full, who is complete and entirely pure, the one fully chosen and fully commissioned, the perfect husband, the perfect ascetic, the perfect friend, the perfect teacher, the perfect instructor, the perfect messenger, the loyal comrade. And what is this product? A nation [umma]! A nation to which God bears witness when He says: "Thus we appointed you a midmost nation, that you might be witnesses to the people" [2:143].

68

The Arab nation must return to all of this, to become the judge/arbiter between East and West, between America and Russia, between America and Europe and Russia, between heaven and earth, so that they may exalt peace in Truth, in the name of Truth, in the name of justice, in the name of goodness.

69

Say: Oh God, make us the people of Islam and of faith [*islām wa imān*].
[Audience: Amen.]

Oh God, prayers upon your Prophet, greatest of creatures [Amen].
Oh God make us those who hold to the Qur'an [Amen].

70

Servants of God, I thank you for your weekly attendance at the mosque of
the Sharī'a Society, and I hope to see you all next week.

Notes

INTRODUCTION

1. Michael M. J. Fischer and Mehdi Abedi, *Debating Muslims: Cultural Dialogues in Postmodernity and Tradition* (Madison: University of Wisconsin Press, 1990), xix–xxxv.

2. Ernst Cassirer, *An Essay on Man: An Introduction to a Philosophy of Human Culture* (Garden City, N.Y.: Doubleday, 1954), 237.

3. Frederick M. Denny, "Islamic Ritual: Perspectives and Theories," in *Approaches to Islam in Religious Studies,* ed. Richard C. Martin (Tucson: University of Arizona Press, 1985), 67–68.

1. THE SOCIAL ORGANIZATION OF THE RITUAL SETTING

1. Victor W. Turner, *The Ritual Process: Structure and Anti-Structure* (Harmondsworth: Penguin Books, 1969), 1–39.

2. John G. Neihardt, *Black Elk Speaks: Being the Life Story of a Holy Man of the Oglala Sioux* (Lincoln, Neb.: University of Nebraska Press, 1979), 43.

3. Juan E. Campo, "Authority, Ritual and Spatial Order in Islam: The Pilgrimage to Mecca," *Journal of Ritual Studies* 5, no. 1 (Winter 1991): 71. See also Juan E. Campo, *The Other Side of Paradise: Explorations of Religious Meanings of Domestic Space in Islam* (Columbia, S.C.: University of South Carolina Press, 1991).

4. *Al-Ahram,* March 29, 1985.

5. "Islam Surges as Communism Recedes," *Chicago Tribune,* March 1, 1992.

6. Marshall G. S. Hodgson, *The Venture of Islam: Conscience and History in a World Civilization,* vol. 1 (Chicago: University of Chicago Press, 1974), 89.

7. Mohammed Arkoun, *L'Islam: Morale et Politique* (Paris: Desclée de Brouwer, 1986), 47–80.

8. Claude Cahen, "The Body Politic," in Gustave E. von Grunebaum, *Unity and Variety in Muslim Civilization* (Chicago: University of Chicago Press, 1955),

132–63; Irving Louis Horowitz, "Religion, the State, and Politics," in *Religion and Politics*, vol. 3 of *Political Anthology* (New Brunswick: Transaction Books, 1984), 5–10; Dale F. Eickelman, "Changing Interpretations of Islamic Movements," in *Islam and the Political Economy of Meaning*, ed. William R. Roff (Berkeley: University of California Press, 1987), 130.

9. Ira M. Lapidus, "The Separation of State and Religion," *International Journal of Middle Eastern Studies* 6 (1975): 363–85.

10. Morroe Berger, *Islam in Egypt Today: Social and Political Aspects of Popular Religion* (Cambridge: Cambridge University Press, 1970), 130. Emphasis in the original.

11. Ali E. H. Dessouki, "Official Islam and Political Legitimation in the Arab Countries," in *The Islamic Impulse*, ed. Barbara Stowasser (London: Croom Helm, 1987), 135–41.

12. Guenter Lewy, *Religion and Revolution* (New York: Oxford University Press, 1974), 443–61.

13. Hamied Ansari, "The Islamic Militants in Egyptian Politics," *International Journal of Middle Eastern Studies* 16 (1984): 123–44.

14. Jean-Jacques Waardenburg, "Islam Studies as a Symbol and Signification System," *Humaniora Islamica* 2 (1974): 267–85; Jerrold D. Green, "Islam, Religiopolitics, and Social Change," *Comparative Studies in Society and History* 27, no. 2 (1985): 312–22; Clifford Geertz, *Islam Observed: Religious Development in Morocco and Indonesia* (Chicago: University of Chicago Press, 1971).

15. Ali Merad, "The Ideologization of Islam in the Contemporary Muslim World," in *Islam and Power*, ed. A. S. Cudsi and A. E. H. Dessouki (Baltimore: Johns Hopkins University Press, 1981), 42–43.

16. W. Montgomery Watt, *Muhammad at Mecca* (London: Oxford University Press, 1953), 123.

17. "Masjid," in *Encyclopedia of Islam*, 1st ed. (Leiden: E. J. Brill, 1931), 3:331.

18. Tor Andrae, *Mohammed: The Man and His Faith*, trans. Theophil Menzel (New York: Barnes and Noble, 1935), 13–30.

19. Eric Wolf, "The Social Organization of Mecca and the Origins of Islam," *Southwestern Journal of Anthropology* 7 (Winter 1951): 329–56.

20. Alfred Guillaume, *The Life of Muhammad: A Translation of Ishaq's Sirat Rasul Allah* (Lahore: Oxford University Press, 1955), 609–10.

21. Fazlur Rahman, *Islam* (Garden City, N.Y.: Doubleday, 1968), 60.

22. Thomas Arnold, *The Caliphate* (London: Oxford University Press, 1924), 19.

23. Hodgson, *The Venture of Islam*, 1:217–18.

24. Max Weber, *Sociology of Religion*, trans. Ephraim Fischoff (Boston: Beacon, 1963); Bryan S. Turner, *Weber and Islam* (London: Routledge & Kegan Paul, 1974). Closely related is the Weberian issue of the "Islamic City"; cf. Dale F. Eickelman, *The Middle East: An Anthropological Perspective*, 2nd ed. (Englewood Cliffs, N.J.: Prentice-Hall, 1989), 261–88.

25. Emile Durkheim, *Elementary Forms of Religious Life*, trans. Joseph W. Swain (New York: Free Press, 1961), 471.

26. Oleg Grabar, "The Architecture of the Middle Eastern City from Past to Present: The Case of the Mosque," in *Middle Eastern Cities*, ed. Ira M. Lapidus (Berkeley: University of California Press, 1969), 26–46. Roger Joseph, "Toward a

Semiotics of Middle Eastern Cultures," *International Journal of Middle Eastern Studies* 12 (November 1980): 319–29.

27. Edward Shils, *Center and Periphery: Essays in Macrosociology* (Chicago: University of Chicago Press, 1975), 4.

28. Dale F. Eickelman, *Moroccan Islam: Tradition and Society in a Pilgrimage Center* (Austin: University of Texas Press, 1976), 211–38; Victor Turner and Edith Turner, *Image and Pilgrimage in Christian Culture: Anthropological Perspectives* (New York: Columbia University Press, 1978).

29. Richard P. Mitchaell, *The Society of Muslim Brothers* (London: Oxford University Press, 1969), 5.

30. Linda G. Jones, "Portrait of Rashid al-Ghannoushi," *Middle East Report* 153 (1988): 19.

2. THE AUTHORITY OF PREACHERS

1. Edmund R. Leach, Introduction to *Dialectic in Practical Religion*, ed. E. R. Leach, Cambridge Papers in Social Anthropology no. 5 (Cambridge: Cambridge University Press, 1968), 1–12.

2. Marc Bloch, *The Historian's Craft* (New York: Vintage Books, 1953), 29.

3. Edmund Burke, III, "Islam and Social Movements: Methodological Reflections," in *Islam, Politics, and Social Movements*, ed. Edmund Burke, III, and Ira M. Lapidus (Berkeley: University of California Press, 1988), 26.

4. Talal Asad, "Religion and Politics: An Introduction." *Social Research* 59, no. 1 (Spring 1992): 5.

5. Clifford Geertz, *The Interpretation of Cultures* (New York: Basic Books, 1973), 87–125.

6. Emile Durkheim, *The Elementary Forms of Religious Life*, trans. Joseph W. Swain (New York: Free Press, 1965).

7. A. R. Radcliffe-Brown, "Religion and Society," in *Structure and Function in Primitive Society* (New York: Free Press, 1952), 160–161.

8. Bassam Tibi, *The Crisis of Modern Islam: A Preindustrial Culture in the Scientific-Technological Age* (Salt Lake City: University of Utah Press, 1988); and Asaf Hussain et al., eds., *Orientalism, Islam and Islamists* (Brattleboro, Vt.: Amana Books, 1984).

9. Ernest Gellner, *Muslim Society* (Cambridge: Cambridge University Press, 1981), 35 ff.

10. Jean-Jacques Waardenburg, "Official and Popular Religion in Islam," *Social Compass* 25, nos. 3–4 (1978): 315–41; Gustave E. von Grunebaum, "The Problem: Unity in Diversity," in *Unity and Variety in Muslim Civilization*, ed. G. E. von Grunebaum (Chicago: University of Chicago Press, 1955), 17–37.

11. Dale F. Eickelman and James Piscatori, "Social Theory in the Study of Muslim Societies," in *Muslim Travellers: Pilgrimage, Migration, and the Religious Imagination*, ed. Dale F. Eickelman and James Piscatori (Berkeley: University of California Press, 1990), 3–25.

12. Dale F. Eickelman, *The Middle East: An Anthropological Approach*, 2d ed. (Englewood Cliffs, N.J.: Prentice-Hall, 1989), 45–62.

13. Edward W. Said, *Orientalism* (New York: Pantheon, 1978), 326. The reconsideration of Geertz appears in *Middle East Report* 151 (January–February 1988): 34.

14. David D. Laitin, *Hegemony and Culture: Politics and Religious Change among the Yoruba* (Chicago: University of Chicago Press, 1986), 24; Henry Munson, Jr., "Geertz on Religion: The Theory and the Practice," *Religion* 14 (1986): 19–32; Talal Asad, "Anthropological Conceptions of Religion: Reflections on Geertz," *Man*, n.s. 18 (1983): 237–59.

15. Abdul-Hamid M. el-Zein, "Beyond Ideology and Theology: The Search for an Anthropology of Islam," in *Annual Review of Anthropology*, ed. Bernard Siegel (Palo Alto: Annual Reviews, 1977), 227–54. Lloyd A. Fallers, Foreword to Abdul-Hamid M. el-Zein, *The Sacred Meadows: A Structural Analysis of Religious Symbolism in an East African Town* (Evanston, Ill.: Northwestern University Press, 1974), xvi.

16. Dale F. Eickelman, "The Study of Islam in Local Context," *Contributions to Asian Studies* 17 (1982): 1–16; Dale F. Eickelman et al., "Islam and the District Paradigm," *Current Anthropology* 24 (1983): 81–87.

17. Dale F. Eickelman, "Changing Interpretations of Islamic Movements," in *Islam and the Political Economy of Meaning*, ed. William R. Roff (Berkeley: University of California Press, 1987), 16.

18. Gabriel Baer, *Studies in the Social History of Modern Egypt* (Chicago: University of Chicago Press, 1969), 30–61.

19. *Al-Ahram*, May 5, 1985, 8.

20. Edward W. Lane, *An Account of the Manners and Customs of the Modern Egyptians* (London: J. M. Dent & Sons, 1908 [1836]), 87.

21. Patrick D. Gaffney, "The Office of the Wāʿiẓ and the Revival of Preaching in Egypt," *Mélanges de l'Institut Dominicain d'Etudes Orientales* 17 (1986): 247–56.

22. Such terms include *mudhakkir*, "one who reminds"; *qāṣṣ*, "one who relates stories"; *ustādh*, a generalized term for "sir" or "gentleman" which also denotes "professor." Other terms which derive more from the tradition of Sufism include *mawla*, meaning "lord" or "master"; *naqīb*, the overseer or presider of the liturgy; *quṭb*, who is the head of a hierarchy of *awliyā* or saints, etc. Johannes Pedersen, "The Islamic Preacher: Waʿiz, Mudhakkir, Qass," in *Ignaz Goldziher Memorial Volume*, ed. S. Lowinger and J. Ssomogyi, (Budapest: 1948), 1:227–51.

23. The term is used in this way, for example, by Dr. Muhammad al-Bahi, himself an Azhari, and one-time Minister of Religious Endowments under ʿAbd al-Nasir. See al-Bahi, *Hayātī fī Raḥab al-Azhar* (My Life in the Setting of the Azhar) (Cairo: Maktaba Waḥba, 1983).

24. Yvonne Y. Haddad, "Muslim Revivalist Thought in the Arab World: An Overview," *The Muslim World* 76, nos. 3–4 (1986): 143–67; Marshall G. S. Hodgson, "A Note on the Millennium in Islam," in *Comparative Studies in Society and History*, supp. 2, *Millenial Dreams in Action*, ed. Sylvia L. Thrupp (The Hague: Mouton & Co., 1962), 218–19.

25. The implications of militancy that surround the term *dāʿiya* may be seen in the titles of two well-known and controversial pamphlets with virtually identical titles but sharply opposing points of view. *Mushkalāt al-Daʿwa w-al-Dāʿiya* (Problems of the Call and the Preacher), by Fathi Yakun (Beirut: Muʾasasa al-Rasāla, 1980 [1968]), is a combination manifesto and handbook advocating the forceful political application of Islam. Dr. Muhammad Hussain al-Dhahabi, at one time Minister of Religious Endowments in Egypt, in 1976 authored an aggressive

condemnation of the excesses of the Islamist tendency entitled *Mushkalāt al-Daʿwa w-al-Duʿāh* (The Problems of the Call and Preachers). In February 1977, its author was kidnapped and subsequently murdered by members of a group that later became known as *al-Takfīr wa al-Hijra* (Condemnation and Holy Flight). Of course, in the history of the Muslim Brothers this term also appears in the significant title of what many have seen as the "revisionist" statement by the second Supreme Guide, Hassan Hudaybi, whose book *Duʿāh Lā Quḍāh* (Preachers, Not Judges), appearing in 1969, was written while he was in one of ʿAbd al-Nasir's prisons.

26. R. Towler, "The Social Status of the Anglican Minister," in *Sociology of Religion,* ed. Roland Robertson (New York: Penguin, 1969), 446.

27. Erving Goffman, *Encounters: Two Studies in the Sociology of Interaction* (Indianapolis: Bobbs-Merrill, 1961), 95.

28. Richard T. Antoun, "Key Variables Affecting Muslim Local-Level Religious Leadership in Iran and Jordan," in *Leadership and Development in Arab Society,* ed. Fuad I. Khuri (Beirut: Center for Arab and Middle East Studies, American University of Beirut, 1989), 92–101.

29. Fazlur Rahman, *Islam* (Garden City, N.Y.: Doubleday, Anchor Books, 1966), 62.

30. Bryan S. Turner, *Weber and Islam* (London: Routledge & Kegan Paul, 1974), 66.

31. Fazlur Rahman, *Islam,* 118 ff.

32. Michael D. Gilsenan, *Recognizing Islam: Religion and Society in the Modern Arab World* (New York: Pantheon, 1982), 27 ff.

33. Lois A. Aroian, *The Nationalization of Arabic and Islamic Education in Egypt: Dar al-Alum and Al-Azhar,* Cairo Papers in Social Science no. 6 (December 1983).

34. Jerrold D. Green, "Islam, Religiopolitics, and Social Change," *Comparative Studies in Society and History* 27, no. 2 (1985): 312–22.

35. Max Weber, *The Sociology of Religion,* trans. Ephraim Fischoff (Boston: Beacon, 1963), 21.

36. Weber, *Sociology of Religion,* 28–29.

37. The use of the word "saint" in the literature on Islamic figures variously known as *walī, shaykh, murābiṭ, ṣāliḥ, agha, murshid, pir,* etc. has been criticized by some, notably by Bryan Turner. The argument is that "saint" conveys a Christian bias inappropriate to the Islamic context. This caution may well be extended to a whole array of terms such as priest, preacher, magician, etc. all of which require qualification. It might also be argued, however, that such terms are not only useful but essential for comparative study although issues of proper translation always need to be discussed. The term "saint" in English is a polyvalent reference that extends to many cultural forms besides the one narrowly defined by Roman Catholic regulations of canonization as Turner exclusively treats it. See Turner, *Weber and Islam,* 56–71; and William M. Brinner, "Prophet and Saint: The Two Exemplars of Islam," in *Saints and Virtues,* ed. John Stratton Hawley (Berkeley: University of California Press, 1987), 36–51.

38. On variations in the structural character of rural and urban societies, especially in the light of "tribal" social dynamics, see Robert A. Fernea, "Gaps in the Ethnographic Literature on the Middle Eastern Village: A Classificatory Explo-

ration," in *Rural Politics and Social Change in the Middle East*, ed. Richard Antoun and Iliya Harik (Bloomington: University of Indiana Press, 1972), 75–102.

39. Marcel Mauss, *A General Theory of Magic*, trans. Robert Brain (London: Routledge & Kegan Paul, 1972), 88–89.

40. Peter Brown, "The Rise and Function of the Holy Man in Late Antiquity," *Journal of Roman Studies* 61 (1971): 100.

41. Michael D. Gilsenan, "Some Factors in the Decline of the Sufi Orders in Modern Egypt," *The Muslim World* 57 (1967): 11–18; and Michael Brett, "The Spread of Islam in Egypt and North Africa," in *Northern Africa: Islam and Modernization*, ed. Michael Brett (London: Frank Cass, 1973), 1–12.

42. Michael Gilsenan, "Lying, Honor, and Contradiction," in *Transaction and Meaning: Directions in the Anthropology of Exchange and Symbolic Behavior*, ed. Bruce Kapferer (Philadelphia: Institute for the Study of Human Issues, 1976), 207.

43. Weber, *Sociology of Religion*, 154.

44. Weber, *Sociology of Religion*, 154–55.

45. Weber, *Sociology of Religion*, 192 ff. For the original text, see Max Weber, *Wirtschaft und Gesellschaft: Grundriss der Verstehenden Soziologie*, 5th rev. ed. (Tubingen: J. C. B. Mohr, 1976), 340.

46. Max Weber, *Sociology of Religion*, 49.

47. Dale F. Eickelman, *Knowledge and Power in Morocco: The Education of a Twentieth-Century Notable* (Princeton: Princeton University Press, 1985); Brinkley Messick, "The Mufti, the Text and the World: Legal Interpretation in Yemen," *Man*, n.s. 21, no. 1 (1986): 102–119.

48. Rémy Leveau, "Réaction de l'Islam Officiel au Renouveau Islamique au Moroc," *Annuaire de L'Afrique du Nord* 18 (1980): 205–218; Patrick D. Gaffney, "The Changing Voices of Islam: The Emergence of Professional Preachers in Contemporary Egypt," *The Muslim World* 81, no. 1 (1991): 27–47.

49. Ali Dessouki, cited in Youssef M. Ibrahim, "Mosque and State: Militant Islam Confronts Secular Egypt," *Wall Street Journal*, August 10, 1987.

50. Jacques Waardenburg, "Islam as a Vehicle of Protest," in *Islamic Dilemmas: Reformers, Nationalists and Industrialization*, ed. Ernest Gellner (Berlin: Mouton, 1985), 34.

51. Fuad I. Khuri, "The Ulama: A Comparative Study of Sunni and Shi'a Religious Officials," *Middle Eastern Studies* 23, no. 3 (1987): 285–98.

52. Salah Abu Isma'il, *Shahdaāt al-Ḥaqq fī Qaḍiyat al-'Aṣr* [Witness to truth amid the predicament of the age] (Cairo: Dar al-'Itisām, 1984), 31 ff.

53. The chapter on the Prophet's military achievements is by far the longest in al-'Aqqad's book. See E. S. Sabanegh, *Muhammad le Prophète: Portraits Contemporains, Egypte 1930–1950* (Paris: Librairie J. Vrin, 1981), 367 ff. Also see Christian Decorbert, *Le Mendiant et le Combattant: L'Institution de l'Islam* (Paris: Seuil, 1991).

54. A. Chris Eccel, "'Alim and Mujahid in Egypt: Orthodoxy versus Subculture, or Division of Labor?" *The Muslim World* 78, nos. 3–4 (1988), 189–208.

55. Such views permeate Sadat's treatment of the October War and later his quest for peace. See Anwar el-Sadat, *In Search of Identity: An Autobiography* (Glasgow: William Collins, 1978), 277–372.

56. John Renard, *"Al-Jihad al-Akbar:* Notes on a Theme in Islamic Spirituality," *The Muslim World* 78, nos. 3–4 (1988): 225–42.

57. Rudolph Peters, *Islam and Colonialism: The Doctrine of Jihad in Modern History* (The Hague: Mouton, 1979), 119.

58. Weber, *Sociology of Religion,* 85.

59. Dale F. Eickelman, "Religion in Polity and Society," in *The Political Economy of Morocco,* ed. I. William Zartman (New York: Praeger, 1987), 85.

60. Norma Salem, *Habib Bourguiba, Islam, and the Creation of Tunisia* (London: Croom Helm, 1984), 103.

61. Michael Brett, "Mufti, Murabit, Marabout and Mahdi: Four Types in the Islamic History of North Africa," *Révue de l'Occident musulman et de la Mediterranée* 29, no. 1 (1980): 14.

62. Fadwa El Guindi, "The Emerging Islamic Order: The Case of Egypt's Contemporary Islamic Movement," *Journal of Arab Affairs* 1, no. 2 (1982): 245–62.

63. The enormous influence of the prolific writer and television personality Dr. Mustafa Mahmud in Egypt and abroad reflects this perspective. See John L. Esposito and John Donohue, eds., *Islam in Transition: Muslim Perspectives* (New York: Oxford University Press, 1982), 155–59. No less dramatic has been the remarkable appeal among many educated Muslims of a book by an eccentric French physician that purports to demonstrate the scientific accuracy of the contents of the Qur'an as contrasted with the Bible. I have heard this book praised from the pulpit in Upper Egypt. See Maurice Bucaille, *The Bible, the Qur'an and Science,* trans. Alastair D. Pannell and Maurice Bucaille (Indianapolis: North American Trust Publications, 1978).

64. Muhammad Khalid Thabat, *Ghaḍab li-Allah* [Outrage for God] (Cairo: Dar al-Thabat, 1983). The author of this pamphlet lashes out at several leading Egyptian intellectuals, notably, Tawfiq al-Hakim, Yusuf Idris, and Zaki Najib Mahmud, whom he condemns for their secular views. The term which forms the work's title is used by Islamists to cover a range of activities from "civil disobedience" to a direct resort to violence.

65. Bryan R. Wilson, *The Noble Savages: The Primitive Origins of Charisma and Its Contemporary Survival* (Berkeley: University of California Press, 1975), 95.

66. Roger Joseph, "The Semiotics of the Islamic Mosque," *Arab Studies Quarterly* 3, no. 3 (1981): 291–92.

67. Ira M. Lapidus, *Muslim Cities in the Later Middle Ages,* 2d ed. (Cambridge: Cambridge University Press, 1984).

68. Juan E. Campo, "Mubarak's Khitat: An Egyptian Nationalist Valuation of Religious Space," paper presented at the meetings of the Middle East Studies Associations, Los Angeles, 1988.

69. Henri Lammens, *Islam: Beliefs and Institutions,* trans. E. Denison Ross (London: Frank Cass, 1968), 102 ff. For a more historically qualified account of this regulation, see Walter Denny, "Contradiction and Consistency in Islamic Art," in *The Islamic Impact,* ed. Yvonne Y. Haddad et al. (Syracuse, N.Y.: Syracuse University Press, 1984), 137–74.

70. Maurice Gaudefroy-Demombynes, *Les Institutions Musulmanes* (Paris: Flamarion, 1946), 79.

71. Jasper Yeates Brinton, *The Mixed Courts of Egypt* (New Haven: Yale University Press, 1930), 116.

72. Gabriel Baer, *Studies in the Social History of Modern Egypt* (Chicago: University of Chicago Press, 1969), 79–92.

73. Morroe Berger, *Islam in Egypt Today: Social and Political Aspects of Popular Religion* (Cambridge: Cambridge University Press, 1970), 18.

74. Gilles Kepel and Kamel T. Barbar, *Les Waqfs dans l'Egypte Contemporaine* (Cairo: Centre d'Etudes et Documentation Economiques Juridiques et Sociales, n.d. [1982]), 35.

75. A. Chris Eccel, *Egypt, Islam and Social Change: Al-Azhar in Conflict and Accommodation* (Berlin: Klaus Schwartz, 1984), 531.

76. Donna Robertson Divine, "The Rites of Nationalism: One Meaning of Egypt's Struggle for Political Independence," *Canadian Review of Studies in Nationalism* 8, no. 1 (1981): 37–54.

77. Morroe Berger, *Islam in Egypt Today*, 111.

78. Nazih Ayubi, *Bureaucracy and Politics in Contemporary Egypt* (London: Ithaca Press, 1980), 456. The texts of the basic laws that provide for the chartering and operation of these societies, including the handling of their finances, are reprinted in Isis Istiphan, *Directory of Social Agencies in Cairo* (Cairo: Social Research Center of the American University at Cairo, 1956), Appendixes 3 and 4, 475–95.

79. This misleading impression is left by a number of authors who associate private mosques directly with Islamic militancy. See, for example, Hamied Ansari, *Egypt: The Stalled Society* (Albany: State University of New York Press, 1986), 218.

80. Gilles Kepel, *Muslim Extremism in Egypt: The Prophet and the Pharaoh*, trans. Jon Rothchild (Berkeley: University of California Press, 1986), 81.

81. John Obert Voll, "Revivalism and Social Transformation in Islamic History," *The Muslim World* 76, nos. 3–4 (1986): 178.

82. Friedemann Büttner, "Political Stability without Stable Institutions: The Retraditionalization of Egypt's Polity," *Orient* 20 (1979): 62.

83. Amira El-Azhary Sonbol, "Egypt," in *The Politics of Islamic Revivalism: Diversity and Unity*, ed. Shireen T. Hunter (Bloomington: University of Indiana Press, 1988), 26.

84. Mohammed Heikal, *Autumn of Fury: The Assassination of Sadat* (New York: Random House, 1983), 232–34.

85. Mohamed Tozy and Bruno Etienne, "Le Modèle Kichkiste et son Impact" in *Radicalismes Islamiques*, ed. P. Dumont, 2 vols. (Paris: L'Harmattan, 1986), 2:17–32.

86. Richard P. Mitchaell, *The Society of the Muslim Brothers* (London: Oxford University Press, 1969), 260.

87. Peter Levi, *The Frontiers of Paradise: A Study of Monks and Monasteries* (New York: Weidenfeld & Nicolson, 1987), 31.

88. Max Black, "More About Metaphor," in *Metaphor and Thought*, ed. Andrew Ortony (Cambridge: Cambridge University Press, 1979), 19–43.

89. Richard T. Antoun, *Muslim Preacher in the Modern World: A Jordanian Case Study in Comparative Perspective* (Princeton: Princeton University Press, 1989), 37.

90. George Lakoff, *Women, Fire, and Dangerous Things: What Categories Reveal about the Mind* (Chicago: University of Chicago Press, 1987), 203.

91. George Lakoff, *Women, Fire, and Dangerous Things,* 60–61.

92. Cited in Hassanayn Krum, "Al-Tayyār al-Dīnī fī Misr: Tarikhihū wa-Mustaqbilihū" [The Islamic Tendency in Egypt: Its History and Its Future], *Al-Manār* 2 (June 1986): 49.

93. Bryan R. Wilson, *The Noble Savages,* 24–25.

94. Pierre Bourdieu, "An Antinomy in the Notion of Collective Protest," in *Development, Democracy, and the Art of Trespassing: Essays in Honor of Albert O. Hirshman,* ed. Alejandro Foxley et al. (Notre Dame, Ind.: University of Notre Dame Press, 1986), 302.

95. Henri Bergson, *The Two Sources of Morality and Religion,* trans. R. Ashley Audra et al. (Garden City, N.Y.: Doubleday, 1954), 31.

3. THE MOSQUE AND THE CULT OF THE SAINT

1. The only major battle fought in Upper Egypt between the invading Arab Muslims and the occupying Byzantine forces occurred in A.D. 651 at a fortress situated at the edge of the Western desert some thirty kilometers north of Minya, near the village of Bahnasa. The Muslims prevailed but not before many had died, among them 'Abd al-Rahman, son of Abu Bakr, the first Caliph. Today a large cemetery, punctuated with shrines amid the ruins, covers the area.

2. His full name: 'Ali ibn Muhammad 'Alī al-Masrī al-Yamanī al-Shahīr bābī Ahmad al-Fulī. 'Ali Bayumi, *Aḍwā' 'ala Tārīkh al-Minyā* (Light on the History of Minya) (Minya: Privately published, n.d.), 87.

3. Edward Lane, *An Account of the Manners and Customs of the Modern Egyptians* (London: J. M. Dent & Sons, 1908 [1836]); chapter 10, "Superstitions" has a long description of "saints." See also Rudolf Kriss, *Volksglaube im Bereich des Islam,* 2 vols. (Wiesbaden: Otto Harassowitz, 1960), 1:53 ff.

4. Bayumi, *Aḍwā',* 87–89.

5. Edward B. Reeves, *The Hidden Government: Ritual, Clientelism, and Legitimation in Northern Egypt* (Salt Lake City: University of Utah Press, 1990). The extensive discussion of contemporary Egypt's saints' shrines in this work includes background on the social history and analysis of their financial and political support.

6. Clifford Geertz, *Islam Observed: Religious Development in Morocco and Indonesia.* (Chicago: University of Chicago Press, 1971), 49. On Ben Badis, see Salah El-Din El-Zein El-Tayed, "The 'Ulama and Islamic Renaissance in Algeria," *American Journal of Islamic Social Sciences* 6 (1989): 261.

7. F. de Jong, *Turuq and Turuq-linked Institutions in Nineteenth-Century Egypt* (Leiden: E. J. Brill, 1978); Gilbert Delanoue, *Moralistes et Politiques Musulmans dans L'Egypte du XIXe Siècle* (Cairo: Institut Français d'Archéologie Orientale, 1982); Michael D. Gilsenan, "Some Factors in the Decline of the Sufi Orders in Modern Egypt," *The Muslim World* 57 (1967): 11–18.

8. Dale F. Eickelman, "Ideological Change and Regional Cults: Maraboutism and Ties of 'Closeness' in Western Morocco," in *Regional Cults,* ed. R. P. Werbner, Association of Social Anthropologists Monograph, no. 6 (New York: Academic Press, 1977): 3–28.

9. D. S. Margoliouth, *Mohammedanism* (London: Williams and Norgate, 1911), 198–99.

10. Mark Twain, *Innocents Abroad, or the New Pilgrim's Progress,* 2 vols. (New York: Harper and Brothers, 1869), 1:231.

11. Pierre Bourdieu, "Une Interprétation de la Théorie de la Religion selon Weber," *Archives Européennes de Sociologie* 12 (1971): 3-21. Mohamed Tozy, "Monopolisation de la Production Symbolique et Hiérarchisation du Champ Politico-Religieux au Moroc," *Annuaire de L'Afrique du Nord* 18 (1981): 219–34.

12. Emile Dermenghem, "Le Saint et le Lieu Saint" in *Le Culte des Saints dans l'Islam Maghrébin* (Paris: Gallimard, 1954), 34–53.

13. Nathan J. Brown, *Peasant Politics in Modern Egypt: The Struggle against the State* (New Haven: Yale University Press, 1990).

14. M. S. Abdel Hakim and Wassim Abdel Hamid, *Some Aspects of Urbanisation in Egypt* (Durham: Center for Middle Eastern and Islamic Studies, University of Durham, 1982), Occasional Paper no. 15; and Gabriel Baer, *Studies in the Social History of Modern Egypt* (Chicago: University of Chicago Press, 1969), 133–48.

15. Central Agency for Public Mobilization and Statistics, *Statistical Year Book, Arab Republic of Egypt* (Cairo: CAPMAS, 1984).

16. These two are identified as Shaykh Ahmad Hatatah and Shaykh Muhammad Mirghani. Unfortunately, no further affiliation is given. See Bayumi, *Aḍwāʾ,* 123.

17. This holiday, called the "national holiday of Minya" (*ʿīd al-minyā al-qawmī*), is celebrated on March 18. Interestingly, Dier al-Mawas has remained something of a backwater compared to many other towns on the direct rail and highway route. Many of the residents claim that their town was deliberately neglected by both European and Egyptian officialdom after this incident. They feel that a tacit continuation of this cold shoulder from the present government has stunted their overall development. This is hardly the reward they think they deserve for those rebel shots of their ancestors upon the foreign oppressors.

18. Marshall G. S. Hodgson, *The Venture of Islam,* vol. 3: *The Gunpowder Empires and Modern Times* (Chicago: University of Chicago Press, 1974), 285.

19. Abdul Rahman Fahmy, "A Place Under the Dome," in *Egyptian Short Stories,* trans. Denys Johnson-Davies (London: Heinemann, 1978), 87.

20. Carl Petry, "Geographic Origins of Religious Functionaries in Cairo during the Fifteenth Century," *Journal of the Economic and Social History of the Orient* 23, no. 3 (1980): 259.

21. Bimbashi [Colonel John W.] McPherson, *The Man Who Loved Egypt* (London: Ariel Books/British Broadcasting Corporation, 1985).

22. [Colonel] John W. McPherson, *The Moulids of Egypt: Egyptian Saints-Days* (Cairo: N. M. Press, 1941), 198.

23. In the magnum opus of the Supreme Council on Islamic Affairs entitled *Masājid Misr wa-Awliyāʾha al-Ṣālihūn (The Mosques of Egypt and Their Blessed Saints),* two bulky volumes published by the Ministry of Religious Endowments in 1971, there is no mention whatsoever of al-Fuli. The work illustrates in this regard the age-old concentration of Egyptian governments upon the capital city. In the first volume, which gives elaborate historical and archaeological accounts of forty-five mosques, including a long section on al-Azhar, only four are from Upper Egypt. In the second volume, the proportion is even smaller. Out of fifty-seven mosques discussed, only three are in Upper Egypt. The selections in these volumes further demonstrate how vital it is for a *walī* to

have a mosque of appropriate dignity (and/or antiquity), since a saint without a monument seems soon forgotten while a monument without a saint may eventually find a patron to suit it.

24. Gabriel Baer, "Ali Mubarak's Khitat as a Source for the History of Modern Egypt," in *Political and Social Change in Modern Egypt,* ed. P. M. Holt (London: Oxford University Press, 1968).

25. ʿAli Pasha Mubarak, *Al-Khiṭāṭ al-Tawfīqīya al-Jidīda,* 20 vols. (Cairo: Bulaq, 1886–1889), 16:51.

26. This statement is heard frequently. It is also given in Bayumi, *Aḍwāʾ,* 87.

27. The name ibn Khasīb does retain a token visibility in Minya since one of the streets in the new quarter bears the name. However, here and elsewhere official street names are seldom if ever used by the local population, nor are they usually marked except on maps, which are rarely available. Also, there is a tourist hotel called Ibn Khasīb located on this same street which caters almost exclusively to Europeans or wealthy urban Egyptians.

28. *Musawīr,* April 6, 1979.

29. Properly speaking the place for ritual ablutions is called a *mīḍāʾa,* from *wuḍūʾ,* meaning the ritual washing itself. However, in colloquial parlance such an area is referred to as the *hammām,* literally, the "bathroom." This second term, like its English cognate, is a euphemism and does not refer specifically to a "bath." The explicit term for a modern toilet, though not used in polite company, is *daurat al-miyāh,* a literal translation of the British W.C., "water closet." Incidentally, there are no public baths in Minya that I could discover.

30. McPherson, *Moulids,* 268. He refers to this shrine as the "Pantheon." See also an extensive treatment in Supreme Council, *Masājid Misrī,* 1:264 ff.

31. Morroe Berger, "The Mosque: Aspects of Government Policy," *Middle East Studies* 6, no. 1 (January 1970): 47–82.

32. Muhammad Rashid al-Rafaʿi, "Makān al-Masjid fī al-Madīnat al-ʿArabīya" (The Place of the Mosque in the Arab City), in *Takhṭīṭ al-Mudun fī al-ʿAlam al-ʿArabīya* (Urban Planning in the Arab World), ed. Morroe Berger (Cairo: n.p., n.d.), 137. This article was written and presented in conjunction with a conference on the Arab city held in Cairo in December of 1960. An English volume with some dozen of these papers was published in English under the title *The New Metropolis in the Arab World,* ed. Morroe Berger (New Delhi: Allied Publishers, 1960). However, the article cited here was printed only in the Arabic collection.

33. Victor Turner, *The Ritual Process: Structure and Anti-Structure* (Harmondsworth: Penguin, 1969), 125.

34. Henri Ayrout, *The Egyptian Peasant,* trans. John Williams (Boston: Beacon, 1971), 93.

35. Michael D. Gilsenan, *Recognizing Islam: Religion and Society in the Modern Arab World* (New York: Pantheon, 1982), 75 ff.

36. Central Agency for Public Mobilization and Statistics, *Statistical Year Book, Arab Republic of Egypt* (Cairo: CAPMAS, 1984), 13.

37. World Bank, *Egypt: Alleviating Poverty during Structural Adjustment* (Washington, D.C.: World Bank, 1991), 191.

38. Richard H. Adams, Jr., *Development and Social Change in Rural Egypt* (Syracuse, N.Y.: Syracuse University Press, 1986), 166.

39. Bayumi, *Aḍwāʾ*, p. 86.

40. R. Arnaldez, "al-Kurtubi," in *Encyclopedia of Islam*, new ed. (Leiden: E. J. Brill, 1982), 5:512.

41. A sometimes high-handed traffic in sacred relics, such as this case suggests, is not uncommon where the boundaries between competing groups even with different types of beliefs intersect. See Michael A. Marcus, " 'The Saint Has Been Stolen': Sanctity and Social Change in a Tribe of Eastern Morocco," *American Ethnologist* 12, no. 3 (1985): 455–67.

4. ISLAMIZATION

1. Nadia Ramsis Farah, *Religious Strife in Egypt: Crisis and Ideological Conflict in the Seventies* (New York: Gordon and Breach Science Publishers, 1986).

2. Saad Eddin Ibrahim, "Islamic Militancy as a Social Movement: The Case of Two Groups in Egypt," in *Islamic Resurgence in the Arab World*, ed. Ali E. Hillal Dessouki (New York: Praeger, 1982), 117–37.

3. William E. Shepard, "Islam as a 'System' in the Later Writings of Sayyid Qutb," *Middle Eastern Studies* 25 (1989): 31–50.

4. Saad Eddin Ibrahim, "Anatomy of Egypt's Militant Islamic Groups: Methodological Notes and Preliminary Findings," *International Journal of Middle Eastern Studies* 12 (December 1980): 452.

5. "Egypt's Khomeini," *The Guardian Weekly*, March 14, 1993.

6. Ibrahim, "Anatomy of Egypt's Militant Islamic Groups," 447. He defines this as "strong achievement motivation, with justified high aspiration, yet little economic and political opportunity."

7. Richard T. Antoun, *Muslim Preacher in the Modern World: A Jordanian Case Study in Comparative Perspective* (Princeton: Princeton University Press, 1989), 235–68; and Antoun, "The Islamic Court, the Islamic Judge, and the Accommodation of Traditions: A Jordanian Case Study," *International Journal of Middle Eastern Studies* 12 (December 1980): 455–67.

8. Rafiuddin Ahmed, "Islamization in Nineteenth Century Bengal," in *Contributions to South Asian Studies I*, ed. Gopal Krishna (Delhi: Oxford University Press, 1979), 115.

9. John L. Esposito, *The Islamic Threat: Myth or Reality?* (New York: Oxford University Press, 1992), 124 ff.

10. Ali E. H. Dessouki, "Arab Intellectuals and al-Nakba: The Search for Fundamentalism," *Middle Eastern Studies* 9 (1973): 187–96.

11. John Waterbury, *Egypt: Burdens of the Past/Options for the Future* (Bloomington: Indiana University Press, 1978), 29.

12. B. L. Carter, *The Copts in Egyptian Politics* (London: Croom Helm, 1986), 256–89.

13. Fazlur Rahman, *Islam* (New York: Doubleday, Anchor Books, 1968), 168 ff.

14. Edward William Lane, *An Account of the Manners and Customs of the Modern Egyptians* (London: J. M. Dent & Sons, 1908 [1836]), 35 ff.

15. Morroe Berger, *Islam in Egypt, Social and Political Aspects of Popular Religion* (Cambridge: Cambridge University Press, 1970), 7–45.

16. Nazih N. M. Ayubi, "Bureaucratic Inflation and Administrative Inefficiency: The Deadlock in Egyptian Administration," *Middle East Studies* 18 (July 1982), 286–99.

17. A. Chris Eccel, *Egypt, Islam and Social Change: Al-Azhar in Conflict and Accommodation* (Berlin: Klaus Schwarz, 1984), 525–37.

18. Henry Munson, Jr., *Islam and Revolution in the Middle East* (New Haven: Yale University Press, 1988), 3–6.

19. R. Stephen Humphreys, "Islam and Political Values in Saudi Arabia, Egypt and Syria," *Middle East Journal* 33 (Winter 1979): 3.

20. Bruce Lawrence, "Muslim Fundamentalist Movements: Reflections and a New Approach," in *The Islamic Impulse*, ed. Barbara Freyer Stowasser (London: Croom Helm, 1987), 32.

21. John A. Williams, "A Return to the Veil in Egypt," *Middle East Review* 11 (Spring 1978): 85–95.

22. Abu Talib al-Makki, "The Beard," trans. E. H. Douglas, *The Muslim World* 68 (April 1978): 100–110.

23. Muhammad ʿAli Qutb, *Risala al-Masjid* (Cairo: Dar al-Ansar, 1977), 6.

24. "Lessons from Iran," a mimeo flyer issued by the Islamic (Student) Association (*al-Jamʿiya al-Islamiya*) of Cairo University was distributed in 1979 at Minya University; a translation is given in *Islam in Transition: Muslim Perspectives*, ed. John L. Esposito and John Donohue (New York: Oxford University Press, 1982), 246–51.

The reference here to the *al-Jamʿiya al-Islamiya* as the source of this citation calls for a clarification that is relevant throughout this study. This name is to be distinguished from the similar title *al-Jamāʿa al-Islamiya*, although both can be translated as "Islamic Society." The first term, *jamʿiya*, connotes a relatively generalized association, whereas the second, *jamāʿa*, suggests a more compact corporate body. This second term also appears in the Qurʾan. While both terms have been used, sometimes interchangeably, with regard to groups of Islamic militants in Egypt, strictly speaking they also have different geographic and historical points of reference that should be mentioned to avoid possible confusion. During the late 1970s the group in Minya and its counterparts on other university campuses that I am discussing here were most frequently identified, including by these activists themselves, as *al-Jamʿiya al-Islamiya*.

Later, in the early 1980s, a radicalized successor organization with considerable overlap in membership emerged that declared itself *al-Jamāʿa al-Islamiya*. Some specialists have been careful to specify that *al-Jamāʿa* leadership consisted of veteran militants who had been imprisoned after Sadat's assassination and who formed this society after their release. But unfortunately, such reviews of the development of Islamism in Egypt may also omit any allusion to its predecessor *al-Jamʿiya*, and in effect ignore this earlier more diffuse phase of the movement that was so prominent in the provinces. See, for example, Abdel Azim Ramadan, "Fundamentalist Influence in Egypt: The Strategies of the Muslim Brotherhood and the Takfir Groups," in *Fundamentalisms and the State: Remaking Politics, Economics, and Militance*, ed. Martin E. Marty and R. Scott Appleby (Chicago: University of Chicago Press, 1993), 161 ff.

However, it has since become the practice in much of the literature to telescope the tangled evolution of Islamic militant groups by referring to those of the late 1970s as well as to later versions by the subsequent name, *al-Jamāʿa al-Islamiya*. For instance, writing on the personal background of Mahmud Abouhalama, born in 1959, indicted for collusion in the bombing of the World Trade Center in New

York, *Time* magazine engages in what might be regarded as an anachronism: "As a teenager, Abouhalama began to hang around with members of the outlawed al-Jamaʿa al-Islamiyya, or Islamic Group, which considered the blind Sheik Omar Abdel Rahman its spiritual guide"; "The Secret Life of Mahmud the Red," *Time*, Oct. 4, 1993, p. 57. For simplicity's sake, I have largely adopted this same manner of referring to this militant movement generally as *al-Jamāʿa* even when discussing its earlier phase when it was also, even more usually, known locally as *al-Jamʿīya*.

25. *New York Times*, May 29, 1977.

26. James B. Mayfield, *Rural Politics in Nasser's Egypt: A Quest for Legitimacy* (Austin: University of Texas Press, 1971), especially chapter 2. See also Nathan J. Brown, *Peasant Politics in Modern Egypt: The Struggle against the State* (New Haven: Yale University Press, 1990).

27. J. G. Peristiany, ed., *Honour and Shame: The Values of Mediterranean Society* (Chicago: University of Chicago Press, 1966); and David D. Gilmore, ed., *Honor and Shame and the Unity of the Mediterranean* (Washington, D.C.: American Anthropology Association, 1987).

28. Carlo Levi, *Christ Stopped at Eboli* (New York: Grosset and Dunlap, 1947), 140.

29. This vivid image has been used by many. I borrow it directly from an unpublished study of Maurice Martin, "Les Courants Extremistes Musulmans Aujourd'hui." He notes: "Ceux qui s'approprient sur ce point l'éxclusivité de l'orthodoxie religieuse exércent une sorte de terreur idéologique qui paralyse la liberté d'autres expressions."

30. I was told by the student who transcribed this chant for me that it originated with Muhammad, and that it was the chant used at the Battle of the Ditch [*Khandaq*], which was one of the most important battles between the Muslims of Medina and the polytheists of Mecca. Further investigation suggests this is an apocryphal attribution, but the claim itself reflects a local perspective.

31. This came to be known as "Jihan's law" after the wife of the president who was active in promoting it; see Fauzi M. Najjar, "Egypt's Laws of Personal Status," *Arab Studies Quarterly* 10 (1988): 318–44.

32. Ann Mayer, "The Shariʿah: A Methodology or a Body of Substantive Rules?" in *Islamic Law and Jurisprudence*, ed. Nicholas Heer (Seattle: University of Washington Press, 1990), 177–98.

5. THE SERMON AS PUBLIC DISCOURSE

1. Nathan J. Brown, *Peasant Politics in Modern Egypt: The Struggle against the State* (New Haven: Yale University Press, 1990).

2. Daryush Shayegan, *Qu'est-ce qu'une révolution religieuse?* (Paris: Michel Albin, 1991), 185–244.

3. Patrick D. Gaffney, "Donner sa Place à la Parole: Mosquées et Prédicateurs en Egypte Contemporaine," in *Modernisation et Mobilisation Sociale: Egypte-Brésil*, Dossier du CEDEJ (Cairo: CEDEJ, 1991), 101–13.

4. Oliver Carré, "Pouvoir et Ideologie dans l'Egypte de Nasser et de Sadat," in *L'Egypte d'Aujourd'hui: Permanance et Changements, 1806–1976*, M. C. Aulas et al. (Paris: Editions du Centre National de la Recherche Scientifique, 1977), 252.

5. Clifford Geertz, "The Integrative Revolution: Primordial Sentiments and Civil Politics in the New States," in *Old Societies and New States: The Quest for Modernity in Asia and Africa*, ed. Clifford Geertz (New York: Free Press, 1963), 105–57.

6. Leonard Binder, *The Ideological Revolution in the Middle East* (New York: John Wiley and Sons, 1964), 137.

7. Robert Bellah, *Beyond Belief: Essays on Religion in a Post Traditional World* (New York: Harper & Row, 1970), 162.

8. Michael C. Hudson, *Arab Politics: The Search for Legitimacy* (New Haven: Yale University Press, 1977), 47.

9. Norma Salem-Babikian, "The Sacred and the Profane: Sadat's Speech to the Knesset," *Middle East Journal* 34 (Winter 1980): 13–24.

10. David E. Apter, "Political Religion in the New Nations," in *Old Societies and New States: The Quest for Modernity in Asia and Africa*, ed. Clifford Geertz (New York: Free Press, 1963), 78.

11. Bruce M. Borthwick, "Religion and Politics in Israel and Egypt," *Middle East Journal* 33 (Spring 1979): 145–63.

12. Saad Eddin Ibrahim, "Egypt's Islamic Activism in the 1980's," *Third World Quarterly* 10, no. 2 (1988): 644.

13. Fadwa El-Guindi, "Veiling *Infitah* with Muslim Ethic: Egypt's Contemporary Islamic Movement," *Social Problems* 28 (1981): 465–85; and Kimberly Faust, et al., "Young Women Members of the Islamic Revival Movement in Egypt," *The Muslim World* 82 (July–October 1992), 55–66.

14. See the speech of Sadat reprinted in *Al-Ahrām*, August 20, 1979.

15. Clifford Geertz, *Islam Observed: Religious Development in Morocco and Indonesia* (Chicago: University of Chicago Press, Phoenix Books, 1971), 90–117.

16. The tendency to neglect, indeed to all but ignore the influence of sermons within the context of Islamic civilization persists in current works including those that are widely acknowledged to be excellent historical surveys; see, for example, Ira M. Lapidus, *A History of Islamic Societies* (Cambridge: Cambridge University Press, 1988). By contrast, virtually the same historical sweep can be approached quite effectively viewed from precisely this marginalized perspective: see Thomas W. Arnold, *The Preaching of Islam* (London: Constable & Co., 1913).

17. It has been noted, for instance, that virtually no record of sermons has been preserved from Ottoman Egypt in the seventeenth and eighteenth centuries; J. Heyworth-Dunne, *An Introduction to the History of Education in Egypt* (London: Luzac & Co., 1938), 7.

18. P. Crone and M. Hinds, *God's Caliph* (Cambridge: Cambridge University Press, 1986).

19. Johannes Pedersen, "Khaṭīb," *Encyclopedia of Islam*, 1st ed. (Leiden: E. J. Brill, 1936), 927–29.

20. Muhammad al-Ghazzali, *Worship in Islam: Being a Translation with Commentary and Introduction of al-Ghazzali's Book of the Ihya' on the Worship*, trans. Edwin Elliott Calverley (London: Luzac & Co., 1925).

21. Rafiq Zakaria, *The Struggle within Islam: The Conflict between Religion and Politics* (London: Penguin Books, 1988), 78.

22. B. Johnson, "The All-Embracing Town and Its Mosques," *Revue de l'Occident Musulman et de la Méditerranée* 32 (1981): 139–61.

23. Marshall G. S. Hodgson, *The Venture of Islam: Conscience and History in a World Civilization,* 3 vols. (Chicago: University of Chicago Press, 1974), 1:235.

24. William Smyth, "Rhetoric and *ʿilm al-Balagha:* Christianity and Islam," *The Muslim World* 82 (1992): 242–55.

25. George Makdisi, *The Rise of Colleges: Institutions of Learning in Islam and the West* (Edinburgh: Edinburgh University Press, 1981).

26. Sam I. Gellens, "The Search for Knowledge in Medieval Muslim Societies: A Comparative Approach," in *Muslim Travellers: Pilgrimage, Migration, and Religious Imagination,* ed. Dale F. Eickelman and James P. Piscatori (Berkeley: University of California Press, 1990), 50–68.

27. The suggestion that "orthodoxy" be replaced, in the case of Islam, with "orthopraxy" represents one manifestation of this difficulty. See Wilfred C. Smith, *Islam in Modern History* (New York: New American Library, Mentor Books, 1959), 78.

28. Samuel M. Zwemer, "The Pulpit in Islam," *The Moslem World* 23 (1933): 221–32.

29. Reuben Levy, *The Social Structure of Islam* (Cambridge: Cambridge University Press, 1970).

30. E. I. J. Rosenthal, *Political Thought in Medieval Islam* (Cambridge: Cambridge University Press, 1962), 217.

31. Jacques Berque, *Egypt, Imperialism, and Revolution* (London: Frank Cass, 1972), 53.

32. Gilles Kepel, "Les oulémas, l'intelligentsia et les islamistes en Egypte: Système social, ordre transcendentale et ordre traduit," *La Révue Française de Science Politique* 35 (1985): 424–44.

6. SECURITY AND BELIEF IN THE RHETORIC OF THE SERMON

1. E. E. Evans-Pritchard, *Social Anthropology and Other Essays* (New York: Free Press, 1962), 80.

2. Kenneth Burke, *A Grammer of Motives* (New York: Prentice-Hall, 1952), xiii.

3. Hans Wehr, *A Dictionary of Modern Written Arabic,* ed. J. Milton Cowan, 3d ed. (Ithaca, N.Y.: Spoken Language Services, 1976).

4. One example of the play of these meanings, belief and security, derived from the cognate root in Hebrew, occurs in Isaiah 7:9: "If ye will not believe, surely you shall not be established."

5. Toshihiko Izutsu, *Ethico-Religious Concepts in the Qurʾan* (Montreal: McGill University Press, 1966), 184.

6. One example of many is on the front page of *al-Ahram* on May 19, 1979. Here President Sadat is pictured praying in the company of other distinguished government and religious personalities at the mosque of Abu al-ʿAbbas al-Marsi in Alexandria.

7. I have tried to be attentive to the insertion of Qurʾan citations embedded in preaching. Often preachers will indicate when they are quoting from the Qurʾan, but just as often they do not do so. When I have recognized the text or suspected its source I have looked it up in the original text with the help of a concordance. I have supplied the chapter and verse number as aids to the reader.

8. In a television program entitled "Sadat's Eternal Egypt," broadcast by C.B.S. on June 22, 1980, Walter Cronkite interviewed Sadat. The latter, speaking in English, referred to his country's land reclamations programs and other schemes supposedly designed to increase Egypt's agriculture to the extent that it would no longer need to import food staples as a "green revolution."

9. These remarks by no means imply that such a naturalist attitude is exclusively Islamic. On the contrary, a very similar conviction has an impressive pedigree in the West. Note the following profession from a minor character in Flaubert's *Madame Bovary:* "I have a religion, my religion, and I even have more than all those others with their mummeries and their juggling. I adore God, on the contrary. I believe in the Supreme Being, in a Creator, whatever He may be. . . . For one can know Him as well in a wood, in a field, or even contemplating the eternal vault like the ancients. My God! mine is the God of Socrates, of Franklin, of Voltaire, and of Beranger! . . . And I can't admit of a God who takes walks in His garden with a cane in his hand, who lodges his friends in the bellies of whales, dies uttering a cry, and rises again at the end of three days; things absurd in themselves, and completely opposed, moreover, to all physical laws"; Gustave Flaubert, *Madame Bovary*, trans. Eleanor Marx-Aveling (New York: Everyman's Library, 1928).

10. Linguistic plays are very frequent in such rhetoric, most, alas, being lost in translation. One item here, however, that should not be missed is the use of the imperative *aqrā*, which I have translated "recite." Not only is this word first used in the verse the Shaykh gives as the introduction to this litany of recitations, but it is also the verbal stem from which is derived the word Qur'an.

11. William A. Graham, "Qur'an as Spoken Word: An Islamic Contribution to the Understanding of Scripture," in *Approaches to Islam in Religious Studies*, ed. Richard C. Martin (Tucson: University of Arizona Press, 1985), 37.

12. Stephen C. Pepper, *World Hypothesis: A Study in Evidence* (Berkeley: University of California Press, 1942), 11.

13. The term Arberry translates here as "signs" (*ayāt*) is also the word for "verses," that is, this people have cried lies to the Qur'an.

14. Muhammad Shawqi, "Limādha ankhafaḍ mastawa al-ṭulāb fī al-lughāt?" (Why is the level of students in languages declining?), *Rūz al-Yusuf* (April 1979): 28–29.

15. Fouad Ajami, "The Struggle for Egypt's Soul," *Foreign Policy* 35 (Summer 1979): 3–30.

16. Michael Silverstein, "Shifters, Linguistic Categories, and Cultural Description," in *Meaning in Anthropology*, ed. Keith H. Basso and Henry A. Selby (Albuquerque: University of New Mexico Press, 1976).

17. Aristotle, *Poetics*, trans. Francis Ferguson (New York: Hill and Wang, 1962).

18. R. Dozy, *Histoire des Musulmans d'Espagne*, ed. E. Levi-Provençal, 4 vols. (Leiden: E. J. Brill, 1932), vol. 3.

19. Without entering here into a potential historical controversy with its attendant problems related to dubious bibliographical evidence, it is nonetheless helpful to point out that Shaykh Umar's rendition is at best an unqualified, gross oversimplification. Apparently he has come across the name of Samuel Ha-Levi in an apologetic pamphlet (which he mentions) and he is exploiting this obscure fig-

334 / Notes to Pages 156–167

ure as a convenient scapegoat symbolizing all that he objects to in current sectarian polemics. Without doubt there were, during this remarkably intellectually vibrant period of Andalusian history, some who expressed various shades of anti-Muslim sentiment. Furthermore it seems that one such was Joseph, the son of Samuel Ha-Levi, who inherited his father's place at court but not his father's piety, literary genius, and discerning respect for religious differences. In addition to Dozy, noted above, see "Samuel Ha-Nagid," *Encyclopedia Judaica,* 14:816–18; and Leon J. Weinberger, *Jewish Prince in Muslim Spain: Selected Poems of Samuel Ibn Nagrela* (Birmingham: University of Alabama Press, 1973), 1–17.

20. R. A. Nicholson, *A Literary History of the Arabs* (Cambridge: Cambridge University Press, 1930), 428.

21. Exodus 34:1. "The Lord said to Moses: 'Cut two tablets of stone like the first, and I will write upon the tablets words that were on the first tablets.' " The point about the ark being empty of all but the tablets is usually interpreted to indicate that the Jews were to worship no image of God. Cf. Bernhard Anderson, *Understanding the Old Testament* (Englewood Cliffs, N.J.: Prentice-Hall, 1966), 71–72.

22. Pierre Bourdieu, *Language and Symbolic Power* (Cambridge, Mass.: Harvard University Press, 1991), 126.

23. G. H. A. Juynboll, *The Authenticity of the Tradition Literature* (Leiden: E. J. Brill, 1969). The author discusses this problem of *ḥadīth* (tradition) as it has been conducted in the Arabic-speaking Islamic world, with special attention to Egypt and Azhar.

24. John Warwick Montgomery, "The Apologetic Approach of Muhammad Ali and Its Implications for Christian Apologetics," *The Muslim World* 51 (1961): 119.

25. T. Sabbagh, *La Métaphore dans le Coran* (Paris: Adrien-Maisonneuve, 1943), 7. Sabbagh begins by making a distinction between the metonym and the figure known as "synecdoche," which is, specifically, "the part for the whole." However, a sentence later he directs our attention to a footnote in which he says he will use the term "metonym" to include "synecdoche" properly speaking. We have followed the same procedure.

26. See Hamed Ammar, *Growing Up in an Egyptian Village* (London: Routledge & Kegan Paul, 1954); Jacques Berque, *Histoire Sociale d'un Village Egyptien au XXème Siècle* (Paris: Mouton, 1957); and John Boman Adams, "Culture and Conflict in an Egyptian Village," *American Anthropologist* 59 (1957): 225–35. Adams concludes with a familiar reflection, for which one might make appropriate allowances, given the time of its observation, but the point is nonetheless widely shared: "But whether conscious or unconscious, piecemeal or systemized, traditional or revolutionary, the villager's basic premises must be absolute. Village basic personality is characterized by a deep insecurity that seeks reassurance through faith in absolutes. Individual responsibility to test and choose between alternative solutions to new problems increases the villager's anxiety" (p. 234).

27. Bronislaw Malinowski, *Magic, Science and Religion and Other Essays* (Garden City, N.Y.: Doubleday, 1954), 101.

7. SECURITY AND BELIEF

1. Muhammad Abdul Rauf, "Some Notes on the Qur'anic Use of the Terms Islam and Iman," *The Muslim World* 57 (1967): 98.

2. Bernard Lewis, "Politics and War," in *The Legacy of Islam,* ed. Joseph Schacht and C. E. Bosworth, 2d ed. (Oxford: Oxford University Press, 1979), 177.

3. Arnold van Gennep, *The Rites of Passage,* trans. Monika B. Vizedom and Gabrielle L. Caffee (Chicago: University of Chicago Press, 1960).

4. There are many varieties of code-switching and different specialists designate them variously. Gumperz distinguishes, for instance, between metaphorical, conversational, and situational code-switching. The object here is not to describe this incidence formally nor to classify it by the criteria of some particular subgroup of this sociolinguistic phenomena. It is merely to demonstrate how it bears on the rhetorical strategy of this preacher's overall ritual performance. See R. A. Hudson, *Sociolinguistics* (Cambridge: Cambridge University Press, 1980), 56–57.

5. The linguistic aspects of diglossia in Arabic have been widely explored in recent years although relatively little research has focused on ritual oratory. Some scholarship is indeed relevant to our discussion of sermons. See, especially, S. A. el-Hassan, "Educated Spoken Arabic in Egypt and the Levant: A Critical Review of Diglossia and Related Concepts," *Archivum Linguisticum* 8 (1976): 108–121. In this unusually detailed and insightful analysis, el-Hassan devotes considerable attention to a transcript from a sermon very much like the ones I heard in the mosques of Upper Egypt. There he examines many of the issues related to a formal description of this usage.

6. Emile Dermenghem, *The Life of Mahomet,* trans. Arabella Yorke (New York: Dial Press, 1930), p. 318.

7. Alfred Guillaume, trans., *The Life of Muhammad: A Translation of Ishaq's Sirat Rasul Allah* (Lahore: Oxford University Press, 1955). I have not made a systematic study of terms of address in the *Sira,* but I suspect a pattern could be demonstrated. Note the following examples chosen more or less randomly: When Abu Talib is on his deathbed, a group of the Quraysh visit him and beseech him to dissuade Muhammad from his preaching. The nonbelievers call the Prophet by name, "Muhammad." Abu Talib calls him "Nephew," while the narrator refers to him as "the apostle" (pp. 191–92). In a discussion between Muhammad and some Jews in Medina, the Prophet is called in the vocative, "Muhammad" (pp. 256–57). In a disputation with Christians of Najran, the Prophet is called "Muhammad" (p. 276). An enemy of the Muslims named 'Uqba is condemned to death, and in pleading (in vain) for his life, he called the Prophet "Muhammad" (p. 308). A blind man named Mirba' ibn Qayzi, while insulting the Prophet, calls him "Muhammad" (p. 372). Another enemy of the Prophet while taunting him calls him "Muhammad" (p. 381). When conducting an armistice with an unbeliever named Suhayl, the latter calls the Prophet "Muhammad" (p. 505). Once when Muhammad is dividing spoils, a certain man named Dhu'l Khuwaysira complains about the distribution and speaks to the Prophet as "Muhammad" (p. 595). However, he is also sometimes called "Muhammad" by his followers, cf., the verses of 'Abbas b. Mirdas, pp. 577 ff. Usually, persons address the Prophet with no vocative, or with the formula "O apostle of God," which is the form Shaykh Uthman puts into the mouth of Sufwan at the end of the narrative.

8. MORALITY AND RELIGION IN IDEOLOGY AND ACTION

1. Max Weber, *The Sociology of Religion,* trans. Ephraim Fischoff (Boston: Beacon, 1963), 271 ff.

2. "It is one of the boasts of Islam that it does not countenance the existence of a clergy, who might claim to intervene between God and man. True as this is, however, Islam, as it became organized into a system, did in fact produce a clerical class, which acquired precisely the same kind of social and religious authority and prestige as the clergy in Christian communities"; Hamilton A. R. Gibb, *Mohammedanism*, 2d ed. (London: Oxford University Press, 1954), 95.

3. Rudyard Kipling, *Kim*, ed. Edward W. Said (London: Penguin Books, 1987), 357.

4. Clifford Geertz, "Religion as a Cultural System," in *The Interpretation of Cultures* (New York: Basic Books, 1973), 90.

5. Abner Cohen, *Two Dimensional Man* (Berkeley: University of California Press, 1976).

6. Raymond Firth, *Symbols: Public and Private* (Ithaca: Cornell University Press, 1975), 205–6.

7. Cohen, *Two Dimensional Man*, 31 ff.

8. Sherry Ortner, "On Key Symbols," *American Anthropologist* 75 (1973), 1338.

9. Wehr, *A Dictionary of Modern Written Arabic*, ed. J. Milton Cowan, (Ithaca, N.Y.: Spoken Language Services, 1976), 424–25.

10. See the Qur'an, 4:94 and 6:54.

11. Muhammad Abdul Rauf, *Islam: Creed and Worship* (Washington, D.C.: The Islamic Center, 1974), 89.

12. The origin, history, and semantics of the word "Islam" are treated in depth in a number of recent studies. Among the most helpful of these for this discussion, see Marshall G. S. Hodgson, *The Venture of Islam: Conscience and History in a World Civilization*, 3 vols. (Chicago: University of Chicago Press, 1974), 1:45 ff.; Wilfred C. Smith, *The Meaning and End of Religion* (New York: New American Library, 1964), 106 ff.; and Jane I. Smith, *An Historical and Semantic Study of the Term "Islam" as Seen in a Sequence of Qur'an Commentaries* (Missoula: Scholars Press, 1975).

13. Muhammad Abdel Rauf, "Some Notes on the Qur'anic Use of the Terms *Islam* and *Iman*," *The Muslim World* 57 (1967): 98.

9. FORMALIZATION AND STRUCTURE

1. Maurice Bloch, *Political Language and Oratory in Traditional Society* (London: Academic Press, 1975), 16.

2. Michael Silverstein, "Shifters, Linguistic Categories, and Cultural Description," in *Meaning in Anthropology*, ed. Keith H. Basso and Henry A. Selby (Albuquerque: University of New Mexico Press, 1976).

3. Arthur J. Arberry, *The Koran Interpreted* (London: Oxford University Press, 1964).

4. There are numerous examples of this genre, but this one has become so well known it might almost be credited as the prototype: Tawfiq al-Hakim, *Journal of a Country Judge* (London: Harvill Press, 1947).

5. Bloch, *Political Language*, 16.

6. Maurice Bloch, "Symbols, Song, Dance and Features of Articulation: Is Religion an Extreme Form of Traditional Authority?" *European Journal of Sociology* 15 (1974): 237–54.

7. Louis Gardet, *L'Islam: Religion et Communauté*, 3d rev. ed. (Paris: Desclée de Brouwer, 1978), p. 295.

8. Richard P. Mitchaell, *The Society of the Muslim Brothers* (London: Oxford University Press, 1969), 223 ff.

9. Jacques Jomier, *Les Grands Thèmes du Coran* (Paris: Centurion, 1978), 61.

10. Rudi Paret, "Die Bedeutungsentwicklung von Arabisch Faṭḥ," *Orientalia Hispanica* 1 (1974): 537–41. In this exemplary piece, Paret eruditely discusses the semantic gap between *fatḥ*, "which normally means 'to open' ('öffnen'), and its use in numerous Qur'anic loci with the special meaning of 'to decide' ('entscheiden')." It is precisely by conflating such semantic extensions that separate the classical and modern usage that this and many preachers achieve remarkable effects.

11. Joseph Schacht, *An Introduction to Islamic Law* (Oxford: Oxford University Press, 1964), especially chapter 10.

12. Reuben Levy, *The Social Structure of Islam* (Cambridge: Cambridge University Press, 1970), 194.

13. Gardet, *L'Islam: Religion et Communauté*, 294.

14. "As the archdeacon stood up to make his speech, erect in the middle of that little square, he looked like an ecclesiastical statue placed there, as a fitting *impersonation* of the church militant here on earth; his shovel hat, large, new, and well-pronounced, a churchman's hat in every inch, declared the profession as plainly as does the Quaker's broad brim; his heavy eyebrows, large open eyes, and full mouth and chin expressed the solidity of his order; the broad chest, amply covered with fine cloth, told how well to do was its estate; one hand ensconced within his pocket, evinced the practical hold which our mother church keeps on her temporal possessions; and the other, loose for action, was ready to fight if need be in her defence; and, below these, the decorous breeches, and neat black gaiters showing so admirably that well-turned leg, betokened the stability, the decency, the outward beauty and grace of our church establishment"; Anthony Trollope, *The Warden* (New York: Printed for Libraries, 1932), 76–77, emphasis added.

15. Fazlur Rahman, "A Survey of Modernization of Muslim Family Law," *International Journal of Middle Eastern Studies* 11 (1980): 451–65.

16. Weber's stereotype, "Kadijustiz," which Fischoff renders "patriarchal justice," is discussed extensively in the context of law and virtually omitted in the context of religion. See Weber, *Wirtschaft und Gesellschaft: Grundriss der Verstehenden Soziologie*, 5th rev. ed. (Tubingen: J. C. B. Mohr, 1976), 563–64.

17. This neologism, "Islamdom," as used by Hodgson, is given an elaborate explanation and a convincing defense. See Hodgson, *The Venture of Islam*, 1:57 ff.

18. Muhamed al-Nowaihi, "Problems of Modernization in Islam," *The Muslim World* 65, no. 3 (1975): 174–185. See also Noel J. Coulson, *Conflicts and Tensions in Islamic Jurisprudence* (Chicago: University of Chicago Press, 1969).

19. The lexeme we translate as "attributes" is *ṣifa*, plural *ṣifāt*, which acquires a technical meaning in numerous fields such as law, grammar, theology, and philosophy.

20. Sayyid H. Nasr, *Ideals and Realities of Islam* (Boston: Beacon, 1975), 104–5.

21. For a good contextualized discussion of this dimension of self-criticism, as a function of the "de-Naserization" and the "open door" policy, as well as insights into the tendency as a national trait, see John Waterbury, *Egypt: Burdens of the Past/Options for the Future* (Bloomington: Indiana University Press, 1978), especially Part III, "Strategies and Solutions."

22. This sermon was preached on March 2, 1979.

10. CREATIVITY AND ADAPTATION

1. Uri M. Kupferschmidt, "The Muslim Brothers and the Egyptian Village," *Asian and African Studies* 16 (1982): 157–71.

2. Wilfred Cantwell Smith, *Islam in Modern History* (New York: New American Library, Mentor Books, 1959), 69.

3. P.J. Vatikiotis, *The History of Egypt,* 2d ed. (Baltimore: Johns Hopkins University Press, 1980), 325.

4. The journal has been published since 1954.

5. An Iranian satirist, living in exile, recently published a collection of articles he called "Friday Prayer Sermons," which he composed in the style of the Ayatollah Khomeini's preaching. Their comic effect flows from the exaggerated merging of exalted pieties and banal trivialities. The result strikes most outside observers as quite funny. But those closer to the scene may not be at all moved to such levity. Indeed, the English translator of these mock sermons notes grimly: "Sometimes one has to examine these carefully to be sure they are not the genuine article." Hadi Khorsandi, *The Ayatollah and I,* trans. Ehssan Javan (London: Readers International, 1987), 4.

6. The implicit code spelling out the proper forms of naming and address are presently undergoing what may be subtle but nonetheless sweeping changes in Egypt. Differences of age and class, along with degrees of familiarity and various cultural orientations have made these issues a sort of mirror of larger shifts in language and social relations. See Dilworth B. Parkinson, *Constructing the Social Context of Communication: Terms of Address in Egyptian Arabic* (Berlin: Mouton de Gruyter, 1985).

7. A. Guillaume, *The Life of Muhammad: A Translation of Ishaq's Sirat Rasul Allah* (Lahore: Oxford University Press, 1955), 485.

8. Guillaume, *The Life of Muhammad,* 145.

9. See, for example, 1 Thessalonians 5:8; Ephesians 6:14.

10. There appeared a somewhat odd, but extremely interesting, feature article on Minya and Upper Egypt generally that gives an especially colorful version of this rough side to the people of this region whom Timothy M. Phelps, the journalist, calls "the poorest, least educated and most uncontrolled geographic group in the country"; *New York Times,* May 29, 1977.

11. There is a well-known maxim in Islamic jurisprudence, *ikhtilāf raḥma* ("differences are a mercy"), which has achieved the status of a slogan in the hands of liberal modernists against traditional conservatives. Its technical meaning is that when a point of law differs between the four classical schools, or *madhāhib,* it is legitimate to adopt whatever ruling is most convenient or suited. Obviously, this axiom has itself been the object of endless interpretation between those who would use it widely and those who use it narrowly; each accuses the other of abuse.

12. An intriguing ancillary issue touching on this reification of Islam is dealt with by el-Zein in an important review we have already discussed. He, a Muslim, argues that "Islam as an analytic category" is meaningless for anthropological discussion and it must be converted into the "facets of the system of which it is part." Obviously this preacher does use Islam as a fixed construct in its surface from, although it is our project to break down this abstraction into more visible social and cultural relations. Abdul Hamid el-Zein, "Beyond Ideology and Theology:

The Search for the Anthropology of Islam," *Annual Review of Anthropology* (Palo Alto: Annual Reviews, 1977).

13. Sadat, *In Search of Identity: An Autobiography* (Glasgow: William Collins, 1978), 233.

14. Guillaume, *The Life of Muhammad,* 674.

15. Guillaume, *The Life of Muhammad,* 429.

16. Guillaume, *The Life of Muhammad,* 427–428. Guillaume has a slightly different translation than ours for this reply. "Zayd answered, 'By God, I don't wish that Muhammad now were in the place he occupies and that a thorn could hurt him, and that I were sitting with my family.'"

17. Guillaume, *The Life of Muhammad,* 428.

18. Khubayb is honored by Muslims as the first martyr of Islam, and as such certain features of his death have become mythical and even set enduring precedent, such as his prayer before dying. His cry for vengeance, because it is so well known, has also called up certain modern apologists who have tried to reinterpret it to make it more palatable to modern sensibilities. It is therefore contrasted to the circumstances and spirituality exhibited in the first Christian martyr, St. Stephen. For an illustrative discussion of this issue, see Emile Dermenghem, *The Life of Mahomet,* trans. Anabella York (New York: Dial Press, 1930), 173.

19. Qur'an 2:178. Although the Qur'an fully condones the eye for an eye retaliation, it also recommends mercy. See W. Montgomery Watt, *Bell's Introduction to the Qur'an* (Edinburgh: Edinburgh University Press, 1970), 6.

20. Guillaume, *The Life of Muhammad,* 485.

21. This term I have translated as "hippies" is an interesting case of etymological and cultural confusion. The term *khunfus,* plural *khanāfis,* is given in the lexicon as "dung beetle, scarab." It is a folk-Arabization of the homonymic "Beatles" referring to the British popular musical group. The connotation of the insect does not persist in the English language pun on "beat" whereas the Arabic term, generalized to a whole perceived movement of decadent youth, is frozen into the term for this low and disgusting pest.

11. UNITY AND COMMITMENT

1. David Parkin, "The Rhetoric of Responsibility: Bureaucratic Communications in Kenya Farming Areas," in *Political Language and Oratory in Traditional Society,* ed. Maurice Bloch (London: Academic Press, 1975), 114–38.

2. Ibid., 116.

3. Ibid., 118.

4. Ralph W. Nicholas, "Social and Political Movements," in *Annual Review of Anthropology,* ed. Bernard Siegel (Palo Alto: Annual Reviews, 1973), 80.

5. Ibid., 80.

6. This story of the national anthem is well told in a book that contains an impressive survey of the social, political, and cultural climate of Egypt at this time, written by the first Israeli journalist to devote himself to first-hand reportage on Egypt since 1948; Amos Elon, *Flight into Egypt* (New York: Doubleday, 1980).

7. Alfred Schutz, "The Contemporary World as an Ideal Type and the They-relationship," in *Collected Papers,* vol. 2 (The Hague: Martinus Nijhoff, 1964), 45. The emphasis is his.

8. Richard H. Adams, Jr., *Development and Social Change in Rural Egypt* (Syracuse: Syracuse University Press, 1986), 53.

9. Martin Luther King, Jr., "A Knock at Midnight," recorded at the Mount Zion Baptist Church, Cincinnati, Ohio, on Golden Words: Dr. Martin Luther King, vol. 2. Airborne Records, 1991.

10. The term used by the Shaykh, *hizb allah,* occurs in the Qur'an where it has the sense of a "band, faction, or troop" although the word *hizb* in modern Arabic is the word for a political party. Hence the meaning "party of God" overlaps neatly with references to modern political parties. Of course, there is no recognized "party" in Egypt that corresponds to that name and on that most obvious level, the *shaykh* is not making a statement about institutional political participation, but rather using the political idiom to advance his religious claims. However, there are fundamentalist groups that have adopted this name as their title, notably among militant Shi'ites in Lebanon and Iran.

CONCLUSION

1. Raymond William Baker, "Afraid for Islam: Egypt's Muslim Centrists between Pharaohs and Fundamentalists." *Daedalus* 120, no. 3 (1991): 43.

2. Barry Rubin, *Islamic Fundamentalism in Egyptian Politics* (New York: St. Martin's Press, 1990), vii.

3. R. Hrair Dekmejian, *Islam in Revolution: Fundamentalism in the Arab World* (Syracuse, N.Y.: Syracuse University Press, 1985).

4. Ahmed Abdalla, *The Student Movement and National Politics in Egypt* (London: Al-Saqi Books, 1985), 198.

5. This policy of non-enforcement was later openly affirmed during a trial in the early 1980s after Isma'il had been removed and a new governor appointed. General Muhammad 'Id, chief of police in Asyut, was asked by the magistrate whether the policy of "accommodation to Islamic groups" was a government decision. He replied: "Yes. We had government orders that we should not stop them or interfere with their activities." See Michael Youssef, *Revolt against Modernity: Muslim Zealots and the West* (Leiden: E. J. Brill, 1985), 102.

6. Johannes J. G. Jansen, *The Neglected Duty: The Creed of Sadat's Assassins and Islamic Resurgence in the Middle East* (New York: Macmillan, 1986).

7. Mohamed Sid-Ahmed, "Egypt: The Islamic Issue," *Foreign Policy* 69 (Winter 1987–1988): 22–39.

8. See Gilles Kepel, *Muslim Extremism in Egypt: The Prophet and the Pharaoh,* trans. Jun Rothchild (Berkeley: University of California Press, 1986); Hamied Ansari, "The Islamic Militants in Egyptian Politics," *International Journal of Middle Eastern Studies* 16 (1984): 123–144; and 'Adil Hamuda, *Qunābil wa-Musāhif: Qaḍiyat Tanẓīm al-Jihād* [Bombs and Qur'ans: the Case of the Jihad Organization] (Cairo: Sina l-al-Nashir, 1985).

9. Hamied Ansari, "Sectarian Conflict in Egypt and the Political Expediency of Religion," *Middle East Journal* 38 (Summer 1984): 408.

10. Gilles Kepel, *Muslim Extremism in Egypt,* 207.

11. Nemat Guenena, "The 'Jihad': An Islamic Alternative in Egypt," *Cairo Papers in Social Science* 9 (Summer 1986): 45.

12. Mohamed Heikal, *Autumn of Fury: The Assassination of Sadat* (New York: Random House, 1983), 247 ff.

13. Lila Abu-Lughod, *Veiled Sentiments: Honor and Poetry in a Bedouin Society* (Berkeley: University of California Press, 1986), 78–79.

14. Nemat Guenena, *The 'Jihad,'* 15.

15. Bertus Henriks, "Egypt's New Political Map: Report from the Election Campaign," *Middle East Report* 17, no. 4 (July–August 1987), 23–30.

16. Gehad Auda, "Egypt's Uneasy Politics," *Journal of Democracy* 2, no. 2 (Spring 1991), 70–78.

17. Saad Eddin Ibrahim, "Egypt's Islamic Activism in the 1980's," *Third World Quarterly* 10, no. 2 (1988): 648.

18. Alexander Flores, "Egypt: A New Secularism?" *Middle East Report* 18, no. 153 (July-August 1988), 27–30.

19. "Muslims' Fury Falls on Egypt's Christians," *New York Times*, March 15, 1993.

20. Abdullah Schleifer, "Sufism in Egypt and the Arab World," in *Islamic Spirituality: Manifestation*, ed. Sayyid Hussein Nasr (New York: Crossroads, 1991), 205.

21. Gerald Butt, "Egypt's Muslim Brothers," *The Tablet*, December 12, 1992, 1560.

22. Habib Boularès, *Islam: The Fear and the Hope* (London: Zed Books, 1990), 129.

23. See Gilles Kepel and Kamil T. Barbar, *Les Waqfs dans l'Egypte Contemporaine* (Cairo: Centre d'Etudes de Documentation Economiques, Juridiques et Sociales, 1982), 59.

24. *Foreign Broadcast Information Service.* As transcribed from Cairo Radio, September 8, 1981.

25. Central Agency for Public Mobilization and Statistics, *Al-A'imma w-al-Wuʿʿāẓ fī Jumhurīya Misr al-ʿArabīya* (Cairo: CAPMAS, 1984), 9.

26. *Arabia*, September 1986, 26.

27. "Mubarak Appeals for Tolerance," *New York Times*, March 21, 1993.

28. F. de Jong, *Turuq and Turuq-linked Institutions in Nineteenth-Century Egypt: An Historical Study in Organizational Dimensions of Islamic Mysticism* (Leiden: E. J. Brill, 1978), 189.

Select Bibliography

Abdalla, Ahmed. *The Student Movement and National Politics in Egypt.* London: Al-Saqi Books, 1985.

Abdel-Malek, Anouar. *Egypt: Military Society.* Translated by Charles Lam Markmann. New York: Random House, Vintage Books, 1968.

Abdel-Nasser, Gamal. *The Philosophy of the Revolution.* Buffalo: Smith, Keynes & Marshall, Publishers, Economica Books, 1959.

Abdel-Rauf, Muhammad. "Some Notes on the Qur'anic Use of the Terms Islam and Iman." *The Muslim World* 57 (1967): 94–102.

'Abduh, Muhammad. *The Theology of Unity.* Translated by Ishaq Musacad and Kenneth Cragg. New York: Arno Press, 1980.

Abu-Lughod, Lila. *Veiled Sentiments: Honor and Poetry in a Bedouin Society.* Berkeley: University of California Press, 1986.

Adams, Charles C. *Islam and Modernism in Egypt.* London: Oxford University Press, 1933.

Adams, John Boman. "Culture and Conflict in an Egyptian Village." *American Anthropologist* 59 (1957): 225–35.

Adams, Richard H., Jr. *Development and Social Change in Rural Egypt.* Syracuse, N.Y.: Syracuse University Press, 1986.

Ahmed, Jamal Mohammed. *The Intellectual Origins of Egyptian Nationalism.* London: Oxford University Press, 1960.

Ajami, Fouad. "The Struggle for Egypt's Soul." *Foreign Policy* 35 (Summer 1979): 3–30.

Al-Husry, Khaldun S. *Three Reformers: A Study in Modern Arab Political Thought.* Beirut: Khayats, 1966.

Ansari, Hamied. "Sectarian Conflict in Egypt and the Political Expediency of Religion." *The Middle East Journal* 38, no. 3 (1984): 397–418.

———. "The Islamic Militants in Egyptian Politics." *International Journal of Middle Eastern Studies* 16 (1984): 123–44.

———. *Egypt: The Stalled Society.* Albany: State University of New York Press, 1986.

Antoun, Richard T. "The Islamic Court, the Islamic Judge, and the Accommodation of Traditions: A Jordanian Case Study." *International Journal of Middle Eastern Studies* 12 (December 1980): 455–67.

———. "Key Variables Affecting Muslim Local-Level Religious Leadership in Iran and Jordan." In *Leadership and Development in Arab Society*, edited by Fuad Khuri, 92–101. Beirut: Center for Arab and Middle East Studies, American University in Beirut, 1989.

———. *Muslim Preacher in the Modern World: A Jordanian Case Study in Comparative Perspective*. Princeton: Princeton University Press, 1989.

Arberry, Arthur J. *The Koran Interpreted*. London: Oxford University Press, 1964.

Arjomand, Said Amir. *The Turban for the Crown: The Islamic Revolution in Iran*. New York: Oxford University Press, 1988.

Arkoun, Mohammed. *L'Islam: Morale et Politique*. Paris: Desclée de Brouwer, 1986.

Arnold, Thoms W., and Alfred Guillaume, eds. *Legacy of Islam*. Oxford University Press, 1931.

Aroian, Lois A. *The Nationalization of Arabic and Islamic Education in Egypt: Dar al-Alum and Al-Azhar*. Cairo Papers in Social Science no. 6 (Cairo: American University in Cairo Press, December 1983).

Asad, Talal. "Religion and Politics: An Introduction." *Social Research* 59, no. 1 (Spring 1992): 1–15.

Auda, Gehad. "Egypt's Uneasy Politics." *Journal of Democracy* 2, no. 2 (Spring 1991): 70–78.

Aulas, M. C., et al. *L'Egypte d'Aujourd'hui: Permanence et Changements, 1806–1976*. Paris: Editions du Centre National de la Recherche Scientifique, 1977.

Austin, J. L. *How to Do Things with Words*. New York: Oxford University Press, 1962.

Ayubi, Nazih N. M. *Bureaucracy and Politics in Contemporary Egypt*. London: Ithaca Press, 1980.

———. "The Political Revival of Islam: The Case of Egypt." *International Journal of Middle Eastern Studies* 12 (December 1980): 481–99.

Baer, Gabriel. *Egyptian Guilds in Modern Times*. Jerusalem: The Israel Oriental Society, 1964.

———. *Studies in the Social History of Modern Egypt*. Chicago: University of Chicago Press, 1969.

———, ed. *The Ulama in Modern History: Studies in Memory of Prof. Uriel Heyd*. African and Asian Studies, vol. 7. Jerusalem: The Israel Oriental Society, 1971.

al-Bahi, Dr. Muhammad. *Hayāti fī Raḥab al-Azhar* (My Life in the Setting of the Azhar). Cairo: Maktaba Waḥba, 1983.

Baker, Raymond William. "Afraid for Islam: Egypt's Muslim Centrists between Pharaohs and Fundamentalists." *Daedalus* 120, no. 3 (1991): 43.

Baljon, J. M. S. *Modern Muslim Koran Intrepretation (1880–1960)*. Leiden: E. J. Brill, 1961.

Banton, Michael, ed. *Anthropological Approaches to the Study of Religion*. A.S.A. Monographs, vol. 3. London: Tavistock, 1965.

Bauman, Richard. "Speaking in the Light: The Role of the Quaker Minister." In *Explorations in the Ethnography of Speaking*, edited by Richard Bauman and Joel Sherzer. London: Cambridge University Press, 1974.

Bayumi, ʿAli. *Aḍwāʿala Tārīkh al-Minyā* (Light on the History of Minya). Minya: Privately published, n.d.

Bell, Richard. *Introduction to the Qurʾan*. Revised and enlarged by W. Montgomery Watt. Edinburgh: Edinburgh University Press, 1970.

Berger, Morroe. *Islam in Egypt Today: Social and Political Aspects of Popular Religion*. Cambridge: Cambridge University Press, 1970.

——. "The Mosque: Aspects of Government Policy." *Middle East Studies* 6, no. 1 (January 1970): 47–82.

Berger, Peter. "Some Second Thoughts on Substantive versus Functional Definitions of Religion." *Journal for the Scientific Study of Religion* 13 (June 1974): 125–35.

Berger, Peter, and Thomas Luckman. *The Social Construction of Reality*. New York: Doubleday & Co., 1966.

Berque, Jacques. *Cultural Expression in Arab Society Today*. Austin: University of Texas Press, 1978.

——. *Histoire Sociale d'un Village Egyptien au XXème Siècle*. Paris: Mouton, 1957.

Bill, James A. "Resurgent Islam in the Persian Gulf." *Foreign Affairs* (Fall 1988): 108–27.

Binder, Leonard. *In a Moment of Enthusiasm: Political Power and the Second Stratum in Egypt*. Chicago: University of Chicago Press, 1978.

Black, Max. "More About Metaphor." In *Metaphor and Thought*, edited by Andrew Ortony. Cambridge: Cambridge University Press, 1979.

Bloch, Maurice, ed. *Political Language and Oratory in Traditional Society*. London: Academic Press, 1975.

Borthwick, Bruce M. "The Islamic Sermon as a Channel of Political Communication in Syria, Jordan and Egypt." Ph.D. diss., University of Michigan, 1965.

——. "Religion and Politics in Israel and Egypt." *Middle East Journal* 33 (Spring 1979): 145–63.

Boularès, Habib. *Islam: The Fear and the Hope*. London: Zed Books, 1990.

Bourdieu, Pierre. "Une Interprétation de la Théorie de la Religion selon Weber." *Archives Européennes de Sociologie* 12 (1971): 3–21.

——. *Language and Symbolic Power*. Cambridge, Mass.: Harvard University Press, 1991.

Brett, Michael. "The Spread of Islam in Egypt and North Africa." In *Northern Africa: Islam and Modernization*, edited by Michael Brett. London: Frank Cass, 1973.

——. "Mufti, Murabit, Marabout and Mahdi: Four Types in the Islamic History of North Africa." *Révue de l'Occident musulman et de la Mediterranée* 29, no. 1 (1980): 14.

Brinton, Jasper Yeates. *The Mixed Courts of Egypt*. New Haven: Yale University Press, 1930.

Bronsveld, Jan. "Some Aspects of the Quantitative Development of Education in Egypt Since 1952." In *Arab Society 1978–79: Reflections and Realities*, 27–78. CEMAM Reports 6. Beirut: Dar El-Mashreq Publishers, 1981.

Brown, Nathan J. *Peasant Politics in Modern Egypt: The Struggle against the State*. New Haven: Yale University Press, 1990.

Brown, Peter. "The Rise and the Function of the Holy Man in Late Antiquity." *Journal of Roman Studies* 61 (1971): 80–101.

Bucaille, Maurice. *The Bible, the Qur'an and Science.* Translated by Alastair D. Pannell and Maurice Bucaille. Indianapolis: North American Trust Publications, 1978.

Burke, Edmund, III. "Islam and Social Movements: Methodological Reflections." In *Islam, Politics and Social Movements,* edited by Edmund Burke, III, and Ira M. Lapidus, 17–35. Berkeley: University of California Press, 1988.

Burke, Kenneth. *A Grammar of Motives.* New York: Prentice-Hall, 1952.

———. *A Rhetoric of Motives.* New York: Prentice-Hall, 1953.

———. *The Rhetoric of Religion.* Berkeley: University of California Press, 1970.

Buttner, Friedemann. "Political Stability without Stable Institutions: The Retraditionalization of Egypt's Polity." *Orient* 20 (1979): 53–67.

Cahen, Claude. "The Body Politic." In *Unity and Variety in Muslim Civilization,* edited by Gustave E. von Grunebaum. Chicago: University of Chicago Press, 1955.

Campo, Juan E. "Authority, Ritual and Spatial Order in Islam: The Pilgrimage to Mecca." *Journal of Ritual Studies* 5, no. 1 (Winter 1991): 71.

Cassirer, Ernst. *An Essay on Man.* Garden City, N.Y.: Doubleday, 1954.

Central Agency for Public Mobilization and Statistics. *Statistical Year Book, Arab Republic of Egypt.* Cairo: CAPMAS, 1984.

Chehabi, H. E. "Religion and Politics in Iran: How Theocratic Is the Islamic Republic?" *Daedalus* 120, no. 3 (Winter 1991): 69–92.

Christelow, Alan. "Ritual, Culture and Politics of Islamic Reformism in Algeria." *Middle East Studies* 23, no. 3 (1987): 255–73.

Cochran, Judith. *Education in Egypt.* London: Croom Helm, 1982.

Costello, V. F. *Urbanization in the Middle East.* London: Cambridge University Press, 1977.

Crecelius, Daniel. "The Course of Secularization in Modern Egypt." In *Islam and Development: Religion and Sociopolitical Change,* edited by John L. Esposito, 49–70. Syracuse, N.Y.: Syracuse University Press, 1982.

Cudsi, Alexander S., and Ali E. Hillal Dessouki, eds. *Islam and Power.* Baltimore: Johns Hopkins University Press, 1981.

Curtis, Michael, ed. *Religion and Politics in the Middle East.* Boulder, Col.: Westview Press, 1981.

Decorbert, Christian. *Le Mendiant et le Combattant: L'Institution de l'Islam.* Paris: Seuil, 1991.

de Jong, F. *Turuq and Turuq-linked Institutions in Nineteenth-Century Egypt: An Historical Study in Organizational Dimensions of Islamic Mysticism.* Leiden: E. J. Brill, 1978.

Dekmejian, Hrair R. *Egypt Under Nasir: A Study in Political Dynamics.* Albany, N.Y.: State University of New York Press, 1971.

———. "The Anatomy of Islamic Revival: Legitimacy Crisis, Ethnic Conflict and the Search for Islamic Alternatives." *Middle East Journal* 34 (Winter 1980): 1–13.

———. *Islam in Revolution: Fundamentalism in the Arab World.* Syracuse, N.Y.: Syracuse University Press, 1985.

Denny, Walter. "Contradiction and Consistency in Islamic Art." In *The Islamic Impact.* Edited by Yvonne Y. Haddad et al. Syracuse, N.Y.: Syracuse University Press, 1984.

Dermenghem, Emile. *The Life of Mahomet.* Translated by Arabella Yorke. New York: Dial Press, 1930.

———. "Le Saint et le Lieu Saint." In *Le Culte des Saints dans l'Islam Maghrébin.* Paris: Gallimard, 1954.

Dessouki, Ali E. H. "Arab Intellectuals and al-Nakba: The Search for Fundamentalism." *Middle East Studies* 9 (1973): 187–96.

———, ed. *Islamic Resurgence in the Arab World.* New York: Praeger, 1982.

———. "Official Islam and Political Legitimation in the Arab Countries." In *The Islamic Impulse,* edited by Barbara Stowasser, 135–141. London: Croom Helm, 1987.

Divine, Donna Robertson. "The Rites of Nationalism: One Meaning of Egypt's Struggle for Political Independence." *Canadian Review of Studies in Nationalism* 8, no. 1 (1981): 37–54.

Douglas, Mary. *Purity and Danger: An Analysis of the Concepts of Pollution and Taboo.* London: Routledge & Kegan Paul, 1966.

Dozy, R. *Histoire des Musulmans d'Espagne.* Edited by E. Levi-Provençal. 4 vols. Leiden: E. J. Brill, 1932.

Durkheim, Emile. *The Elementary Forms of Religious Life.* Translated by Joseph W. Swain. New York: Free Press, 1961.

Eccel, A. Chris. "Rapidly Increasing Societal Scale and Secularization: A Century of Higher Muslim Education and the Professions in Egypt." Ph.D. diss., University of Chicago, 1978.

———. *Egypt, Islam and Social Change: Al-Azhar in Conflict and Accommodation.* Berlin: Klaus Schwarz, 1984.

———. "'Alim and Mujahid in Egypt: Orthodoxy versus Subculture, or Division of Labor?" *The Muslim World* 78, nos. 3–4 (1988): 189–208.

Eickelman, Dale F. *Moroccan Islam: Tradition and Society in a Pilgrimage Center.* Austin: University of Texas Press, 1976.

———. "Ideological Change and Regional Cults: Maraboutism and Ties of 'Closeness' in Western Morocco." In *Regional Cults,* edited by R. P. Werbner. New York: Academic Press, 1977.

———. "The Study of Islam in Local Context." *Contributions to Asian Studies* 17 (1982): 1–16.

———. *Knowledge and Power in Morocco: The Education of a Twentieth-Century Notable.* Princeton: Princeton University Press, 1985.

———. "Religion and Policy and Society." In *The Political Economy of Morocco,* edited by I. William Zartman, 84–97. New York: Praeger, 1987.

El Guindi, Fadwa. "The Emerging Islamic Order: The Case of Egypt's Contemporary Islamic Movement." *Journal of Arab Affairs* 1, no. 2 (1982): 245–62.

Elon, Amos. *Flight into Egypt.* New York: Doubleday, 1980.

Encyclopaedia of Islam. 1st ed. Leiden: E. J. Brill, 1931.

Esposito, John L. *The Islamic Threat: Myth or Reality?* New York: Oxford University Press, 1992.

Esposito, John L., and John Donohue, *Islam in Transition: Muslim Perspectives.* New York: Oxford University Press, 1982.

Evans-Pritchard, E. E. *Social Anthropology and Other Essays.* New York: Free Press, 1962.

———. *Theories of Primitive Religion.* New York: Oxford University Press, 1965.

Fallers, Lloyd A., assisted by M. C. Fallers. "Notes on an Advent Ramadan." *Journal of the American Academy of Religion* 42 (March 1974): 35–52.

Farah, Nadia Ramsis. *Religious Strife in Egypt: Crisis and Ideological Conflict in the Seventies.* New York: Gordon and Breach Science Publishers, 1986.

Fernandez, James. "The Mission of Metaphor in Expressive Culture." *Current Anthropology* 15 (June 1974): 119–45.

Fernea, Robert A. "Gaps in the Ethnographic Literature on the Middle Eastern Village: A Classificatory Exploration." In *Rural Politics and Social Change in the Middle East,* edited by Richard Antoun and Iliya Harik. Bloomington: University of Indiana Press, 1972.

Fischer, Michael M. J., and Mehdi Abedi. *Debating Muslims: Cultural Dialogues in Postmodernity and Tradition.* Madison: University of Wisconsin Press, 1990.

Flores, Alexander. "Egypt: A New Secularism?" *Middle East Report* no. 153 (July–August 1988): 27–30.

Gaffney, Patrick D. "The Office of al-Wāʿiẓ and the Revival of Preaching in Egypt." *Mélanges de l'Institut Dominicain d'Etudes Orientales* 17 (1986): 247–56.

———. "The Local Preacher and Islamic Resurgence in Upper Egypt: An Anthropological Perspective." In *Religious Resurgence: Contemporary Cases in Islam, Christianity, and Judaism,* edited by Richard T. Antoun and Mary E. Hegland, 35–66. Syracuse, N.Y.: Syracuse University Press, 1987.

———. "Authority and the Mosque in Upper Egypt: The Islamic Preacher as Image and Actor." In *Islam and the Political Economy of Meaning: Comparative Studies in Islamic Discourse,* edited by William Roff, 199–225. London: Croon Helm, 1987.

———. "Magic, Miracle and the Politics of Narration in the Contemporary Islamic Sermon," *Religion and Literature* 20, no. 1 (Spring 1988): 111–38.

———. "The Changing Voices of Islam: The Emergence of Professional Preachers in Contemporary Egypt." *The Muslim World* 81, no. 1 (1991): 27–47.

Gardet, Louis. *L'Islam: Religion et Communauté.* 3d rev. ed. Paris: Desclée de Brouwer, 1978.

Gaudefroy-Demombynes, Maurice. *Les Institutions Musulmanes.* Paris: Flamarion, 1946.

Geertz, Clifford. *Islam Observed: Religious Development in Morocco and Indonesia.* Chicago: University of Chicago Press, Phoenix Books, 1971.

Gellner, Ernest. *Muslim Society.* Cambridge: Cambridge University Press, 1981.

Ghazzali, Mohammad al-. *Our Beginning in Wisdom.* Translated by I. R. el-Faruqi. Washington, D.C.: American Council of Learned Societies, 1953.

Ghazzali, Muhammad al-. *Worship in Islam: Being a Translation with Commentary and Introduction of al-Ghazzali's Book of the Ihya' on the Worship.* Translation, commentary, and introduction by Edwin Elliott Calverley. London: Luzac & Co., 1925.

Gilsenan, Michael D. "Some Factors in the Decline of the Sufi Orders in Modern Egypt." *The Muslim World* 57 (1967): 11–18.

———. *Saint and Sufi in Modern Egypt.* London: Oxford University Press, 1973.

———. "Lying, Honor, and Contradiction." In *Transaction and Meaning: Directions in the Anthropology of Exchange and Symbolic Behavior,* edited by

Bruce Kapferer. Philadelphia: Institute for the Study of Human Issues, 1976.

————. *Recognizing Islam: Religion and Society in the Modern Arab World.* New York: Pantheon, 1982.

Gluckman, Max, ed. *Essays on the Ritual of Social Relations.* Manchester, Eng.: Manchester University Press, 1962.

Goffman, Erving. *Encounters: Two Studies in the Sociology of Interaction.* Indianapolis: Bobbs-Merrill, 1961.

Goldziher, Ignaz. *Vorlesungen über den Islam.* 2d rev. ed. Heidelberg: Carl Winter's Universitätsbuchhandlung, 1925.

Grabar, Oleg. "The Architecture of the Middle Eastern City from Past to Present: The Case of the Mosque." In *Middle Eastern Cities,* edited by Ira M. Lapidus. Berkeley: University of California Press, 1969.

Grainger, Roger. *The Language of the Rite.* London: Darton, Longman & Todd, 1974.

Green, Jerrold D. "Islam, Religiopolitics, and Social Change." *Comparative Studies in Society and History* 27, no. 2 (1985): 312–22.

Guenena, Nemat. "The 'Jihad': An Islamic Alternative in Egypt." *Cairo Papers in Social Science* 9, no. 2 (Summer 1986): 45.

Guillaume, Alfred. *The Life of Muhammad: A Translation of Ishaq's Sirat Rasul Allah.* Lahore: Oxford University Press, 1955.

Gulick, John. "The Religious Structure of Lebanese Culture." *Internationales Jahrbuch für Religionsoziologie* 1 (1965): 151–87.

Haarmann, Ulrich. "Islamic Duties in History." *The Muslim World* 68 (January 1978): 1–24.

Haddad, Yvonne Y. "Muslim Revivalist Thought in the Arab World: An Overview." *The Muslim World* 76, nos. 3–4 (1986): 143–67.

Hadj-Sadok, Mahammed. "De la Théorie à la Practique des Prescriptions de l'Islam en Algérie Contemporaine." *Social Compass* (1978): 433–43.

Hairk, Iliya F. *The Political Mobilization of Peasants: A Study of an Egyptian Community.* Bloomington: Indiana University Press, 1974.

Hamid, Wassim Abdel, and M. S. Abdel Hakim. *Some Aspects of Urbanisation in Egypt.* Durham: Center for Middle Eastern and Islamic Studies, University of Durham, 1982.

Hamuda, 'Adil. *Qunābil wa-Musāhif: Qadiyat Tanzīm al-Jihād* (Bombs and Qur'ans: The Case of the Jihad Organization). Cairo: Sina l-al-Nashir, 1985.

Hanifi, M. Jamal. *Islam and the Transformation of Culture.* New York: Asia Publishing House, 1970.

el-Hassan, S. A. "Educated Spoken Arabic in Egypt and the Levant: A Critical Review of Diglossia and Related Concepts." *Archivum Linguisticum* 8 (1976): 96–122.

Heikal, Mohammed. *Autumn of Fury: The Assassination of Sadat.* New York: Random House, 1983.

Henriks, Bertus. "Egypt's New Political Map: Report from the Election Campaign." *Middle East Report* 17, no. 4 (July–August 1987): 23–30.

Hodgson, Marshall G. S. "A Note on the Millennium in Islam." In *Millennial Dreams in Action,* edited by Sylvia L. Thrupp. The Hague: Mouton & Co., 1962.

————. "The Role of Islam in World History." *International Journal of Middle Eastern Studies* 1 (1968): 99–123.

———. *The Venture of Islam: Conscience and History in a World Civilization.* 3 vols. Chicago: University of Chicago Press, 1974.

Holt, P. M., ed. *Political and Social Change in Modern Egypt.* London: Oxford University Press, 1968.

Hopkins, Nicolas. "Popular Culture and State Power." In *Mass Culture, Popular Culture, and Social Life in the Middle East,* edited by Georg Stauth and Sami Zubaida, 225–42. Frankfurt am Main: Campus Verlag, 1987.

Horowitz, Irving Louis. "Religion, the State, and Politics." In *Religion and Politics,* vol. 3 of *Political Anthology,* edited by Myron J. Aronoff. New Brunswick, N.J.: Transaction Books, 1984.

Hourani, Albert. *Arabic Thought in the Liberal Age, 1798–1939.* London: Oxford University Press, Oxford Paperbacks, 1970.

———. *A History of Arab Peoples.* Cambridge, Mass.: Belknap Press of Harvard University Press, 1991.

Hudson, Michael C. *Arab Politics: The Search for Legitimacy.* New Haven: Yale University Press, 1977.

Humphreys, R. Stephen. "Islam and Political Values in Saudi Arabia, Egypt and Syria." *Middle East Journal* 33 (Winter 1979): 1–19.

Hussein, Taha. *The Stream of Days.* Translated by E. H. Paxton. 3 vols. London: Longmans Green and Co., 1948.

———. *The Future of Culture in Egypt.* Translated by Sidney Glazer. Washington, D.C.: American Council of Learned Societies, 1954.

Ibrahim, Saad Eddin. "Anatomy of Egypt's Militant Islamic Groups: Methodological Notes and Preliminary Findings." *International Journal of Middle Eastern Studies* 12 (December 1980): 423–53.

———. "Egypt's Islamic Activism in the 1980's." *Third World Quarterly* 10, no. 2 (1988): 639–51.

Isma'il, Salah Abu. *Shahādat al-Ḥaqq fī Qaḍiyat al-'Aṣr.* (Witness to truth amid the predicament of [our] age). Cairo: Dar al-'Itisām, 1984.

Iqbal, Allama Muhammad. *The Reconstruction of Religious Thought in Islam.* Lahore: Muhammad Ashraf, 1965

Izutsu, Toshihiko. *Ethico-Religious Concepts in the Qur'an.* Montreal: McGill University Press, 1966.

Jama'īya Islāmīya. *Al-Jihād fī Sabīl Allah.* Cario: Maṭaba' al-Kilani, 1977.

Jansen, Johannes J. G. *The Neglected Duty: The Creed of Sadat's Assassins and Islamic Resurgence in the Middle East.* New York: Macmillan, 1986.

Jomier, Jacques. *Les Grands Thèmes du Coran.* Paris: Centurion, 1978.

Joseph, Roger. "Toward a Semiotics of Middle Eastern Cultures." *International Journal of Middle Eastern Studies* 12 (November 1980): 319–29.

———. "The Semiotics of the Islamic Mosque." *Arab Studies Quarterly* 3, no. 3 (1981): 291–92.

Juynboll, G. H. A. *The Authenticity of the Tradition Literature.* Leiden: E. J. Brill, 1969.

Kaye, Alan S. "Modern Standard Arabic and the Colloquials." *Lingua* 24 (1970): 374–91.

Keddie, Nikkie, ed. *Scholars, Saints, and Sufis: Muslim Religious Institutions in the Middle East Since 1500.* Berkeley: University of California Press, 1972.

Kepel, Gilles. "Les oulémas, l'intelligentsia et les islamistes en Egypt: Système social, ordre transcendentale et ordre traduit." *La Revue Française de Science Politique* 35, no. 3 (1985): 424–44.

———. *Muslim Extremism in Egypt: The Prophet and the Pharaoh.* Translated by Jon Rothchild. Berkeley: University of California Press, 1986.

Kepel, Gilles, and Kamel T. Barbar. *Les Waqfs dans l'Egypte Contemporaine.* Cairo: Centre d'Etudes et Documentation Economiques Juridiques et Sociales, n.d. [1982].

Kerr, Malcolm H. *Islamic Reform: The Political and Legal Theories of Muhammad ʿAbdu and Rashid Rida.* Berkeley: University of California Press, 1966.

———. *The Arab Cold War: Gamal ʿAbd al-Nasir and His Rivals, 1958–1970.* 3d ed. London: Oxford University Press, 1971.

———. "The Political Outlook in the Local Area." In *The Economics and Politics of the Middle East,* edited by Abraham S. Becker. New York: American Elsevier Publishing Co., 1975.

Khalid, M. Khalid. *From Here We Start.* Translated by I. R. el-Faruqi. Washington, D.C.: American Council of Learned Societies, 1953.

al-Khawali, Muhammad ʿabd al-Aziz. *Aṣlāḥ al-waʿẓ al-dīnī* (Reform of the Religious Sermon). 7th ed. Cairo: al-Maktaba al-Tijarīya al-Kubra, 1969.

Khuri, Fuad I. "The Ulama: A Comparative Study of Sunni and Shiʿa Officials." *Middle East Studies* 23, no. 3 (1987): 285–98.

Kupferschmidt, Uri M. "The Muslim Brothers and the Egyptian Village." *Asian and African Studies* 16 (1982): 157–71.

Laitin, David D. *Hegemony and Culture: Politics and Religious Change among the Yoruba.* Chicago: University of Chicago Press, 1986.

Lakoff, George. *Women, Fire, and Dangerous Things: What Categories Reveal about the Mind.* Chicago: University of Chicago Press, 1987.

Lammens, Henri. *Islam: Beliefs and Institutions.* Translated by E. Denison Ross. London: Frank Cass, 1968.

Lane, Edward William. *An Account of the Manners and Customs of the Modern Egyptians.* 1836. London: J. M. Dent & Sons, 1908.

Langer, Susanne K. *Philosophy in a New Key: A Study in the Symbolism of Reason, Rite and Art.* New York: New American Library, 1952.

Lapidus, Ira M. *A History of Islamic Societies.* Cambridge: Cambridge University Press, 1988.

Laroui, Abdullah. *The Crisis of the Arab Intellectual: Traditionalism or Historicism.* Translated by Diamid Cammell. Berkeley: University of California Press, 1976.

Lerner, Daniel. *The Passing of Traditional Society: Modernization in the Middle East.* New York: Free Press, 1958.

Leveau, Rémy. "Réaction de l'Islam Officiel au Renouveau Islamique au Moroc." *Annuaire de L'Afrique du Nord* 18 (1979): 205–18.

Levy, Reuben. *The Social Structure of Islam.* Cambridge: Cambridge University Press, 1970.

Lewis, Bernard. *The Arabs in History.* Rev. ed. New York: Harper and Row, Harper Torchbacks, 1966.

———. "Politics and War." In *The Legacy of Islam,* edited by Joseph Schacht and C. E. Bosworth. 2d ed. Oxford: Oxford University Press, 1979.

Lewy, Guenter. *Religion and Revolution*. New York: Oxford University Press, 1974.

Lings, Martin. *A Sufi Saint of the Twentieth Century*. 2d ed. Berkeley: University of California Press, 1971.

McPherson, J. W. *The Moulids of Egypt: Egyptian Saints-Days*. Cairo: N.M. Press, 1941.

Madelung, Wilfred. "The Origins of the Controversy Concerning the Creation of the Koran." *Orientalia Hispanica* (1974): 504–25.

Mahmud, ʿAli ʿAbdal-Halim. *Al-Masjid wa-Atharahu fi al-Mujtamaʿ al-Islāmi* (The Mosque and Its Influence in Islamic Society). Cairo: Dar al-Maʿarif, 1976.

al-Makki, Abu Talib. "The Beard." Translated by E. H. Douglas. *The Muslim World* 68 (April 1978): 100–110.

Marcus, Michael A. " 'The Saint Has Been Stolen': Sanctity and Social Change in a Tribe of Eastern Morocco." *American Ethnologist* 12, no. 3 (1985): 455–67.

Marsot, Afaf Lutfi al Sayyid. *Egypt in the Reign of Muhammad Ali*. Cambridge: Cambridge University Press, 1984.

Martin, M., and R. M. Mascad. "Return to Islamic Legislation in Egypt." *CERAM Reports*. Islamic Law and Change in Arab Society (1976): 47–71.

Martin, Richard C., ed. *Approaches to Islam in Religious Studies*. Tucson: University of Arizona Press, 1985.

Massignon, Louis. "Notes sur l'Apologétique Islamique." *Revue des Etudes Islamiques* 6 (1932): 491–92.

Mayfield, James B. *Rural Politics in Nasser's Egypt: A Quest for Legitimacy*. Austin: University of Texas Press, 1971.

Merad, Ali. "The Ideologization of Islam in the Contemporary Muslim World." In *Islam and Power*, edited by A. S. Cudsi and A. E. H. Dessouki. Baltimore: Johns Hopkins University Press, 1981.

Messick, Brinkley. "The Mufti, the Text and the World: Legal Interpretation in Yemen." *Man*, n.s. 21, no. 1 (1986): 102–19.

Mitchaell, Richard P. *The Society of the Muslim Brothers*. London: Oxford University Press, 1969.

Mitchell, Timothy. *Colonizing Egypt*. Cambridge: Cambridge University Press, 1987.

Montgomery, John Warwick. "The Apologetic Approach of Muhammad Ali and Its Implications for Christian Apologetics." *The Muslim World* 51 (1961): 114–27.

Mottahedeh, Roy. *The Mantle of the Prophet: Religion and Politics in Iran*. New York: Simon & Schuster, 1983.

Mubarak, ʿAli Pasha. *Al-Khiṭāṭ al-Tawfiqīya al-Jidīda*. 20 vols. Cairo: Bulaq, 1886–1889.

Munson, Henry, Jr., "Islamic Revivalism in Morocco and Tunisia" *The Muslim World* 76, nos. 3–4 (1986): 203–18.

Nader, Laura. "A Note on Attitudes and the Use of Language." *Anthropological Linguistics* 4, no. 6 (1962): 24–29.

Neihardt, John G. *Black Elk Speaks: Being the Life Story of a Holy Man of the Oglala Sioux*. Lincoln, Neb.: University of Nebraska Press, 1979.

Nicholas, Ralph W. "Social and Political Movements." In *Annual Review of Anthropology*, edited by Bernard Siegel. Palo Alto: Annual Reviews, 1973.

Nicholson, R. A. *A Literary History of the Arabs.* Cambridge: Cambridge University Press, 1930.

al-Nowaihi, Muhamed. "Problems of Modernization in Islam." *The Muslim World* 65, no. 3 (1975): 174–85.

Paret, Rudi. "Die Bedeutungsentwicklung von Arabisch Fatḥ." *Orientalia Hispanica* 1 (1974): 537–41.

Parkinson, Dilworth B. *Constructing the Social Context of Communication: Terms of Address in Egyptian Arabic.* Berlin: Mouton de Gruyter. 1985.

Parsons, Talcott. "The Professions and Social Structure." In *Essays in Sociological Theory.* Rev. ed. New York: Free Press, 1964.

Partin, Harry B. "The Muslim Pilgrimage: Journey to the Center." Ph.D. diss., University of Chicago, 1967.

Pedersen, Johannes. "Khaṭīb." In *Encyclopedia of Islam,* 3:927–29.

———. *The Islamic Preacher: Waʾiz, Mudhakkir, Qass.* Ignaz Goldziher Memorial Volume. Edited by S. Löwinger and J. Somogyi. Budapest: n.p., 1948.

———. "The Criticism of the Islamic Preacher." *Die Welt des Islam* 36 (1953): 215–31.

Pepper, Stephen. *World Hypothesis: A Study in Evidence.* Berkeley: University of California Press, 1942.

Peristiany, J. G., ed. *Honor and Shame: The Values of Mediterranean Society.* Chicago: University of Chicago Press, 1966.

Peters, Rudolph. *Islam and Colonialism: The Doctrine of Jihad in Modern History.* The Hague: Mouton, 1979.

Petry, Carl. "Geographic Origins of Religious Functionaries in Cairo during the Fifteenth Century." *Journal of the Economic and Social History of the Orient* 23, no. 3 (1980): 259.

Piscatori, James P. *Islam in a World of Nation-States.* Baltimore: Johns Hopkins University Press, 1986.

Pullapilly, Cyriac K., ed. *Islam in the Contemporary World.* Notre Dame, Ind.: Cross Roads Books, 1980.

Qutb, Muhammad ʿAli. *Risāla al-Masjid.* Cairo: Dar al-Ansar, 1977.

Qutb, Seyyid. *The Religion of Islam.* Translated by the "islamdust." Palo Alto: Almanar Press, 1976.

Qurʾan. Arabic text established by the Egyptian High Council of Islamic Affairs. Cairo: n.d.

Radcliffe-Brown, A. R. *Structure and Function in Primitive Society.* New York: Free Press, 1952.

Rafaʿi, Muhammad ʿAli. *Al-Tarbīya al-Asasīya fī al-Khuṭub al-Minbarīya.* Cairo: Maktaba wa matbaʿīya Muhammad ʿAli Ṣabiḥ wa Awlāduhu, n.d.

———. *Kayfa Takun Khaṭīban.* 7th ed. Cairo: Maktaba wa matbaʿīya Muhammad ʿAli Ṣabiḥ wa Awlāduhu. 1972.

al-Rafaʿi, Muhammad Rashid. "Makān al-Masjid fī al-Madīnat al-ʿArabīya" (The Place of the Mosque in the Arab City). *Takhṭīṭ al-Mudun fī al-ʿAlim al-ʿArabīya* (Urban Planning in the Arab World). Edited by Morroe Berger. Cairo: n.p., n.d.

Rafiq, Zakaria. *The Struggle within Islam: The Conflict between Religion and Politics.* London: Penguin, 1988.

Rahman, Fazlur. *Islam.* Garden City, N.Y.: Doubleday, Anchor Books, 1968.

———. "Islam: Challenges and Opportunities." In *Islam: Past Influence and Present Challenge*, edited by Alford Welsh and Pierre Cachia. Edinburgh: University of Edinburgh Press, 1979.

———. "A Survey of Modernization of Muslim Family Law." *International Journal of Middle Eastern Studies* 11 (1980): 451–65.

Reeves, Edward B. *The Hidden Government: Ritual, Clientelism, and Legitimation in Northern Egypt.* Salt Lake City: University of Utah Press, 1990.

Reid, Donald Malcom. *Cairo University and the Making of Modern Egypt.* Cambridge: Cambridge University Press, 1990.

Renard, John. "*Al-Jihad al-Akbar:* Notes on a Theme in Islamic Spirituality." *The Muslim World* 78, nos. 3–4 (1988): 225–42.

Ricoeur, Paul. *The Conflict of Interpretations: Essays in Hermeneutics.* Evanston, Ill.: Northwestern University Press, 1974.

Rida, Muhammad Rashid. *Tarīkh al-Ustādh al-Imām al-Shaykh Muhammad ʿAbdu.* Cairo: Matbaʿa al-Manār, 1931.

Robertson-Smith, W. *Lectures on the Religion of the Semites.* 1st series. New ed. London: Adam and Charles Black, 1894.

Rosenthal, E. I. J. *Political Thought in Medieval Islam.* Cambridge: Cambridge University Press, 1962.

Roussillon, Alain. "Sociologie Egyptienne, Arabe, Islamique: L'Approfonissement du Paradigme Reformiste." *Peuples Méditerranéens* 54–55 (1991): 111–50.

Rubin, Barry. *Islamic Fundamentalism in Egyptian Politics.* New York: St. Martin's Press, 1990.

Sabanegh, E. S. *Muhammad le Prophète: Portraits Contemporains, Egypte 1930–1950.* Paris: Librairie J. Vrin, 1981.

Sabbagh, T. *La Métaphore dans le Coran.* Paris: Adrien-Maisonneuve, 1943.

el-Sadat, Anwar. *In Search of Identity: An Autobiography.* Glasgow: William Collins, 1978.

Salem-Babikian, Norma. "The Sacred and the Profane: Sadat's Speech to the Knesset." *Middle East Journal* 34 (Winter 1980): 13–24.

Schacht, Joseph. *An Introduction to Islamic Law.* Oxford: Oxford University Press, 1964.

Schacht, Joseph, and C. E. Bosworth, eds. *Legacy of Islam.* 2d ed. New York: Oxford University Press, 1979.

Schimmel, Annemarie. *Mystical Dimensions of Islam.* Chapel Hill: University of North Carolina Press, 1975.

Schleifer, Abdullah. "Sufism in Egypt and the Arab World." In *Islamic Spirituality: Manifestation*, ed. S. H. Nasr. New York: Crossroads, 1991.

Shaban, M. A. *Islamic History: A New Interpretation.* 2 vols. Cambridge: Cambridge University Press, 1971 and 1976.

Shariʾati, Ali. *On the Sociology of Islam.* Translated by Hamid Algar. Berkeley: Mizan Press, 1979.

Shayegan, Daryush. *Qu'est-ce qu'une révolution religieuse?* Paris: Michel Albin, 1991.

Shils, Edward. *Center and Periphery: Essays in Macrosociology.* Chicago: University of Chicago Press, 1975.

Sid-Ahmed, Mohamed. "Egypt: The Islamic Issue." *Foreign Policy* 69 (Winter 1987–1988): 22–39.

Silverstein, Michael. "Shifters, Linguistic Categories, and Cultural Description." In *Meaning in Anthropology*, edited by Keith H. Basso and Henry A. Selby. Albuquerque: University of New Mexico Press, 1976.

Skorupski, John. *Symbol and Theory: A Philosophical Study of Theories of Religion in Social Anthropology*. Cambridge: Cambridge University Press, 1976.

Smith, Donald Eugene. *Religion and Political Development: An Analytic Study*. Boston: Little, Brown, & Co., 1970.

Smith, Jane I. *An Historical and Semantic Study of the Term "Islam" as Seen in a Sequence of Qur'an Commentaries*. Missoula: Scholars Press, 1975.

Smith, Wilfred Cantwell. *Islam in Modern History*. New York: New American Library, Mentor Books, 1959.

Sonbol, Amira El-Azhary. "Egypt." In *The Politics of Islamic Revivalism: Diversity and Unity*, edited by Shireen T. Hunter. Bloomington: University of Indiana Press, 1988.

Stetkevych, Jaroslav. *The Modern Arabic Literary Language: Lexical and Stylistic Developments*. Chicago: University of Chicago Press, 1970.

Stoddard, Philip H., et al., eds. *Egypt: Islam and Social Change in the Modern World*. Syracuse, N.Y.: Syracuse University Press, 1981.

Stowasser, Barbara F. *The Islamic Impulse*. London: Croom Helm, 1987.

Supreme Council on Islamic Affairs. *Masājid Miṣrī wa-Awliyā'ha al-Ṣalīhūn*. 2 vols. Cairo: Ministry of Waqfs [Religious Endowments], 1971.

Swartz, Merlin L., ed. and trans. *Studies on Islam*. New York: Oxford University Press, 1981.

Talmoudi, Fathi. *The Diglossic Situation in North Africa: A Study of Classical Arabic*. Göteborg, Sweden: Acta Universitatis Gothoburgensis, 1984.

Tambiah, S. J. "The Magical Power of Words." *Man* 3, no. 2 (1968): 175–208.

Tawfiq al-Hakim. *Maze of Justice*. London: Harvill Press, 1947.

Thabat, Muhammad Khalid. *Ghaḍab li-Allah* (Outrage for God). Cairo: Dar al-Thabat, 1983.

Tibi, Bassam. *The Crisis of Modern Islam: A Preindustrial Culture in the Scientific-Technological Age*. Salt Lake City: University of Utah Press, 1988.

Towler, R. "The Social Status of the Anglican Minister." In *Sociology of Religion*, edited by Roland Robertson. New York: Penguin, 1969.

Tozy, Mohamed. "Monopolisation de la Production Symbolique et Hiérarchisation du Champ Politico-Religieux au Maroc." *Annuaire de L'Afrique du Nord* 18 (1981): 219–34.

Tozy, Mohamed, and Bruno Etienne. Le Modèle Kichkiste et son Impact." In *Radicalismes Islamiques*, 2 vols. (Paris: L'Harmattan, 1986), 2:17–32.

Trimingham, J. Spencer. *The Sufi Orders of Islam*. London: Oxford University Press, 1971.

Troll, Christian W. *Sayyid Ahmad Khan: A Reinterpretation of Muslim Theology*. New Delhi: Vikas Publishing House, 1978.

Turner, Bryan S. *Weber and Islam*. London: Routledge & Kegan Paul, 1974.

Turner, Terence S. "Narrative Structure and Mythopoesis: A Critique and Reformulation of Structuralist Concepts of Myth, Narrative and Poetics." *Arethusa* 10, no. 1 (1977): 103–63.

Turner, Victor W. *The Forest of Symbols*. Ithaca, N.Y.: Cornell University Press, 1967.

———. *The Ritual Process: Structure and Anti-Structure.* Harmondsworth: Penguin, 1969.

Turner, Victor, and Edith Turner. *Image and Pilgrimage in Christian Culture: Anthropological Perspectives.* New York: Columbia University Press, 1978.

van Gennep, Arnold. *The Rites of Passage.* Translated by Monika B. Vizedom and Gabrielle L. Caffee. Chicago: University of Chicago Press, 1960.

Vatikiotis, P. J. *The History of Egypt.* 2d ed. Baltimore: Johns Hopkins University Press, 1980.

Vatin, Jean-Claude. "Seduction and Sedition: Islamic Polemical Discourses in the Maghreb." In *Islam and the Political Economy of Meaning,* edited by William R. Roff. Berkeley: University of California Press, 1987.

Voll, John Obert. *Islam: Continuity and Change in the Modern World.* Boulder, Col.: Westview Press, 1982.

———. "Revivalism and Social Transformation in Islamic History." *The Muslim World* 76, nos. 3–4 (1986): 178.

von Grunebaum, G. E. *Modern Islam: The Search for Cultural Identity.* New York: Random House, Vintage Books, 1964.

Waardenburg, Jean-Jacques. *L'Islam dans le Miroir de l'Occident.* Paris: Mouton, 1962.

———. "Islam Studies as a Symbol and Signification System." *Humaniora Islamica* 2 (1974): 267–85.

———. "Official and Popular Religion in Islam." *Social Compass* 25, nos. 3–4 (1978): 315–41.

———. "Islam as a Vehicle of Protest." In *Islamic Dilemmas: Reformers, Nationalists and Industrialization,* edited by Ernest Gellner. Berlin: Mouton, 1985.

Waterbury, John. *Egypt: Burdens of the Past/Options for the Future.* Bloomington: Indiana University Press, 1978.

———. "Egypt: Islam and Social Change." In *Change and the Muslim World,* edited by Philip H. Stoddard et al. Syracuse, N.Y.: Syracuse University Press, 1981.

Watt, W. Montgomery. *Muhammad at Mecca.* London: Oxford University Press, 1953.

———. *Muhammad at Medina.* London: Oxford University Press, 1956.

———. "The Closing of the Door of Ijtihad." *Orientalia Hispanica* 1 (1974): 14–107.

Weber, Max. *The Sociology of Religion.* Translated by Ephraim Fischoff. Boston: Beacon, 1963.

———. *Wirtschaft und Gesellschaft: Grundriss der Verstehenden Soziologie.* 5th rev. ed. Tübingen: J. C. B. Mohr, 1976.

Wehr, Hans. *A Dictionary of Modern Written Arabic.* Edited by J. Milton Cowan. 3d ed. Ithaca, N.Y.: Spoken Languages Services, 1976.

Weinreich, Uriel. "On the Semantic Structure of Language." In *Universals of Language,* edited by Joseph H. Greenberg. 2d ed. Cambridge: M.I.T. Press, 1966.

Williams, John A. "A Return to the Veil in Egypt." *Middle East Journal* 11 (Spring 1978): 85–95.

———, ed. *Islam.* New York: George Braziller, 1962.

Wilson, Bryan R. *The Noble Savages: The Primitive Origins of Charisma and Its Contemporary Survival.* Berkeley: University of California Press, 1975.

Wolf, Eric. "The Social Organization of Mecca and the Origins of Islam." *Southwestern Journal of Anthropology* 7 (Winter 1951): 329–56.

World Bank. *Egypt: Alleviating Poverty during Structural Adjustment.* Washington, D.C: The World Bank, 1991.

Youssef, Michael. *Revolt against Modernity: Muslim Zealots and the West.* Leiden: E. J. Brill, 1985.

el-Zein, Abdul Hamid M. *The Sacred Meadows: A Structural Analysis of Religious Symbolism in an East African Town.* Evanston, Ill.: Northwestern University Press, 1974.

———. "Beyond Ideology and Theology: The Search for an Anthropology of Islam." In *Annual Review of Anthropology,* edited by Bernard Siegel. Palo Alto: Annual Reviews, 1977.

Zonis, Marvin. *The Political Elite of Iran.* Princeton: Princeton University Press, 1971.

Index

Compositor: Impressions, a Division of Edwards Bros., Inc.
Text: 10/13 Aldus
Display: Aldus
Printer: Edwards Bros., Inc.
Binder: Edwards Bros., Inc.